A Recent Portrait of Doctor Vaughan

A
DOCTOR'S MEMORIES

By *Clarence*

VICTOR C. VAUGHAN

ILLUSTRATED

INDIANAPOLIS
THE BOBBS-MERRILL COMPANY
PUBLISHERS

Printed in the United States of America

PRINTED AND BOUND
BY BRAUNWORTH & CO., INC.
BROOKLYN, NEW YORK

B
V369d

CONTENTS

CONTENTS

LIST OF ILLUSTRATIONS

Facing page

A DOCTOR'S MEMORIES

CHAPTER I

ANCESTRY

M Y LIFE has been determined by heredity and environment. These are the factors that have molded my being, given direction to its development, marked out the course of its growth and set bounds to its activities. Had either been different from what it was, better or worse, I would have been different from what I have been and from what I am. Heredity supplies the seed and this contains the potentialities of life. Environment conditions the growth, supplying the soil and all else concerned in the conversion of the potential into the actual.

Some years ago Galton coined the word *eugenics,* which he defined as being well born. Many centuries ago a wise man wrote: "The felicity of being well born is the richest gift the gods may bestow upon mortals." My maternal grandmother was wont to say to me, long before Galton put the word *eugenics* into the dictionary, "Victor, never forget that you come of a good family." I once asked her what she meant by "good family." She replied that there had been in her family, as far back as tradition and history reached, no criminal, no insane person, no drunkard and no pauper. Grandmother might have added "no man of great distinction." Knowing my grandmother. as I did, I am sure that she would have struck from the family list the name of any individual who, in her judgment, dishonored it. If Grandmother's statement was strictly true I feel that there has been some deterioration in the family since her time, as I have known some who were inclined in pre-Volstead days to drain the cup too deeply. Rare is the tree whose every bud develops into perfect fruit and if there be such a family tree I find no adequate evidence of it.

I can not omit a brief account of family tradition and history. As I have indicated, were I to do so, this would not be a true story of my life. I believe in these things and I wish to testify to their beneficial effects upon me all the way through life. I heard them in my childhood from the lips of three generations and they became a part of my very being. They have stayed my steps when tempted to go astray and they have cheered and stimulated me in every good work. Their strict truth in detail is a matter of no vital importance. When family history and tradition lead one to acquire a sense of superiority they are harmful. When they hold one to duty they are the most priceless possessions man can have. At the outset I wish to state that I have no claim to birth of distinction. On both sides I came from families which at no time, covered by tradition or history, have been other than plain people. Still, I state that family ideals planted in my soul in earliest childhood have had a stronger hold on me and have done more for me than the catechism and all other forms of religious instruction.

At birth the child is only a small bundle of potentialities, seeking adjustment to its new environment. At the age of two or thereabout the physical adjustment has been fairly well established. From two to six, the pre-school age, is the time for the implantation of moral and intellectual principles. During this period the child learns more, absorbs more rapidly and assimilates more thoroughly than in any subsequent period. Intelligence expands, imagination awakens, grows by leaps and bounds, and ideals take root. It is what the child acquires at its mother's knee that becomes the most potent factor in shaping its future life. During the first two years, the child remains, in large part at least, physically a part of the mother, receiving its sustenance from her breasts and even possessing immunity to those diseases to which she is immune. During the next four years its moral and intellectual training is determined by the mother or her substitute. A family of good ideals may pass through generations of adverse environment, of poverty and even of illiteracy and still transmit the seeds of good and honorable citizenship. This was the fate of the families that gave birth to such men as Thomas Carlyle and Abraham Lincoln. Similar examples might be multiplied indefinitely. I am not a Chinaman and do not practise ancestor-worship, but I do respect my forebears and acknowledge my indebtedness to them. They have transmitted to me no spark of genius. I am not aware that any of them ever possessed such a gift, be it in the form of a blessing or a curse, and I am sure that I have never acquired it by inheritance or through environment. My family, so far as I can ascertain, bred constantly plain people, honest according to the standards of its several generations, and rebellious to dictation from others in religion, morals and politics.

My father was a Welshman and my mother a French Huguenot with a liberal mixture of English blood. I will first give briefly the tradition and history of my French ancestry. Tradition along this line begins in the year 1033 when Conrad II became King of Burgundy. One of Conrad's lieutenants at that time was Raphael Du Puy, who was given an important post. Raphael's son, Hugh Du Puy, went on the first crusade with Godfrey of Bouillon in 1096. In recognition of his services on this expedition he was made Governor of Acre. According to family tradition Hugh took his wife and three children to Syria where he resided for some years. According to history, Acre, or Saint Jean D'Acre, a seaport of Syria, anciently called Ptolemais, on a promontory at the foot of Mount Carmel, was captured by the first crusaders in 1104, recaptured by the Saracens in 1187 and retaken by the Christians under Richard the Lion Hearted in 1191 and given to the Knights of St. John of Jerusalem. This Hugh is said to have built the Abbey of Aiquebelle of the Order of St. Bernard. The second Hugh Du Puy was in the second crusade in 1140.

In the twelfth and thirteenth centuries there came into existence in Southern France a sect of heretics known from a local town as Albigenses. These people were denounced by the Catholic church and for a time were protected by Raymond, Count of Toulouse. In 1207 Innocent III excommunicated Raymond and under the Inquisition was supposed soon thereafter to have exterminated the heretics. Exactly at what time the family left the Catholic Church can not be determined, but the continuance of Protestantism in Languedoc is certain. The family record states that it skips nine generations from Hugh, the second crusader, to Jean Du Puy, who was a leader in a Protestant colony in upper Languedoc in 1583. The Edict of Nantes promulgated by Henry IV, April 13, 1598, granted toleration in religion to all French subjects. A period of comparative freedom from religious persecution continued until the revocation of this edict by Louis XIV, on October 22, 1685. During this time three generations of the family came and passed away.

With Bartholomew Du Puy more reliable family information begins though I have no doubt that romance continues. Bartholomew was born in 1650 and was about thirty-five years old when the edict was revoked. At that time he was a trusted lieutenant in the household guard of the king on leave of absence at his country home. The royal decree ordered all Protestants to abjure their faith, to submit themselves and all their dependents to the rites and ceremonies of the Catholic Church and to proclaim their sole allegiance to this institution. The alternatives were loss of property, torture, and possibly death.

The following, which purports to be a translation of a message sent by Louis XIV to Bartholomew Du Puy, is treasured in the family records:

"This to our trusted and well beloved Bartholomew Du Puy, one of our guardsmen, who has amnesty granted him with his household until the first day of December. Any annoyance of the said Seigneur Du Puy will be at the peril of the officer who commands it. Such is our royal will. Moreover, we pray our said trusted friend, Du

Puy, to abjure his heresy and return to the bosom of the holy church, in which alone is rest.

"Done at Versailles, this thirtieth day of October in the year 1685.

"To the Seigneur Bartholomew Du Puy at his château of Velours in Saintonge. Ride in haste."

I shall spare the reader the details of Bartholomew's flight with his recently acquired bride, Susanne Lavillon, to Germany whence after some years of residence he passed through Holland into England. Here Bartholomew and his family remained for a short time and in 1699 under the "commission and providing" of King William came to America. A partial list of the families accompanying the Du Puys on their voyage to this country has been preserved and includes the following names: Dameron, Tribue, Flournoy, Meaux, Maury, Bowdoin, Latiné, Du Valls, Jarnette and Clay. The last mentioned is said to have been the only English family in the group. Some of these names have been so changed in spelling and pronunciation during the two centuries that have elapsed since their coming to this country that recognition is often quite impossible. My mother's family name, Dameron, has undergone the least change and this is now sometimes spelled without the *e*.

This group of French Huguenots located temporarily on the James River, about seventeen miles above Richmond, and in the family record this location is given the name of "Monacon," though the name has different spellings in the chronicles. However, this was only a temporary resting place and the families soon dispersed throughout Virginia and North Carolina.

So nearly as I can trace my direct ancestral line the

first three American generations lived in Hanover County, Virginia. Here Joseph Dameron was born, grew up and married Mary Ball. This name has given the family opportunity to claim relationship with Mary Ball, the mother of George Washington. The claim, so far as I know, is founded upon nothing more than the name and the proximity of the families. Joseph Dameron was a revolutionary soldier and was wounded at Guilford Court House. After the war he moved to Dinwiddie County and later "down on the Dan river." One of his sons, my great-grandfather, George Ball Dameron (1771-1848), married Mary Moore (1781-1870), who lived to the advanced age of eighty-nine, preserving much of her physical and mental alertness to the end. I knew her, rode and drove with her, and listened with great eagerness to her stories of the family. My other great-grandmother on my mother's side was Mary Clay, "a daughter of Edward C. Clay, whose father was a brother of Reverend John Clay, the father of Henry Clay." This good lady gave me in my boyhood days "Henry Clay's whiskey glass" which I still possess, but it has long been void of the ancient beverage. Probably it is one of the many glasses from which this illustrious statesman took his toddy.

From the autobiography of the late James P. Dameron (my mother's brother) of San Francisco, published privately in 1877, I take the following:

"Edward C. Clay's wife was a Tribue, whose mother was a daughter of Count Bartholomew Du Puy, one of those noble and great men who, with his accomplished wife disguised as a page, fled from home and country rather than abjure their religious faith and escaped from

France to Germany where they resided fourteen years and then went to England and stayed two years, and then emigrated to Virginia in 1699 or 1700 and settled at a place called Monican Town, some twenty miles above Richmond on the James River."

From the same source I make the following extracts concerning two of my ancestors: "Joseph Dameron was a large, fine looking man and a school teacher by profession but kept a farm for his family to live on. He had five sons and three daughters. He was in the Revolutionary War under Captain Rainey and was at the Battle of Guilford Court House, North Carolina."

"George Ball Dameron (Joseph's son)' was an old school Virginia gentleman. He wore knee breeches, straight breasted coat and queue; but toward the close of his life he had his queue cut off as he said it made him too marked. He was a stout built man, about five feet ten inches in height, broad shoulders and thick set, fair complexion and blue eyes. He was a very good man and every one respected him; a deacon in the Methodist church and an old Jeffersonian Democrat, a well-to-do farmer, had a large farm and some ten or fifteen negroes to do the work; but he taught all his children to work on the farm, saying it was a disgrace to be idle and lazy. His house was always open to his children and grandchildren. On Saturday evening it was always full and rang with the shouts of laughter, but at bedtime all were to come in to prayers. He read a chapter in the Bible, sang a song, all standing; then all knelt down and he offered up a fervent prayer. He had perfect control of his passions, and never gave expression to them. His wife was tall and slender, had a fair complexion and blue eyes, and was very active and industrious; always kept her cupboard full of sweetmeats and good things for the children. As soon as any of the children got married father and mother had laid by money to purchase a home for them, with horses, cows, sheep and pigs; and a negro, to help them start in the world, was loaned, but seldom returned. His wife had her daughters well supplied with linen, beds and bedding. She would say: 'I don't want my daughters to go to housekeeping like turtles with their outfits on their backs. Love is well enough in its place, but when poverty comes in at the door love flies out at the window. Nothing like a plenty of good food, warm rooms and nice soft beds to keep cupid at home. Do this, my daughters, and treat your husbands kindly and they will be good to you; try to help them to lay by for the rainy day and you and your children will never stand in want of the necessities of life.'"

William Moore Dameron (1799-1839, a son of George Ball) married his cousin, Eliza I. Dameron (1800-1873), and became a tobacco grower in Caswell County, North Carolina. The family Bible, now in my possession, shows that he was twenty and she nineteen when they were married. Both inherited slaves and life seemed fair in prospect, but soon the young husband realized that an old enemy to the family, pulmonary tuberculosis, had its grip upon him. Even at that time there was a well founded belief that an outdoor life was best for a victim marked by this disease. Therefore, with his wife, five children, four brothers, all of his negroes and much of his live stock, William Dameron migrated to Missouri in 1829. Two daughters, one of whom was my mother, were born to him after this migration. He purchased a farm in Randolph County and continued his former occupation of growing tobacco. The journey benefited him but did not secure the complete suppression of the disease. Therefore he began the practise of buying a drove of mules each year and taking them overland to New Orleans. Here these animals were converted into coffee, sugar and other staple merchandise and the return trip made by boat to St. Louis. In the Black Hawk War, William Dameron served with the rank of colonel. After his death (1839) his widow received some back pay from the government. This she converted into silver tablespoons bearing her late husband's name and these were distributed among their children. My grandmother leased her negroes to her sons and sons-in-law by the year. During the last years of her life she made her home with my mother. From this grandmother and the two great-grandmothers mentioned, also from my mother and other members of the family, I heard the story of my French ancestry as I have outlined it. One of my mother's brothers, the late James P. Dameron of San Francisco, published for private distribution in the seventies three papers on this subject: (1) *Count Du Puy's Escape to America;* (2) *The Du Puys in America;* (3) *Autobiography.* In the D. A. R. magazine of January, 1921, there may be found confirmation of this story by Edith Roberts Ramsburgh. It is said that an article by J. Esten Cooke in an early number of Harper's Magazine, entitled *The Huguenot Sword,* is founded on this story. One may read a further confirmation of my story in *Kith and Kin* by John R. Sampson, William Bird Press, Richmond, Virginia.

This is not a boastful story. It is not improbable,

though I have no doubt that it is colored with romance, and it is not inconsistent with historical records. Be it true or fictitious I am sure that it has had a most potent influence upon my life and conduct. When I have turned instantly, instinctively and with horror from a bad suggestion coming from someone else or having birth within myself, I like to think that my action is determined by inheritance. It is due to a reflex born in me and is an essential function of my being. Most of the critical moments in life are determined by impulse and not by the slower processes of reasoning. The one who stops to reason, to weigh the pros and cons, is likely to meet disaster. On the crowded highway of life each driver must look out not only for himself, but for all others at the wheel. It is not enough to know and practise the rules of the road. There are sure to be some who either do not know or who do not practise. It is well to exercise caution, but the possession of skill enhances safety. The reflex must work promptly and correctly. There are mental and moral impulses as well as physical, and fortunate is the man whose moral reflexes are prompt in action and correct in direction. I admit that it is debatable as to the extent to which moral impulses are inherited and I would not deny the importance of training in their development.

The Virginia Huguenots dropped all titles and prefixes to their names. Jacques de la Fontaine became plain James Fontaine and Count Bartholomew Du Puy became Bartholomew Du Puy. Even the titles Mr. and Mrs. were reserved for strangers. Those of like age addressed one another by the first name while the terms, uncle, aunt and cousin, were extended to all members of the community and had but little significance in showing blood or marriage relationships. When a stranger came to reside in the community, at first he was designated as "Mr." If he continued his residence and was approved he became one of the community and was addressed as "Uncle" or "Cousin" as the relative ages of the speaker and the addressed indicated. This custom was in consonance with the French people's practise during and after the Revolution when every man was a citizen. I grew up with this habit firmly fixed and I have usually addressed my intimates, my colleagues, and my better known students by their first names. On some occasions this has embarrassed me and possibly my friends to an even greater extent.

My French ancestry had been, as far back as tradition goes, an agricultural people. In France, they grew grapes, fruit, grain and stock, and for the most part the family continued these pursuits in this country. I can find actual evidence of only one lawyer in all the generations, and he, the late James P. Dameron of San Francisco, was more successful as a rancher than as a lawyer. There have been one or more physicians in nearly every generation, but most of these have been village doctors practising in rural communities. Doctor John James Du Puy, a lineal descendant and the inheritor of the sword of Bartholomew, served as a surgeon in the Confederate Army. The sword was "irrevocably lost" by the burning of the home of Mrs. Julian Ruffin near Petersburg in the Civil War. That my people have been farmers so continuously accounts for the fact that the locations for several generations are given by the names of counties and not by those of towns or cities. Indeed this condition largely prevailed throughout the South until the Civil War. Up to that time the South was almost exclusively an agricultural country. A manufacturer was rare and a small tradesman was not highly esteemed. Social position was largely determined by acres and slaves owned. Of course all this has greatly changed and even the descendants of the slow-going Huguenots, like all others, are now flocking to the cities. Both by inheritance and environment I am a ruralite. In fact, I suffer from an urbophobia—a dislike for residence in a large city. I prefer Ann Arbor to New York and Old Mission to Atlantic City. I shun crowded thoroughfares and seek rural lanes. I prefer a cottage in the woods to a mansion in the city. I hope that the bungalow will win in the contest with the apartment house. My picture of heaven is a land where each family owns its little home with a modest house, a fertile vegetable garden and beautiful flowers in bloom the year around. A city paved with gold has no allurement for me.

I am told that the name Vaughan is an Anglicized Welsh word, a term of endearment, best translated by the phrase "a dear little fellow." Since I am absolutely ignorant of Welsh speech, which was "a fine old language when ours was young," I am perfectly willing to accept this translation, or, if it be wrong, I am equally willing to accept the appellation given to the Welshman in an immortal ditty, "Taffy is a Welshman," first published in *Punch* many years ago. This refers to the Welshman as a "jolly little brick."

All I know about my Welsh ancestry is that after the battle of Waterloo and after the little Corsican had been safely housed at St. Helena, when England was no longer in need of Welsh protection, my grandfather, Sampson Vaughan, having some leisure, married Mary Jones, a worthy compatriot, and came to America on his honeymoon. He bought a scrub oak farm, which I have no doubt he called an estate, near Durham, North Carolina, and with the aid of some negroes, spent the remainder of his days in cultivating that weed which was introduced into England by Sir Walter Raleigh. My father, John Vaughan, it appears, grew tired of hoeing tobacco; and working with an uncle in Durham became quite an expert cabinet maker. Later, wishing to see something of the fabulous West, he enlisted in the quartermaster's department of the United States Army and did his bit in the construction of Forts Laramie and Kearney.

Recently I motored into the thriving city of Laramie, Wyoming, with wide open eyes seeking for some evidence of my father's handiwork, but seeing nothing which by the widest stretch of my imagination I could convert into a fort, I asked an apparently intelligent citizen. "Oh!" says he, "Old Fort Laramie! It is a hundred miles or more from here." When father's term of enlistment expired he found himself in old Missouri and in love with Adeline Dameron, whom he married, after which momentous event he returned to the occupation of growing tobacco.

In my boyhood days when I came across the family name in English history or in literature it was my habit to take it to my father and ask if the name mentioned indicated a relative of his. One day he replied to one of these interrogations something as follows: "Great men, indifferent men and even bad men have borne that name. Pick out the good ones and emulate them; neglect the

indifferent ones and despise the bad ones." This sage
advice I have followed. It gives me the unique opportunity of selecting my own ancestors. I can claim relationship
with every good Vaughan and deny all others, and since
among my ancestors there have been as many females as
males I can claim kinship with any good Welshman, be he
living or dead. Should I be rude enough to claim kinship
with Lloyd George he would have more trouble in dis-
proving it than he did in bringing England safely through
the World War. Indeed, I do not believe that he would
undertake so Herculean a task; therefore I will not put
him to the test.

Some years ago my wife and I made an inspection
trip through Wales. I wanted to see something of my
cousins. I had telegraphed to a hotel at Llandudno and
when we alighted from the train at that delightful resort
a porter with a pushcart for our baggage met us. We followed him along Vaughan Street and at the hotel the
proprietor greeted me as "Major Vaughan," as he assured
me that he had reserved his best room for us. I was entitled to that appellation, but I wondered how it happened
that my Welsh host was so well acquainted with the heroes
of the Spanish-American War. It was not until three days
later that Major Vaughan of the British Army arrived
and my wonderment was relieved. I may add that there
was no suggestion from either the Boniface or the English
Major that we vacate the best room. I have no doubt
that there were many *best* rooms in that small hostelry.

The guide book told us that Corsygedol "the old family seat of the Vaughans, descendants of an Irish noble-
man" had passed into the hands of a rich Australian by
the name of Dangerfield, but that the present proprietor

would grant visitors permission to inspect the premises on the receipt of a written request. Of course it went against the grain of an American to ask of an interloper permission to visit his own ancestral halls. After a few days at the hotel at Barmouth we had learned all the details about the occupants of Corsygedol. So one morning we drove to the lodge gate. A woman appeared. I said "Good morning, Mrs. Jones. Bring the keys to the church." She asked, "I suppose that you are a friend of Mr. Dangerfield?" I ignored her question and repeated my request. In the chapel are stone effigies of a Vaughan of the year 1620 with his wife, two sons and four daughters. If there be any truth in these images, I prefer kinship to the good-looking Mrs. Jones who brought the keys and served as our guide. Near the mansion is a stone known as Arthur's Quoit, said to have been thrown by that Prince from the top of a mountain. "There can be no doubt about the truth of the story for there are the marks of the royal fingers eighteen inches long."

On one of the roads between Barmouth and Dolgelly the tourist passes quite a forest of splendid trees and is told that they were planted by Colonel Vaughan's soldiers during the "Short Peace" with Napoleon. This area is known as the "Peace Plantation" and may be regarded as a national Welsh cemetery for soldiers of the Napoleonic wars. Planting trees was no doubt a happy interlude in the battles against the "Little Corporal."

Nannau, another residence of the Vaughan family, "is said to stand on the highest ground of any gentleman's estate in Great Britain, and undoubtedly the situation is one of the most romantic kind with Moel Cynwd and Moel Orfrwm standing as sentinels over it." I am told that

Moel is a Welsh word for mountain. On inquiry at Nannau we were told that a dispute over the succession to the estate had recently been decided in favor of an American claimant. This information quite elated us and we had visions of being entertained, but on sending in our cards we were informed that the owner, having established his claim, returned to the United States and was then hunting wild cats in Wyoming or attending the horse races in Kentucky, for these pastimes are among the allurements which attract English gentlemen of leisure to this country.

The Welsh are strong on tradition, since this and their scenery are about the only things they have to occupy their minds, when they are not engaged in protecting England against the rest of the world. The Vaughan family tradition runs back to the time, if there ever was such a time, when the Scotch, Irish and Welsh were all one, at least in language, and that, of course, was the Welsh tongue. Once in schoolboy days I was called an Irishman. I did not know whether to regard this as a reproach or as a compliment, so I took the matter to Father. He assured me that the Vaughans had originally lived in Ireland, but that centuries ago Taffy had swum across the sea and built a home on the Welsh hills where lights were kept burning every night to pilot any of his friends who might be attempting the same feat. This story is confirmed by the following lines from the *Punch* ditty already referred to:

> "If Taffy rides to my house
> Or unto Pat's doth *swim*,
> I think my Taffy will remark
> That we might learn of him."

Once on a somewhat prolonged stay in Boston a good doctor friend invited me to exchange my hotel bed for a more comfortable one in his home. At dinner the doctor's wife put me through a social catechism. She wanted to know what county in England my ancestors came from. I answered that they did not come from England but from Merionethshire in Wales. She then asked me if they came over with William the Conqueror. I told her that they did not come from Normandy but that they were on the reception committee at Hastings when William landed. I added that our family tradition claims that my ancestors performed a like function on the arrival of Julius Cæsar some years before. The tradition continues, saying that the weaker Welsh, those who could not swim the sea, were left in Ireland to be tormented by the snakes until Saint Patrick, of blessed memory, came and relieved them of these pests.

Having claimed the privilege of selecting my Welsh ancestry I might go into detail, but this would be largely fiction; and an autobiographer should shun this so far as possible. I will close this section with the statement that the family name has not been altogether free from stain. I was once introduced to a Belgian who pronounced my name correctly. When I expressed some surprise at this he said, with some hesitation: "You must be aware of the fact that your name is not without notoriety in my country," referring to the scandal about Leopold II and the Baroness Vaughan. But she had acquired the name by marriage and not by birth.

In France and Germany the name is pronounced Vō-gan, with the accent on the last syllable. I was once attending a clinic in Paris conducted by my friend Doctor

Pozzi. The speaker referred to me, his guest, as Doctor Vō-gan. There were three or four American doctors in attendance. One of these touched me on the shoulder and asked, "Who in the devil are you?" When I told him that at home I was Vaughan, he exclaimed, "Victor Vaughan!"

I have had great fun in selecting my cousins among the Vaughans. In the eighties I was waiting one oppressively hot night at the Union Station in Chicago. I saw across the street a sign, "Saloon, J. Vaughan." I crossed over and entered. The only man in the room was behind the bar. I asked him to bring two mugs to a table and as we sipped the cooling beverage we talked about the Vaughan family. He learned that I was on my way to Missouri, that I would return next Wednesday with my wife and that I would attend the laying of the corner stone of the then new Federal building. When I left, he said: "You and Mrs. Vaughan will be here next Wednesday. The hotels will be crowded. Come here and let me entertain you." His name went down on my list of cousins.

More recently I was motoring through a prosperous southern city where I called at a palatial bank and sent in my card to the president, Mr. Vaughan. He received my wife and me in his office and we had a pleasant chat, but he had an air of expectancy, counting on me to draw a check and ask for cash. He could not be a cousin for three reasons: (1) He was handsome; (2) he was rich; and (3) he did not invite us to dinner.

From the Vaughans I have selected a number of cousins among whom I may mention with pride, T. Wayland Vaughan, now Director of the Institution of Oceanography at La Jolla, California, and Doctor Tully

Vaughan of Washington, D. C., who rode the *Leviathan* as surgeon during the war and rendered other valuable service to our Navy.

When I visit France, Wales and England I feel at home and seem to be reviewing people and scenes once seen in dim outline. I wonder if there may be an inherited subconsciousness, or does this sensation result from stories told me in early childhood? A Frenchman once wrote a book showing that unicellular organisms are potentially immortal. On reaching a certain stage of development they split into two and then continue their existence until interrupted by lack of food. Is not this equally true of human germ plasm, and while men are mortal, man is immortal?

In human beings, as in bacteria, the thread of life is continuous. Enrichment or impoverishment of the soil may modify growth but does not readily alter the essential qualities of the seed. However, I am ready to admit that bad environment long continued may weaken and possibly obliterate desirable qualities.

Of personal, conscious, continuous existence I am uncertain. Of racial perpetuity, so far as limited human comprehension can go, I have no doubt. Man transmits his actual qualities. These may differ widely from those assumed by himself or attributed to him by others. A donkey may be covered with a lion's skin but its progeny will continue to be donkeys. A childless man said: "When I see the manly sons and womanly daughters of Richard Roe I am filled with regret. When I see the degenerate offspring of John Doe I thank God." Heredity and environment are not antagonistic, but are complementary, factors in race betterment.

CHAPTER II

THE OLD MISSOURI FARM

I WAS born—so the family Bible says—on the twenty-seventh of October, 1851. I first saw the light of day in my grandmother Dameron's house which lay about three-fourths of a mile east of Mount Airy, Randolph County, Missouri. During the first year of my life, Grandmother's farm became the property of another of her sons-in-law, Robert Smith, and my father bought and took possession of a farm at Mount Airy and this was my home so long as I lived under the parental roof. Randolph County is in the second tier of counties north of the Missouri River. On the east it lies adjacent to Monroe County and there in the village of Florida, not larger than Mount Airy, Mark Twain was born. So far as I know, this is the nearest point to Randolph County that ever gave birth to a great man. The chief distinction of Mount Airy was that it was on the plank road that led from Huntsville on the north, to Glasgow on the south, a distance of about twenty-five miles.

The population of Mount Airy has fluctuated from time to time, and although there are no official statistics, I can safely say that it has never exceeded fifty; an approach to this figure is determined by the number of adjacent or near-by farms included in the census. Its industries also have fluctuated. In my early recollection there was a woolen mill owned by a Pennsylvanian by the name of Sutliffe. The machinery was moved by oxen, horses, or mules, or a mixture of these animals on a tread-wheel. Enoch Sutliffe, a boy of about my age, played in the fleece and learned to crack the whip and keep the animals going. In this arduous occupation I often assisted him. When this method of propulsion became anti-quated Mr. Sutliffe moved down on to Silver Creek and used water power when the stream was not dry. Later he transferred his factory to Huntsville and steam drove his spindles and shuttles. Enoch continued as my fellow student through college. When I went on a summer vacation in Cuba in 1898 I took as part of my impedi-menta a red woolen blanket made by Sutliffe. If I do not forget it, I will tell what became of this blanket, and the important part it played in the Santiago campaign.

In its history Mount Airy has had, either immediately on the Mount or near by, three considerable tobacco fac-tories, though I believe that all these were not contem-poraneous. To these the farmers in the olden days brought their tobacco after the leaves had been stripped from the stalks, sorted and tied in bundles. In the fac-tories the bundles were packed in hogsheads with the aid of a screw press. The weight of a hogshead varied with the kind of tobacco from fifteen hundred to three thousand pounds. These were hauled in the earliest days to the river at Glasgow and in later times to the railroad by teams of from four to six mules. The driver, gener-ally a negro, rode the near mule and guided the leaders by one line and by word of mouth, emphasized when necessary by the lash of a black snake whip. The little boys boasted that "Uncle Dan" could kill a fly annoying a lead mule with his lash without touching the animal. Before the Civil War these tobacco consignments went via river and ocean to Liverpool where they were first broken and their contents sold. Later they went by rail to commission merchants in St. Louis. The commission merchant was the pioneer middleman, stepping in between the producer and the consumer. His descendants have filled the land, raking in the profits with both hands.

Near the woolen mill was a barn in which the relays of stage horses were kept. The two great daily events on the Mount were the stage arrivals, the one from the north in the morning and the one from the south in the afternoon. However, the natives of that time did not employ the word "afternoon" and its use betrayed the stranger. Until noon it was morning. From noon until sundown it was evening, and after sundown it was night. "In the beginning God created the heaven and the earth. And the earth was without form, and void; and darkness was upon the face of the deep. And the Spirit of God moved upon the face of the waters. And God said, Let there be light: and there was light. And God saw the light, that it was good: and God divided the light from the darkness. And God called the light Day, and the darkness he called Night. And the evening and the morning were the first day."

From afar the approaching stage driver blew a blast; the negro hostlers brought out four fresh horses, all resplendent in their highly polished, brass-mounted harness; the great swaying vehicle came to a stop; mail bags were exchanged; occasionally a passenger alighted, or a departing one mounted; the foam-covered horses were detached; the fresh ones were attached. The reins were handed to the driver; the hostlers left the bits of the excited animals; the whip cracked; the last reverberations of the coach lumbering down the plank road died away. Mount Airy had a few hours of complete isolation from the great world. The celerity with which all this was done and the skill with which the driver handled the reins were at once the wonderment and admiration of the small boy and his companions. There seemed nothing more desirable as a future career than to be a stage driver.

When there was a passenger for the home, the stage stopped at the road gate, the driver blew a loud and joyous call which brought all the household to the front door or yard in joyous anticipation. The keen eyes of the children were usually the first to identify the visitor and they ran screaming, "It's Uncle [or Aunt, or Cousin] from St. Louis." Moreover, the children's eyes were not confined to the person but embraced numerous boxes and other articles being removed from the top and inside of the coach. Yes! It's Uncle Logan Dameron, Aunt Sue Melton or Cousin Harper, and sure enough there is the box of oranges and candies which he or she always brings. Then, having received the visitor's embrace with kiss or pat on the head and with eyes averted from the coveted box the children next thought of the contents of the family larder and the possibility of proper gastronomic entertainment for the visitor. How lucky that Uncle Dick had just brought in a hatful of partridge eggs which he had found while mowing or, according to season, there is a basketful of crisp and luscious persimmons recently ripened by the first killing frost! Then there were the pigeons' nests in the barn, vociferous with squabs, just of the right

The Old Missouri Farm

age and size, crying for liberty or death. Whatever the
season, in due time the visitor was seated at the bountifully laden table with dishes not usually included in the
menu of the Laclede or the Planters. Fried chicken with
cream gravy and hot biscuit, or equivalents of roast goose
or turkey, were always in season and besides they were
cooked and served with a perfection that never failed
Irene.

The most popular stage driver of the time was Lou
Hether, whose cheerful face and jolly laugh were seen and
heard daily, as he drove either south or north. Some
days he would tarry at the barn long enough to give an
exhibition with his whip to the music of which the little
negro boys danced a jig. One day in his reckless haste
the coach went over the embankment south of the house
along the line of the woodland pasture. Passengers were
more or less cut with the broken glass but the only one seriously hurt was the Jehu, whose leg was broken. But after
a few weeks, with a limp that never left him, he mounted
the box again and became a greater hero than ever. Since
that time I have fraternized with the rough men of the
London busses, sat with the driver on the old road from
Geneva to Chamonix, passed over the Tête Noir and
down into Martigues and enjoyed the descent from
Mount Hamilton into the beautiful Santa Clara Valley,
but none of these rides has ever thrilled me as did an occasional one on the box with the picturesque and big-
hearted stage driver of the old plank road. Many years
after the planks of the old road had disappeared and the
coaches had gone into the waste heap, I saw "the postil-
lion" on the great stage at Kroll's Garden in Berlin, and
while the audience applauded the music of the whip

I looked and listened and my memory was with Lou Hether, who drove the stage on the plank road when I was a child.

From my earliest recollection until recent years there has been continuously at Mount Airy a blacksmith shop; now it is a garage. Formerly it was more than a blacksmith shop. Wagons, plows, hoes and other agricultural implements were made there. However, it is true that this factory never rivalled Studebaker in wagons or Oliver in plows. Indeed, its products could hardly be called finished, but they were strong and durable. The returning tobacco wagons brought iron in rods, bars and sheets, and these were worked into form. The native forests supplied the wood. For some years Father owned this shop and with the aid of Louis and other servants he kept it busy. To me it was a kind of rudimentary technical school. I spent many hours in it and by no means were all of these passed in play. I worked the bellows, and as I grew older and stronger other jobs fell to me. However, I never became enamored of either carpentry or blacksmithing.

Before the Civil War there was no general store, such as is now found at nearly every cross road. There was no need of one. The farmer bought coffee by the sack; flour, if purchased at all, by the barrel, and brown sugar by the hogshead. The small package is a device by which the cost of living has been increased.

I recall with much pleasure the monthly comings of the preacher of the circuit. The one whom I best remember, Brother Root, weighed more than three hundred pounds and was due at the farm on the afternoon of the Saturday before the fourth Sunday in the month. At this time all watched anxiously for the gig and the old gray mule, the vehicle and motive power by which this man, big in body, mind and soul, made the round of his circuit. In the pulpit he was great on theological dogma but in the family circle he was a jolly friend, bringing good cheer, telling and enjoying a good joke, ready to help the boy in the translation of lines of Virgil or an Ode in Horace, explaining some principle in mechanics, making intelligent inquiry about progress in lessons, and recommending books of biography, fiction, science, or travel. He had a snowy white beard and black hair, the contrast of colors being marked. He explained the difference by saying that he worked his jaws more than he did his brain.

Once a quarter came the presiding elder. He arrived on Friday afternoon, for quarterly meeting meant service on both Saturday and Sunday. This dignitary was so great that he was regarded with awe by the children on the farm, and while many good men of this rank visited the home, no one of them ever favorably touched the life of the small boy. Indeed the coming of so exalted a personage cast a cloud over the home. Parents were too deferential; the old minister told no stories, gave no instruction; and worst of all the children were sentenced to the second table. Were you ever compelled to wait for the second table on account of company at your father's house? If not, you have no adequate appreciation of the severity of the resulting pain. The meal has been delayed beyond the usual hour by the tardiness of the guests and the extent of the preparation in the kitchen. The children are told to play in the yard, run down into the pasture, or pick fruit in the orchard. But what attraction has yard, pasture or orchard for the small boy in whose stomach there are a million peptic glands swollen to the point of bursting with gastric juice? What fascination has the yard, when the odor of fried chicken, cream gravy and hot biscuits floats from the dining room window? Why go to the pasture when the incense of its fattest mutton rises from the kitchen chimney? What raw product of the orchard can attract when a stack of pies, every one a magnet of great strength, pulls on every cell in the body with immeasurable force toward the pantry? Oh! The torture of having to wait for the second table! How slowly the guests eat. They are certainly oblivious of the cruel torture they are inflicting. At last human nature prevails and the small boy ventures to the kitchen door and casts a wistful eye on the cook who stops for a moment, and preparing a place on the kitchen table, says: "Come, honey, come and eat these scraps before they get cold." After that the choicest samples of each course are placed on the boy's platter before the change is made in the dining room.

The early Missourian was strong in his convictions and unyielding in his creed. His ancestors fought the battles of Protestantism in France. In this struggle he lost his home and became an exile, but he never for one moment thought of modifying his creed. His nature would not permit his doing so, certainly not at the command of someone else. The right to think for himself and arrive at his own conclusions he has always regarded as a possession from which he could never part, even at the cost of life itself. If I correctly understand the primitive Missourian, it was his right of choice rather than what he chose, of which he was so tenacious. He began as a Protestant and he has continued to protest. In this country of religious freedom, finding themselves without a common enemy, the descendants of the old French

Huguenots broke into factions in their creeds and differed earnestly on free will, predestination and forms of baptism. I have listened to many a warm discussion of these points. I well remember a most amusing termination of one of them before the open fire at the old home. The antagonists were eating juicy Northern Spies. One had cut a nice bit from his apple and holding it aloft on the point of his knife he said: "I believe that it was fore-ordained before the world was created that I should eat this piece of apple." His antagonist, resorting to an argument more forceful than polite, knocked the piece of apple into the midst of the blazing logs.

I also remember how warmly the disputations concerning forms of baptism were waged. Some held that immersion was a positive command and that entrance to the celestial city would be permitted only to those whose sins had been washed away in this manner. Fortunately, however, these differences in theological dogma had no effect upon their practical Christianity, and Methodists and Baptists lived side by side in brotherly love. Their sons and daughters married and intermarried and wisely left nice distinctions in creed to be settled in another world where we may be sure they will not have much weight one way or the other.

One of my earliest lessons in theology came when I could not have been more than seven years old. Mother had permitted me to spend the night with a neighbor boy whose father was a Baptist. After family prayers Mr. B. took me on his knees, told me what a good man and neighbor my father was, but assured me that he could never go to heaven because he had not been immersed. I was horrified at this statement. By the side of my boy friend I sobbed myself to sleep. In the early dawn I slipped out of the bed, crept out of the still slumbering house and fled to my home. On Father's neck I told my story and wildly begged that he be immersed forthwith. To my surprise Father was not disturbed. Indeed, he seemed greatly amused. He told me that Mr. B. was a good and well meaning man, but a religious fanatic. It took some days to allay my anxiety but after much thinking I became calm and afterwards listened to stories of future rewards and punishments much as I did to those told me by Black Mammy of "raw head and bloody bones."

The mistress of the Missouri farm of ante-bellum times had her days filled with duties. It was for her to direct the busy and somewhat complicated machinery of the household. Meals were provided under her direction. The dairy products must pass through the usual routine. The poultry yard demanded frequent visits. The flower and vegetable gardens were under her supervision. The products of the orchard must not be permitted to go wholly to waste. The fibers, from which the clothing for both whites and blacks was made, must pass through every stage of their manufacture under her inspection. The carding, spinning and weaving of both the coarser and finer textures depended upon her experience and skill. She served as nurse, and in many ailments as physician to both whites and blacks. One of her duties was to instruct her daughters in the art of housekeeping, and that meant much in those days. Her hospitality was unbounded in quantity, if plain in quality. Guests were frequent and welcome. On account of the distance between friends and relatives, visitors often prolonged their stay for days.

Camp and protracted meetings were frequent, and well filled lunch baskets were a necessity. In all this busy life mothers did not neglect the intellectual and moral education of their children. Good manners and refinement in behavior were inculcated and practised. These mothers knew nothing of women's clubs and did not discuss woman suffrage but they did the duties that fell to their share and this is all that can be expected of mortal man or woman.

In these days of special labor, of machine-made goods, and of facility of interchange, one is inclined to doubt the veracity of his own memory as he recalls the old farm and the occupations of its inhabitants. All the ordinary clothing worn by both whites and blacks was made from home grown fibers, flax and wool. Attempts were made to grow cotton and these were not without some success. The hand cotton gin, something like a diminutive clothes wringer, and homemade, served to remove the seeds. Spinning wheels for flax and wool, reels that cracked at every one hundred rounds, and looms for both plain and fancy fabrics were busy in providing clothing, blankets and carpets. The working day garments for summer were of coarse flax and those for winter were linsey and jeans. Sumac berries and walnut hulls supplied the ordinary dyes. Straw hats for summer and cloth or fur caps for winter were the products of the unskilled labor of the farm. As I have already said, plows, harrows, corn planters, wagons, and even the family carriage were joint productions of the carpenter and blacksmith; the cradle in which the child was rocked was a section of the gum tree; and the coffin in which both the young and the aged were laid to rest was shaped of black walnut boards sawed partly through and bent after being treated at the right place with boiling water.

The practical chemistry of soap making in all its details was well-known to the early Missourian. The ashes stored in great wooden hoppers and leached with water supplied the alkali and this boiled with the scraps of fats obtained at hog killing time, made the soap. Candle making was a fine art, and the iron lamp with its twisted wick gave out a dim light and much bad odor.

With the exception of coffee, tea and sugar, most of the food consumed on the farm was the product of its own growth. Sorghum often served the purpose of cane sugar, and coffee substitutes in the form of roasted rye or wheat were not unknown. The big kitchen fireplace was a wonderful laboratory and the memory of its products stimulates my digestive secretions even now. There was the great swinging crane on which hung boiling pots of vegetables and meats. The broad stone hearth was covered with the baking ovens with live coals underneath and piled on the lid, all aglow. From these came the great pones of cornbread and the toothsome beaten biscuits. On winter nights the prizes of the hunter, rabbits, "possums," quail and larger birds, as wild geese and turkeys, were suspended in front of the blazing logs and basted with melted butter and spices applied with swabs on long sticks as they swung about, first one side and then the other, turned to the culinary artists. Sweet and Irish potatoes never tasted better than when roasted in the ashes, and it may be added that their sterilization was complete. While these delectable dishes were being prepared the winter winds moaned and sighed through the great locusts in the yard, and black Mammy told grewsome stories of "raw head and bloody bones." I have seen imitations of the old kitchen in the Creole quarters in New Orleans, and, I may add, have enjoyed their well-prepared dishes, but the greatest pleasure came from the awakening of memories of the old Missouri home.

One of the duties of those too young to do heavier work was to cure the meat that hung in tier upon tier to the rafters in the smokehouse. A smoldering fire was kept going for weeks. Chips from the woodpile furnished the fuel and the fire must not blaze but generate as much smoke as possible. The task of keeping these fires going just right so frequently called the small boy from play or entertaining book that he has ever since had an aversion to the odor of creosote.

The methods of farming were crude and wasteful. "What does not go into the granary goes into the smokehouse" was a favorite saying, and implied that the hog picked up and converted into pork whatever grain was left in the field or dropped from the wagon. The grain was cradled, bound, shocked and stacked. In the barn was a large room floored with puncheons laid as smoothly as the crude workmanship of the day permitted. On this floor the wheat was spread and trampled by a troop of horses, the leader of which was ridden by the small boy. The trail was kept near the wall, and men stood in the middle of the room and kept tossing the grain in front of the trampling horses. The grain, crudely and imperfectly separated, was winnowed in a fan mill turned by hand and then carried to the old grist on the creek and ground. The flour thus produced could have awakened even in the mind of my friend, Doctor Harvey Wiley, no suspicion that it had been bleached.

There were fields of corn, wheat, oats, rye, tobacco, flax and meadowland. There were broad acres of open woodland where the scaly barked hickory, the spreading oak and the graceful elm reared their massive trunks and spread their green branches high above the beautiful carpet of blue grass painted in shades of color, shifting with light and shadow and more beautiful than any texture that ever came from the looms of the Orient. On this carpet so beautifully spread over hill and dale in the woodland pasture the farmers' horses, cattle and sheep fed to repletion and then rested for more perfect digestion in the shade. The oak and hickory supplied without stint the fast-growing porkers, which, happily oblivious of the fact that hog killing day would be due in December, lazily divided their time between the mast-strewn ridge and the cooling waters of the pond. The grass, both carpet and food, ever renewed itself. With the coming of winter it only changed its color and, retaining all its nutriment, lay buried beneath the white blanket of snow and when this had been imperceptibly lifted by the magic hand of spring, there it lay, an abundant supply for the quadrupeds of the farm, until through its roots it should convert the richness of the soil into a new growth of proteins and carbohydrates.

The woodland pasture was not devoid of gastronomic enticement for the farmer's boy. Down in the deepest parts of the shade on the slope toward the creek, near where the lime kiln had been operated, modestly sheltered under more pretentious neighbors, grew the mulberry trees for whose rich but fleeting gifts the red-headed woodpeckers and the sun-tanned boys contended. The boy quite equalled the bird in reaching the topmost boughs, and in capacity was equal to a dozen of his winged competitors. The contest was soon over, for the black mulberry ripens suddenly and disappears into the stomach of boy or bird quickly. Then for a few days longer it is only a memory in the form of stains on the hands and cheeks of the former, and on the white collar of the latter. The next thing in the woodland pasture to direct the bare feet and stimulate the digestive secretions of the boy was the wild plum. The trees grew best in thickets along the rail fence and the fruit ripened in the dog-days. The hogs rooted up the ground in the clump of trees and the thorns were sharp, but the boy first filled his distensible stomach and then a less capacious basket and promised to return to-morrow with an empty stomach and a more generous basket. I can testify from personal experience that the prize products of the best orchards of the Santa Clara Valley failed to produce the same effect on the gustatory nerve of the man of fifty that the wild plum of Missouri did upon the same nerve in the barefooted boy of ten. I shall refer this matter to the National Research Council for investigation.

With the first severe frost another gastronomic feast was prepared for the small boy. In the open field the thoughtful ax of the pioneer had left a few trees which bore a fruit fit for the feasts of Olympus. In my boyhood days I imagined that the manna upon which the children of Israel were fed in the wilderness was something like the persimmon after the killing frosts had, through the magical chemistry of nature, converted its acid substances into the richest and daintiest of sweets. Then there were haws, red and black, and the flavor of the Missouri wild grape has been wafted to me across the wide ocean, even as I have lingered in the vineyards of the Italian Riviera.

There was the winding creek with its fringe of hazel, willow and towering sycamores, with its deep pools in which dwelt the homely and elusive catfish, ever tempting, generally evading the youthful Izaak Walton. The creek had other irresistible attractions for the youthful dweller near its banks. In summer its cool waters were ever inviting the small boy to a plunge and in winter its coat of ice had its fascination, and the possibility that one might break through and undergo baptism without sanction of the church added to the allurement. In summer the feathery songsters of the hazel fringe were constantly calling to the small boy, especially if some task in lesson or work had been placed upon him, and the possibility of meeting with a blue racer in the bushes increased the zeal with which he searched for the bird's nest. Then there was the plaintive cry of the whip-poor-will as the shadows of evening were falling, and what success was secured when the eggs of this mysterious bird were found lying in the dead leaves without form of nest! In autumn hazel nuts must be gathered, and farther down, where the creek broadens and loses its shrubby fringe, where it flows through the massive timber, there grew the great hickory, and in late October it literally strewed the ground with the big creek nuts. Here on Saturday afternoon came the whole family with a wagon which was filled with bags of these, the most delicious of the native nuts of Missouri. These, with the black walnuts that grew near by, were stored away in the cellar to furnish refreshments for the long evenings of the coming winter. In winter the banks of the creek and the woods of the ridge became the haunts of rabbits and quail, the pursuit of which, with snare or net or gun, quickened the currents of red blood that flowed through the muscles of the Missouri boy of sixty years ago.

In the fall, clouds of wild pigeons flew so near the earth that with a shotgun many could be brought down at one discharge. At night so many of these would alight on small trees that the limbs were often broken. This bird has suddenly and unaccountably become extinct. In the winter, flocks of wild geese came to rest in the corn field, and hunters, hidden in the shocks, had at least one good shot. Wild ducks were numerous on the lakes in the fall and there were no laws forbidding their being killed. Along the heavily wooded ridges wild turkeys tempted the hunter by responding to his call. Food on the old farm was unstinted in quantity, diversified in kind and not wanting in vitamines.

Patches of potatoes of both kinds supplied the family. In the orchards, apples, peaches, pears, cherries and plums were free to all, including the hogs and birds. Berries of all kinds came in season and in abundance. In our community no one ever thought of limiting white or black in consumption of food of any kind, and no vegetables, fruits or berries were ever sold.

At one time I had a horse which was never ridden save by mother or myself. With mother in the saddle, he would be a gentle, ambling gray, never shy and never going faster than a moderate pace, or at most in a rhythmic lope. With the boy astraddle, the horse was off like a flash dodging among the trees and leaping fences and gullies. When I approached this horse in the pasture he would come and rub his head against my breast, apparently anticipating fun. I would jump on his back without saddle or bridle and away he would go. At one place there was a low fence and about a rod beyond and parallel to it was a deep ditch with soft clay banks. The ditch was too wide for the horse to attempt, but he delighted in leaping the fence and, with a sudden turn, running between the fence and the ditch. More than once this manoeuver resulted in my landing in the ditch, which the horse seemed to enjoy more than I did. I am deeply grieved to say that this horse-play of mine caused another boy's death. The other boys on the farm had been repeatedly told not to follow my example, but the son of a tenant tried it. He was thrown against a tree and his skull was fractured. The degree of my responsibility in this accident has given me serious moments.

The neighborhood boys became quite expert in bareback riding. In summer there was a long stretch of sand, left by the drying up of a stream. Here the boys were wont to assemble with their horses. Bareback riding with or without a surcingle is quickly learned by a nimble boy. With a surcingle supplied with handles, getting on and off a horse in full gallop is jolly fun. Without a surcingle the grasp must be on the mane. Even standing with bare feet on the broad hips of a horse going at a rhythmic gait is easily done and costs only a few falls.

An innocent amusement consisted in swimming horses across the large mill pond in Sweet Springs. A horse goes into deep water timidly and with evident apprehension, but when firmly urged he takes the plunge and then devotes his whole attention to his strokes. The wash of the water over the shoulders of the horse and against the bare body of the boy rider is most agreeable to the latter.

It is better to guide the horse since he does not always show good judgment in the selection of his landing place.

Another pastime occasionally indulged in was not free from danger, and I do not advise its practise. Near the barn there was a large straw stack. On sunny wintry Sundays when neither boy nor beast had enough to do to break the monotony of the day, horses, mules and cattle would stand with their heads and necks up to their shoulders hidden in the straw, which they munched slowly and with apparent satisfaction. The boys would climb to the top of the stack and each selecting his animal, slide down and drop on its back. Then the fun began. The first time a horse or a mule met with this shock the reaction was immediate and violent. But these animals soon got on to the trick and the sudden thud on the back no longer disturbed their feeding. From this I concluded that horses and mules have memories and learn by experience. One day having exhausted these animals, I tried a drop on a lusty young ox. The animal responded immediately and forcefully. The result was disastrous to the boy and the experiment was never repeated; therefore, I do not know to this day how far an ox profits by past experience.

In 1925 I witnessed at Tucson, Arizona, a three days' rodeo. As I looked on I recognized that practically every detail was an evolution from the old straw stack play of sixty years ago. I am sure that if at the age of sixteen I had been transplanted to Arizona instead of going to Central College, I would have become a cowboy and the story of my life would be quite different.

The boys of my childhood days never heard of tennis nor did they know of golf, but their lives could not be said to have been wholly devoid of sport. I believe that had I remained on the old farm and continued my active exercise, the tubercle bacilli would not have troubled the body cells in the apex of my lung; but when I went to college, studied in a small unventilated room, and neglected exercise in the open, the sleeping bacilli awoke and began the contest, which was finally terminated in my favor by the improved appetite stimulated by riding and the cold baths.

Telling a wilful lie was counted among both whites and blacks a most heinous and unforgivable sin. Temporarily I once fell under this ban. I spent the whole of one rainy Sunday morning in trying to comprehend the description by Julius Cæsar of the wonderful bridge he claimed to have built. In fact for some weeks I had been trying to make a model of this structure. The whole family had become interested in it. The afternoon came on cloudless. I saddled Golden and rode into the forest. The woods have always had a special fascination for me when the sun comes out after a heavy rain. The foliage, free from dust and debris, is at its best; the birds sing their sweetest songs. Rabbits and other small quadrupeds leave their damp burrows and scamper in joy through the brush. All nature renders thanks to heaven for the long needed and fructifying rain. I will acknowledge that I have some remnant of the spirit of tree worship, possibly transmitted to me through the Welsh line from my Druidian ancestors. I came to a bend in Sweet Springs. On the side on which I stood the bank was low and the area was frequently overflowed. The opposite bank rose perpendicularly to a height of twenty feet or more. My astonished eyes saw a rude foot bridge across the stream, one end resting on the low shore and the other terminating abruptly against the bank on the other side. For some time I sat on Golden rubbing my eyes and wondering if I was asleep or awake.

When I returned, the family was at the supper table. I took my place and told my story. Father's questions showed plainly that he thought I was lying. More charitably, Mother suggested that I lay aside all thought of Cæsar's bridge. The subject was dropped so far as Father and Mother were concerned, but the attendants took my story to the cabins. I did not sleep well that night and my dreams were filled with all kinds of bridges, including the Pons assinorum. The following week days brought their pressing duties. But I knew especially from questions asked by the negroes that my story had been widely distributed and that I was suspected of either lying or insanity. Towards the end of the week there was a lull in the work and Father proposed that we take a ride. I noticed that he turned immediately into the forest and when we reached the creek he gently asked me to lead him to the spot where I had seen the bridge. I complied with a benumbed brain, doubting my own sanity. When we reached the point there was no bridge, but lying on the low bank were the poles which had supported it and the boards which had constituted the flooring. More astounding still, where the point of the farther end of the bridge had touched the cliff there was a tunnel, some feet square, dug into the earth. The excavated soil had evidently fallen into the creek. My heart rejoiced for there was visible truth that I was neither a liar nor was I insane. The matter became for some time a neighborhood mystery, which was finally solved by ascertaining that a prospector had tested the bank in his search for a vein of coal; similar bluffs not far distant were then yielding an inferior grade of bituminous coal. This experience has made me more tolerant of improbable stories told me by my own and other boys, and less ready to pronounce every big story teller a liar.

Being a physician I have been interested in collecting all possible information concerning the prevalence of diseases in the Huguenot branch of my family. Since coming to America three diseases have caused the majority of deaths; one in childhood, one in early adult life, and one in old age. Naturally I am not able to give exact figures since my information comes from tradition, confirmed in part by records in family Bibles. The most fatal childhood disease is designated in the family records as "bloody flux." It is a bacterial dysentery and in some generations has killed quite one half the children, mostly before they reached five years of age. I am the eldest of a family of ten children, five of whom succumbed to this disease, and the fatality among my first cousins was about the same.

My wife and I had a serious experience with this disease in our youngest son. In 1894, she with our five boys went to Missouri to make her father a visit. In about two weeks she called me on account of the serious illness of the baby, then about eighteen months old. I arrived at Huntsville at two P. M. My wife's uncle, Doctor W. H. Taylor, was in attendance and told us that he had at that time some forty children with "bloody flux" under his care and that the mortality was great. The weather was intensely hot, day and night. Even a breeze was like a breath from a blast furnace. By eight o'clock that evening my wife and I with the baby were in a stateroom on the fast train for Chicago. The next morning we took the child to a room high up in a hotel facing the lake and by six P. M. we were on a boat and moving northward. During the long vigil of that night we kept the baby on a cot on deck. Strangers in their unwise sympathy crowded about us, cutting off the cool air which we were seeking so desperately. I think that I have never been so ferocious as I was that night. With words as gentle as I could make them I begged the crowd to let the child have air. In my deepest soul I cursed their stupidity. All kinds of suggestions as to treatment came from the kind-hearted people. In words I thanked them; in my heart I damned them. During the next afternoon there came one of those storms which so frequently sweep over Lake Michigan. As darkness was deepening we took the child, still alive but barely so, from the boat to a hotel in Charlevoix where a former and beloved pupil, Doctor Armstrong, rendered us every aid possible. Early the next morning Doctor George Dock, my colleague from Ann Arbor, arrived. A few days later we were in our cottage at Old Mission watching with joy the child's speedy return to health. The memory of this is one of the ties that binds us to Old Mission. This is not a medical essay, but I beg to say that I am thoroughly convinced that the intense and prolonged heat of the Missouri summers is a factor in the high mortality from "bloody flux" in that region. Fortunately improved sanitary conditions have done much towards the elimination of this disease.

Consumption, or pulmonary tuberculosis as we now call it, has been a frequent cause of death in the early adult in my family. I have told of my grandfather's attempts to rid himself of this disease by living an outdoor life. Of his seven children who reached maturity three developed consumption; two succumbed and one overcame it after two overland trips from Missouri to New Orleans and a subsequent journey across the plains to California.

In my twenty-first year, my great uncle, Doctor Warren Dameron, recognized the fact that I had pulmonary tuberculosis. At that time I was losing flesh rapidly, my minimum weight being 108, coughing badly and suffering from exhaustive night sweats. This was long before Koch identified and isolated the tubercle bacillus. My good uncle went over the family history with me and gave advice to live an outdoor life. Then with a smile on his lips and a tear in his eyes he said: "Victor, postpone dying as long as possible; let it be the last thing you do." I am consistently following this advice now in my seventy-fifth year.

The treatment which I adopted with my uncle's approval was more heroic than I have ever dared prescribe for any patient. About two miles from my father's house was a sulphur spring, which had some local reputation for its medicinal virtues in which neither my uncle nor I believed. The water welled up into a box which reached to my chin when I stood in it. Every morning during an entire summer and late into the fall before breakfast I rode to the spring, stripped in the open and stood for a few moments in the ice cold water. As cold weather approached I frequently found thin ice in the cow tracks about the box. Soon I began to gain flesh and other unfavorable symptoms gradually faded away. Now the only evidence of the presence of the tubercle bacillus in my body is a lesion in one apex.

An old saying which has run in our family for many generations is as follows: "If you escape consumption in early life you will die of cancer in old age." Of my grandfather's seven children who reached adult life four died after fifty of cancer. It is worthy of note that of these no two had the malignant growth in the same organ. The same grim and remorseless reaper has been equally busy in other branches of the family.

I hope that no one led by my description will attempt to find the old Missouri home. As I have described it, it does not exist; in fact, it has never existed except to me. A wise man centuries ago wrote: "To me things are as they seem to me; to you they are as they seem to you." I have described the old home colored by the imagination of Walter Scott, the stately lines of Virgil and the eloquence and wisdom of that great pagan, Cicero.

CHAPTER III

THE CIVIL WAR IN MISSOURI

BEFORE the Civil War my father was not a Democrat, but a Conservative or Whig, the platform of which party stated that "they recognized no political principle other than the Constitution of the country, the Union of the States and the enforcement of laws." In the state and presidential elections of 1860, which I remember well, the contest in Missouri was between the Whigs and the Northern (Douglas) Democrats, the Southern Democrats and Republicans polling only small numbers.

One morning in April, 1861, my father entered the school room of Hazel Hill Academy with a pained and anxious expression on his face. I was startled and feared the announcement of some family disaster. In a tremulous voice he announced that the secessionists had fired on Fort Sumter and asked that the school be dismissed for the day. The local militia, organized and commanded by my grandfather, Colonel William Dameron, in the Black Hawk War, assembled and was addressed by the leading men of the community. The burden of these speeches was that they must prepare to go and whip South Carolina back into the Union as Andrew Jackson had once threatened to do. Once or twice a week these potential

46

soldiers were drilled and harangued. In the meantime
many things were happening in the state and nation.
Governor Jackson labored at first to keep the state neutral,
but the intemperate speech made by General Lyon, the
commander of the United States troops in the state, at a
conference with the Governor, drove the latter with a
large following into the waiting arms of the Confederacy.
Besides, the dominance of the German element of St.
Louis in the Union cause made the natives turn to the
other direction. *"Die schwartze Garde"* and *"mit Siegel"*
became terms of reproach. The tone of the talks to the
local militia rapidly changed and in early June this small
troop joined the Governor in his futile attempt to aid the
South.

A lasting impression was made upon at least one small
boy as he witnessed these events. One man in the militia
stood out for the Union to the end. At every meeting,
after the change in purpose became apparent, he protested. He appealed to sentiment and to reason. When
the final day came, when the ladies presented a Confederate flag, he made a last appeal, which was met with
laughter. Then the order to move came. He swung into
his saddle and rode with the troop. A shout went up:
"What! Bill, are you going with us?" "Yes, you are all
going to hell, but you are my friends and I am going
with you." He never came back but he deserved a better
destination than he predicted. When the conflict is on,
the call to stand by friends is well nigh irresistible.

Four years of my childhood were spent in the midst
of an internecine war, with brother against brother, neighbor against neighbor, with opportunity to avenge every
real or imagined affront, with privilege to plunder and

murder, with at least a partial return to the barbaric and savage state, with the revival of the brute instincts which still linger in the best of men. I learned to hate war and to love peace so dearly that I have been willing to do my small bit in fighting for it. I agree with General Sherman in his definition of war; certainly no one was more competent than he to give the definition he did.

So long as regular troops occupied our area, family privacy and property were protected. Guards were placed about the buildings and we felt safe. I remember with pleasure a Colonel McKay, who slept and ate in our home as an honored guest. At that time I had two beautiful golden-chief horses. One day during the Colonel's stay I rode one of these some miles beyond the outer guards. I was riding along Silver Creek with the stream on one side and high rocks on the other when the shout "Halt!" came from the hills. I looked up and saw "a cousin" who had joined the rebel guerrillas standing above me with a gun in his hand. He said: "Victor, I will have to take that horse." I knew that I had nothing to fear from him, so leaning forward I touched Golden's neck and shouted back, "You will have to catch us first." As the horse fled down the stream a shot rang out far above me but soon I was safely within the Union lines. Of course I did not inform the colonel of my cousin's proximity.

One of these horses saved me from great injury and demonstrated the marked intelligence of the equine species. I had ridden to a neighbor's house and was hitching the horse when a large dog sprang at me. As the dog came the horse kicked him but the beast recovered his footing and giving the horse's heels a wide berth seized me by the arm. The horse struck the dog across the back with a forefoot and made him loosen his hold. Later both of these horses were "commandeered," one by southern and the other by northern thieves. One morning nearly a year after it had been "confiscated" the latter was found, broken and crippled, standing at the woodland pasture gate, mutely begging recognition by its old friends and admittance to its home. It received both but it never again carried me over the fence or across the ditch. A blooded, coal black mare with silvered fetlocks, lovingly known as "Silver Heels," disappeared from the pasture, and some months later was recognized by father in the lot of a farmer, about five miles distant from our home, whose sons thieved in the livery of Uncle Sam. Father made a claim, but the jury branded him as a "southern sympathizer," and the matter rested there and the mare in the possession of the Union man.

During the last months of the war we preserved a few horses by keeping them in the woods down on Sweet Springs. At that period rebel guerrillas were nonexistent in northern Missouri except in the imagination of the state militia, but the groundless fears of the latter were of service to the natives, since under them, the militia, "the brave protectors of our homes and firesides," did not dare to venture into the woods. As a blind we kept old and crippled horses in the barn lot. When a squad of soldiers came to "impress" horses we showed this bunch and said: "Take your pick." The woody recess on Sweet Springs served not only for the preservation of horses, but there we stored away the family carriage, the best wagon, harness and other farm valuables. We kept at the "woodpile" an old wagon without a body and with harness made with pieces of rope. One Sunday afternoon a squad of militia came and ordered us to bring immediately a load of corn to Huntsville, their camp. We showed them the old wagon without a body and the corn standing on the stalk and told them that we would gladly comply with their order if they would tell us how. They did not know that we had made a collapsible wagon body out of fence rails, tied together with rope, when we were compelled to gather corn to feed the animals, both the crippled ones in the barnyard and the sound ones in the woods. Surely adversity is a great teacher. During the fall and winter of 1864-65, cribs stood empty and the ears of corn remained on the stalks from which they were plucked as necessity demanded, or I should say, as the hunger of man and beast required.

We did not altogether escape the rebel guerrillas. One day "Bill Anderson" at the head of his desperadoes and cutthroats rode into Huntsville, the village in which he had been reared, shot down peaceful citizens against whom he had a boy's dislike, robbed the bank and rode away.

The day before the Centralia massacre (September 27, 1864)¹ Quantrell breakfasted, as an uninvited guest, at my father's table. His men were gaily bedecked. Some carried gold watchcases as cap boxes. At Centralia he took a troop of paroled Union soldiers from the train, lined them up and shot them dead. Then setting fire to the train, he ordered the engineer to start it and jump at his own risk.

With the exception of Colonel McKay and his command, I saw no regular United States soldiers during the Civil War. I saw no regular Confederate soldiers, except during the few days in 1864 when General Price made his raid and attacked Glasgow, eighteen miles from my father's home. The night before that event Price's scouts tore down the telegraph lines along the plank road in front of our home. This done, they did not tarry.

Missouri never seceded from the Union. This matter was referred by the legislature to a committee elected by the people and this body never severed the relation of the state to the Union. It is true that a minority of the legislature met at Neosho in October, 1861, passed a secession act and appointed two senators and eight congressmen to the Confederate Congress but this was clearly illegal. The Federal government never regarded the state as a part of the Confederacy and Missouri slaves were not emancipated by Lincoln's proclamation, but by act of the State Legislature passed in 1865. The number of soldiers furnished by Missouri to the Union Army was one hundred and ten thousand. How many of these were colored I do not know. How many enlisted in the Confederate forces is not known but is estimated at about forty thousand.

So far as I know, the most despicable and brutal act inflicted upon the people of the state was that of General Ewing of the 11th Kansas Volunteer Infantry in Order Number 11. This order compelled the residents of three counties (Jackson, Cass and Bates) and a part of the fourth (Vernon) to desert their homes. Those who were willing to swear allegiance to the Union were permitted to live within an area of one mile from a military post, while those who would not take the oath became outcasts and their homes were plundered and burned. This man, and not General Weyler of Cuban fame, was the instigator, in modern times at least, of the establishment of

"Reconcentrados Camps." It is said that one of his own officers, Colonel Bingham, remonstrated, and when repulsed, swore that he would make the name of his superior infamous. At least Colonel Bingham painted a reconcentrados scene, prints of which hung in many a Missouri home for long years and helped to keep alive the fires of sectional animosity, now happily extinguished. How far Federal authorities were responsible for this order I leave to historians to debate.

One day I was throwing wood from the wagon. Hearing a horse charging toward me I turned my head. A militiaman sat on his horse beside the wagon. His right hand held the reins, his left elbow rested on the rim of a rear wheel and in this hand he held a cocked pistol with the barrel almost touching my upturned face. Through his closed teeth he growled into my ear: "Where are those damned rebels you have been feeding in this house?" Terror such as I have never known before or since, seized me. Tears came to my eyes. My tongue became inarticulate. My heart seemed to stand still. I clutched a stick of wood to support my trembling frame. It seemed an eternity before I could find words to answer. I assured him finally that I had not seen a rebel since the night that Price's scouts had torn down the telegraph lines. This time I told the truth, the whole truth, and nothing but the truth. But this experience was so often repeated that I learned to tell a lie with a cocked pistol in my face as readily as under other conditions. In fact I came to find enjoyment in lying in these cases. Such is the power of education and training. The small family, Mother, a younger brother, Sister and I, sitting before the blazing logs in the great fireplace at night would hear the rush of horses under the leafless trees in the yard. We knew what was happening. The house was being encompassed by soldiers. Then there was an interval of intense and oppressive silence, sometimes broken by screams of terror from the negro women and children, but even they learned to keep mute. Then the butt of a musket would strike against the front door. I as the eldest child and man of the house, for I had recently completed my thirteenth year, opened the door and faced the inevitable pistol. "Where is your father?" Then I lied with ease and readiness. We all lied; even the negroes lied. Irene would say as the searching party went through her cabin: "'Fore God I hain't seen Mars John for weeks," when the truth was that she had prepared his dinner not two hours before and he was then in the woods down on Sweet Springs.

As I have said elsewhere my father had served in the quartermaster's corps before his marriage. A falling tree had caught him, breaking both legs, one in two places. One of these fractures never entirely healed and left a suppurating sore from which spicules of bone frequently worked their way through the tissues, causing great pain and at times complete temporary disability.

Shortly before the war, a man giving his name as Young came into the neighborhood, and served a Mr. Philpot as a day laborer working with the negroes and as one of them. Naturally he was not received as a guest in the country homes. He had served in this capacity but a few days when he and Mr. Philpot's best horse simultaneously disappeared. Both were captured, the horse returned to its owner, and the man sent to the Missouri penitentiary. Father had been foreman of the jury that convicted and sentenced this man. In the fall of 1864 Young, now as lieutenant-colonel of a marauding band of home guards, revisited the scenes of his former activities. He was no longer dressed in prison stripes but in the striking livery of Uncle Sam. He shot Mr. Philpot in the barnyard from which he had taken the horse. His next victim was to be my father, hence his frequent visits to our home.

Failing in his purpose he came with his troop late in January or early in February, 1865, and took possession of the farm and all that was thereon. He did not burn the buildings because they gave him and his men shelter. He permitted Mother and her children the occupancy of one room but even in this there was no privacy as soldiers passed through it day and night. One evening four men spread their blankets before the fire, when Mother seized a musket from the corner, drew a bead on them and ordered them from the room. I may say that this was not mere bravado on Mother's part. She was an accomplished shot, as she had frequently demonstrated to the family by killing an occasional stray cat or a vicious dog. The soldiers took up their blankets and beat a hasty retreat, leaving Mother in possession of their guns, with a threat that she would use one of them on any man who entered her room without permission. They threatened Mother with no other show of personal violence, but she was subjected to every other conceivable insult. The soldiers gathered the negroes from the cabins, seated them at Mother's table and ordered her to wait on them as they had done for her. On her refusal to comply with this demand the soldiers performed this function themselves. They boxed up books, linen and other valuables before our eyes and shipped them to their homes.

A neighbor boy became, after the war, a Methodist preacher. He was assigned to a circuit in one of the northern border counties. One Sunday afternoon after preaching in a rural church he was invited to tarry over night in the home of one of the elders. That night he was handed the family Bible and asked to read a chapter and lead in prayer. He was surprised on opening the holy book to find that it was his own family Bible and contained a record of his own birth. He says that he prayed loudly and earnestly for the conversion of thieves.

During Colonel Young's domination of our home and especially after the insult directed at my mother, I swore that the chief function of my life should be to kill this man, but fate soon relieved me of this obligation. Shortly after the escape of the family, about which I am soon to tell, a train passed over his drunken body. I am sure that Satan welcomed him as an efficient coadjutor.

At that time there was said to be an organized society of southern sympathizers, known, if I remember correctly, as Knights of the Golden Circle, in Illinois. I know nothing about the truth of this statement, but whisperings of the existence of such an organization came to us over the "grapevine telegraph" and we believed them. I do know that in our loyal sister state Father found friends and helpers. In Montgomery County, Illinois, he had refuge during most of the time that Colonel Young was lying in wait for him in Missouri. From this haven Father made occasional excursions to see how we were doing. Finally having made all preparation for our flight into Egypt (a name for southern Illinois), he returned to his straw pallet on Sweet Springs and watched for a chance. In these movements he was accompanied by one of Mother's brothers, Uncle Green Dameron. The opportunity came sooner than we expected. Colonel Young, having exhausted the visible resources of the old farm, led his men away to richer fields. We were kept informed of his whereabouts by "grapevine telegraph."

On the night of February 14, 1865, a memorable date in my life, all were astir in the old home. Two wagons, the family carryall and riding horses were brought from Sweet Springs. Uncle Jeff, the only negro man left on the place, was instructed so far as he could comprehend as to our destination and given charge of the farm and all that remained on it. Sometime in the night we were on the way. The party consisted of Father, Mother, the three children, including myself, Uncle Green Dameron, Doctor Perkinson, the neighborhood physician, and two neighbor boys, both about fifteen, Claibourne Jackson and William Birge. We took our breakfast at a friendly farm house some miles away and then avoiding the chief highways and as many towns as possible continued eastward. We crossed the Mississippi River at the village of Louisiana without question. Father had arranged for our crossing the Illinois River at Apple Creek Ferry, not far from Louisiana. But when we arrived at this place we found the flimsy ferry, a flat boat guided by poles, quite unable to stem the current and withstand the blocks of floating ice. We continued our weary journey through the day and throughout the long night up the western bank of the Illinois. We were among total strangers and feared that we might fall into the hands of enemies. We made cautious inquiry as to the possibility of crossing the river at every hamlet, but were compelled to proceed to Peoria before we found possible chance of transportation. I never visit this city, famous in pre-Volstead days for its distilleries, without an initial shudder. There must have been some corn juice there as early as 1865, for we were questioned, suspected and threatened by drunken men at the wharf. But we gave gentle answer and were allowed to move on to the boat, one bystander expressing the hope, which did not seem groundless, that we would go to the bottom instead of the other shore. Without mishap we landed and continued on our way.

The first night after leaving Peoria I had an extremely unusual experience. We had traveled some hours after dark. The last thing that I remember that night was tying my horse in a fence corner and supplying it with an armful of corn thrown on the frozen ground. When I became conscious again I was in bed with the doctor and he was trying to awaken me. By the light of the kerosene lamp in the farmhouse I found my clothes, placed more carefully than I would have arranged them had I been awake, on a chair. The doctor told me that I had eaten supper and behaved as a normal boy, but the long journey of the night before had rendered the desire to sleep irresistible.

A few days later we arrived at our destination and were installed in a double log cabin, which Father had previously provided. The McDavids and other friends supplied our immediate wants while our scanty stores from the wagons furnished our cabin.

As soon as we were installed in our new home, Father sent me to the rural school. At the first recess, the boys selected one of their own number of about my size and age, formed a ring about us, and told us to fight it out.

My opponent began by hurling at me all the vile epithets in which his vocabulary was rich. He called me a rebel, a secessionist, a white livered scoundrel, a puke and other names unfit for this page. I showed no resentment. Finally emboldened by my attitude, half squatting, with his hands on his knees, he peered into my face and said: "He is a pretty decent boy for the upbringing he has had." This was too much, since it implied a slur on my family and my ancestors. The fight was on. For some minutes it raged. I will not give the details since the boy is not here to tell his story and I am not an impartial narrator. Suffice it to say that this was my only fight in that school. From that time I was one of the boys and I must pay tribute to the fairness with which the "sucker" boys initiated the "puke." I have seen less honor displayed in contests between older and more intelligent males of the genus homo.

That summer Jackson, Birge and I broke the ground and cultivated sixty acres of corn. Father worked as a carpenter as his lame leg did not permit his following the plow, but did not incapacitate him for the more arduous labor of converting huge sections of oak trees into clapboards and making roofs of the same.

The southern Illinois of 1865 was quite different from that of to-day. Then there were vast expanses of virgin prairies. Here and there small clumps of trees indicated the location of farmhouses, which for the most part were small wooden buildings, but with abundant hospitality within. The prairies were broken at long distances by sluggish streams with heavily wooded shores, varying in width with the size of the stream and its smaller tributaries. The dwellers in the open lands were quite as different from those on the creek bottoms as were their surroundings. The former were of the ordinary American farmer type, mostly from Ohio, Indiana and farther east, though with a goodly sprinkling from Kentucky and Virginia. Those along the streams were the most primitive people I have ever seen in this country. In fact they were but little better supplied with creature comforts than the present peasants of the Balkans and quite as ignorant and shiftless. I have ridden through the mountains of Kentucky, Tennessee and North Carolina and know something of the "poor white trash" of these regions and I saw more of them in Camps Sevier and Wheeler during the war. Their intellects impressed me as fertile soil lying fallow, ready to prove productive under skilful cultivation, and then I recall that they have produced an Andrew Jackson and an Abraham Lincoln. But it was different with the people that I knew on the creek bottoms of southern Illinois in 1865. To me their brains seemed absolutely sterile. I have often wondered what has become of these people. If I could be convinced that their descendants have become worthy citizens I should have less faith in heredity and more in environment. Our cabin lay on the edge of a forest and I made acquaintances in both directions. A ride of a mile to the west carried me to the residence of farmer Brown whose intelligent sons and daughters I respected; while a ride of less distance to the east brought me to the windowless hut of neighbor Trelawney, whose half grown children roamed in the forest with less clothing than a modern fashionable woman wears. These children gathered acorns for the winter and berries for more immediate consumption.

One day I drove to Hillsboro, the county seat of

Montgomery County, and went to the hotel for lunch. The proprietor asked if I did not live near McDavid's Point and if a young lady, recently arrived, could ride with me to that place. Although I was at the girl-shy age I accepted the responsibility. Seated in the buggy by the side of a handsome girl, I was informed that she had recently graduated at a seminary in New York State and that she was making a visit to her father's brother, Mr. Trelawney. I assured her that I knew her uncle and should safely conduct her to his door. At our cabin I told her that it would be necessary to continue our journey on horseback. She asked if there was no carriage road to her uncle's. I lied—a habit acquired during the war—and told her that a bridge was down. Mounted, we proceeded through the roadless forest. I drew rein at the door of the Trelawney hut. She exclaimed: "My uncle does not live here?" I told her that we were before the residence of the only Trelawney I knew. She asked me to wait. She went into the house as stark naked children stared from the doorway and retreated in fright at her approach. Returning she asked if my mother could give her shelter for the night. The next morning Mr. Trelawney brought his eldest daughter, with her nakedness decently hidden, and I drove the pair to the railroad station. Did the daughter ever return, and what became of the other little Trelawneys, are questions for which I would greatly like to have answers. They would be of sociological and eugenic interest.

During the summer Father interrupted the making of clapboards long enough to purchase a drove of hogs and a number of young horses. As soon as the corn was "laid by," I became for a short time a herder of horses.

It was my business to see that individuals did not stray and to keep the bunch together. It was at this time that I had my first experience with malaria. In 1865 every man, woman and child in southern Illinois, at least within my range, shook with ague every other day. Father, as a precursor to later Italian savants, believed in and practised the prophylactic use of quinine. He had a great demijohn filled with chopped Peruvian bark, while the interspaces were occupied by *spiritus frumenti*. Of this noxious mixture each member of the family had to swallow a liberal draught every morning before breakfast. I shunned the mixture on the plea that I had to ride with the horses. Besides, some nights I did not get home, since the herd often led me far away.

On a hot August morning as I sat on my horse in the treeless prairie, I felt cold chills playing hide and seek up and down my spine. As the sun's rays became more vertical the chilly sensations grew in strength. Soon my teeth were chattering. I dismounted, removed the saddle, staked my horse, and using the saddle as a pillow, I wrapped my blanket about me and sought comfort but found none. The sun did its best to warm me but failed. In my misery I heard the horses moving. The sun was driving them to shade and water. In single file and at a lazy trot they were making for the creek bottom, some miles distant. My horse, impatient to follow, was straining at his tether and calling to his fellows. There was but one thing to do and soon I was loping after the herd with every joint and ligament in my body out of gear and with my teeth clattering like castanets with every footfall of my horse. After miles of agony and about high noon, my herd, having quenched their thirst, were standing with heads down, tails switching and hoofs stamping, fighting the innumerable hosts of every genus and species of insect created to make miserable the life of man and beast. I had again taken to the ground with the saddle for a pillow, busy fighting the voracious mosquitoes. Rather abruptly the chilly sensation left me and another tormentor came. The fever laid its tight grip upon me. Currents of heated blood under high pressure flowed through my throbbing arteries, ringing in my ears and benumbing my senses.

The sky became overcast with clouds. An ominous silence pervaded the air. Not a leaf moved, and as the gloom deepened the swarms of insects grew more voracious. The heavy artillery of heaven began a bombardment which shook the earth while vivid flashes of lightning awakened terror in my fevered brain. Suddenly the frightened herd with a snort made a stampede in the direction of the open prairie. My horse attempted to follow but the rope held. As soon as I could girth the saddle with my trembling hands I was on his back and rushing away in pursuit. By the time I reached the prairie the flood gates were open and the water falling in torrents. I made no attempt to guide my horse, but held the reins tight in my left hand to support my trembling frame and to check as far as possible the dangerous speed at which my wild horse was carrying me. With my right hand I clutched a bunch of his mane and leaned forward as much as the high pommel of the saddle permitted. I recall having a fear that the girth might loosen and wishing that I had left the saddle under the trees. Repeatedly I felt that I must fall, but this sensation resulted only in a firmer grip on mane and rein. By the flashes of lightning I could occasionally see the fleeing herd, at first far away and then nearer. I realized with some grain of satisfaction that my fleet footed horse had not lost his sense of direction and was gaining on his fellows. I have never been able to figure out satisfactorily how many hours or how many miles I rode that night. As suddenly as it had come, the storm passed. What remained of the cloud dispersed and the harvest moon stood revealed in all its beauty. The man in it smiled down benignantly and by his light I tried to count the horses now leisurely feeding on the rich grass, but I could not be sure that my still fevered brain registered the numbers correctly. As the God of Day heralded his coming by flaming banners in the east my fever left me and was followed by the sweating stage. As fast as the sun dried my clothes on the outside the flowing pores of my skin wet them within. When this had passed I felt quite normal and was wholly unconscious of the preparation already in progress by the plasmodium for the invasion and destruction of other thousands of my red blood corpuscles.

Late that afternoon I led a troop of tired and docile horses into the corral at the log cabin. This was my first and last personal experience with malaria in Egypt. Before I had finished the relation of my experiences, I began to swallow double doses from the demijohn and these were repeated at frequent intervals during the night and the following days, and at longer intervals during the following weeks.

That summer I saw enough of a people held in bondage by malaria to make a lasting impression upon a boy's mind. How much the present dwellers in southern Illinois owe to the open-eyed and keen-witted Jesuit who penetrated the interior of Peru and to his patroness, the

Princess Chinchon, I will not attempt to estimate; but if quinine has clothed and redeemed the recent generations of Trelawneys, I am willing to pronounce it a gift from heaven.

When the corn had grown sufficiently mature, the stalks were cut close to the ground and with their hanging ears and green blades hauled to the pens and thrown to the hogs. These animals with eager relish converted this provender into pork and at the proper time were sold at fair profit.

Mr. Trelawney had a few razor-back hogs which, tired of the scanty mast found in the woods, would collect about our pen with covetous eyes on the luscious corn being devoured by our porkers. One, a tall, long, lean, red boar, managed to find a weak rail and broke into the pen. Here Brother and I found him one day at feeding time. I took one of Father's heavy, green clapboards and stationed myself near the broken fence. Brother, from the other side of the pen, set up a shout. The great boar came leaping over the tame animals and as he was in mid air I struck. The heavy edge of the board landed across the hog's forehead and it fell stone dead at my feet. Brother and I were in consternation. Our little play had grown serious. We greatly feared the anger of Trelawney and we dreaded to go to Father with our story. We harnessed a horse and dragged the dead body far into the forest and hid it in the bushes. But we had heard that "murder will out," and for days we carried our guilty consciences in our trembling bodies. Waking and sleeping, that dead boar was before us. Trelawney came, hunting for his prize animal. We assured him that we had not seen it, adding the crime of lying to that of murder. Trelawney evidently did not suspect us and after our denial he turned back into the woods saying: "Wall, I guess he's left the world and clumb a tree." But our sense of guilt grew enormously and finally we made a full confession to Father who immediately rode to Trelawney's house and paid him for the hog. Thus the sense of guilt was removed and the wild red boar no longer troubled our dreams.

In October, 1865, accompanied by other exiles, we turned our caravan westward and within a short time reached our old Missouri home where Uncle Jeff rendered a satisfactory account of his stewardship and where we began life under new conditions.

Although General Lee had surrendered at Appomattox, Jefferson Davis was in prison at Fortress Monroe and the slaves of the South had been emancipated, war conditions had not ceased in Missouri and were to continue for five years more. It is true that marauding bands no longer rode through the state but the bad element wielded a more powerful weapon than a cocked pistol— that of legal enactment.

In January, 1865, a Constitutional Convention, composed for the most part of delegates who came from oblivion and having signed a document prepared by one Charles Drake, now of odious memory, returned to the realm from which they came. From the name of its author and from its likeness in severity to the laws written by Draco of ancient Greece, the Missouri Constitution of 1865 is known as the Draconian Law. If a more iniquitous constitution has been written within the Christian era I am not aware of it. Some of its provisions were:

(1) The ousting ordinance.—

This ordinance which was passed by the Constitutional Convention on March 17, 1865, provided that the offices of the judges and the clerks of the Supreme Court and of all the Circuit Courts of the state, and also certain county offices, such as recorders, circuit attorneys, and sheriffs, should be vacated. It also gave the Governor authority to fill all these places with his own appointees (see Violette's *History of Missouri,* page 413). Most of the men thus deposed were Union men; at least they had been elected by Union voters, since southern sympathizers in the state had been disfranchised in 1862. This ordinance was put into operation without having been submitted to the vote of even the restricted electorate and it placed in the hands of the Governor every judicial office in the state.

(2) Voters' disqualifications.—

Every man wishing to vote was required to appear before a registrar and subscribe to an ironclad oath. At first the registrars were elected, but when it was found that they were occasionally too lenient, they became in 1868 appointees of the Governor. Even when one swallowed the "ironclad" the registrar endorsed his application to vote or rejected it as he saw fit.

(3) Professional disqualifications.—

No lawyer could advise with a client, plead a case at the bar or accept a fee; no minister could preach a sermon, lead in prayer or officiate at a christening or perform a marriage ceremony; no one could give instruction in the state university or in any public school, without subscribing to the "ironclad" oath. Strange to say, physicians and undertakers were not mentioned in these disqualifications.

(4) County courts were authorized to bond their respective counties for prospective railroads on a two-thirds vote of the restricted electorate and some courts issued these bonds without submitting the question to any vote.

By these means the Republican party attempted to fasten its grip on the state in perpetuity. Is it any wonder that I cast my first vote in 1872 for Horace Greeley in preference to General Grant, although I never admired the old egotist of the New York Tribune, or that I adhered to the Democratic party until detached therefrom by the vagaries of Mr. Bryan in 1896?

However, these shackles on citizenship became obnoxious to many individuals in the party which forged them, and under the leadership of Carl Schurz, Joseph Pulitzer, Gratz Brown and others the Republicans split into what were known locally as Liberal and Black Republicans. Finally the former group affiliated with the Democrats and in 1872 a Democrat, Silas Woodson, was elected Governor and this office was held continuously by that party until 1909, when Herbert S. Hadley, a gentleman and a scholar although a Republican, occupied the Governor's residence at Jefferson City and now presides with honor and dignity over the destinies of Washington University, St. Louis.

The first of the above mentioned measures to be mollified was that pertaining to professional disqualifications. Father Cummings, who said mass, heard confession, administered the last rites of the church and prayed for relief from purgatory, without taking the oath, was fined five hundred dollars and sentenced to jail until it should be paid. The last of the obnoxious measures to pass into oblivion was the bond issue, which, according to a historian, aggregated fifteen millions of dollars for which the people received no benefit. The United States Supreme Court—that oracle of unerring wisdom and divine justice enshrined by our forefathers—pronounced these issues constitutional and ordered their payment. Some of the bondholders built castles far east of the Mississippi. However, those thus enriched have long since deserted their earthly mansions and, if our accepted theology be true, are now sojourning in a climate where ice is unknown and the average temperature of which exceeds that of old Missouri in the worst dog days.

It was not until 1875 that Missouri had a constitution more consonant with present day civilization, but before that time I had ceased to be a resident of this state.

CHAPTER IV

EDUCATION

I RECEIVED my first training in spelling, reading, writing and figures from my mother. I recall the colors of the paper bound books: Webster's spelling book in blue, McGuffy's readers in yellow, and Ray's arithmetic in brown. The first school I attended was at the home of the neighborhood physician, Doctor William Watts, about one mile down the plank road from my father's house. Ordinarily I went alone and walked. The plank road was new then and no one had dreamed at that time of an automobile. In bad weather I rode behind Father or one of the servants on horseback. My remembrance of the Watts family is most pleasing. The doctor and his wife were educated and refined. They had a commodious house located in a locust grove, with a detached schoolroom in the yard. In the family there were seven or eight children, and Mrs. Watts instructed these with myself and two or three other children of the neighborhood. The environment was ideal. During the allotted hours we were strictly held to our lessons, but it was not all work. During the recesses we played "poor pussy wants a corner" or other games under the great trees in the yard, romped about the barn or went farther afield on the farm. Each season offered its special attractions and we were unconsciously appreciative. My continuance in this fascinating kindergarten was, after some two years, interrupted by the decision of the doctor that he would sell his farm and take his family to Fayette where his children could have the advantages offered by Central College. His eldest son became quite a linguist and finished his university training at Heidelberg, but died in early manhood. The second son studied medicine and came back for a time to practise in the old neighborhood. The third is now a successful and justly reputed lawyer in St. Louis.

After the departure of the Watts family, my parents with others of the community became solicitous about the schooling of their children. Finally they decided to build a schoolhouse. This was located in my father's woodland pasture, not more than a quarter of a mile from the house, and was given the somewhat pretentious name of Hazel Hill Academy. I have before me as I write a printed program of an "Exhibition of the students of Hazel Hill at Sweet Springs Church, Thursday, June 14, 1860."

On this program my name is down for a declamation under the title of "An appeal from our constitution." It will be understood that this was nothing more than a recitation, but I would greatly like to know what it was that I, a boy in my eighth year, declaimed. I must in justice to the memory of my childhood friends add that the orator on the occasion announced by this program was A. F. Denny, the son of a local farmer, who had recently returned from a period of study and residence at Oxford and who in the Civil War became a colonel in the Union Army.

All my schooling until I went to college was received at Hazel Hill Academy. With one exception all the teachers at this institution were women and to one of them

I owe a tribute not only for her breadth of learning and ability as a teacher but for her excellent judgment and the enthusiasm she awakened in her students. Besides, there is a glamour of romance connected with her history. As my teacher she was Miss Lucy Gamble; now she is the widow of Captain Coudrey. Practically all of her students were the children of southern sympathizers. Some had fathers and more had brothers in the Southern Army. Therefore when a handsome Federal officer showed unusual interest in Hazel Hill Academy and especially in its fair mistress, the students were all aghast. They had to admit that personally he was charming and a suitable suitor for the hand of their beloved teacher, but could she be in love with one of the enemy? This courtship proceeded under our eyes. Our teacher could not conceal the joy with which she greeted her visitor and probably he could not have been blind to the aversion with which her students regarded the progress of his suit. Suddenly she resigned her position and announced her engagement to the captain. Then the fathers and mothers took up the matter and it was wisely decided that Miss Gamble had the right to choose her own husband. One of my uncles, Robert Smith, the most outspoken rebel and the possessor of the largest house in the community, offered to open his home for the ceremony and even to act as her guardian and give her away. The older students were at the wedding and with mingled tears and smiles we saw the gallant captain lead away our beloved teacher.

The only male teacher at Hazel Hill in my day was Colonel Strong, a Scotchman, whom I always likened to Dominie Sampson. He was uncouth in person and dress, tall, angular, with a mass of unkempt red hair and beard.

With his inimitable Scotch accent he talked to me in Latin and demanded immediate reply. He began his instruction with simple sentences, such as *"Puer colubam habet,"* which I was to translate without hesitation. These sentences grew longer and more complicated and I had to give by number the rule in the grammar governing the ablative or dative or whatever the case might be. He claimed that he used the English pronunciation but I have never heard such jargon in any language. Whatever it was I had to forget it or drop it when I went to college and this was more difficult than acquiring it.

While nominally I had my schooling at Hazel Hill I received the better part of my education at home. My wise mother did not pretend to dictate my instruction. She simply placed the books she desired me to read within my reach and supplied no others. I sat many a night into the wee small hours and absorbed, by the light of a sycamore ball floating in a cup of grease, the wonderful stories of Walter Scott. I knew every one of his characters in detail and sought their prototypes among those about me. I clothed the farm and the neighboring hills and dales with romance. Rob Roy's cave was a certainty. I discovered it in a high bluff on the creek. I read the works of Dickens and Thackeray with like avidity and recited the *Prisoner of Chillon* and the *Corsair*. These and books of like character filled my library shelves. There were also volumes of ancient history and I remember with what eagerness and enthusiasm I read the *Decline and Fall of the Roman Empire*. "Poor training," a present day educator would say for one whose adult life was to be devoted to science. This may be true, but I am reciting facts. I can not deny that my scientific work might have been more productive had my early training been different. However I am not making a plea for a handicap, and I remain grateful to my mother for the books I read in childhood. They continue to be associated with her hallowed memory. I never open one of these now ancient volumes without seeing her face, as with lighted candle she came to my room and gently urged me to go to bed. For religious instruction I had the Bible, the family copy of which I still treasure. I have always been thankful to my mother for her lack of interest in insipid Sunday school books awarded to children for the recitation of so many biblical verses. My aversion to this kind of literature is inherited.

In my sixteenth year I entered Central College, Fayette, Missouri. This is a Methodist school. It had been closed during the Civil War and was recently opened when I went there. I did not do well at Central, recognized this fact myself and withdrew of my own volition at the end of the first semester. The fault was not with the college but in myself. I was immature, and my immediate associates having no strong inclination to work, I did nothing. Only one of the Faculty made an impression upon me. This was Professor F. X. Foster who taught Latin. Through the mists of nearly sixty years I see him huddled up in his big chair, with his great coat drawn over his shoulders, in the inadequately heated class room, discussing Virgil. "Take the two word sentence, *Troja fuit;* this means that Troy was, but is not; that Troy was once powerful, now is impotent; that Troy was once glorious, now is in ashes; that Hector is dead and Ilion is no more. Gentlemen: The Latin language not only denotes; it connotes." I am sorry that I did not appreciate Professor Foster more fully at the time. I am sure that a longer pupilage under him would have been beneficial to me. Recently in riding along that wonderful scenic California-Oregon highway over the Siskiyou Mountains, I caught a glimpse over a precipice which recalled something which Professor Foster had once said and had lain dormant in my mind through the many intervening years. I leaned forward to ask the chauffeur to turn and drive back when I realized that the narrow rim admitted no turning back. Then I thought to say, Drive more slowly that I may catch another glimpse around the next corner, when I saw that the pressing line of cars behind denied even this prospective pleasure. The revolving cylinders of our memory cells play us inexplicable tricks.

The best thing I took away with me from Central College in the sixties was the friendship of a red-headed, freckled-faced boy by the name of John Shafroth. Companionship formed at that time was renewed at Michigan University and later still in Washington where he was successively Congressman and Senator from Colorado. Until age had ripened both of us we never agreed about anything. Our visits, all too infrequent for me, were wholly devoted to argumentation. In early life, he was a Republican and I a Democrat; then he was a Silver Republican and I a Gold Democrat; for a few years he was a Democrat and I a Republican. But during the World War, he in the Senate, and I in the Army, were both Wilson Democrats. On most other points we differed quite as consistently. After one of his elections to Congress he became convinced that some of his supporters had employed questionable methods. He refused to make a contest and conceded the election to his opponent. This won for him the sobriquet of "honest John" and no man was ever more worthy of this honorable designation. Although neither of us ever acknowledged that the other had made an impression upon him, I will now admit that our arguments often broadened my view, making me less certain in some and more certain in other convictions.

My chum at Central College was a handsome, winning, big-hearted boy, but too fond of pouring libations to Bacchus. However, his potations never interfered with his Latin lessons. The deeper he drank the more sonorously the stately lines of Virgil fell from his lips. Some forty years or more later the corner stone of the Parker Memorial Hospital at the University of Missouri was laid. This had been done accompanied by the impressive ceremonies of the State Masonic Lodge, when a line of march was formed to proceed to the chapel where I was to deliver the dedication oration. The cadets were drawn up on each side of the walk and the procession, headed by the Governor and other state officials with President Jesse and me leading the faculties, was in motion. I felt a hand on my shoulder and a voice in my ear. *"Tempora mutantur; nos mutamur"* was the message. Recognizing my old chum I asked President Jesse to walk ahead and I escorted the dear old boy to a front seat in the chapel.

I did learn one thing at Central College which has been of value to me. As in most small colleges of that time, and I believe in some big ones, both then and now, there were innumerable rules bearing on the conduct of students both on the campus and elsewhere. I shall content myself with giving only one as an illustration. At roll call on Monday each student said "Church" or "Not church," signifying his attendance or non attendance at divine worship on the previous day. Many boys would stand on the steps of the church for a few minutes, possibly enter the vestibule, or more rarely sit on a back seat for a short time and answer "Church" loudly the next morning. Multiplicity of rules of personal conduct is an incentive to lying, especially when boys are concerned.

In 1910 I gave the commencement address at Central College and was rewarded by the degree of LL.D. This shows that it required something like forty-three years for me to obtain a diploma from the college in which I first matriculated.

In my seventeenth year I enrolled at Mount Pleasant College, Huntsville, Missouri. This was only seven miles from my father's home. It was a Baptist school which had been founded in the late fifties, flourished for a few years under the presidency of Dr. Rothwell, an able man, and had been closed during the Civil War. In 1868 the building, somewhat wrecked, was leased or otherwise put into the possession of the Reverend James W. Terrill, who, within the next five years, made it one of the best educational institutions in the state. He added commodious wings to the main structure, enlarged the campus by several acres and erected what would now be called a dormitory for girls; then it was designated as "the girls' boarding house." He brought to this institution some of the ablest teachers in the state, drawing for a time largely from the faculty of the newly established State Normal School at Kirksville. He made the college undenominational and filled it with earnest and intelligent boys and girls drawn from the families of every Protestant creed, not only in Missouri but from adjoining states. The time was propitious. The youth of the state, for years deprived of educational privileges, were athirst for knowledge and here it was offered. Political and religious ideas were submerged and the children of those who had worn the blue and those who had worn the gray, of Baptist and of Antibaptist, drank from the same spring and ate at the same table.

The college was a one-man institution and James W. Terrill was the greatest educator I have ever known; but like many others he was great only in the face of obstacles and became weak when these were removed. He was a successful builder but he did not keep his buildings in repair. He was a success in construction but a failure in maintenance. For some years the farmers of the surrounding counties and the business men of the village, impoverished as they were by the war, contributed gladly small sums for the building up of the college. The president employed excellent teachers at the beginning of the year at decent living salaries and at the close of the first semester informed them that their pay must be reduced. Under these conditions the best instructors left immediately and others of like grade could not be secured. The President was sole owner and dictator. There was no appeal from his decision. The school lost its prestige. The whole thing went to wreck. President Terrill finally left, for a while conducted a private school in Tennessee and later built up a similar institution in Texas. The deserted buildings burned in the early eighties. Like Troy, Mount Pleasant College *was* but *is* not. It was never more than a small thing, but I am inclined to ask if there may not yet be college presidents, both small and big, who starve scholarship in their lust for material growth.

President Terrill had been a southern soldier, had suffered several serious wounds and on one occasion had been left as dead on the field of battle by his comrades. After Lee's surrender, he, with others, fled to Mexico, where he soon mastered the Spanish language sufficiently to become a teacher in a boys' school in the capital. In 1868, as I have indicated, he returned to Missouri and became owner and president of Mount Pleasant College. At this school, although the students wore no uniform, all movements en masse were in military form. In the morning, the girls from one side and the boys from the other filed into chapel to the music of the organ. The president or some member of the faculty gave a short talk, a prayer was spoken and the students left the chapel for their several rooms, to music. Classes in all subjects used the blackboard. The class filed into the room, each student taking his position with a piece of chalk in his right and an eraser in his left hand. The teacher stood in the middle of the room. Except in small classes no teacher was permitted to sit. The students counted off into sections of three or five. At the call "attention" each in the section stood ready. At the call "one" he turned half way to the right; at "two" he faced the board and at "three" began to write. The theory of President Terrill was that no one knows anything until he can clearly state it in writing. His criticisms of the selection of words were scathing. So deeply did some of these burn into my being that I can not now hear certain words used without a jar on my nerves. This is true, notwithstanding the fact that many of his strictures would not have the approval of the highest authorities. He was wont to question even the most direct and correct statements. In doing this he felt at liberty to resort to the worst kind of sophistry. Nothing delighted him more than to make a good student acknowledge his error when in fact he was right. Then with great glee he would point out the fallacy in his own argument and chide the student for being so easily "brow-beaten." He taught by disputation, a method of education beloved by the ancients but now fallen into desuetude. It has been of service to me, especially when on the witness stand.

The only direct instruction I had from President Terrill was in Latin and what was then called "mental and moral philosophy." The disputations in the latter were most varied in scope and forceful in statement. Nothing within the wide range of human conduct escaped us. There were ten in the class, divided equally between the sexes. By the time we reached this subject, which was in our senior year, each student had been well trained in disputation and we constituted a small debating society, frequently employing the sophistry in which our teacher had so long trained us. Often the hour closed after the statement of eleven different religious creeds. The one good effect this course had on me is that I have never since combatted any one's religious belief.

President Terrill made no pretention to a thorough knowledge of Latin and he plainly told me of his limitations the first day I met him. In fact his reading in this language had scarcely exceeded mine at that time. He had read Cæsar, Cicero, Sallust, Virgil and a few of the

Odes of Horace. With this knowledge I accepted him as a teacher and I admit that for the first few months I received from him the most atrocious flagellations that were ever showered upon my shoulders by a teacher. Up to that time I had known only the so-called English, more correctly Scotch, pronunciation. At this he hurled all forms of ridicule. To him it was barbarous and abhorrent. If it should reach the ears of the dead Cicero he would forget the torture of Hades, but scream in terror at the sound. The unrivaled orator and great philosopher of classical Rome spoke with what is now known as the "continental" pronunciation and this I must learn. At every lapse into the dialect of Colonel Strong the verbal lash fell upon my naked soul and figuratively the blood trickled down until it bathed the nethermost parts of my being. At last after weeks of trial the devil was exorcised and I was congratulated on being fully prepared to converse with Cicero without giving him torture after old Charon had ferried me across the Styx.

I was the Alpha and Omega of the advanced class in Latin. The president and I read Ovid, Horace, including *Ars Poetica* and parts of Livy. There were no assignments of lessons. "Read as far as you wish for the next hour" was his usual parting injunction. Sometimes on entering the room he would say: "I have been too busy to look at the book, read on." I had the advantage because I had read the text which he had never seen. There were the usual disputations but most frequently he yielded to my interpretation. The instruction I received in this course was most satisfactory to me.

In my first or second year at Mount Pleasant I became instructor in Latin, and from that time I had charge of all the Latin classes except the one I have described. Before and after my graduation, as long as I remained in Mount Pleasant College, I was "in charge of Latin and Chemistry," an incongruous professorship! However, President Terrill had the good taste not to employ the word "professor" in any of his catalogues, nor was this title used by teachers or students.

Lest I may give an exaggerated impression of my classical attainments I wish to state that I never knew more than the elements of Latin and still less of any other ancient language. In making this confession I am conscious that I am complimenting myself, since Ben Jonson said of Will Shakespeare: "He knew small Latin and less Greek."

In 1917, Dean West of Princeton University had a day for the glorification of the classics. He wished to see these studies restored to their former position in the curricula of our colleges and universities, and I was in sympathy with him in this particular. He invited a number of learned men, some of whom, no doubt, could translate simple Latin phrases, to come to Princeton and read short papers. In mine I had a joke for the good dean. I said something like the following: "Although my adult life has been given to the sciences, I wish to testify that the first author to stimulate the pyramidal cells of my cerebral cortex was old Virgil, and even now in my old age when I seek mental recreation there is only one book which I prefer to Virgil, and that is Dryden's translation which I read with less effort."

Before I went to Mount Pleasant College I had only a vague idea of physics and chemistry. I did not hear of these at Central and they did not appear in the curriculum of Hazel Hill Academy. But at home there were some old books on natural history with crude illustrations of Newton under the apple tree, Galileo and the leaning tower of Pisa, Franklin with his kite, the Magdeburg cups with horses trying to pull them apart, an oxy-hydrogen blow pipe, Leyden jars, frictional electric generators, and so forth. These figures and their accompanying texts I had studied and read with eagerness and wonderment.

In the main building at Mount Pleasant there was a room which had been found locked when President Terrill took possession and I believe it had not been opened until I had permission to investigate. It was not a closet but a room of at least twelve feet square. Great was my surprise when I entered and found the walls on three sides lined with glass cases and in these were most of the apparatus I had seen figured in the old book and many more. Besides the instruments there were bottles of chemicals wrapped in paper and plainly labeled. Everything was new; nothing had been used; even the outside papers on the bottles containing chemicals were not broken. Here were chemically pure mineral acids and many of the salts and alkalis. I never was able to learn who was responsible for this collection. Most certainly it had been secured by some teacher in the college shortly before the building was closed during the Civil War. The responsible person evidently had some understanding of chemistry. The room contained the nucleus of a chemical laboratory. All my spare hours were spent in this room, at first secretly, zealously guarding it against intrusion. With Barker's *Chemistry* and its clear statement on nomenclature, it was easy to ascertain the composition of the contents of the bottles and to perform simple reactions, such as the precipitation of soluble salts of silver and lead with sodium chlorid. The first time I made hydrogen sulphid the odor penetrated the whole building, and my embryonic chemical studies were threatened with complete annihilation. However I learned discretion and finally I had permission to offer a course in elementary chemistry, at first limited to two or three students. During my last years at Mount Pleasant I came into possession of a copy of the first edition of Douglas and Prescott's *Qualitative Analysis* and this decided the question long debated in my mind as to whether I should choose the classics or science for my life work, and where my education should be continued when I left Mount Pleasant.

President Terrill was not the only great educator whose instruction I enjoyed at Mount Pleasant. Another man who could be justly called great in this direction was my instructor in higher mathematics, solid geometry and calculus, James M. Greenwood, who in later years, as superintendent, gave to the public schools of Kansas City an enviable reputation. He came from the State Normal School at Kirksville and, if my memory serves me right, remained at Mount Pleasant only one year. There were only two students in his classes, U. S. Hall and myself. We made a wager that we could skip a point in a demonstration without detection by the teacher, but the wager was never won. Greenwood was wont to stand with his right hand playing with his watch chain, his left deep in a trouser pocket and his eyes on the window, apparently totally absorbed in something outside and wholly oblivious of us and what we were saying. But the moment one of us attempted the break he would cry "Hold on, that will not do." He was a man of affable manner, broad culture, and probably no one of his time was more thoroughly versed in educational methods.

I graduated at Mount Pleasant College in 1872. I had filled the requirements a year earlier, but as no one else had done so, and as the usual four years since the reopening of the school had not elapsed, the conferring of the degree was delayed with my consent. My most intimate friend in the class was U. S. Hall, who served one term in Congress in the late eighties, stuck to President Cleveland on the gold standard and failed of renomination. Since that time he has given himself to teaching, for a while at Pritchett Institute at Glasgow, Missouri, and later in a private preparatory school for boys at Columbia, Missouri. His father, William A. Hall, represented our district in Congress for a part of the time at least during the Civil War. An uncle, Willard Hall, was once Lieutenant Governor of the state, and my classmate's brother, General Willard Hall, won his stars in fighting the Apaches and in capturing Geronimo.

After my graduation I continued teaching Latin and chemistry until February, 1874. Then came the inevitable break with President Terrill. The school was in apparently a most flourishing condition but in the middle of the year the president announced his intention of adding to the buildings and cutting the salaries of his teachers into halves. The result was that four of the teachers resigned. I met my last classes in Mount Pleasant one Friday afternoon and began teaching the same subjects at Hardin College the following Monday morning.

I desire at this point to say a few words concerning one of my fellow teachers at Mount Pleasant. Among others who came from the State Normal at Kirksville with Professor Greenwood were a young man by the name of Fluhart and his wife. Mr. Fluhart developed tuberculosis and died within two years after coming to Mount Pleasant. His wife filled the function in the college which is now assigned to the dean of women. However, there were no deans at Mount Pleasant. At the present time in each pretentious institution there are a round dozen or more deans, engaged for the most part in some form of administrative work. Once the title indicated some degree of scholarship; now it suggests supervision of non-scholarly student activities, such as acting as a chaperon at dances, etc. Mrs. Fluhart filled the bill most admirably as it was then understood. A lifelong friendship has made me most appreciative of her learning and wisdom. She left Mount Pleasant at the same time that I did, and for the same reason, and the next Monday she began teaching in Stephens College, Columbia, Missouri. After a year or two she went to Athens to take charge of a school for native girls supported by an English society. When this school was closed by the Turkish authorities, she opened another under the same auspices on the Island of Cyprus, which at about that time came under English control. Her work here was continued with marked success for many years. She spent most of her vacations in England, France, or Germany but she passed some time, unaccompanied save by her Arab servants, in visiting the more remote districts of Asia Minor. Her Arab attendants were most loyal, treating her with respect and even with reverence. She now resides in Kansas City where for years she has been a kind of godmother to the Greeks and other immigrants from the eastern coasts of the Mediterranean.

Hardin College, to which I went on leaving Mount Pleasant, was founded and built by Governor Hardin as a school for girls. It had been open a little more than a year and was under the able management of Wood Terrill, a brother of President Terrill, and his wife, both of whom had been my classmates at Mount Pleasant. A few years later Mr. Terrill developed tuberculosis and died. The school continues as a junior college and I believe that the present head is a man of my name though I have never had the pleasure of meeting him. I went to this school for only one semester and the only impression that I carried away was that I enjoyed talking to girls. But my wife, to whom I was then engaged, says that I developed that defect before I went to Hardin.

Although my people were plain Missouri farmers, tilling the soil, wearing homespun, eating pork and hominy when they tired of chicken, turkey, goose, duck and squab, they were not altogether indifferent to the importance and value of an education. It was the usual thing, or at least not the unusual thing, for the neighborhood boys to go to college. There was at the time of which I write not less than six so-called colleges within a radius of fifty miles from my father's farm, but most of these were of no better grade than the high schools of to-day. This list includes the State University which had been greatly retarded in its development by the Civil War, while from the same cause most of the denominational schools had been temporarily closed. Besides there was, at the time of which I am writing, a ban on the State University, because only those who would take an oath that they had never sympathized with the South could teach in the University or in any of the public schools of the state.

Under these conditions I found it necessary to look outside my native state for my university training. Before the war the University of Virginia had been a favorite with our people, but disaster, temporarily at least, had come to it. Dartmouth for Episcopalians and Princeton for Presbyterians were of good repute, but at that time neither of these had developed their scientific schools. Harvard and Yale were but little known among us since Unitarians were non-existent and Congregationalists rare in our latitude. Besides, the flavor of religious sectarianism clung to the names of most of our great eastern universities.

At that time, Michigan was the great state university. Simple people as we were, we knew of Watson and of the asteroids he had found in the sky. Winchell had shocked the elders in our church by his conservative interpretation of creation. Cooley was emerging as the great authority on constitutional law. Frieze had issued a most excellent edition of Virgil, which had a special fascination for me. Fasquelle's *French Grammar* had found its way into our colleges. Olney had flooded the schools with his mathematical texts replacing older authors. The St. Louis *Republican,* which came to our house daily, announced that President Angell had suspended the greater number of a class for insubordination, showing that discipline would be maintained at Michigan. Hillgard, one of the greatest scientists of the South, had been called from the University of Mississippi to a chair in Michigan. However my final decision was made when I learned that there was a large and well-equipped chemical laboratory at Michigan University. The book on qualitative analysis by Douglas and Prescott, already referred to, proved to be the most attractive force that guided a Missouri boy to Michigan in the early seventies. It is true that at that time there was no Professor Fielding Yost, and his football teams had not then won their laurels. In September, 1874, accompanied by another Mount Pleasant youth, Edward Samuel, who was intending to enter the pharmacy school, I travelled via the Wabash Railroad through Toledo and Detroit to Ann Arbor.

My companion and I spent a forenoon in youthful admiration of the beautiful homes on Fort Street, Lafayette, Woodward, Jefferson Avenues and other thoroughfares in Detroit. Our bucolic eyes had never realized that earth could be so fair. Certainly in the seventies and eighties Detroit in the early fall was one of the most fascinating of cities. A wider observation led me to the belief that there was only one other city and that was Cleveland which could favorably compare with it. It was an intoxication of the imagination to visit either. Now, I drive miles to avoid penetrating them. "The banners of industry," in the form of great volumes of smoke, now shut out the sunlight which at that time kissed their pavements and played "hide and seek" on their beautifully wooded lawns. Fair vistas have been obliterated by the marts of trade, some colossal, some small, some gaudy in exterior, some plain, but all offensive to the esthetic sense. The inhabitants of Detroit, who as children played on the spacious lawns, are now living in blocks of cells, some plain, some gilded, but all cramped and prison like. In part, the inhabitants of today are moving "woodward" in

The Chemical Laboratory of the University of Michigan in the 'Seventies

attempting to renew for themselves and secure for their
children the joys and comforts they once knew. Big
business continues to expand apparently with irresistible
force pressing hard upon the heels of retreating family
life. However there are signs that this expansion will find
relief, and both employer and employee will again know
something of the joy of semi-rural life. But this is not
an essay on rural versus city life, and I find myself
digressing.

After alighting from the train at Ann Arbor in the
late afternoon and entering the disreputable station of
that time, and especially after dining at the "Cook
House," we, boy-like, cursed the lack of wisdom which led
the early authorities to select Ann Arbor instead of Detroit as the seat of the University. This opinion was
strengthened by a night of attempts at sleeping and a
scanty breakfast at the famous hostelry named above.
One man, who has won great distinction in science, confided to me recently that one night at the "Cook House"
ended his intention of matriculating at Michigan. I
should hasten to say that the Cook House under the name
of the Allenel has greatly improved, while other hotels
have developed during the half century which has elapsed
since the time of which I write. Besides, the weary trav-
eler may now find rest and comfort at the Michigan
Union.

After breakfast Samuel and I started out to make a
survey of the village and to look for the campus. We
walked east on Huron Street to State. With every step
our spirits rose. The street was lined with great oaks
and modest dwellings stood back a few paces from the
walk. The lawns were not so spacious as those that had

won our admiration in Detroit, but were neat, well-grassed, partly wooded and well-kept. At the junction of Huron and State Streets we came upon a building, not so large as Mount Pleasant College, and with less extensive grounds, but somewhat imposing. Nervously we asked a passer-by if this was the University, and were relieved when told that it was the High School and that if we would walk two blocks south we would come to the campus. This gave us a few more moments of doubtful anticipation. Soon we were at the northwest corner of the campus. Its area of forty acres was at that time enclosed by a high picket fence. Whether this was to keep students in or others out I never learned. Certainly it accomplished neither of these purposes. The only useful function I ever observed was that in freshman-sophomore rushes the contest was determined by the number hoisted over it. Evidently the authorities finally became convinced that this function did not justify the waste of so much lumber and the fence was removed.

On the west side of the campus there were the law and literary buildings, the former small and ugly and the latter differing from it only in size, which at that time seemed to us colossal. On the north and south sides of the campus were two residences, said to have been built for professors' homes and probably once used for this purpose. The west one on the south side was then, and is now, with additions and adornments, the President's residence. The other one on the south side soon after our first visit housed an embryo dental school, and the space is now occupied by the beautiful and classical Clements Library. The two dwellings on the north side for a time became hospitals. The space then covered by them is now occupied by the science building and the new chemical laboratory. On the east side was the old medical building, which, with its fluted classical columns, displayed the only architectural merit on the campus.

Hidden away behind the medical building was the chemical laboratory, then the largest and best equipped chemical laboratory in the United States, and with but one in the world to compare with it—the laboratory of Fresenius at Wiesbaden. Harvard and Yale, and possibly the other eastern universities, had had for years small, special chemical laboratories for the professors in this branch and some epoch-making researches had been done in them, but Michigan was the first university in this country to offer the facilities and require laboratory courses of students. The laboratory was a bud from the Medical School and was primarily for medical students. Up to the opening of this institution the only laboratory instruction required of medical students of any school in this country was that in anatomy. The chemical laboratory had a small beginning but demand for tables forced almost annual additions until further extension was impossible and the new chemical building was erected. The old building, with its grotesque additions, still (1926) stands and houses physiology and pharmacology, besides supplying some class rooms for other courses. But I am writing of the old laboratory as I saw it in 1874 and through the immediately following decades. During these years many embryonic great men handled their first test tubes and received their elementary instruction in this building. During these same years Albert B. Prescott, with a benignant smile and a genial voice, answered the students' queries, both the wise and the unwise. Often he would raise his eyebrows as if astounded at the profundity of the students' knowledge. His most frequent advice was: "Go to your table and do this and your question will be answered." Prescott made no startling discoveries in chemistry but all his work stands. Besides, he nourished many who have made great contributions. The University of Michigan chemical laboratory had its inception in the brain of Silas H. Douglas, who was for many years professor of general chemistry in the Medical School. He was not a great teacher, either in the lecture room or in the laboratory, but he built the laboratory and saw that it functioned. In my opinion, he justly deserves the credit of introducing required laboratory instruction in chemistry into the curricula of medical schools.

The present day (1926) visitor to the University of Michigan will have difficulty in conceiving of the campus as I saw it in the seventies. The old fence has disappeared. The law building has been enlarged and this department is soon to move into the unrivaled dormitories, libraries and lecture rooms erected and donated by one of its most intelligent and successful alumni. The unique Michigan Union, designed by Pond and Pond, also alumni and distinguished architects, and built by subscriptions from the alumni and friends, affords social opportunities for all students and delightful housing for visitors. The Memorial Building across the way commemorates the deeds of those alumni who have fallen in wars in defense of home and country. The colossal main building now presents a new and more dignified front and at the same time supplies ample offices for the administrative force and lecture and class rooms. The

President's home has been enlarged and improved beyond recognition. The Martha Cook dormitory as well as similar buildings for the housing of women students give to these opportunities for living in the midst of esthetic surroundings. The classical Clements Library contains the most complete and valuable collection of Americana in the country. The new School of Education permits the application of laboratory methods in pedagogy. The Engineering College, which unfortunately, in my opinion, remains a college and has not advanced to the position of a school, has spread its class rooms and shops on both sides of the street and now accommodates more students than were enrolled in the whole university when I began my studies there. The Medical School, somewhat more modest, has also passed beyond the bounds of the original campus. The great gymnasium with its detached Ferry Field, both under the supreme direction of Professor Yost, provides for athletics, which in the opinion of some have taken on the aspects of the highest form of university training and culture. The new chemical laboratory, had it a conscious being, would deny its descent from the humble building provided by Silas Douglas and furnished with scientific pabulum by Albert Prescott. The Hill Auditorium, donated by an alumnus, renders it possible for every student to become acquainted with the best music. Then there is the new hospital built by the state at a cost of four millions. These are only some of the material improvements in the University. I sometimes wonder if mental growth on the campus keeps pace with expansion in brick and stone. If this be the case, the professors and students of my days at the University were pigmies.

While the original chemical laboratory at Michigan was built and equipped primarily for medical students, it soon attracted those from other departments. Shortly before I went to Ann Arbor a School of Pharmacy was established and Prescott made dean of the school and director of the chemical laboratory. Later I shall attempt to show that Michigan did not prove a laggard in the development of laboratory instruction in other directions.

I had gone to Ann Arbor in 1874 some days before the session was to open. I was to work in the chemical laboratory, that was certain, but I wished to enter the graduate school and, if possible, secure a higher degree. According to the specifications at Mount Pleasant I was entitled to an A. B., but as no one else in my class had done enough work in the classics to secure this degree, I did not seek differentiation and accepted a B. S. This was a mistake. If a college degree has a definite value the student should take the best to which he is entitled and not be content with any other. I admit that there was enough reverence in me for the classics to feel somewhat ashamed of my B. S. and later when I became a member of the Academy of Medicine I was compelled to show that I had done collegiate work equivalent to the A. B. requirements, but this was done on my own statement of the facts.

The burning question with me during those days of waiting in September, 1874, for the return of President Angell from his vacation was, would he admit me to graduate work on a diploma from an unknown college? At last I learned that the President would receive me. I knocked timidly at his door and having been so invited

Northwest Corner of the Campus, University of Michigan, in the 'Seventies

by a voice from within, I entered. I stood in the presence of two men who evidently were finishing an agreeable conversation. One was a striking figure, with a mass of snowy white hair and full beard. Only his heavy eyebrows were dark. Beneath these, cold, sharp gray eyes seemed to penetrate me. He was tall and angular but evidently with powerful muscles, strong and quick in action. I scarcely observed the other man, but timidly addressed this aged Hercules as Mr. President. With a gracious smile and a courtly wave of his hand he referred me to the other man and withdrew. He proved to be the Reverend Benjamin Cocker, then professor of mental and moral philosophy.

Evidently I was now alone with President Angell. In figure he did not compare favorably with his recent guest. His head was bald with a scanty fringe of reddish brown hair and a Horace Greeley beard of like color and texture under his chin. His smoothly shaven face was youthful, and his eyes and smiles showed amusement at my mistake. He asked me to be seated and soon had me at ease, asking me all kinds of irrelevant questions about men and affairs in Missouri. When he saw that my nervousness had left me he listened gravely to my statement, and, scanning my diploma, he said that the University could not recognize it, but that he would ask me to talk with three men and if they so advised, I would be permitted to do graduate work and, if I did well the first semester, I might consider myself a candidate for a master's degree the following June. I informed him that his proposition was eminently fair and wholly satisfactory to me.

I wished to major in chemistry with geology and

biology as minors; consequently the three professors named by the president were Prescott, Hilgard and Harrington. After five minutes' talk with Prescott I had his approval. Harrington was brusk and would not listen to me or question me but dismissed me with the statement: "I suppose you know about as much biology as our freshmen do." Evidently I must win the support of Hilgard, but I was told that he was in California and would not meet his classes for some weeks. This gave me ample opportunity for preparation. I knew that my weak points would be in mineralogy, especially as to the forms of crystals. I secured a half bushel of potatoes, and with Dana's *Mineralogy* I cut out the shapes of all crystals therein described. I never studied a subject more intensely. In my waking hours crystals hung in mid air about me. They bedecked my dreams. When Hilgard returned he posted an hour for examination of those who wished to do advanced work with him. When the hour came I found three or four waiting young men. Hilgard began quizzing the boy next to me. This poor fellow did not know much, and in his despair he whispered to me for help and I attempted to render it. Hilgard's keen eyes through his green goggles saw my lips move. "Sit down!" he shouted. "The young man next to you thinks he knows so much about this subject that I will give him a chance." He quizzed me without mercy and apparently to me throughout eternity, but he might have handed me the crystals one at a time and asked me to describe them. The next day I became Hilgard's student assistant and so continued throughout the year. When he went to the University of California permanently he offered to take me with him, but Prescott and the

chemical laboratory held me at Michigan. The task
Hilgard gave me, with two other student assistants for
the year, was the identification and relabeling of all the
minerals in the Museum. This was of course done under
his supervision. When we found a specimen which we
believed to be incorrectly named, we laid it aside with
the name we believed it should have and a written statement of our reasons. Hilgard came daily and passed on
these.

I had a thorough course in mineralogy and temporarily learned much, all of which I have forgotten.
However, much as I advanced in knowledge of mineralogy I learned more from my associates in the work
and though both have been long dead I have forgotten
neither them nor the lessons they taught me. One was
George G. Groff, who having served Bucknell University as a teacher for many years, became its president.
The other was the first and most intellectual Japanese
student who came to Michigan. In later years he became
Dean of the Scientific School of the Royal University
at Tokyo and later still Minister of Education. Coming
from a slave state as I did, I was slow to believe that
any man of color could possess a high degree of intelligence. Toyama soon convinced me of my error. Daily
he exhibited unconsciously his possession of powers of
accurate observation and logical reasoning. While we
were at this work there came to the Museum many contributions from Japan. No one could be more competent
to arrange these than Toyama, and Groff and I became
his menial assistants. Good naturedly we would twit
him about his gods. With equal good humor he would
deny that he or any intelligent Japanese had ever wor-

shiped these or any other images. They were only symbols. Then he would turn on us and ask: "What is the religion of this land? Your people believe literally the story of creation as told in Genesis, the story of the crossing of the Red Sea, the miraculous conception, and so forth. If we are idolaters, so are you." One day he said, "I will tell you a little story: Once in the lowlands near a river was a small pool in which there were a few fish. One, the largest, thought that the pool constituted the world, and that he was the biggest fish in the world. There came a great flood and the river overflowed the pool, sweeping its fish into the ocean. The big fish learned that the world was larger than he had supposed and that there were other big fish. So it is with you Christians. You think that you have the only great religion. But go out into the world and you will learn the same lesson the big fish of the pool learned." Toyama never accepted Christianity and was anathema to Christian missionaries in Japan. Thus I had from Toyama another lesson in religious toleration.

In June, 1875, I was granted the degree of Master of Science. I wrote a thesis on "The Separation of Arsenic and Antimony." This was published in the *American Chemical Journal* and was abstracted, as all such papers are, in certain European chemical journals, but I observed no evidence that it startled the great men in science who continued in the even tenor of their ways.

In the fall of 1875 I continued in the same graduate work as a candidate for the degree of Ph. D. This was the first time that this degree was offered "in course" at Michigan. Hitherto it had been given, if at all, as an honorary degree, but about this time, it appears that

the leading universities in this country decided to drop
it as an honorary and offer it as a working degree. In
this they followed the German universities. It had
become quite the proper thing for American professors
to go to Leipzig and return after two years' residence
with a Ph. D. There were two of us, the other being
William H. Smith, who had graduated at Michigan and
had taught one year at Vassar. Both of us received the
coveted honor and entered the Medical School in the fall
of 1876.

My most pretentious thesis for the Ph. D. degree
was entitled: "The Osteology and Myology of the
Domestic Fowl." An Ann Arbor bookseller, S. C.
Andrews, somehow acquired an insane idea that he could
publish this thesis in book form and make money. I,
having no such illusion, gave him a copy of the manuscript. Andrews never confessed to me how much he
lost on this enterprise. It made a neat little volume,
some copies bound in green and some in red. Andrews for
a while carried these in his pockets exhibiting them to
anyone whom he could detain. He sold at least two
copies. I know this because I bought them, one green
and one red, but I never showed them to anyone. However this little book did have one merit. The illustrations
of the bones and muscles of the barnyard bird are
excellent. They were done by a student friend, O. C.
Simonds, for many years and now the great Chicago
authority on landscape gardening. He has had much
to do with the creation of the unrivaled park system
of the metropolis of the Great Lakes, his special pet
being Garfield Park. I never take the park drive in
Chicago (and I do so at every opportunity I have; no

one who loves the beautiful can afford to miss it) that I do not linger at Garfield Park whose beauty I interpret as an expression of Simonds' life and character. I advise any friends of mine who should find a copy of this supposedly extinct book in a junkshop, to buy it—the cost will not be more than ten cents—because it contains Simonds' illustrations. Its value will be enhanced if the text has been lost.

The second thesis that I presented for a doctor's degree in 1876 was another paper on the separation of arsenic and antimony. This went the way of its predecessor. The third was a learned thesis on certain fossils found in the vicinity of Ann Arbor. It fortunately has eluded the printer and lies buried with hundreds of other theses, of equal value, in the basement of the University library. Possibly it may be discovered sometime in the distant future by some prowling antiquarian who will make known its contents to a waiting world.

In December, 1875, a storm broke loose in the chemical laboratory, spread a threatening cloud over the campus and quickly encompassed the whole state. The Regents were evenly divided and therefore could do neither right nor wrong. The legislature investigated and enacted. Religious prejudice was aroused and political sympathies were evoked. The only official apparently not disturbed was President Angell. He never became excited, expressed no opinion which either party could quote and smilingly said that the matter must be referred to the courts. They alone could solve the questions involved. Of course the matter came to this at last.

It is not my purpose to go into the details of the Doug-

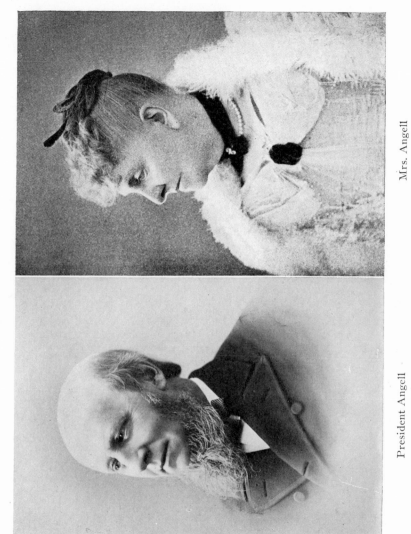

President Angell

Mrs. Angell

las-Rose controversy. Douglas was director of the laboratory and responsible to the Regents for all receipts. Rose
conducted the work in physiological chemistry and received in cash for material used a few dollars from each
student. Occasionally Douglas came around and Rose
turned the cash over to him. Douglas acknowledged
the receipt only by writing a "D" on the stub. This had
gone on for years and the aggregate now stood at some
thousands of dollars. Each individual transaction had
to be reviewed and the trouble began. Knowing both
men as I did I have never thought that either stole a
dollar. Both went through years of litigation and both
lost their positions. I was the chief beneficiary of this regrettable affair, since Rose was dismissed and I was made
instructor in physiological chemistry. I needed the salary,
small as it was, but I needed the opportunity more. I
suppose that one of my Huguenot ancestors would have
attributed this matter to the hand of Providence working
"in a mysterious way" for my good, but I never could
so regard it. I have always looked upon my first appointment to the teaching force of the University of
Michigan as due to a regrettable and sorrowful affair.

I was informed of Rose's dismissal and my appointment by Doctor Prescott in the last week before the
Christmas vacation, and was instructed by him to meet
the medical students in the class room on the first day
of the resumption of work. The students were divided
in their allegiance to the Douglas-Rose factions. Rose
held a medical degree and was deservedly popular in both
class room and laboratory. I had not then even matriculated as a medical student, though I had occasionally
acted as a voluntary and temporary demonstrator in the

dissecting room, and had many friends among the medical students. I was kindly informed that at my first appearance there would be present not only the section assigned to physiological chemistry for that period but the entire body of medical students, and that there would be a Rose demonstration. My informant was particular to say that I must not regard whatever happened as against me but as for Rose.

One may imagine with what intensity I worked during that short vacation. I knew that it would not do to give my initial talk along chemical lines, since the students would grant that I was competent in that direction. I must convince them that I was able to approach the subject from other directions. I wrote enough to fill many lecture hours on: "The Structure and Functions of the Kidney." I so familiarized myself with this material that it became a part of my being. On the appointed day I stood before the closed door of the lecture room and listened to the uproar within. Seniors were "passing up" underclassmen who had trespassed upon the front seats. The sound was a familiar one and bore no ominous foreboding. When I stepped upon the rostrum there was silence but neither applause nor hissing. Without prelude I began. The silence deepened and I was honored and encouraged by the closest attention. When I closed, the walls rang with approval and the crowd filed out singing "He is a jolly good fellow." During the forty-five years that I continued to lecture to medical students not one has ever shown me the slightest disrespect in class room or elsewhere. Give to American student audiences what they have a right to demand, and no teacher will have cause to complain.

In 1878 I put in book form my lecture notes in physiological chemistry and this book passed through three editions in as many years. As I write I have before me a copy of the third and last edition published in 1880. Holding this date in mind I am not ashamed to have anyone read it. I revised and rewrote this work many times, but never satisfied myself with the product. So rapidly has this science progressed and so lamentably have I fallen behind in it that I hesitate to state that I once taught it. I was fortunate in some of my early students in this branch. They include such names as John J. Abel, Frederick Novy, Donald Van Slyke, Frank Mall and Moses Gomberg. When I ceased giving laboratory instruction in this branch, this duty fell upon the stronger shoulders of Doctor Novy. Even the designation "physiological chemistry" has fallen into oblivion and is now found only in ancient tomes, such as my old books. It is now *biochemistry*. The coining of new words is sometimes mistaken for progress in science.

When I went to Ann Arbor, and for some years thereafter, the Medical School was greatly agitated by the legislative attempts to engraft homeopathy on its teaching. At first the legislature demanded that chairs of practise and materia medica in this cult be established in the Medical School. The Regents denied the right of the legislature to dictate appointments in the University and in this contention they were sustained by the Supreme Court. Finally the legislature made all university appropriations contingent on the establishment of a full Homeopathic School, quite independent of the Medical School in the University and provided a special appropriation for that purpose. The medical professors hurled anathemas at the accursed heresy. The State Medical Society and the American Medical Association joined in and threatened non-recognition to all medical graduates of the University provided this unholy alliance was consummated. But the Legislature held the purse strings and the independent school opened its doors in 1875. The new school was not in fact wholly independent of the old one. The students in the former always did their fundamental scientific work, especially their laboratory courses, with their enemies. So far as I know there was but little friction between the students in the two schools. The homeopaths were never numerous and for this reason were negligible in student affairs. They bore with resignation the good natured jibes tossed to them by the "old liners" as they lived often in the same rooms, ate at the same tables, and did their tasks side by side.

In later years, as dean of the Medical School, I had only three difficult problems in connection with homeopathy which, as most difficult problems have a way of doing, settled themselves. For a while, especially during the years in which the Medical School was frequently increasing its requirements, the Homeopathic School did not keep pace, and students who were not qualified to enter the Medical School matriculated in homeopathy and then came into our classes. This was galling but hurt homeopathy more than it did scientific medicine. The opprobrium fell upon the homeopathic students and finally by mutual agreement between the deans of the two schools, sanctioned by the Regents, the requirements were made identical and a student failing of admission to one school could not enter the other. The second difficulty was of the same nature but concerned the requirements for graduation. In the Medical School no student could graduate until he had passed every subject. A few men did graduate in the Homeopathic School who had not passed in some (one or more) subjects in the scientific branches. This difficulty was arranged as was the first by agreement between the deans. The third difficulty which, as I look back upon it, was the most serious and the one which was never removed, at least under my régime, was never openly settled. I, and I am sure that some of my colleagues did the same, passed homeopathic students on a lower grade than I did my own students. I did not demand from them the same thoroughness and I knew that if they failed before state boards of licensure their failure would not be charged to my school. I am sure that Dean Hinsdale would never approve of this had he been aware of it. Hinsdale was dean during most of the time that I held the same office in the Medical School. He and I were always friends and I had great respect for his judgment in all things except in medicine.

Many good, conscientious men graduated in homeopathy during my time and some of them are now, or were during their lives, competent, conscientious physicians. Most of them soon dropped their allegiance to the sect. Since my resignation from the University the Homeopathic School, as such, has been discontinued and two chairs in this form of medical practise have been established in the Medical School. Thus it will be seen that the Regents, after more than forty years, have adopted the plan advised by the legislature in the seventies. In this way the world moves.

I never objected to the establishment of the Homeo-pathic School nor to its maintenance in the University. In fact I looked upon it as I would regard a laboratory experiment, and held that if scientific medicine could not successfully compete with sectarianism it deserved to fail. I regarded the experiment as costly and useless, and I had no doubt as to the final outcome. Medicine is the application of those scientific discoveries which can be utilized in the prevention, alleviation or cure of disease. Medicine is not based on theory nor does it constitute a system of philosophy. It can grow only as the sciences which supply its pabulum develop. There can be but one medicine. Medical sects are all parasitic growths and must fail in the end.

I have not the bitterness toward medical cults that some of my colleagues show. I regret their acceptance by the people as evidence of unbalanced mentality. Naturally I am speaking of the honest believer in the so-called schools of medicine and not of the man who deliberately plans to dupe his fellows. Accept the dictum of Hahnemann, *"Similia similibus curatur,"* as an in-fallible and invariable law—true in the same way and to the same extent as the law of gravitation—then one can be honestly a homeopath. Indeed he could be nothing else. Accept the claim that all diseases, or even many, are due to dislocated vertebrae, and osteopathy is rea-sonable. Accept as literally and invariably true all the statements in the Bible and the followers of Mrs. Eddy have a valid claim to a respectful hearing. The minds of many people are so constituted that they must have some axiom of supposed truth and infallibility upon which they can found their beliefs. Some of the most popular systems of religion and philosophy are based on this common human defect. Grant that God created us knowing that some would obey and others violate his laws, then the Calvinistic doctrine of predestination is wholly logical. Accept the teachings of Freud and his apostles that dreams are always of import, that they are founded upon some sex experience or repression, that even the nursing infant has sexual orgasm, and that most horrid of all human concepts, the Œdipus complex, becomes a possibility.

During my graduate and medical years at Ann Arbor a small number of students formed a scientific society. I am not sure that we had a name for it, but each gave from his own specialty what he thought might interest and instruct the others. At that time Richard Corwin, who had worked with Wilder at Cornell, was Curator of the Museum, housed at that time in the north wing of the main building. Our little group usually met in his room where we had our chats and exhibited our collections. For two years Corwin and I were roommates and were known to our intimates as "Dick and Vick." He is now, and has been since his hospital year, the medical chief of the Colorado Coal and Fuel Company. He designed and built the unique hospital at Pueblo in which he has done excellent surgical work. Toyama and Groff were members of our club. Among the others I recall Charles Beecher, who became professor of paleontology at Yale and died with his great work only begun; Paul Hanus, now professor of education at Harvard; J. B. Johnson, who became dean of the engineering school at Wisconsin and was killed in an accident; O. C. Simonds, the Chicago authority on landscape gardening to whom I have already referred, and William Greeson, now over seventy and still teaching Latin in the Grand Rapids High School.

When I began teaching physiological chemistry in January, 1876, there were only two microscopes for students' work and these were well nigh worthless. The students in sections of thirty or more did their chemical work at the tables and each with his slide prepared came to my room for microscopical examination. This caused great delay and students were compelled to stand in long waiting lines. So far as I know, these were the only microscopes at the service of the students in the University. Some of the professors in scientific subjects had their individual instruments, mostly quite antiquated, seldom used even by their possessors and most of the time stood under glass cases. Professor Ford did show us sections of bone and awakened our wonderment at the Haversian canals.

In September, 1876, I went to the Centennial Exposition at Philadelphia and was authorized by President Angell to spend a few hundred dollars for microscopes for students in physiological chemistry. The make and the number were left to me, my only limitation being the amount of money authorized. I bought six. These were of English make and if my memory serves me right, they were known by the name of Crouch. At any rate they proved satisfactory. When they came I placed them on a table in my room and set out to teach each medical student how to use the instrument beginning with diatoms, vegetable fibers, yeast, blood, and so forth. I had had but little experience and felt the need of instruction for myself. This came from an unexpected quarter. I learned that the engineer who drove the accommodation train from Jackson to Detroit and back each day was an amateur microscopist and a student of diatoms. I made his acquaintance and asked him to help me. This he gladly did, and greatly enjoyed the nice new instruments which magnified quite beyond his belief. From this man I had my elementary lessons in microscopy. I owe his memory much, and admit with shame that I have forgotten his name. For this work, which was given on Saturdays and Sundays since our artificial lights at that time were but poorly adapted to microscopical study, I accepted no pay. So the students invited me to a lunch one night and the girl who passed the rolls was particular to see that I took a certain one. When I opened it I found that it contained a pair of gold cuff buttons and shirt studs. This girl became the wife of Harry Gradle, the late distinguished professor of ophthalmology in Northwestern University and the mother of the younger Harry who fills his father's chair with honor.

One year later I was authorized to purchase six more microscopes. This time they were Zentmayers. As early as that time medical students began to purchase their own microscopes. Now (1926) Professor Huber estimates that the university has in its various laboratories fourteen hundred and nineteen microscopes, invoiced at $70,000.00; while practically all the medical students and many others own their individual instruments.

In June, 1877, I was unanimously recommended by the medical faculty for promotion, with the understanding that I was to teach histology in addition to physiological chemistry. At that time this was not an unusual combination. While the Board of Regents was in session Dean Palmer came to me quite agitated, saying: "The charge of atheism has been brought against you. If I can return to the board and say that you deny this charge the promotion will be granted. Otherwise I fear that it will not." I reacted as if I had been struck in the face. Reason was not in my answer. It came as a reflex. It was not I who answered, but my Huguenot ancestry. "Tell the board that I decline to make a confession of faith to them. The position concerns the teaching of science and has no relation to religious belief." The dear old dean did not argue; did not advise me to modify my statement, but, with his hand on my shoulder said: "You are right, and I will stand by you." The medical Faculty did stand by me. The Regents discussed the matter at odd intervals through two days and several times sent a request to the faculty to name someone else to teach histology but the faculty returned my name each time. Finally the board postponed action and adjourned. I may say that in the fall another man was appointed to teach histology. After a service of some years he was asked to resign, after letters which he had indiscreetly written to a fair companion in a church choir were revealed.

That night I cursed myself bitterly for being a fool. I could have truthfully denied the charge of atheism because I did not then and have never since held that belief. However, the next day two letters came which amply repaid me for my distress. There were then at the University two men whom I had admired from a distance. It had never occurred to me that I might sometime know them. These men were Thomas M. Cooley, then

THE THREE DEANS WHO PRECEDED DOCTOR VAUGHAN

Doctor Corydon L. Ford,
Dean 1887–91

Doctor Abram Sager,
Dean 1850–75

Doctor Alonzo B. Palmer,
Dean 1875–87

dean of the Law School, and James C. Watson, then professor of astronomy. The letters were from these men
and both were to the same effect: "Call to see me when
convenient." From that time so long as they lived I
enjoyed their friendship and profited by their wise
council. The loss I had suffered by my rash statement
was a mere bagatelle; the gain I had won was above all
price. Professor Watson who, in his periods of rest
from bagging asteroids and computing the orbit of the
still uncertain planet, Vulcan, owned and edited a local
paper. In this he flayed the Regents for their action.
One of the board, the chief instigator of the charge
against me and a physician, wrote me threatening letters
if Watson did not desist. Of course Watson saw these
letters and spoke in his paper more emphatically. Cooley
with his great authority as a constitutional lawyer, was
ready for my defense but it was never needed. To
finish up this story I may say that later, and while I was
dean, the ex-regent, the man who had made the charge
against me, wrote me suggesting his own name as proper
for a chair then vacant in the Medical School. It is
needless to say that he never occupied the chair. Another
member of the board, active in the charge against me,
died from a disease which the Volstead law is said to
prevent, and I as his physician aided him in his frequent
combats with snakes.

In the early summer of 1877 Groff and I, with others,
lectured in the summer session at the Normal School
at Westchester, Pennsylvania. The president of this institution at that time was George Maris, a graduate of
Michigan. My lecture hour was from seven to eight
P. M., immediately after supper. Most of the students

and teachers lived and ate in the building. Among the lecturers was Professor Bailey of Yale with whom, together with his wife, I formed a pleasant acquaintance. Professor Cope, the eminent paleontologist of Philadelphia, gave one or two lectures. My acquaintance with him was afterward renewed, much to my pleasure and profit, when he, with his rivals, Professor Marsh of Yale and Doctor T. Sterry Hunt, were co-guests at my house in Ann Arbor.

My first talk at the Normal School was on the chemistry of the alcohols. In closing this lecture I stated that I had not discussed the use of alcohol as a beverage, but that I approved of letters on that subject then appearing in the Philadelphia *Ledger* under the pseudonym of John Ploughshare. The audience broke into tremendous applause and I left the rostrum much embarrassed. President Maris came forward and introduced me to a handsome elderly gentleman whom I had seen on a front seat, as Alfred Sharpless, alias John Ploughshare. This was the beginning of a long friendship, and Sharpless sent his two sons to Michigan University. He and I spent many days riding about that beautiful region watered by the historic Brandywine, collecting minerals. When the noon hour approached we would turn in at some Quaker farmhouse where my companion was sure of a hearty welcome and a savory repast. I was charmed with the intelligence, simplicity and hospitality of these gentlemen farmers. Many of them had cabinets of minerals and we soon learned that we must not too enthusiastically admire a specimen. If we did so it was pressed upon us as a gift. One fine old lady, who was feasting us, quizzed me about Watson, his asteroids and his observatory, revealing a depth of interest and intelligence in astronomical matters that embarrassed me, lest my paucity of knowledge convince her that I was a sham. I have since had occasion to observe how deeply real knowledge has penetrated some of our rural districts. All learning is not confined to our great cities. Sharpless and I visited Valley Forge, Washington's headquarters and the home of Mad Anthony Wayne. We made a pilgrimage to Kennet Square, although we knew that the distinguished citizen who gave reputation to that hamlet, Bayard Taylor, was then in Germany as American minister. Taylor died in Berlin in 1878. In 1877 Mr. Jeffries, a banker in Westchester, owned a most valuable mineralogical collection, which I am told, has since gone to Philadelphia. In an old quarry near the village of Westchester the best samples of Chesterite were found, and we were fortunate in our search. On Sundays we went to "meeting" and listened to Lydia Childs and others moved by the spirit. My subsequent visits to Westchester have been short and infrequent.

Notwithstanding the pleasant and profitable time I had in Westchester I hailed with delight the last day of the session. I am sure that my last lecture was not so good nor so interesting as the first, and I have no recollection of what it was about. I only know that I was aglow with joyous anticipation when I left the rostrum. I perfunctorily bade my good Quaker friends good-by and temporarily forgot the beautiful drives, the savory viands and even the faultless minerals. All thoughts of George Washington, Anthony Wayne and Bayard Taylor were gone. I took the fastest train for old Missouri because there "the sweetest girl on earth" awaited me. The day after my arrival I did the best and wisest thing I have ever done in my somewhat long life. I married Dora Catherine Taylor. We had grown up together, I being about five years her senior. We had made mud pies, built dams across spring rivulets and hunted the whip-poor-wills' eggs in the great forest. She had been my star student in Latin at Mount Pleasant from which she graduated a year after I did. In her sixteenth year I had placed a plain gold ring with a boyish inscription "Amo Doram" on her finger. She still wears the ring and I still subscribe to the sentiment. Soon our golden anniversary will be here. She has been my wise counselor in all the affairs of our joint lives. She has a mind of her own, as I have known since mud pie days, and I have honored and respected it. She has borne and reared to manhood five worthy sons, the eldest of whom sleeps in the soil of France. I will not embarrass the others with either praise or blame. Their journeys through life are recently begun while we are on the last lap.

We took up our residence in Ann Arbor in September, 1877, and there we had our home until June, 1921. We have lived modestly, suffering no financial privation and desiring no luxury. We have been able to entertain our friends and to take an occasional excursion out into the wide world. We have ridden in a Ford (our own) without shame and in a Pierce Arrow (our friends') without pride.

CHAPTER V

INASMUCH as this chapter deals with intellectual and social affairs, it will be convenient for me to change my pronouns from the singular to the plural, thus including my wife and later the boys who came to broaden and bless our lives. When my wife and I left our old Missouri home, the kindly agent, a friend from childhood, checked our numerous trunks to St. Louis saying nothing of extra baggage. Feeling that we had plenty of money to carry us comfortably to our future home, we took seats in the parlor car. On the way an acquaintance of mine asked an introduction to my handsome sister. Although I recognized this supposed relationship as a reflection on the features of my bride, we gladly accepted the deception and thus escaped the brand of newlyweds. The young man did his best to entertain my "sister" and we had a jolly time. When we reached St. Louis a villainous baggage agent heaped every piece of our luggage on the scales and took my breath away by demanding a large sum for extra weight. I had to pay, and we rode that night in a day coach to Chicago. Fortunately the trunks were now checked to Ann Arbor and we had no fear of another wicked baggageman; so we removed the stains of travel so far as possible and again seated in a parlor car we finished our journey.

In Ann Arbor we rented a cottage on Jefferson Street and entered upon the cares and joys of housekeeping, about which we were quite ignorant. It is exhilarating to sail on unknown seas, keeping a sharp outlook for hostile shores and hidden rocks. The courage of youth is an alluring, if not an altogether trustworthy, guiding star. Some follow it recklessly without regard to the beacon lights built and maintained by nature at danger points, and are wrecked; while those who heed the signals reach the harbor of safety.

A few days after our installation in the cottage, a farmer whom we met on the street suggested that we would need some nice Hubbard squash for winter provender. We agreed. On our return we found that the farmer had transferred a wagon load of these esculent gourds to our cellar. When he came for his pay we remonstrated at the liberality with which he had provided for our sustenance, stating that we were only two in number and were not from Battle Creek and not exclusive vegetarians. Besides we preferred some variety in our dishes derived from plant life. This conference ended in the transference of a ridiculously small sum of money from our limited hoard to the farmer's exchequer and the retention of the wagon load of Hubbard squash in our cellar. Laughingly we told our good and wise baker and grocer, Mr. Hendrickson, on State Street, of our predicament. He advised us not to be disturbed, that the cottage cellar was nice and dry, and that he would draw on our supply as needed through the winter and would credit our account at current prices. If our subsequent small investments had yielded equivalent profits we would now be riding in a Lincoln or a Pierce Arrow instead of a Ford. It is but a slight exaggeration to say that we lived that winter on Hubbard squash without cutting more than three. Our Huguenot ancestors would have attributed this good fortune to a special act of Providence on our behalf, but we have attributed it to the wisdom of the grocer and have held his name in blessed memory. At any rate this is an illustration of how Fate protects newlyweds and other incompetents.

Our adventures into the social field were even more propitious than our investment in Hubbard squash, but in quite a different way. They brought us friendships which not only nourished our intellectual lives through the winter but still after quite fifty years are returning rates of interest far above the legal limit. These friendship certificates are not quoted on the stock market, nor are they recorded in our pass book at the bank, but their face value is beyond the power of gold to purchase; their coupons are endless and may be clipped not only by us but by our descendants.

In my student days I was attracted to the Unitarian Church by the Sunday evening lectures of Charles Brigham, the pastor. He was an erudite man; his subjects were well chosen; his diction was pleasing. The year of our marriage he died, and his mantle fell temporarily upon the shoulders of the Reverend Joseph Allen, professor in the Harvard Divinity School, and joint author with Greenough of Latin texts. Mr. Allen was our first table guest and we well remember our solicitude that all should go well and so it did. He partook of our simple fare, without Hubbard squash, with ease and grace. I introduced my bride to his small congregation and she was immediately accepted as she well deserved to be.

At that time there were but few Faculty members in the Unitarian congregation, among whom I may mention Doctor Donald Maclean, professor of surgery; Doctor John W. Langley, professor of general chemistry; Dean Charles E. Greene, of the Engineering School; and Professor William H. Pettee, head of the chair of geology. The last mentioned, with his charming wife and their only daughter, occupied the cottage next to ours. All these names have been transferred from the records of the living to the larger volumes of the dead, but the memory of their gracious reception of the boy and girl from old Missouri lingers with us as a priceless heirloom, which we wish to transmit to our children.

Outside of the Faculties there were others to whom we were equally indebted. To one of these I wish to pay a special tribute. This was William D. Harriman, known to all his neighbors as Judge Harriman. We gave the title with a loving, lingering intonation. At our modest club dinners he supplied the intellectual vitamines. Being a man of leisure he devoted most of his time to reading wisely and deeply of English and American literature. He knew the old time poets of both nations intimately and thoroughly. My interest in him and admiration for him were awakened by a paper read by him before the club, on Whittier, with selective readings. He was Mayor of Ann Arbor when I had the honor of representing the sixth ward on the Board of Aldermen.

In January, 1925, my wife and I, while spending a few weeks in St. Petersburg, Florida, learned that the judge was at Bradentown, that he was in his ninety-fourth year, and so benumbed by that great anesthetic, old age, that he seldom recognized his most intimate friends. We discussed the question of visiting him; we had not seen him for many years and feared that the visit would leave with us a painful impression. We had always known him as neat in dress, courtly in manner and witty in conversation. We did not wish to mar this memory picture which we had so long cherished. After much debate and many pros and cons we, with other old friends of his, eluded for a day the realtors of St. Petersburg and drove over the splendid Gandy Bridge on the excellent highway to the fair and flourishing city of Bradentown. We pulled the bell at a neat, vine-covered cottage and were welcomed by the judge's daughter, with her charming face framed in snowy white hair. She welcomed us; said that he was at his breakfast; that he retired at eleven P. M. and arose at eleven A. M. She took me to the breakfast room saying, "See if he will recognize you." At the table I found the familiar, graceful figure, smoothly shaven and neatly dressed. He seemed to be doing full justice to the large and savory dish of scalloped oysters in front of him. I pulled a chair close beside his and putting my lips to his ear I asked if he knew me. Blankly he inquired my name, what I wanted and where I came from. I whispered: "You dear old heathen; it does my soul good to see you devouring these bivalves." I could almost see the memory cylinders in his brain turn as an old time courtly smile passed over his face; then, he said: "You are a doctor but I can't recall your name." I repeated my whisper with some modification. His face lighted up: "You are my doctor from home." For some minutes he became the friend of old, radiant in countenance and fluent in speech. He said: "Being a Democrat in Florida is more popular than in Michigan; but being a Unitarian in Florida is anathema. There will always be one Unitarian so long as God lives." On leaving, he said: "Come again; you will find me here; I am not going to die soon."

I left the cottage bearing in the memory chamber of my brain a portrait of a saint, such as no old master ever painted.

One of the homes into which we had an early introduction was that of Professor Henry Frieze. The house, with a large garden, occupied the space now covered by St. Joseph's Hospital. Doctor Frieze was professor of Latin language and literature from 1852 until his death in 1889. He was twice acting president of the University and was once urged to accept this position permanently, but preferred to limit his burdens and to devote his time to study. His ideals concerning the University have not yet been realized and there is no reason for believing that they will be in the near future. He believed in the divorcement of the undergraduate and the graduate teaching, confining the University to the latter, and the establishment of graduate schools in mathematics, science, philology, and so forth. The medical and law departments have become in part graduate schools, but the engineering department continues undergraduate teaching and no provision has been made for other graduate schools, but all graduate students are lumped together. The provision for junior colleges has partly relieved the burden thrown on the University. How far this will go I am not in a position to forecast. I am sure that the realization of Doctor Frieze's dreams will not come so long as our universities are ranked by the number of students and not by the excellence of work

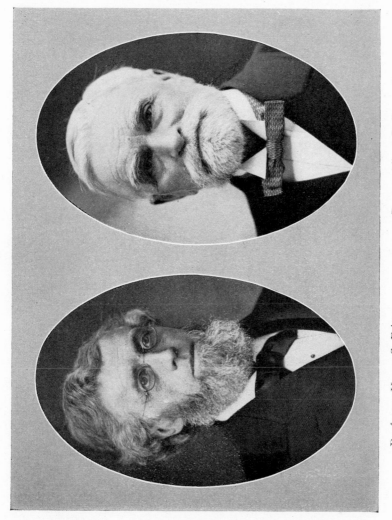

Professor Henry S. Frieze   Doctor Albert B. Prescott

done in them. In most of them at present elementary instruction dominates and, may I say it, cripples productive scholarship. However this is not an essay on the functions of a university; I have written several essays on this subject, but being a man of peace, I have refrained from printing them.

At the time of which I am writing (1877-89) Doctor Frieze was engaged in revising his Virgil and writing of Italian artists and their works. We spent an evening or two a week, sometimes more, in his parlor. He would read us what he had written since our last visit, illustrating Italian art with photographs, and then he would play Beethoven, of whom he was a great admirer, and of whose compositions he was a skilful interpreter. He told us of the first time he, Andrew D. White and Thayer (the author of the *Life of Beethoven*) studying together in Berlin, heard Wagner's music. It was so different from that of Beethoven that they compared the two and passed judgment on the future estimation in which each would be held. After arguing he played a Beethoven sonata and the three agreed that Wagner would never supplant their adored master.

Doctor Frieze was responsible for the purchase of the Columbian organ by the University and for the founding of the Musical Society and the School of Music. Of the latter I was one of the Directors for many years. This honor is, however, no evidence of my musical ability. The function of the Board of Directors was to look after financial needs, while Professor Stanley, the real Director, cared for the professional accomplishments. In the early days the School of Music was seriously threatened with financial disaster. We were in debt to the extent of many thousands of dollars and the Directors were individually responsible. The students did not care for classical music and would not buy tickets. It was proposed that we open the season with a concert by a popular band of national repute. Professor Stanley protested and in doing so addressed me: "Doctor, how would you like to have homeopathy taught as a part of the medical curriculum?" I had never before understood that the musician regards ragtime as the physician looks upon a cult. I took Stanley's side and joined him in his protest. Then some wise man on the Board suggested that we make the first concert so good that no one could afford to miss it. With the help of Madame Schumann-Heink we did this and within a few years were out of debt. The purpose of the University Musical Society was to educate the members of the faculties, their families, the students and the citizens in good music. Any excess in one year's receipts has been spent in making the program for the next better. In this way Professor Stanley has met with great success. His firm stand for the best in music has educated even his own Board of Directors. The first time I sat on this Board I learned something. The Board was negotiating with the greatest prima donna of the time. She submitted her contract, or her agent did, stating that she never sang for less than a thousand dollars a night. When I read the first claim in the contract I said that it was impossible; but I was advised to read further on, and in doing so found that reductions for cash and other provisions made the charge quite within our means. Thus there are, or at least were, advertising tricks to which even prima donnas resort. I know nothing of the present market price at which great singers sell their musical wares. From the first the

Chicago Orchestra, under Theodore Thomas and later under Frederick Stock, has rendered valuable aid to the University of Michigan Musical Society.

However my purpose is to record the fact that the University of Michigan owes its present development in musical education to the initiation of Professor Henry Frieze, whose interest in this direction has been carried on since his death by Professor Francis Kelsey, to whom the University also owes its present reputation in archeological research. To both of these men I owe much. In the early days when my studies led me to seek a new word I sought the help of Professor Frieze and later that of Professor Kelsey. With their approval I have ventured to introduce into the dictionary of science new words, some of which, at least, have become standard terms. Before turning back into the lines suggested by the title of this chapter I wish to say that my training in the appreciation of good music has entered so far into my inward self that when I hear jazz, even Whiteman's improved variety, in a hotel dining room, I am either seized with acute indigestion or my proclivity to forceful expression is restrained with difficulty or not at all.

Doctor Frieze had the unconscious habit when walking with one, of throwing an arm about the waist or shoulder of his companion. He, my wife and I often sauntered through the campus, along State Street, or among the roses in his garden, my wife in the middle, he with his arm about her waist, and I on the other side or following behind, proud of his affectionate attitude toward my bride. There were several newlyweds on the Faculties at that time and the males would brag about the attitude of the beloved master toward their mates.

To be with Professor Frieze was to receive lessons in grace and courtesy. He was my ideal of a learned man. I could not make of him a Trojan hero; not even an Æneas; he was Virgil himself. The admiration of Doctor Frieze, held by my wife and myself, led us to give to our fourth son, born about the time of Doctor Frieze's death, his name. During the World War an engineer officer (Colonel Crocker) said to me in the Cosmos Club: "I have just voted into our society a man about whom I know little besides his name." I said that that was not a safe procedure. "No," he replied. "It usually is not, but this man's name is Henry Frieze Vaughan." After all there is something in bestowing a good name on a son.

In the old days which my memory is now reviewing, the center of intellectual and social life in Ann Arbor was in the home of President and Mrs. Angell. Doctor Angell's presidency extended through thirty-eight years (1871-1909) and he died in 1916. The President's house on the campus, was not quite so large or so pretentious as it now is, but during the years mentioned thousands enjoyed its hospitality. The Faculty was not so large then and even assistants knew personally and drew inspiration from their seniors, not only in their own specialties, but in all. The Faculty was one large family group, the members mingling with no stressed formality. Students in groups were received and given occasion to observe the social amenities of life as dispensed by their cultured host and hostess. Professor Frieze once remarkd to me that the greatest pleasure he found in being a teacher was to watch the growth mentally and socially of the students from their freshman to their senior years. **Even now** when I meet learned lawyers, skilled engineers and wise physicians at alumni gatherings I recall the social as well as the intellectual conditions of their student lives. Deans and professors and their wives followed the example set by President and Mrs. Angell, and socially entertained their assistants and students.

There were at that time in Ann Arbor no nice hotels, and the Michigan Union, that experimental college of social training, was still in the womb of the future. During the thirty-eight years of which I am writing, men and women of all degrees and varieties of greatness, from all parts of the world, came to the University and were entertained in the home of the President or in those of the professors, most frequently in the former. It became the custom of each host to see that such of his colleagues as might be interested in the visitor should have the opportunity to see him. The venerable President Eliot said to me a few years ago to this effect: "You were fortunately situated at Ann Arbor; every man of intellect went to Ann Arbor to see Doctor Angell and no one went without returning richer." The man who spoke these words was one of our most highly prized visitors and he never came without leaving us richer. I remember his coming into my laboratory one afternoon when the splendid Harvard medical buildings were being planned and asking me to show him the arrangement that we had made for the care of our experimental animals in our much simpler laboratories, recently constructed. There was nothing in an educational way foreign to the mind of this great college president. I also recall his showing me the Harvard medical buildings when they were completed. He took me through every laboratory and as we stood in the splendid court, he asked if I felt a pang of jealousy. I said, "No; I am glad to see medicine properly housed in at least one great university." I felt no pang of jealousy but a spirit of elation in the recognition of the esteem in which this eminent college president held medical science. Medical education in this country owes much to Doctor Eliot and the splendid school which developed so greatly under his fostering care. One feels that medicine has broken the shackles of empiricism when it receives the recognition and help of such men as he.

In my opinion, there were three great university presidents at that time. They were Charles Eliot of Harvard, Andrew White of Cornell and James Angell of Michigan. There were other worthy men performing this function at that time and there are worthy successors, but I am sure that I am disparaging no memory nor discounting the service of any living man by giving these names.

In the early morning of a spring day in 1911, I was hurrying along the diagonal walk across the campus, on the way to my laboratory to see how my guinea pigs and rabbits were responding to my treatments, when I saw a man behaving queerly. He seemed to be consulting a sheet of paper which he carried in his left hand; then he went from tree to tree, patting each in a caressing manner with his right hand. Thinking that I had detected a patient escaped from the psychopathic ward I left the walk and approached the strangely behaving individual. He was standing by a tree and patting it when he heard me approach and turned quickly. In my surprise I cried out: "Mr. White! What does this mean?" He said: "Yesterday while sitting in my library at Ithaca I happened to think that fifty years ago to-day the class of 1861 planted these trees under my direction. I had among my papers a plot of the ground, the location of each tree and the name of the student who planted it." Then he added, with tears in his eyes: "There are more trees alive than boys."

In those days we entered the President's residence by the back door on the campus; the front door was only for strangers or when receptions were being given. Not infrequently the bell brought the President himself to the door in his slippers and with a gracious welcome on his face. Informal lunches and dinners were frequent and we were invited to meet distinguished guests.

When I read a book by Lord Bryce, and I believe that I have read all that he has written, I have a memory picture of this great Englishman. He sits in a Morris chair in the Angell drawing room; he wears a worn smoking jacket of uncertain, but varied color; his feet in carpet slippers, with gray woolen socks down to the ankles, rest on a stool; his necktie is all awry and he is anything but a fashionably dressed man, but he is talking about his travels in strange and remote parts of the earth, in Iceland, in the Polish and Hungarian Alps, in Transcaucasia, or he is discoursing on Democracy. We are listening; his talk is an informal and most instructive lecture.

Every one who has written about Sir Frederick Pollock emphasizes his silence. In this respect his reputation quite exceeds that of President Coolidge. Sir Frederick is silent not only in voice but in facial expression; President Coolidge does smile. Sir Frederick is a most learned man; he knows more about law than Lycurgus did because he knows all the laws that Lycurgus gave the Spartans and all that have been given since; at least so far as they are worth knowing. This is a heavy burden for any man to bear and I have noticed that even a jolly Irishman is not given to talk while he has a loaded hod on his shoulders. In other words, my guess is that Sir Frederick's silence is due to the fact that he knows too much. I am not sure that this diagnosis will hold in the case of President Coolidge. My training as a physician causes me to recognize that similarity in symptoms does not always imply identity in etiology. I may ask the National Research Council to induce some erudite scientist to investigate the etiology of silence.

In the meantime, I may relate that Sir Frederick was the guest of President Angell for some days while giving a course of lectures in the Law School. I should interject that both he and President Coolidge can talk in public but are strangely silent socially. One afternoon a note came to the laboratory from Mrs. Angell. The import was as follows: "Bring Mrs. Vaughan to dinner and do make Sir Frederick talk; he sits at the table, stares into vacancy but says nothing. Make him talk if you have to be rude to him." We sat at the table with our hostess between us. I made many attempts to fulfil my mission but all were failures. The distinguished guest did not even look at me. Finally in a desperate effort I said: "Sir Frederick, why is it that there are no great schools of law in England and that all barristers read in Inns of Court as they did a century ago; is this due to English conservatism?" The great man dropped his knife and fork. He brought his fist down on the table with sufficient weight to endanger the dishes; he fairly shouted: "English conservatism! It is damned stupidity." Then through the dinner and evening we listened to a most

Viscount Bryce

learned disquisition on methods and systems of legal instruction.

The engineers of his day regarded Francis Hopkinson Smith a great novelist while the novelists admitted that he was a great engineer. He once told me that his greatest ambition was to rebuild the fallen Campanile in Venice, but at that time he was engaged in the lighter occupation of sketching the picturesque spots of the city in the sea. I do know that in pre-Volstead days he was a most entertaining companion, especially as the midnight hour approached or receded; then he would give most inimitable readings from *Colonel Carter of Cartersville*.

The great and original Joseph Jefferson came occasionally, only too rarely for us. After answering a knock at the President's study door one day I informed him that a bevy of college girls begged a presentation and I added that every girl admired him. Graciously bidding me to usher them in, he said: "It is not Joseph Jefferson that they admire. It is old Rip. I never knew a girl who did not love the old scamp."

Wu Ting Fang was a picturesque and entertaining visitor. In his full Chinese regalia his social discourse, sparkled with wit, revealed a breadth of view and a spirit of toleration seldom expressed by either American or European, and showed an intellectuality that would have done honor to a man of any race. One of his witticisms, as I remember it, was something as follows: "Shanghai is the best place to be born in, because there is made a superior baby cradle; Pekin is the best place to live in on account of the excellence of the food and the skill of its cooks; Canton is the best place to die in because there are made the most comfortable coffins."

Both Doctor and Mrs. Angell were intolerant of any exhibition of self superiority. In 1885 Charles Kendall Adams, previously professor of history at Michigan, became president of Cornell. Some months after assuming his new duties, he made a visit to Ann Arbor, and my wife and I were invited to dine with him at Doctor Angell's. As we pulled our chairs out at the table, he asked: "Mrs. Angell, do you think fifteen dollars apiece enough for a university president to pay for dining room chairs?" The answer came without hesitation: "I do not know, President Adams; mine cost two dollars apiece but they have been occupied by some very nice people." Later in the dinner President Adams took up a salt cellar and spoke of it as a fine sample of cut glass. "Yes," said the hostess, "it is pretty. I bought it at the ten cent store."

On another occasion a young man from New York came with a letter of introduction and gave a parlor talk in the President's house. The large drawing room was filled with professors and their wives. The young man talked about New York society and the famous Four Hundred of that time. The sum and substance of his speech was that only millionaires contributed to society in the metropolis. I sat near Doctor Angell. He was plainly irritated by the views expressed by the speaker. He whispered to me: "When he stops I am going to ask you to say a few words. Hit him and hit him hard." When the man stopped, Doctor Angell said: "Doctor Vaughan goes to New York occasionally and I am asking him to say something about New York society as he sees it." I stated that I knew nothing of the society described; I had recently visited the city. I was on professional business and as the weather was warm I went rather scantily

and cheaply clothed. Doctor Abraham Jacobi, seeing me
at the professional meeting, insisted that I dine with him.
I accepted. The night was very hot and we dined in our
shirt sleeves. The other guests were George P. Putnam
and Nathan Straus, and I was foolish enough to think
that I was in good society.

An instructor on a small salary brought his bride to
Ann Arbor. She gave a ladies' luncheon to which Mrs.
Angell was invited. The courses were many and boun-
tiful. On bidding her hostess adieu, Mrs. Angell said:
"Will you and your husband dine with us informally at
seven o'clock Friday? Be sure, however, that our meal
will be simple. My husband's salary is small."

Grover Cleveland came more than once and had in
the Faculty many supporters, although the University was
supposed to be a stronghold of Republicanism. President
Cleveland for a time hesitated between Princeton and Ann
Arbor as a place of residence on his retirement. At least
he spoke to me once on this matter during his second term.
He appreciated life in an intellectual atmosphere; he approved of plain living and high thinking; he was democratic not only in politics but in his daily life. One night
during his second term I was at a play in a Washington
theater. When the curtain went down there was a somewhat unseemly and a certainly unnecessary rush for the
doors. Caught in the crowd I found myself thrown,
though not roughly, against Mr. Cleveland. I apologized
as together we pushed our way out. I remarked that it
was too bad that the President of the United States should
be subjected to so much rudeness. He replied that he
was not there as the President, but as an ordinary citizen,
and expected to be treated as such. He was willing to

take his chance; he was in no way superior and was among his equals.

Some have said that Benjamin Harrison wore his grandfather's hat. From the glimpses I had of him this insinuation is wholly without warrant. He wore his own hat and it covered good brain tissue. I once had quite a long chat with him. It was about the time when President Roosevelt took a somewhat arbitrary course in the deal about the Panama Canal. Mr. Harrison castigated President Roosevelt rather severely and I said that had he (Mr. Harrison) been president the action would not have been taken. "No," said Mr. Harrison, "nor would it have been done if Grover Cleveland had been president." Then he launched into an eulogy of Cleveland which quite surprised me. Mr. Harrison was a man of great legal ability, which he exhibited in his practise and in his arguments in international matters. His inaugural address in 1889 almost reconciled me to his defeat of Mr. Cleveland.

Theodore Roosevelt came, with his military attaché in full uniform, while he was Governor of New York. I had much respect for Mr. Roosevelt and voted for him for President in 1904, but I never was a hero worshipper. On his visit to Ann Arbor, Doctor Angell gave a luncheon at which I had the honor of a seat next to the distinguished visitor. A few weeks later Doctor Angell and I rode with Governor Roosevelt from Albany to New York, pleasantly renewing our acquaintance. Both at the luncheon and on the train Governor Roosevelt reminisced about the Cuban Campaign in 1898. He had recently published an article or given an interview in which he said that he had encouraged the charge at San Juan Hill,

cheering some and swearing at others. Some clergyman
had asked him to deny that he had sworn at any one.
At this Governor Roosevelt laughed most heartily. The
military display which accompanied President Roosevelt's
public appearances irritated me. I recognized that the
persons of our chief executives were entitled to special
protection. We had had our lessons in this matter in the
assassinations of Garfield and McKinley, but I queried if
this protection could not have been even more efficiently
given with less display. That President Roosevelt had no
personal fear was plainly shown by his behavior at Mil-
waukee when an attempt was made upon his life. When he
accepted the nomination of the Bull Moose faction in 1912
my critical attitude of mind toward him developed into
one of hostility.

Woodrow Wilson came twice, once while president of
Princeton and again soon after the announcement of his
candidacy for the presidency. Indeed his lecture at Ann
Arbor was one of the first after this important event. A
delegation of citizens met him at the station as he came
up the platform carrying a heavy valise. We relieved
him of his burden, took him to make a call upon President Angell, then somewhat infirm, and conducted him
to the Opera House filled with Ann Arborites of all political creeds and to whom I introduced him. His address
was a literary gem and awakened the greatest enthusiasm.
Of course in introducing him I predicted that the ides of
November would see his election, but I had no idea at
that time that my prediction would come true. At the
luncheon following, he and I discussed Princeton affairs
and especially the recently appointed president, Dr. Hib-
ben, of whom Mr. Wilson spoke in praise.

A few weeks later at the annual meeting of the American Medical Association at Atlantic City I sat by the side of Professor Councilman of Harvard, while Governor Wilson addressed the audience. Councilman thought that there was only one other man in America who could give so scholarly an address and that man was President Eliot; while I expressed the opinion that the other man was President Angell. At his first election I voted for Mr. Wilson with greater enthusiasm than I had ever felt in the exercise of that function. I appreciated the great things he accomplished in his first term, especially did I approve of the establishment of Federal Reserve Banks. My long experience on the Board of Directors of one of our local banks had given me some right to hold an opinion on this matter. But I was greatly irritated by his apparent tardiness to help our European friends. His failure to enter the contest after the sinking of the *Lusitania* drove me wild, and I joined in more than one telegram or memorial to him. These were met with only polite acknowledgments by Mr. Tumulty.

I was somewhat cheered by President Wilson's request to the National Academy of Sciences in April, 1916, to appoint a committee to advise him on scientific matters in case of emergency; but the shout that "He has kept us out of the war" during the campaign rekindled my antagonism. When Mr. Hughes was nominated I said, "There is the man for whom I will vote." Every speech made by Mr. Hughes rendered this decision more doubtful; the day before the election arrived with my vote still uncertain. There is in Washtenaw County a township, Freedom, in which at that time few of the voters spoke anything but their Swabian dialect. I had frequently been called

The President's House in the 'Seventies

to their homes in consultation and among them I was known as the "Prussian doctor" on account of the brogue I employed in endeavoring to ascertain their symptoms. My wife and I talked the matter of our votes over, and on the day before the presidential election in 1916, we drove through Freedom in our Ford eating fruit and drinking cider with our Swabian friends. At each home we asked, "What about your vote to-morrow?" The invariable reply was: "We vote for Hughes." This settled the matter with us. The next day we voted for Wilson.

I am not competent to pass judgment on President Wilson. Time alone can do that and what the verdict of the future will be no one of the present can know. Mr. Lansing's book, in my opinion, condemns its author quite as strongly as it labors to convict his chief. Even the Page letters which I enjoy greatly, rasp on my nerves and I believe them to be unfair. Mr. Page, a most able man in London, among his English friends, practically in the midst of the war, saw one side of the shield. President Wilson in Washington, with his hand on the pulse of the nation, made up of many nationalities, with diverse heredity and environment, with conflicting social, intellectual and economic interests, saw both sides of the shield. Indeed the crystal of divination through which he looked had many facets and each gave a different picture.

During the presidential campaign in 1896 there was a big Republican rally in Ann Arbor. McKinley, Alger, Thurston, Mason and others, high in the party council, were there. The distinguished visitors were assigned to several homes without regard to party affiliations. All citizens were to be Republicans for that day at least. Senators Mason and Thurston, with the latter's wife, were our guests. At the mass meeting I sat between Mrs. Thurston and my wife. McKinley discussed the tariff; Alger appealed to the old soldiers; Thurston denounced the solid South; Mason and others told stories, some good, some bad. I joined in the applause most vociferously. Mrs. Thurston evidently had heard her husband's speech before and now and then she would whisper: "Listen, something good is coming." Then the distinguished senator from the Sunflower State would hold before our astonished gaze and wave most frantically the bloody shirt. In the applause which followed I joined with increased vigor. After the speaking a group repaired to our dining room. My colored office boy and family butler, neat in his tuxedo, drew upon the wine cellar, then fairly replete with the vintages of France and California; alas! I did not then know that wine cellars, like Troy, were soon to be known only in tradition. Mrs. Thurston told exultantly how her escort had led the applause, especially when her husband was speaking. Then I confessed that I had been born a Democrat, that I did not believe a word that her husband or others had spoken, and that my behavior at the mass meeting had been prompted solely by my gallantry towards her. This confession detracted in no way from the jollity of the occasion but in fact increased the merriment. I voted for McKinley at the election, but it was Mr. Bryan and not the speeches I heard that night that led to my deflection from that party whose standard I had supported since my first presidential vote in 1872 for Horace Greeley.

On my return from Cuba in 1898, General Alger, Secretary of War, took me to President McKinley and asked me to tell him my opinion of the defects in the

campaign which had contributed so greatly to the priva-
tions of our soldiers.   This I did without hesitation and
without reserve.   The President heard me with patience
and dismissed me with thanks.   I am sure that our country was fortunate in having McKinley instead of Bryan
at the helm in the Cuban crisis.   This view I adhere to
notwithstanding my full recognition of the fact that in
many respects the Spanish-American War was conducted
in a manner of which we have no cause to be proud.

Professor Paul Ehrlich, the discoverer of salvarsan
(606), which, with its congeners, has proven so valuable
in the treatment of syphilis and a few allied diseases, was
with his wife once a guest at our home for some days.
He lectured to the medical students, met the Faculty and
proved to be a most desirable and interesting guest.   He
spoke no English, though his wife was most proficient in
the use of our tongue.   On his return to Germany he
advised his friends, contemplating a visit to this country,
not to admit any knowledge of English.   If you follow
this advice, said he, your American friends will make full
provision for your traveling and accommodation and will
send an escort with you.   When in Ann Arbor he made
frequent requests to see an Indian and was most surprised and disappointed at our inability to satisfy his
desire.   At a dinner in Berlin a few years later he told
the story as follows: "I wanted to see an Indian.
Vaughan said there were none thereabouts; I asked him
if he had ever seen one. 'Oh yes, I saw one at Buffalo
Bill's show in Berlin.'"   One morning at breakfast, finding a shredded wheat biscuit on his plate, Ehrlich looked
at it from all sides and inquired: *"Was ist das?"* He
was told that it was *"weizen."* *"Ich werde es diskutieren;*

es schmeckt gut." He ate two. Professor Welch once asked me how it was that while Johns Hopkins paid Ehrlich's way over here and Chicago University gave him a degree, on his return he talked more about Ann Arbor. I will now confess how we won the heart of this great scientist. My colleague, Professor Huber, had once worked in Ehrlich's laboratory and knew that he was limited to three cigars a day by his physician. We sent to New York and secured a box of the strongest, blackest cigars in the market. It was through these that we won the great man's affection, but I will not swear that he followed his physician's advice in their use.

In 1907 I went to Berlin and soon hastened to the Institute for Infectious Diseases where Professor Wassermann was perfecting his scientific test in the diagnosis of syphilis. He welcomed me; said that he would instruct me in his technique, and I could carry it to America. We went to work immediately and continued without interruption until he, looking at his watch, announced that it was four o'clock and that we would go out and find a lunch. In our walk we came to the military barracks. He inquired if I knew the purpose of the great building. On my replying in the affirmative he became eloquent and declaimed as follows: "There are fifty thousand soldiers quartered in Berlin and a proportionate number in other German cities. They do nothing but scatter gonorrhea and syphilis." Growing more intense in his words he added: "I fear that the time may come when the militarism of Germany will endanger the peace of the world and possibly wreck the empire." During the war I often thought of this prophetic speech and expressed the hope that I might live to see the day when

I would walk with Professor Wasserman along the streets of Berlin under the flag of a stable German republic. Alas, that time has not come and my friend is dead!

It was my good fortune to meet several times the great Russian scientist and biologist, Elie Metschnikoff. He might have sat for a portrait of a typical nihilist. His long hair and heavy beard, as black as a crow in earlier life, tinged with gray in advancing years, evidently received but little attention. He would sit for minutes apparently in deepest thought and utterly oblivious of those about him, biting his nails. Then he would break into most fluent and correct French, always apologizing for being compelled to speak in a foreign language. His words were at times profound and at times biting with satire. In science at least he was anything but a nihilist. His work was constructive and rational. He was the founder and defender of the phagocytic theory. I believe that the essential facts of this theory, as he discovered and interpreted them, will not be discarded by the scientific world. They may be modified, since the discovery of absolute and perfect truth is hardly within the realm of human endeavor. In 1907 I was at a dinner at Wassermann's house. Besides the wise host and the fair hostess there were Metschnikoff, Erhlich, Wright, Strong and myself. Metschnikoff said there is dogma in science as well as in religion. If a German does not believe in Erhlich's side chain theory, he is damned.

In 1891 my wife and I attended an International Congress of Hygiene in London. We reached England some weeks before the session and leisurely journeyed from Liverpool, visiting Oxford, Stratford, Kenilworth

and other points of historic interest and natural love-
liness. In London I found an invitation to attend a
gentlemen's dinner to be given by Sir Joseph Lister to
those who were to read papers in his section at the Congress. This quite elated me and filled me with anticipation. On the afternoon of the day named for the dinner
we attended a garden party at the beautiful home of
Baroness Burdett-Coutts at Holly Lodge, Highgate.
Her handsome husband, Mr. William Ashmead-Bartlett,
as an American, took us in tow and showed us the
indescribable beauties of the place.

On returning to London I found that I had short
time to dress and reach Lister's home. I hurriedly made
the change in apparel, called a hansom, and was on my
way to 12 Park Lane when I discovered that I had no
small money. Fortunately I had time to cerebrate, a
function which I exercise slowly; the cab stopped at the
curb; a man in livery stood ready to open the cab door
and another to perform a like function at the door of
the mansion. I alighted, asked cabby the fare and being
informed that it was a shilling, I held out a gold
sovereign. He had no change. I had figured in my
painful moments of cerebration that this would happen.
I was a few minutes late and I had been told that in
England it was held to be a crime to be late at a formal
dinner. I had not been informed of the penalty attached
to this crime, but I knew that English justice was speedy
and uncompromising. I could not run around the corner
and have gold transmuted into silver. I had already,
during the drive, decided on the action I should take in
the emergency. With as lordly an air as I could assume,
another painful process, I handed the sovereign to the

Sir Joseph Lister

man in livery, told him to give cabby a shilling and to pocket the remainder. This seemed wholly satisfactory. During the dinner this servant stood behind my chair, and, do my best, I could not lower the levels in my wine glasses.

Everything was going well and I was congratulating myself upon the successful result of my cogitations when Professor Carl Frankel, of the University of Berlin, who had been my instructor in bacteriology in Koch's laboratory three years before, announced that he had a joke on the Americans. Knowing something of Frankel's jokes, my knees began to tremble and I sent up a silent but fervent prayer that the Lord might strike Frankel dead. But there was no divine interposition and Frankel ruthlessly and murderously proceeded. He informed the expectant diners that on the day before when the American delegates to the Congress were being presented to the Prince of Wales, the representative of the crown of England, one of these uncouth and uncultured aborigines said, "My dear Sir, I am glad to meet you. My name is Wales and I think we must be related." I am sure that if I had arisen and shouted an oath there could not have been more consternation among the English at the table. A few foreigners who had understood the story laughed; but most of their faces were covered with interrogation points. They knew that something had happened but they had not the remotest idea what it was. Frenchmen, Italians, and even Germans, since Frankel had spoken in broken English, sought the eyes of their compatriots. I sought surcease from sorrow by trying to empty all my wine glasses at once but my faithful servitor frustrated this plan. In my pain I realized that Lady Lister's eyes were tracing the faces on my side of the table and finally I was conscious that they rested on me. Then I heard her voice, soft and sweet, as the tone of a fair hostess should be, inquiring: "Doctor Vaughan, you are the only American at the table, and what have you to say about the story?" This seemed my death knell. I made no attempt to reply. In my extremity the Lord sent relief. At the table was Doctor W. D. Miller, then dean of the Dental School of the University of Berlin, an American by birth, a graduate of Michigan and an old friend of mine. He replied to Lady Lister's interrogation saying: "Pardon me, Lady Lister, Doctor Vaughan is not the only American at the table. Although I represent a German university, I am an American, and while my colleague's story is a good one, there is no truth in it." I revived sufficiently to call the function of the servitor behind my chair into operation again, and later when our hostess had retired I saw peace in rings of smoke from a fine Havana.

When Doctor Miller and I left the house I embraced him and told him that he had saved my life; the story that Frankel had told was true. The surgeon general of our Navy at that time was Philip Wales and he perpetrated the joke as Frankel told it. The Prince of Wales (afterward Edward VII) said, "Yes, we are cousins; come and meet your other cousins," and our surgeon general had the honor of being introduced to the whole royal family, or as many of them as were within reach. There is an account of this dinner with a list of guests in the excellent life of Lord Lister, but the book makes no mention of the story I have told.

It would be superfluous, and in a sense incongruous, for me to speak in praise of Lord Lister. It would be like a pigmy pouring a libation to a god. In person Lord Lister was most imposing, his fair face beaming with the intelligence and benignity of generations of inherited Quaker refinement, learning and culture. Lady Lister was the daughter of the great Syme, the surgeon of Edinburgh of the preceding generation. My first teacher in surgery and subsequently my colleague in the Michigan Faculty, Donald Maclean, like Lister, was a product of Syme's teaching; and I had heard stories of this original character since my freshman days. I fancied that I could detect a striking resemblance between Lister and Maclean and as I looked into the face of the former, I recalled the old days in the seventies, when, as Maclean's assistant, I had spent hours drenched in the poisonous sprays of carbolic acid. The lesser son of Syme had attempted to follow in the footsteps of his greater brother.

At this Congress I met many distinguished men of various nationalities. I desire to mention here the names of three Englishmen who were then doing good work and who subsequently added to their laurels. Professor Adami, at that time professor of pathology in McGill University, Montreal, is now Chancellor of the University of Liverpool. He gave the oration at the laying of the cornerstone of our new medical building in 1901. G. Sims Woodhead became professor of pathology in the University of Cambridge and was knighted. He once made me a short visit in Ann Arbor. He died a few years ago. Doctor A. Ruffer became medical adviser to the Egyptian government, did epoch making work on the diseases of the ancient Egyptians by studying their remains, thus creating the science of paleopathology, and became Sir Armand. He was lost in the Mediterranean during the war. I came in pleasant but brief contact with Blanchard, long professor of biology in the University of Paris. His personality was charming and his knowledge wide and diverse. At the Congress he discussed a paper of mine on meat poisoning and gave me valuable information concerning the poisonous fish of the West Indies.

On my first visit to England in 1888 I had the good fortune to meet Lauder Brunton, afterwards Sir Lauder. Our acquaintance began in the musty atmosphere of an old book shop. Both were poring over ancient tomes when, without letter of introduction or other formality, we began to talk. He invited me to dinner that evening at his home at 7 Portland Place. He added, "Without formality. My wife is at the seashore and only my niece and I will be present." I arrayed myself in a Prince Albert with white vest and striped trousers and covered myself with a high hat. In this costume I was admitted to the vestibule and conducted to the drawing room by a servant. I found Doctor Brunton and his handsome niece in full dinner attire and was graciously requested to conduct the young lady to the dining room. The second edition of Brunton's great work on pharmacology had just come from the press and I was presented with a copy. I was perfectly familiar with the first edition and the advance in this science, embryonic at that time, supplied abundant material for conversation. However I was somewhat ill at ease and when the lady had retired and I was being consoled by the wine, tobacco and the closer intimacy of my host, I laughingly said to him: "Our great American essayist and philosopher, Emerson, has written: 'There is a consolation in being well dressed that religion does not afford, and now I could testify that there is a misery in the soul due to being improperly dressed that all the consolations of religion can not relieve." The conversation grew more personal and intimate and this great doctor detailed to me his early struggles in establishing himself in a consultation practise in London. In my classes I used his second edition as I had done with the first and our acquaintance through occasional correspondence continued as long as he lived, but I never saw him again until 1897 in St. Petersburg. We were standing in line awaiting the stamp of approval by a bearded Russian official on our credentials. Over my shoulder he caught my name on my paper and acquaintance was renewed most pleasantly but too shortly. At that particular time for some trifling political reason, which I have long since forgotten if I ever knew, Americans were more popular in Russia than Englishmen and on account of my nationality I was able to be of some slight service to him. In my opinion, Sir Lauder Brunton has never been so highly honored by scientific men as his work deserves, but in the annals of pharmacology his name will occupy a most distinguished place. At least his memory will ever be green among his friends so long as they live. Brunton gave me a letter of introduction to Professor J. Burdon-Sanderson, but my acquaintance with this eminent man was regrettably short. He at Oxford, and Professor Michael Foster at Cambridge, did much to develop modern biologic research in these ancient and honorable universities.

In 1888 Doctor Novy and I, with the prospect of opening our laboratory of hygiene that fall, hastened to Berlin
to take the course in bacteriology in Koch's laboratory.
We were advised to secure letters from the President of
the United States or from the Secretary of State, and were
told that without such we certainly would not be admitted,
since applications were pouring in from all parts of the
civilized world. However we went without troubling
these dignitaries and found places without question. At
that time Koch's laboratory occupied a hastily converted
dwelling at 36 Klosterstrasse and the laboratory instruction was given by Professor Carl Frankel with the assistance of Docents Kirchner and Herter. Professor
Koch gave general lectures on hygiene and carried on his
researches in a private room. Frankel was a most capable instructor, did good research work, wrote a book
on bacteriology which we used in our first course and later
became professor of hygiene at the University of Halle.

I can say nothing that would enhance the reputation
of Robert Koch. He stands next to Pasteur as the
founder of the science of bacteriology. As a village
doctor in East Prussia he discovered the use of solid
media in the growth of bacteria, and demonstrated their
value in the identification and isolation of these low forms
of life. He formulated the rules, compliance with which
must be shown before a given bacterium may be recognized as the sole and sufficient cause of a given disease.
He did much to convert the germ theory of disease into
a science. In 1882, after many months of untiring research, Koch identified, isolated and grew in pure cultures the bacillus of tuberculosis. His studies in Egypt
and India enabled him in 1884 to announce like success

in his pursuit of the vibrio of Asiatic cholera. In later years he won other laurels and received the highest rewards that can come to a man of science.

While I was at work in the laboratory, Professor Koch summoned me to a conference in his private room. I felt highly honored to be thus distinguished, but the burden of his talk was the condemnation of the University of Michigan for retaining as its professor of pathology a man who did not accept the well established fact that bacteria cause disease, referring to Professor Gibbes, whose name Koch pronounced with bitterness, biting it into two syllables. I tried to explain that I was an antagonist of Professor Gibbes' teaching and that my purpose in seeking instruction in Koch's laboratory was to fit me better to combat my colleagues' erroneous teachings, but I did not succeed in mollifying his anger. Robert Koch was a great man, but in many respects a typical German, ready to stamp upon those who did not acknowledge his authority. While I admired his work I could not be altogether pleased with his personality.

At the completion of our laboratory course, following the custom of the time, the students gave Professor Frankel and his assistants a *kneipe,* which might be defined as a "drinking bout." If there were eatables they were negligible. The special drink at our feast was denominated *pfirschebowle* and consisted, so I was told, of fresh, peeled and chopped peaches, plentifully sprinkled with sugar, covered with Moselle wine and the whole allowed to ferment for some days in large earthen jars. This drink was served in long stemmed goblets. At the call *ein* one took hold of one's glass; at *zwei* one raised the glass to one's lips; and at *drei* one drained the contents. The inspector made a *Nagel-probe*. In other words there must not be enough wine left in the glass to moisten the thumb nail, but needless to say that as the feast progressed the test was neglected. We made speeches in the order of our sitting. Fortunately my time came second and consequently when I was not intoxicated. I began my speech in German, intending to drop into English, but my German proved so mirth-provoking that I was not permitted to make the transfer. I soon saw that my training in drinking would not permit me to drain my glass at every toast. I therefore bribed the waiter behind my chair to take my glass each time I raised it. He accepted both the bribe and the function, and my fellows were now too far gone to detect the deceit. In this way I managed to keep fairly conscious of what was going on throughout the feast. There were at the table Germans predominantely, a few Italians, two Mexicans and two Americans. One by one my comrades went under the table. Frankel arose and made a speech—I think his twentieth. This time he referred to the triple alliance and shouting *"Noch einen Krieg! Noch einen Krieg!"* he joined the majority. The police came uninvited by us. They may have had an invitation from our landlord. The feast ended, and Herter and I procuring a cab took our distinguished instructor home and put him to bed.

After recovering from the feast Doctor Novy and I took our departure from Berlin; he, always pursuing knowledge with more zest than I, to the Pasteur Institute in Paris while I, with my old friend Dennison, visited Dresden, Vienna, Salzburg and spent some weeks in the Tyrol and Switzerland. Later I joined Novy in Paris and through Roux's kindly intercession I was presented to the man who, in my opinion, was the greatest product of the nineteenth century, Louis Pasteur. This judgment must be just if human greatness be estimated by benefits conferred upon one's fellows. Pasteur demonstrated that it is within the range of possibility for man to eradicate from the earth every infectious disease which may afflict himself or other living creatures. Man may never reach this great achievement but the demonstration of its possibility indicates that intellectually he has reached a stage in which he may become a co-worker with his creator in leading his race toward the mountain tops of human perfection. But the ascent to these heights is steep and stony, while the alluring valleys of ignorance and indolence lying below are always tempting the masses.

In the early eighties an Englishman, already advanced to middle life, entered the Medical School. He was an ideal gentleman, prepossessing in manner and speaking fluently French, German and Spanish. His name was Francis W. Brewer and it was rumored that he might legally attach a prefix to this name. Of this I do not know, but I do know that he would not have disgraced such a title. He was poor and I was able to help him financially by having him serve as an attendant to some of my more wealthy male patients. After his graduation he was in my office for a time. During the Chicago Exposition he served as sanitary supervisor of the buildings and grounds. Later he was made professor of hygiene in the State College of Utah at Logan, where he died. Recently I tarried for a short time in that prosperous looking little city and made inquiry for my old friend, but the present generation knew only the name and could give no particulars.

When I went to Europe in 1888 Brewer gave me two letters of introduction. One was to a director of the Kosmos Line at Hamburg, Germany. This letter I presented. It was graciously received with expressions of the highest esteem for its writer, and the German gentleman dined me at the Hamburg Club. He gave me advice as to my conduct in Germany, saying: "Do not tell any of your American stories. People will not believe them and will pronounce them lies. In a club like this one would expect to hear good stories, but I have heard only two. A member said that he had two of the best anecdotes in the world. One was too long to tell and the other rich beyond compare, but he had forgotten it." Thus my friend belied his own advice. I found German wit by no means insipid and my lies were often believed while my truths were discredited. When I told my fellow students that there were houses in New York twenty or more stories in height they thought and sometimes said that I was lying. Then I told of a roadsign in Virginia having the inscription: "This is the road to Richmond; that is the road to Petersburg; those who can not read should consult the blacksmith nearby." This statement led to the applause of the care and consideration displayed by the road superintendent.

Brewer's second letter was to the Lord Mayor of London. I carried this to the Mansion House, handed it to the lackey and awaited its reception. The Lord Mayor himself came to the waiting room, greeted me most cordially and said that the bearer of a letter from his old friend Brewer would be the recipient of any favor he could bestow. I wished to attend a murder trial at the Old Bailey. I saw three under the escort of the lord

Pasteur at Work
Etching done by Mr. Louis Orr, from painting by Edelfelt

high sheriff in the picturesque regalia of his office. One day I went to see St. Bartholomew's Hospital. Doctor Brunton was not in, and the superintendent treated me rather rudely. I jumped into the waiting cab, drove to the Mansion House and expressed a desire to see "St. Barts." With a letter from the Lord Mayor I returned and handed it to the superintendent. I was most graciously shown through that ancient institution. I am sure that to-day I would be welcomed by my friend, Sir Thomas Horder, were he not attending His Majesty.

In 1891 my wife and I were guests at a garden party at the home of Sir Spencer Wells at Hempstead Heath. Some years later when I heard a German professor state in a lecture that Billroth was the first to perform an ovariotomy I protested in memory of Ephriam McDowell, Nathan Smith, the Atlees and Spencer Wells.

One Sunday afternoon, after listening to Canon Farrar at Westminster, we were wandering through the tombs of the mighty when a lady and gentleman approached, introduced themselves and insisted that we take Sunday evening tea with them. Thus I became acquainted with Mr. Ballance, an English surgeon, and was the recipient of a presentation copy of his work on the ligation of arteries. Americans sometimes speak of the lack of cordiality among the English and I admit that they are not so demonstrative as the French, or as we are, but for real friendship and genuine hospitality they are unsurpassed. I have always felt as much at home, unless it be in some trivial custom, in England as I have in Boston and I am sure that some of my best friends live in the Hub. Socially and ethnologically, we are as much a part of the British Empire as is Canada. It is true that the

good mother, quite unwisely as she now admits, about a
century and a half ago, attempted to dictate the tea drinking habits of her youngster, but like Troy, this is in the
past.

About the middle of the nineteenth century Munich
was a hotbed of typhoid fever. From 1857 to 1867 the
annual death rate from this disease in that city averaged
two hundred and three per one hundred thousand. The
city was honeycombed with privy vaults and shallow
wells. The contents of the former leaked into the latter,
from which the people drank. About the later date there
came to this city a young, intelligent epidemiologist, one
of the first of his kind, by the name of Pettenkoffer. He
induced the people to abandon their privy vaults and cess-
pools, to build a system of sewers and to bring a pure
water supply from a mountain lake. By these means the
prevalence of typhoid fever was within a few years reduced to almost zero. Pettenkoffer did other great things
beneficial not only to his fellow citizens but to the entire
world. He and a colleague, Voight, devised an apparatus
for determining the calorific value of foods and laid the
foundation for the formulation of rational diet tables.
No king ever did for Munich and Bavaria what this modest scientist did. In 1888 I spent some days with
this great man. It was at the beginning of the long
vacation. He and I sat in his room smoking Virginia
cheroots—cheap cigars containing straws to improve
the draft—while his students came in, one by one, to
thank him for his instruction and to wish him a pleasant
holiday. One was profuse in his thanks. He said: "Professor, it has seemed to me that you have taken a personal
interest in me and that you have spoken directly to me in

your lectures." Since Pettenkoffer was known as a great
teacher as well as a great investigator I was much interested in the statement of this student, and on his retirement I asked what basis of truth there was in his
assertion. "Perfectly true," said the old teacher, "I
always pick out the biggest fool in the class and talk
directly to him, feeling that if he comprehends others
will." I had a valuable lesson in methods of instruction
which I adopted with some success.

One morning in emerging from my hotel on my way
to Pettenkoffer's laboratory, I found the houses bedecked
with flags, bands playing and soldiers marching. I engaged in the following conversation with an intelligent
looking by-stander:

"What is it all about?"

"It is our king's birthday."

"I did not know that you had a king; I thought that
Bavaria is ruled by Prince Luitpold, acting as regent;
where is your king?"

"He is in an insane asylum, but this is his birthday."

I decided to ask each intelligent loiterer on my way
to direct me to the laboratory of Herr Professor von
Pettenkoffer. I asked many before I found one who had
ever heard the name. The man who had so greatly lowered the death rate was unknown while the name of the
crazy Ludwig II was on the lips of all.

In 1894 Doctor Novy and I attended the International
Congress on Hygiene at Budapest and heard Roux read
his paper on diphtheria antitoxin. This was given in an
unventilated classroom of the musty old university. There
were present many of the great men in preventive medicine from various parts of the world. At the conclusion

of the reading these men stood on their seats, shouted applause in all civilized tongues and threw their hats toward the ceiling. I have never before nor since seen such a demonstration at a scientific congress. Each delegate returned to his home with a bottle of this marvelous curative agent in his possession. Soon extensive laboratories for its production came into being on both sides of the Atlantic and in Japan and during the more than thirty years that have elapsed since that time the death rate from diphtheria has continuously declined. Similar preparations for the treatment of other diseases have been evolved and serum-therapy now has an important place among the achievements of science. Our sojourn in the double city on the Blue Danube was not given solely to attendance on the sessions of the Congress. One day we visited the beautiful and extensive estate of Count Esterhazy at Totis and lingered in his great wine caves. On another day we were entertained by the Countess Hunyadi Janos. Under the canopies erected for the comfort of visitors, wine and champagne flowed more freely than the justly celebrated laxative waters supplied by the wells near by.

The delegates to this Congress were invited to a court reception at the picturesque castle on the Buda side of the river. Our invitations told us how we were to be clothed, how we were to come and left but little chance for individual choice. We were received by an Archduke, a brother to the Emperor. In single file I found myself immediately behind the representative of Cambridge University, England, bearing on his person the highly colored academic robes. When he was presented I overheard the conversation. The Archduke spoke to him in Italian; the Cambridge man said that he did not understand

Italian. Then the host spoke in German and meeting with a similar reply he drew himself up and said in correct English most bitingly: "What, the representative of Cambridge University and speak only English!" Hearing this my heart was going pitapat, but it gave me time to think. I said to myself: "Old man, you can speak to me in any European language. I think I can recognize the language and can say 'Yes' or 'No' in it and that will be all that will be required of me." So it was a toss up whether my answer should be "Yes" or "No." He spoke to me in German, saying: "I understand you are a member of Congress." I answered in the affirmative, thinking that he referred to the Hygienic Congress, or more probably I was too confused to think at all and my lips just formed the word of their own accord. Then he asked me to explain the difference between the House of Representatives and the Senate and the functions of each. I do not know how much misinformation I gave the archduke of the Austro-Hungarian empire. I was not concerned with the truth of my statements but gave my undivided attention to the correctness of my German.

In 1882, we (my wife and I) built a modest but commodious home of stone and brick on South State Street in which we were to live until 1921 when we left Ann Arbor. The house was the first residence designed by Mr. Irving Pond, now of Pond and Pond, Chicago architects. Mr. Pond points with interest to the designs on the old mantels which foreshadowed his future works. We built for permanency, dreaming that the house might serve as a family home through generations, but we considered only the corrosion of the elements and the crumbling hand of time. We did not have in mind the

more rapidly progressive and the more irresistible en-
croachments of business. When, within a few years, we
saw this approaching menace, we bought an adjacent lot
and built a brick wall with stone pillars about the whole.
We encysted ourselves, the new accession being converted
into a small but beautiful garden under the skilful direction of our old time friend, O. C. Simonds, the landscape
artist. The garden could be entered only through the
house and became in summer the living and reception
room, thus serving the family and enlarging our facilities
for the entertainment of friends. No friend in the Faculty or among the citizens and no medical student escaped
an invitation to a garden party. Indeed the uses to which
we put the garden were many, not the least of which was
that of a shower bath room. At bedtime the boys and I
would strip and turn the hose up and down our spines. I
have broken the ice to take a plunge, dived into the cold
waters of Lake Superior, rushed from a steam bath to a
cold pool in Russia, rolled in a bank of snow and fled to
a hot tub, but I know nothing more cooling than a garden
hose played on the spine on a hot night. Satisfaction
comes quickly and completely.

In this house and garden we entertained our friends
from near and from afar, while our boys profited by the
imparted wisdom, wit and good cheer. Indeed, had some
of our guests realized how critical five pairs of young ears
may be, they would have been more cautious in some of
their statements. Such entertainments were often followed by consultations of Webster, Worcester and other
dictionaries for correct pronunciation and of the *Encyclo-
pedia Britannica* and other reference books for facts.
With the purpose of broadening their intellectual horizons

Glimpses of the Ann Arbor Home from the Garden

and at the same time making them content to eat what they found before them at table without asking questions, we placed each boy when he finished high school in a French boarding school in Switzerland. I am not sure about success in the first direction, but in the second the result was highly satisfactory. However, speaking more seriously, when the Great War came and the five sons were in the army and three of them in France, we recognized that their French pupilage had not been altogether in vain.

The family owes much to the men and women who honored us with their visits to the old home. Rare indeed was the one who did not leave with us some grain of good. Now we are compelled to entertain our friends at the club or in the hotel. This is not satisfactory. With friends in one's own home there is a sense of personal possession that is foreign to a club or a hotel; it seems more transient and artificial; it is only the rind of hospitality; the meat of it is wanting; it is but the shell with the kernel gone.

Some of our friends did us the honor of dropping in unannounced. We considered this as a special compliment since they showed their perfect confidence in the sincerity of our welcome. One Sunday afternoon upon returning from a drive we found Doctor Abraham Jacobi sitting in the garden. He welcomed us by saying that, tiring of the bustle of New York, he had come to spend a few days in our garden. This dear man was always a most welcome guest, full of wit, wisdom and pathos. He came to us first in 1898. The University was to give him an LL. D. I went to Cuba and my wife expressed some apprehension of her ability to entertain one about whom she had heard so much but had never seen. At the first breakfast, she reprimanded the youngest son who came to the table with but scanty attention to his dress. The kind guest said: "Do not scold the boy; he will connect me with the reprimand, and I want him to like me." This relieved her embarrassment and won the love of all the boys. He told them of his imprisonment and escape from Germany in 1848; how he hid a short pencil in his abundant hair, and how he planned revenge. This he won in a way he did not dream of in 1848, when he declined a professorship in the University of Berlin, saying that he could not accept an honor from a country which had treated him and his fellows so unjustly. On account of his small frame and large head so richly stored with knowledge our boys among themselves gave him the appellation of "Atlas," bearing the world on his shoulders. They treasured some of his sayings, such as: "I have been too busy all my life to do anything." "I know that the world is growing better because my East Side Jewish patients bear less vermin than formerly."

Baron Takaki and Doctor Suzuki, fleet surgeon in the Russo-Japanese war, once paid our hospitality a compliment. Before dinner the Baron informed me that it was absolutely essential that they should reach Chicago early next morning. Their berths were secured and I divided my time between the conversation and consulting my watch. At last I informed the Baron that his cab was waiting. "Oh well," said he, "let the train go. We can go to Chicago sometime to-morrow."

We were entertaining Mr. Fletcher, the man who taught that each mouthful of food should have a grinding for every tooth, hence the verb "to fletcherize." The boys were keen in watching and one of them managed to say to me that he could not see that Mr. Fletcher was eating differently from the rest of us. It was too good to keep and I passed it on to Mr. Fletcher. Our jolly guest said: "Boys, I am not making a demonstration to-night. I am simply enjoying myself."

My old comrade of the Typhoid Commission, Walter Reed, fresh from his brilliant research on the transmission of yellow fever, came, met our friends, lectured to the Faculties and students and received from the Regents an LL. D. Each year for many years I asked the Regents to bestow an honorary degree upon some eminent American physician or scientist. I have before me a list of these men but it is too long for insertion.

For the greater part of the more than fifty years which have passed since I voted for Horace Greeley for President of the United States, I lived in the modest home in the peaceful village of Ann Arbor. I am aware of the fact that in calling this justly famed seat of learning a village I shall bring upon myself the wrath of many of my highly esteemed and dearly beloved neighbors, but when I took up my residence in Ann Arbor in the seventies it was certainly only a village and since, unlike many American cities, it has not had a phenomenal growth, I still prefer to call it a village and I linger over this designation most lovingly. It was never a Gopher Prairie, as described by the talented author of *Main Street,* but for the most part at least it has consisted of a collection of modest homes in which has dwelled an appreciation of learning. However it is not my purpose, now at least, to do more than indicate that my neighbors have been interesting and intelligent; in other words, my environment has been good. I have been fortunate in my neighbors and friends. My own position has been that of teacher in a limited branch of chemistry and hygiene. As I have told elsewhere, for some twenty years I practised medicine among my students, colleagues and neighbors, so far as they were willing to trust their bodily ailments to my professional skill. Many years ago I discontinued my medical practise, and a colleague has on more than one occasion called my attention to the fact that the local death rate has fallen since that time. This I freely admit, but would be willing to combat any claim that there is causal relation between the two facts.

In this peaceful village, somewhat removed from the great throbbing world, I have spent a quiet life. My name has occasionally appeared in print on the program of some scientific meeting but never in the society columns or among the celebrities. Financially I have sailed only in quiet waters and should have escaped all sharks, but the reminiscences which I am about to relate will furnish other and more detailed information on this point.

It was when our respected, martyred President McKinley and his invalid wife occupied the White House that the experience now to be related occurred. The month was February, when old Boreas is likely to be most dominant in Michigan; the sun had appeared above the horizon accompanied by his dogs, seen only when the mercury falls far below zero. The day had grown colder with each hour and the north wind cut the face of the wayfarer like the lash of a heavy whip. During the forenoon I had seen a few patients in the office, lectured to my big class in hygiene, and struggled through the deep snowdrifts to visit the homes of my more seriously ill patients. During the afternoon I had worked in my laboratory among my rabbits and guinea pigs, in my attempts to solve some of the many problems concerning the nature and processes of infection. Usually I saw some of my students or patients in my library after supper, but this evening the cold was so intense, the walks so deep in snow and the wind so biting that I expected no one and anticipated keen enjoyment in the study of a ponderous tome lately arrived from Europe. To the student there is no joy quite comparable to that of feeling sure that he is to have a few hours, unbroken by the coming of even his best friend, to give to the perusal of some interesting volume. Saturated with this sense of pure contentment, thankful for the raging storm without for bringing me the highly prized opportunity, I exchanged my coat for a somewhat worn smoking jacket, my damp shoes for soft slippers and with a good cigar I drew my great chair in front of the grate of glowing cannel coal and thanked the storm gods for the howling night.

The volume eagerly expected for months and lately arrived, was the complete works of a peripatetic doctor of the early part of the sixteenth century who wrote under the euphonious name of Theophrastus Bombastus Paracelsus. In view of what happened to me that evening I may mention the fact that this author was a Swiss and that the city in which he began his work, Basel, after having pronounced him a sorcerer, a corrupter of morals and one possessed by the devil, after driving him beyond its walls in his lifetime, has recently placed on one of its public squares a handsome monument in his memory and now proudly claims to be his native city. Among the heresies of which he was accused was the teaching that at least some of the processes going on in the human body are chemical; that the efficiency of certain drugs, like opium, might be improved by the extraction and utilization of their active principles; that miners in the Tyrol were poisoned with the vapors of arsenic and antimony; that syphilis, then recently introduced into Europe, is a venereal disease and might be cured by mercury; that the children of goitrous parents are likely to be cretins (fools); that without air all living things would die from suffocation. These were some of his professional heresies, but his immoral teachings were worse. He went so far as to say, "He who is able to be his own master should not allow himself to be led blindly by another." The chapter which I had promised myself the pleasure of reading that night is entitled *De Generatione Stultorum* (The Begetting of Fools). My promised hours of pleasure were abbreviated to a few minutes. I had not read more than two or three pages when I heard the storm house door open and close. Someone in the vestibule was stamping the snow from his feet. "Alas!" I thought. "Someone is dying or a child is to be born. In either case I am called upon to officiate. The population of this village will be decreased or increased by one before morning. Nothing else could drive man, woman or child out into this storm."

Before these cogitations had been fairly registered on my brain cells the doorbell had sounded and I had admitted to my study a most interesting stranger. At my bidding he was laying aside his overcoat, which evidently was of costly fur, and removing his heavy arctics. Then he stood in the glow of the grate fire, the most prepossessing man it has ever been my lot to meet.

During these seconds I was only a self interrogation point. "Who is he?" On entering the room he had asked: "Have I the honor of meeting Professor Vaughan?" The form of the question, its intonation, the accompanying smile and the graceful inclination of the body, all were complimentary to the person addressed. I admit that the subtle flattery, expressed in manner more artistically than in words, quite captivated me, unsophisticated as I was. The question, "Who is he?" did not cease knocking at every cell in my conscious being. His English was faultless, and he had pronounced my name correctly, as no Frenchman or German could have done. No Englishman, so far as I have observed, could have been so graceful in bearing or so felicitous in speech. These hasty mental notes led me to the conclusion that my visitor was a fellow countryman of a variety with which I had but little acquaintance. We of the Middle West had heard much of the superiority of Harvard graduates, but there were several of these on my own Faculty, and once or twice I had ventured out in the world as far as Boston, where I had met members of the Harvard Faculties on their native heath, and I had concluded that there is among them no pretension to superior culture. They are, it is true, a fine type of the American, but with insufficient differentiation in speech or manner from the common stock to justify their classification as a new species or even as a new variety. That my visitor could be a medical confrère from one of our great cities—New York, Philadelphia, Chicago—I did not entertain for a moment, because these have acquired from their environment a directness in speech and manner which has been no small factor in making them quite

equal in skill and accomplishment to the medical practitioners and professors of Europe.

With my question as to his identity still unanswered,
my visitor, after warming his hands and after making a
few desultory remarks concerning the inclemency of the
night, addressed me as follows: "I have come from
Geneva, Switzerland, and I bring you an important message from the great scientist, Pictet."

With this statement he handed me an unsealed letter.
On the envelope and on the letter sheet, these words in
French were engraved: "Laboratory of Professor Raoul
Pictet, Geneva, Switzerland." The letter was in French
and I admit that I had some difficulty in reading it. Although I was fairly familiar with scientific and medical
French, I had had but little opportunity to read letters in
this language and I was unacquainted with many French
idioms. Moreover I could hardly believe that I was correctly interpreting the parts which seemed perfectly plain.
The whole scientific world knew that at that time Professor Pictet was reducing many gases to the liquid state.
Even the daily press had an occasional exaggerated
account of the scientific wonders being wrought in his
laboratory at Geneva.

The writer of the letter, as indicated by the signature
affixed, was Professor Pictet, and I was informed that
in his work he had mixed equal parts of sulphurous acid
gas and carbonic acid gas and on reducing this mixture to
liquid under pressure he had obtained, much to his surprise, a compound which had properties quite different
from those of either component. The corrosive action
of the sulphurous acid gas had wholly disappeared, while
its germicidal action was greatly intensified. In other

words, the experiment had resulted in the preparation of a marvelous compound, as bland as water but most deadly to microbic life. Under pressure it was a liquid, which passed into the gaseous state on opening the stop cock. The ideal and long-sought disinfectant had been discovered. In a hospital room or ward it would be necessary only to pipe the gas around the walls, and when disinfection was deemed necessary one or more stop cocks could be opened. The writer desired, so the letter stated, that a stock company should be formed in this country for the manufacture of this wonderful agent. The bearer of the letter to me was authorized to proceed to organize such a company, to sell stock, and I was requested in courteous terms to supply said bearer with a letter of endorsement. I fear that I finished deciphering that letter with incipient cranial enlargement. That Professor Pictet had ever heard of me and that he should have selected me among all the scientists of America to introduce his epoch-making discovery to the Western Hemisphere threatened to disturb my mental equilibrium. Fortunately my long scientific training saved me. I must have the evidence. I consented to make a test of the wonderful discovery and so informed my visitor. I had observed that he had brought with him a roll which he had carefully placed on the table. From this my friend—I had reached this degree of intimacy by this time—took a siphon bottle, such as I had first seen an English host use in the preparation of brandy and soda for his guests, and which more recently could be found on American bars. Pressing on the spring there was an outgush of gas which could be identified as sulphurous acid by the smell with no need of laboratory equipment in confirmation. On the strength of the letter and the odor of the gas my visitor insisted in a gentle but persuasive way that I should immediately write for him the endorsement requested by the Geneva scientist. He argued that promptness was desirable; that carefully graduated apparatus and skilled workmen would need to be imported from Switzerland, and that Professor Pictet was highly desirous that American production should follow as soon as possible.

At that time no shadow of a doubt in the authenticity of the letter or in the composition of the liquid crossed my mind, but I refused to give the endorsement because I had not made a complete examination. With my training I could not have done otherwise. There was no moral question involved. A chemist could do naught else. My visitor sat with me for some hours, and, when not insisting on my giving him immediate endorsement, he talked most charmingly, not about himself, but about many places in Europe, both small and large. Some of these I had visited and I knew he was correct in his statements. When the hands of the little clock on the mantel, a gift from a grateful patient, approached the hour of midnight, my visitor insisted on facing the storm and finding his way to the Cook House, then our most sumptuous hostelry, although I gladly and rather insistently offered him room, bed and breakfast in my home. Reluctantly he consented to leave the siphon and its precious contents with me, and it was arranged that he was to return a week later when I would be ready to report.

At the appointed hour he was again in my library. I told him that I had satisfied myself that the siphon contained liquid sulphurous acid, known long before the researches of Pictet; that I could find no evidence of the presence in the fluid of carbonic acid; that I had compared his preparation with liquid sulphurous acid which had stood in my laboratory for some years, both chemically and as to their germicidal properties, and that I could find nothing distinctive in his preparation. Sitting in front of the fire, he dropped his head with his chin clasped in his hands and for some minutes he was apparently absorbed in deep contemplation of the dancing flames. In his attitude and in his face, so far as I could see it, I could discover nothing but an honest attempt to solve the mystery. There was not the slightest indication of conscious guilt or intended deception. Suddenly he raised his head, turned his face all aglow with satisfaction towards me and spoke as follows: "I know just how it happened. I left Geneva in a great hurry. There was much confusion. Professor Pictet instructed his laboratory attendant to prepare my traveling bag and supply the proper siphon. The careless man picked up the wrong container. That is all there is to it. You can see that there could be no other rational explanation. The next train from Chicago to New York passes Ann Arbor at 9:30. I shall go to the hotel, pack my belongings and take that train. This is Thursday. I shall reach New York to-morrow evening, catch a boat Saturday morning and go directly to Geneva. This is too bad! Such delay! Professor Pictet will be greatly vexed! Could you not give me the endorsement?" Gently, but positively, I said that I could not. With parting words containing much subtle flattery and with a smiling but disappointed face he went out of my house for the second time without the coveted endorsement.

I had a suspicion that the gentleman from Switzerland would not visit me again; therefore, I was surprised when on a beautiful spring day, when the maples that line the streets of our village, making its name so appropriate, were displaying to great advantage their half-grown leaves, he entered my library. He came in with joy on his face and with words something like the following on his lips: "It was as I suspected; I left here on Thursday night, February 27; in New York I caught the *Burgoyne* on Saturday morning; reached Havre in ten days; traveled to Paris the same day and took the 6:10 Lyons express for Geneva that evening. Professor Pictet has sent you another letter. He approves of your caution and hopes that there will be no further delay. I brought the right siphon this time; it is in my trunk in New York and I will have it forwarded, if you insist, but I am sure that after reading the letter you will no longer hesitate to give the endorsement."

I am somewhat reluctant to admit that at this juncture I lost my temper and spoke harsh words. I fear that I hurled upon my visitor insulting epithets. I told him that on a certain night, which, according to his story, he had spent in mid ocean, I had ridden on the same sleeping car with him from Grand Rapids to Detroit. I declined even to accept the letter. In short, I did what I should not have done. I became violent and abusive. On the contrary he showed no anger. He was simply hurt; there had been a grievous mistake. If I would only read the letter, all would be explained. I could not question the written statements of so eminent a man as Professor Pictet. The demon of anger dominated me and I rudely and harshly requested him to leave, and the gentleman from Switzerland passed out of my house for the third time and out of my life forever.

For years I looked for him on trains and in hotels. I did not forget him on my subsequent visits to Europe and other foreign lands. I wanted to apologize for my rudeness. I made inquiries for him, and I was told that he finally found permanent residence in a certain well-known national asylum for the insane. Never since have I written a letter of recommendation or given approval of any scientific procedure without recalling my experience with the gentleman from Switzerland, and this has in more than one instance been the source of much humor.

I must add a few words concerning the gentleman from Switzerland. He was an American of Irish descent, the most affable and persuasive variety of the genus homo. He had been educated partly in France, which no doubt contributed greatly to his skill in speech and grace in manner. He had probably stolen the engraved envelope and sheets of paper from the laboratory of Professor Pictet. He lied with great plausibility and occasionally gave attention to details. At the time of his visits to me one of my sons was in a French boarding school at Château de Lancy near Geneva. I probably informed my visitor of this fact, and this accounts for his taking the 6:10 Lyons express from Paris. This was the best train between these cities. I knew the time tables of the French road quite as well as I did those of the Michigan Central.

Some years after the occurrence of the instance here mentioned I observed in one of our large cities, high up on the wall of what appeared to be an old unoccupied warehouse, the following inscription in bold, black letters:

"Pictet Germicidal Fluid." Upon inquiry I was told that the gentleman from Switzerland had visited a chemist in that city and as a result of this visit had organized a stock company for the manufacture of the germicide, but that the existence of this corporation was cut short by legal procedures instituted in behalf of the interests of Professor Raoul Pictet of Geneva, Switzerland.

In the nineties there were in the village of Milan, about fifteen miles from Ann Arbor, four struggling churches of as many denominations, each with its pastor. It is needless to say that all these churches were cheap in construction, inadequately maintained, attracting but few to their services and paying the pastors niggardly salaries. The life of the pastor under these conditions could not be said to be highly stimulating in any material way. Three of these village parsons apparently felt the great responsibility placed upon them by the Lord, seemed content with the lot assigned them, and with the care of the souls of the flocks under their guidance. The fourth parson became restless, dissatisfied, and felt that he deserved a better assignment than the Lord had given him. He wanted to get out into the big world, meet more sinners, have a broader field for operation and possibly it occurred to him that he might be able to hold his own even in a game with sinners. He resigned his pastorate, went to New York City, to which he had frequently referred in his sermons as a modern Babylon, the home of all kinds of iniquities. Having reached the city and secured a room in one of its great hotels he visited the more important and well-known sugar importers. He bought small quantities of their best grades of sugar, took these to his room, prepared small white paper boxes lined with blue, giving especial atten-

tion to the lining of the top of the box which was hinged
and so arranged by being attached to the bottom with a
blue ribbon on each side that the top could not be taken
off, and could not be raised beyond a certain desirable
angle, which he determined experimentally with the greatest exactitude. The sugar in one of these little boxes with
the blue lined cover raised to exactly the right position and
with proper exposure to the light acquired a degree of
whiteness unrecognizable in the same sugar not provided
with the reflected light from a blue surface. With these
samples he went back to the sugar importer, demonstrated
to him the superior appearance of the sugar in the little
box contrasted with the best the importer could show in
his stock. The parson said that he had produced this
superior grade of sugar by the discovery of an electric
process of manufacture. He stated that by the application
of his discovery crude brown sugar was converted into
the product which he displayed in the blue lined boxes.
The importer, admitting that he had never seen such
sugar, became deeply interested. Within a few weeks a
stock company for the manufacture of a high grade sugar
by electricity was formed and the parson appointed as its
general manager. He had no difficulty in selling stock in
New York, but even this city became too small for the
village parson. He sailed across the ocean and found the
sugar importers of Liverpool quite as eager to invest in
the electric process as were their brothers in New York.
A large warehouse in Brooklyn was secured as a suitable
factory. The parson insisted, and if I remember correctly, provided in the contract that the secret of manufacture should remain his and that not even a stockholder
could, without his permission, enter the factory and

acquaint himself with the machinery and its operation.
Great hogsheads supposed to contain crude brown sugar
were carted into the factory and lifted into an upper floor.
From time to time the general manager invited the stockholders to a demonstration. Under his guidance they
were shown through the plant, but shown only those
things which he wished them to see and the use of which
he explained. After a hurried tramp through the machinery room on the upper floor where they saw and examined
the crude brown sugar, they were assembled below, the
machinery was put in operation and soon small quantities
of a high grade product trickled from a tiny spout into
blue lined boxes. Each stockholder left the plant with a
sample in his pocket and with visions of big dividends
which would soon fill his coffers. This condition continued for nearly two years. During this time the parson
had not wholly neglected his Michigan home. He still
claimed residence, bought a desirable site in the outskirts
of the village, erected a handsome house and drove about
the country in a smart carriage drawn by a pair of handsome dappled grays. The stockholders became more and
more impatient. More frequent demonstrations were
demanded and less satisfaction found in the samples supplied them. Finally some of the stockholders actually
grew unreasonable in their demands. Suit against the
general manager of the company was begun. Finally the
court ordered the general manager to throw open the
manufacturing plant to the inspection of stockholders.
When this was done its emptiness was revealed. All the
brown sugar was found in the loft with a few boxes of
Havemeyer's best. Then the parson was prosecuted for
fraud and for getting money under false pretenses. My

part in this prosecution was small but essential. I analyzed the sugar in the blue lined boxes and compared its chemical composition and its physical properties with those of the best market sugar and there was no difference. After a bold but futile attempt to escape, the village parson, who had valiantly gone out into the wicked world thinking that he migh successfully play a game with sinners, was convicted and sentenced to a residence for a number of years in the imposing state hotel known as the Sing Sing Prison. His name, prominent for a short while among New York financiers and for a shorter time still more prominent in the proceedings of the criminal court, has not since, so far as I know, occupied a prominent place in the columns of the metropolitan dailies.

For three successive years in the late eighties and early nineties I gave a short course of special lectures in the University of Toronto. These lectures were, so far as I can judge after more than thirty years, of no special credit to the lecturer or benefit to the hearer. The invitation to give them supplied the opportunity for me to make the acquaintance of members of the Faculty and physicians in the city. I formed ties of strong friendship, many of which have been broken by death while others continue. Since that time I have gone to Toronto on at least two occasions; once to give the opening address for the medical school, and once to talk to the medical society. The latter event occurred in the late winter of 1917, and that visit was a sad one for me. Nearly every friend made in the late eighties and early nineties had gone overseas to engage in war activities, had lost his own life, or had suffered the loss of a brother or son. At the little dinner given me on the occasion of the 1917 visit, while I admired the courage of my friends about the table, I recognized that each carried a heavy burden of sorrow. The thing, however, which disturbed me most deeply was the attitude of my own country towards the World War. I felt sympathy for my friends who were still "carrying on," but for myself and for my country I felt the deepest shame. In the following April our President relieved the nation of the sense of shame under which it was shuddering and called the people to arms. Anticipating this event, I was in Washington when the call came and enlisted as soon as possible. I had been in uniform but a few days when General Gorgas informed me that he wished to send a medical commission from our army to Canada in order that we might advise with Canadian medical officers, come to some arrangement concerning harmony and uniformity of action, visit the army camps and hospitals, and learn whatever we could that might aid us in our mobilization which was soon to follow. I asked that I might be made a member of the proposed commission. I desired to go to Canada in uniform. I thought that it was doing something to remove the stain which I had felt to be deeply implanted on my person and on my country. Within a few hours the commission, consisting of Colonel Goodwin (later surgeon general of the British army), Major Rist of the French army, Colonel Frederick Reynolds of our army, and myself were on our way to Canada. We visited Toronto, Ottawa, Montreal, Quebec, and Camps Borden and Cartier.

I must return to the time of my early visits to the University of Toronto. At that time the president of this university was Sir Daniel Wilson, a native of Edinburgh, the historian of that ancient city, and an archeologist of

Top—Pavilion Hospital, 1875
Center—University Hospital, 1890
Bottom—Front of Hospital, 1925

wide and deserved repute. He did much for higher education in Ontario, and under his direction this university
became the educational crown of the province. Sir
Daniel was known for the accuracy of his spoken and
written word. Every morning the Faculty, including myself as a temporary member, assembled, donned our
academic regalia, and proceeded to the chapel, where Sir
Daniel read a chapter and pronounced prayer. One morning while disrobing, Sir Daniel's attention was called by
Professor Ellis, the learned professor of chemistry, to the
fact that a quotation he had made in his prayer was to be
found in the gospel according to St. Luke and not in that
according to St. John, as Sir Daniel had accredited it.
The New Testament was consulted and Sir Daniel, with
some evident confusion, acknowledged his error. We
thought nothing more of it. Imagine then our surprise
when on the following morning Sir Daniel began his
prayer: "Oh Lord, in the words of St. Luke, which in my
petition to you of yesterday morning I erroneously attributed to St. John . . ."

In 1888 yellow fever appeared at Decatur, a village of
some two thousand five hundred or three thousand souls
in northern Alabama on the Louisville and Nashville
Railroad. There were not more than twelve cases and not
more than three deaths, but at that time even a suspicion
of yellow fever was sufficient to agitate and disturb the
whole country. As soon as the disease was reported at
Decatur, Doctor Jerome Cochrane, at that time state
health officer, hastened to the stricken village. The
Mayor of Decatur issued through the Associated Press
an appeal for food and clothing. The state health officer,
through the same agency, advised that no donations be

shipped into the village. The reason for the advice of the health officer was that there was no one in Decatur suffering for food or clothing and that the shipment of these articles into the place would attract the ne'er-do-wells, tramps, and beggars from all the surrounding country. This proved to be true and before the first train of provisions and clothing had been unloaded the population of the village had doubled. Every worthless scamp, male and female, in northern Alabama and southern Tennessee, rushed to Decatur in order to participate in the distribution of the charities. The state health officer became highly unpopular among the inhabitants, both the old and new, both the permanent and transient, of the village. He cared with the best scientific information of the day for the sick and provided against the spread of infection, but when he appeared on the streets he was hissed and hooted. I believe he was burned in effigy, but no physical harm was done his person.

With the first killing frost the further spread of the disease discontinued. During the winter of 1888-89 the matter of epidemics of yellow fever in the South was discussed in Congress, and that body placed at the disposal of the President of the United States five millions of dollars for the purpose of preventing the reappearance of the disease in the South during the summer of 1889. The people of Decatur petitioned the President to burn and rebuild their village on the ground that the infection of the preceding summer was only hibernating for the time and with the oncoming of hot weather would awaken and manifest itself even more violently than in the previous season. In answer to this petition the President expressed his willingness to comply with the request to burn and rebuild the village, provided that a requisition to this effect was made by the Governor of Alabama. This placed a heavy burden upon the shoulders of the Governor who was besieged on every hand and by practically every interest in the state to make the requisition. Being in doubt as to what he should do, early in March, 1889, the Governor invited a few sanitarians to come to Montgomery, hear the evidence, and advise with him concerning the matter. I was fortunate enough to be one of those called to this conference.

The Commission met in the State House at Montgomery on a beautiful day in early March when peach trees were in blossom in Alabama. We were on historic ground; from the window of the room in which we sat Jefferson Davis had delivered his inaugural address as President of the Southern Confederacy. For nearly two days we listened to the impassioned oratory which comes most voluminously and torrentially from southern lips, in favor of the requisition. An official of the Louisville and Nashville Railroad stated that his company would not await the oncoming of hot weather for the reappearance of yellow fever at Decatur but would proceed immediately to change its line and leave the village twenty-five miles from the nearest station. Representatives of many southern cities joined in the plea that the Governor sign the requisition. The Mayor of Decatur in vivid colors pictured the distress caused by the epidemic of the preceding season. Then he turned the canvas and on the other side, in still more lurid tints, he portrayed the economic, physical and moral disaster which only awaited the revivifying influence of warm weather to burst the seeds in which it had been slumbering during the winter and send forth over the helpless people the miasmatic vapors which were to cut short many lives.

We had reached the middle of the afternoon of the second day of the hearing before the speakers in favor of the requisition had discharged their final appeal. The Governor occupied the chair and when there was nothing more to be said in favor of burning and rebuilding the village he called upon the state health officer for his opinion. Doctor Jerome Cochrane, a keen, alert, attractive man with gray hair and beard, for two hours, in a quiet conversational tone, reviewed briefly but clearly, the history of every invasion of the United States by the virus of yellow fever. It will be well to recall that at that time we had nothing more than theories concerning the cause or the transmission of this disease. Among us there sat Doctor Carlos Findlay of Havana, who had already suspected but had failed to convict the stegomyia as a distributor of the virus. For many years Findlay's search kept him close to the great discovery which he lived to see Reed and his coadjutors make. As another member of our advisory board there was George M. Sternberg, who later contributed largely to our knowledge of this disease, not only by his own work but by sending Reed and his assistants, properly equipped, to Cuba to continue the search for this virus. To these men and to other members of the committee, Doctor Cochrane addressed his words. He argued that in every invasion of the United States by yellow fever the disease was arrested by the first frosts and that in no instance had the virus hibernated in this country. He therefore felt justified in saying with certainty that yellow fever would not appear in Decatur with the advent of summer unless reimported. He concluded his remarks by turning to the Governor and saying: "Mr. Governor, you may have my resignation as state health officer this minute or whenever you wish it. But so long as I am health officer I shall not advise you to squander the money which would be unnecessarily and unwisely expended in burning and rebuilding the village of Decatur." As he said these words I saw about his head a halo.

It is needless to add that the Conference terminated in advising the Governor by unanimous vote of its members that the requisition should not be made. Decatur was not burned and there has been no case of yellow fever in the village since 1888. There was every personal inducement for Doctor Cochrane to ask the Governor to sign the requisition, but his scientific training and his expert knowledge of the epidemiology of yellow fever would not permit him to do so. This explains why in my mind's eye I saw a halo about his head, as I recognized the fact that his words were determined by his scientific convictions and not by his personal interests.

The Columbian Exposition in Chicago was planned for 1892, but there were delays in preparation and the directors found themselves with weighty problems on their hands during that summer. In some of these I had a personal interest and some minor obligation. From the earliest conception of the Exposition I had been consulted concerning the safety of the water supply furnished by the city of Chicago upon which apparently the Exposition wholly relied. At that time there were thirty public and innumerable private sewers pouring their infected contents into the lake from which the water supply of the city was taken. The London *Lancet* had caused samples of Chicago water to be sent to England where they were examined by a special commission appointed for that purpose and which reported the water badly contaminated. To-day we know that the methods of analysis employed by the *Lancet* Commission were faulty but no demonstration was necessary in order to show that Chicago's water supply at that time was unsafe. In addition to the sewers of which I have spoken, other evidence of water contamination could be found in the high morbidity and mortality at that time among the inhabitants of Chicago from typhoid fever. I may add that before the Exposition was finally opened in 1893 a pipe line from a spring near Waukesha, Wisconsin, to the Fair grounds was laid; it having been decided that it was impossible within any reasonable time to secure otherwise a pure or a safe water for drinking purposes.

In the midsummer of 1892 I had fled from my laboratory to the north woods and was anticipating much pleasure and some relaxation in chasing the festive trout. I had been but a few days at my cottage at Old Mission and was enthusiastically preparing for a fishing excursion along the Rapid River when I had urgent telegrams from a friend, then a member of Congress, asking me to meet him at a certain hour at a certain hotel in a certain city. When I arrived I found an assembly of prominent men; some were high government officials; others were rich business men; and all were in a state of excitement. In addition to the Chicago water situation, Asiatic cholera had reached New York, had been denied admission, and was confined to a few transatlantic liners held in quarantine. One of the men present about whom the excitement seemed to center was a diamond merchant. He had been to Amsterdam, as was his custom, to buy diamonds, and while in Europe he had fallen into the meshes of a French promoter. This gentleman had a recipe which was guaranteed to kill typhoid and cholera bacilli at long range and in unlimited numbers. The diamond merchant had signed a contract with the promoter in which he promised to pay one hundred twenty-five thousand dollars for the recipe. There was, however, in the contract a provision that the germicide was to make good the claims for it, and I was called to make the test.

The proposition was that I was to improvise in the city where we were a small laboratory, that I should test the preparation, with a newspaper reporter nearby ready to send to an expectant world full confirmation of the discovery which was to free the Chicago water supply from its typhoid bacilli and to destroy valiantly any dangerous microbes that might be imported from India or elsewhere. I said that I could not make my tests under such conditions; that it would be necessary for me to take the fluid which the French promoter had prepared to my laboratory in Ann Arbor, mobilize my helpers, and that within two weeks I hoped to be able to make a report. I especially stipulated that during the two weeks I was not to be disturbed by any visitor or by any message. So far as visitors were concerned the arrangement was not violated, but I am compelled to say that telephone and telegraphic messages poured into my laboratory during the two weeks in great numbers. With the help of Doctors Novy, McClintock and others, I was able to complete the task within the time specified. The men with the French promoter arrived in a special car. Their intention was to form a stock company, manufacture the

germicide, have it officially recognized and employed by
national, state and municipal authorities. When the
crowd came into my laboratory I had on tables in a
large room four hundred demonstrations. These consisted of as many test tubes containing beef tea or other
nutrient fluid to which the specific agent had been added
in varying dilutions. Some tubes contained one part per
thousand, others one part per hundred. Some contained
similar preparations of well-known disinfectants, such
as mercuric chlorid and carbolic acid. I explained how
the results of the experiment could be interpreted. If
there had been no bacterial growth or if the germicide
added had a decidedly positive action, the contents of the
tube would be found clear. The extent to which bacteria
had grown in spite of the addition of the various agents
could be estimated by the comparative cloudiness of
the contents of the tubes. The Raymond fluid, under
which name the French promoter introduced his preparation, had some germicidal action, but this was not comparable with that exhibited by our ordinary disinfectants.

While others, most of whose faces showed keen dis-
appointment, were inspecting the tubes, the Frenchman
asked to have a few words with me in private. I took
him to my study; here he became highly voluble. He
spoke not only in words, but in gesticulations and muscular movements. He demanded to know how my
demonstration could be true. Did I know that one of
the ingredients of his fluid was mercuric chlorid? How
then could it be less effective as a germicide than mercuric
chlorid by itself? The truth is that Professor Raymond
had overdone his attempt to make a perfect germicide.
He had taken every chemical compound known to have

any germicidal action and had mixed all these in his fluid. One had neutralized the other and the most powerful germicidal constituents had been rendered insoluble and were found in the deposit and not in the fluid.

The great corporation was not formed. Professor Raymond with his secretary and valet had a trip to the United States, lived at the expense of his would-be dupes and also at their expense returned to his native country, where it is to be hoped he acquired some knowledge of chemistry before he again attempted to prepare a universal germicide.

CHAPTER VI

THE UNIVERSITY OF MICHIGAN MEDICAL SCHOOL

THAT the original Board of Regents which was appointed by Governor Mason and began to function in 1837 had a distinct appreciation of science is shown by their first appointment to a professorship in this University. The man selected was Doctor Asa Gray, a graduate of the medical school founded by the Board of Regents in the state of New York and located in the village of Fairfield, Herkimer County, in 1812. Doctor Gray was appointed professor of botany and zoology in 1838, and was commissioned by the Regents to go to Europe and collect scientific books and a herbarium. In 1842 he resigned this position without ever giving instruction in this University and became professor of botany in Harvard and won for himself the distinction of being the supreme authority on this subject in this country, a position which he maintained throughout his life. When he resigned from this University in 1842 Doctor Abram Sager was selected to fill his place. Before this Doctor Sager had served as chief of the botanical and zoological department of the Michigan State Geological Survey.

The second appointment to a professorship in this University showed the same appreciation of scientific

184

work indicated by the first. Doctor Douglas Houghton, at that time head of the Michigan State Geological Survey, was in 1839 made professor of chemistry, mineralogy and geology. Like Gray, Houghton never gave instruction in the University but made collections for the Museum. He was drowned in Lake Superior while exploring the copper region, October 13, 1845. A broken shaft still stands on the campus in commemoration of the life and work of this brilliant young scientist. In 1844 Silas H. Douglas, who was to build up the chemical laboratory, was made Houghton's assistant and subsequently became his successor.

To what influences may we attribute this marked tendency towards science on the part of the Regents who launched Michigan University at a time when classical and humanistic studies still dominated New England universities? To me the source of this influence is plainly visible, though, as far as I know, no university historian has perceived it.

There were two real scientists on that Board, and while the majority of them may have been, as one historian says, without special fitness for the work before them, these two evidently knew what they were doing. These men were Henry R. Schoolcraft, the great explorer and naturalist as well as the best versed student of Indian lore in the region of the Great Lakes, and his companion and fellow student, Doctor Zina Pitcher. Furthermore behind the Regents were the Governor and the Superintendent of Public Instruction, since all important acts of the Board required the approval of these officials before becoming effective. Indeed the Regents were named by the Governor and he was the President of the Board.

Stevens T. Mason was Governor of the territory and state of Michigan practically all the time from 1831 to 1840, and had much to do with the foundation and inauguration of the University. The Superintendent of Public Instruction, the Reverend John D. Pierce, a graduate of Brown University, was an appointee of Governor Mason and the two seem to have been in agreement on educational matters, in which both were deeply interested. Mason was a Virginian and it is not probable that he was unacquainted with the scientific activities and ideals of Thomas Jefferson. Hinsdale and Demmon in their history of the University say: "Ex-President Jefferson had founded the University of Virginia on new lines in 1825, but that excellent institution was at the time practically unknown in the West."

It is undoubtedly true that to the mass of the people in the Northwest at that time the work of Thomas Jefferson in founding the University of Virginia was unknown; but that Schoolcraft, Pitcher and above all Governor Mason, himself a Virginian, were ignorant of it is highly improbable. The details followed in the development of the two universities are too similar to have been accidental. Both provided preparatory schools and both stressed scientific training. The claim that the ideals of a state university as developed in Michigan in 1837 came from a study of the Prussian system of education seems to me to have been unduly stressed. Indeed when Thomas Jefferson committed to writing his plan for the organization of the University of Virginia in 1812 Prussia had no system of education. The first professor of modern language in Michigan University (1846) was Louis Fasquelle; and French, Italian and Spanish were taught in this University before any provision was made for the teaching of German.

Still another evidence of the scientific spirit of the original Board of Regents lies in the fact that one of their first appropriations was the sum of ten thousand dollars for the purchase of scientific apparatus and books. This is exactly what one would expect of such men as Mason, Schoolcraft and Pitcher.

It will be seen from what I have said that during the forties two of the strongest men on the University Faculty had been trained scientifically and had medical degrees. These were Abram Sager and Silas H. Douglas, and they constituted the leaven in the Faculty which led to the development of the Medical School. The departments of literature, science and the arts had been organized in 1837 and the charter indicated that the law department should be the first professional school provided for, but this did not happen. The Law School was not organized until 1859 and I at least can see plainly the reason why the Medical School took precedence. One cold, snowy February day in the late forties there arrived in Ann Arbor a young man who was to become a tower of strength to Sager and Douglas in their efforts to provide for a medical school. This newcomer in my opinion, was inferior to both Sager and Douglas, certainly to the former, in both native and acquired ability in scientific work. But he had a strong personality and a genius for organization and constructive work. While a student in a medical school at Geneva, New York, he read about the organization of the University of Michigan and the provision that a medical department would, sooner or later, be attached to this institution. Immediately on receiving his medical diploma he started for Ann Arbor, carrying in his grip several dissecting cases and, among his grosser impedimenta, a box of suspicious shape and size and unmarked content.

On arriving in Ann Arbor he hung out a shingle offering his surgical skill to the public and more discreetly he let it be known to the University students that, in his back office after a certain hour, he was prepared to initiate any of them, who might have the profession of medicine in view, into the mysteries of the structure of the human body. He was soon recognized as a most desirable addition to the small group of intellectuals then constituting the faculty and student body of the University. There is no record of his surgical success as a private practitioner but his class in anatomy was soon in a flourishing condition. His best students in his back office were Robert Kedzie, who later became the distinguished professor of chemistry in the Michigan Agricultural College, and Edmund Andrews, who, in later life, became the leading surgeon of Chicago, one of the founders of the first graded medical school in this country, the Chicago Medical College (now the Medical School of Northwestern University), and recognized as an authority both here and abroad on the geology of the Great Lakes. This newly arrived ally to Sager and Douglas in their attempts to hasten the organization of the Medical School was Moses Gunn.

Personally I did not know Moses Gunn until some thirty years after his coming to Ann Arbor. However it was his custom in his later years to come to Ann Arbor on the anniversary of his first coming in the forties. On these occasions I, as his host, listened attentively to the stories of his early manhood. He told me that when he read about the prospective medical school in connection with the University of Michigan he and Corydon L. Ford were roommates at the medical school in Geneva; that they talked over the possibilities that might lie in the West; that he said to Ford that he would come to Ann Arbor, aid in founding the school and that he would become professor of surgery and Ford should be professor of anatomy. As I knew him Moses Gunn was a most striking figure, one which would attract attention on the street, in an assembly or at a social function. He was more than six feet tall, spare and muscular, with deep blue eyes, snowy hair and beard which he wore à la Burnside. He wore a Prince Albert coat, a high hat, generally a white vest, and striped trousers. Pending from his neck was a long, slender, gold watch chain. His hair hung about his neck in curls. In fact, as I once sat in an assembly hall beside one of the most eminent medical men of the time, Moses Gunn appeared on the stage. My companion asked, as he leaned toward me, "What old mountebank is that?" That his peculiarity in person and dress was not a foible of his old age is shown by a description of him by the late Doctor Norman Bridge of Los Angeles, California, who entered the Medical School in 1866. "Doctor Gunn, the professor of surgery, was an inspiring man; tall, erect with a reddish beard which he wore à la Burnside and which was being tinged with gray. His graying hair was very long, and hung in large depending ringlets, each of which every morning was wound about the moist finger of his adoring wife. This gave him a fantastic appearance and a reputation for foppishness that he hardly deserved. He was a rapid and elegant operator and had made some striking additions to his art."

Urged, no doubt, by Sager and Douglas, with Gunn's outside help, the Board of Regents, in 1847, appointed a Committee with Doctor Pitcher as Chairman whose duty it became to consider the expediency of organizing a medical department and to ascertain the expense that would be incurred should such a step be taken. In January, 1848, this Committee made a favorable report which was supplemented by a more detailed communication to the Board of Regents in January, 1849. The last mentioned report went into detail concerning needed buildings, equipment, the selection of a Faculty, entrance requirements for students, length and character of course, and other matters. Doctors Sager and Douglas were transferred to the embryo Medical School, and Sager made Dean, or, as the title was, President, and continued in this office for twenty-five years, or until he resigned in 1875. In July, 1849, Moses Gunn was made professor of anatomy and surgery, and in January, 1850, J. Adams Allen was appointed professor of physiology and pathology and Samuel Denton, professor of the theory and practice of medicine. On the first Wednesday in October, 1850, the first session was opened by addresses by Doctor Sager and Regent Pitcher. Thus the School was begun with nothing to occupy the time and energy of the students save lectures, quizzes and a short course in anatomy. In fact this schedule constituted the curricula of all medical schools in this country at that time. Fortunately there were two men on the original Faculty whose foresight and wisdom did not permit the School to remain long in this primitive condition. These were Doctors Douglas and Gunn. The former began laboratory instruction on his appointment in 1844 and soon secured from the Regents a fund sufficient to erect a small, one-story laboratory and in this the students were soon busy in a field hitherto unknown and unvisited by medical students in this country at least. This small laboratory, well equipped for the times, grew year by year until it soon became the largest and best equipped chemical laboratory open to students in this country.

The University of Michigan Medical School was from its start a scientific, in contradistinction to a practical or clinical, institution. This was not altogether due to preference on the part of its founders and professors, but was a necessity. For twenty-five years it had no hospital—not a building which by any stretch of courtesy could be so denominated. The task of developing clinical facilities fell upon Doctor Gunn and was heavier than that resting upon the shoulders of Doctor Douglas. Indeed for many years the criticism of the School of most weight was that it had no hospital connection. This deficiency was urged against the School even by some of its best graduates, who, while students, had felt it and had established themselves in large cities after graduation. As late as the eighties one of these urged me to leave Ann Arbor, arguing that the School must fail on account of its lack of clinical opportunities, and I did not deny the weight of his argument, but I saw the matter from another angle—the deficiencies in the city schools at that time in scientific training.

Another argument against the School was that it

is supported by the state. It was held that it is not
a state function to provide a professional education. In
the eighties I spent many an hour discussing this point
with some of my most esteemed friends who were serving
on the faculties of city schools. My reply to this criticism ran along the line that formerly universities had
been founded and supported in the interest of some
theological dogma. More recently and often in connection with this purpose wealthy men have built and endowed universities in order to perpetuate their names.
I acknowledged that both of these motives have been
honorable, but I held that the state university owes its
origin and secures its maintenance because the people
believe that higher education improves its citizenship
and therefore should be available to all at a small cost.
The state needs wise lawyers to enact and enforce its
laws, intelligent physicians to prevent and cure disease,
skilful engineers to build roads and bridges and otherwise to develop transportation, and intelligent agricul-
turalists to improve the fertility of its soil; therefore it
offers professional training. Now state education along
professional lines is not questioned by anyone; forty
years ago it was most earnestly and honestly contested
by many wise men. Then the state university medical
school was founded upon simple resources and inadequately supported. In fact, for many years Michigan
University Medical School was the only successfully
managed institution of its kind supported by the state.
The University of Pennsylvania was a state institution
in name only and for many years received no grants
from the state. Now state university medical schools
are many, and some of them at least compare favorably

with the best in the country, and indeed all of the best
medical schools now have some connection with either
state or endowed universities. In short, medical education is unanimously admitted to be a university function
and an important one. Every medical school is seeking
or has found university connection and every great
university is seeking or has found a medical department.
Forty years ago all my best and most esteemed friends
and colleagues in medical education, outside of my own
Faculty, were teaching in proprietary schools, a few at
their financial advantage, most of them at financial sacri-
fice. The proprietary medical school was a step in the
evolution of medical education; it was a vast improvement on the old apprentice system. It had the services
of the best in the profession; it made many contributions to science; and it supplied the people with thousands
of capable physicians, but, like Troy, it belongs to the
past.

When the Medical School opened in 1850 Gunn, with
Kedzie, Andrews and other back office students, took
charge of anatomy and taught it thoroughly. In 1854
Gunn was able to keep his promise to Ford and the
latter was called to the chair of anatomy, which he
held for forty years. After giving his last lecture in
1894, Ford fell from an apoplectic stroke on his way
home and died a few hours later.

During the last century there were many great
teachers of descriptive anatomy and among these Ford's
name did not stand at the bottom of the list. He never
practised medicine and was a full time teacher throughout his life. His services as a teacher were in great
demand, and until within a few years of his death he

gave two courses annually, one at Michigan and one in some other school. He knew anatomy, both human and comparative. He lived it and he taught it in a way that held the individual attention of every student. He not only taught the subject but he awakened a love for it in his hearers. Among his old students I may mention such names as Lewis Pilcher, Frank Mall, William J. Mayo and Carl Huber. I sat under his spell and felt its fascination to such an extent that my thesis for Ph. D. was on an anatomical subject. He lectured every day, beginning with the bones and then covering every tissue in the body. In demonstrating a foramen or a duct a favorite expression was: "Finger on it; probe in it." Professors and students from other departments crowded the upper seats in his lecture room, and how many young men he attracted to medicine I can not say. Even the janitor in the dissecting room, old Nagele, became a most proficient demonstrator and a reliable help, as hundreds of doctors now grown gray can testify.

As I have already indicated, laboratory instruction in chemistry developed by leaps and bounds. Frequent additions were made to the first small building. It grew in every direction, both in height and depth, since the basement was supplied with tables. Each table was furnished with reagents. In fact, I have visited many chemical laboratories in various countries and I can say that I have never seen one which did not bear a close similitude to that in which I began my work in 1874, but long before my time medical students at Michigan pursued much the same courses as I did. Nor was laboratory chemical teaching confined to medical students. Students in the collegiate department anticipating medicine or any other calling in which this science might be useful availed themselves of the opportunities. Above all chemistry was taught as a science and not as applicable to some practical problem. Prospective medical students soon became aware of the fact that it was well to do their laboratory work before entering a medical school, either at Michigan or elsewhere. It should be plainly understood that Michigan University owes its past and present eminence in chemistry to the initiative of the Medical School. Chemical teaching grew out of no want felt for it in the collegiate department. It was thrust upon the university by the initiative and insistence of the Medical School; nor is this the sole instance in which the University has been benefited by the Medical School.

I am sure that the reader will want to know how the Michigan University Medical School managed to thrive for twenty-five years without a hospital. Samuel Denton (professor of medicine, 1850-1860) was a member of the first Board of Regents and, with Mason, Schoolcraft and Pitcher, possibly had something to do with the inauguration of the Medical School, but so far as I can learn he contributed but little to its reputation. During his professorship little was done in building up a clinic in internal medicine. The intellect and energy expended in the development of clinical facilities and teaching were largely supplied by Moses Gunn. He announced to the physicians of the state that the forenoons of Wednesday and Saturday would be devoted to consultations with them over their difficult cases. Emergency cases would be seen at any time. There would be no charge to either the doctors or their patients so far as these consultations were conducted in the presence of the students. In this wise and mutually helpful way began that flow of the stream of the sick and injured citizens of Michigan to Ann Arbor. Small at first, this stream has grown until now (1926) it fills to over-flowing the splendid University Hospital of many hundreds of beds. Indeed it has been found necessary at times to check and regulate the incoming material. Herein lies a difficulty which has given and will continue to give to an increasing degree the Medical School cause for wise counsel. The clinical teachers in the School should never lose sight of the fact that the facilities they now enjoy had their origin and their continued growth in the mutually helpful cooperation between the physicians of the state and the medical Faculty. There can be no departure from this contract without injury to both parties. This unwritten agreement, originated in the brain of Moses Gunn, was accepted and endorsed by the physicians of the fifties and on the whole has operated to the satisfaction and benefit of the successors of both parties.

At first the number of patients brought to the consultations on Wednesday and Saturday mornings was small, but they were wisely and profitably used. I employ the words "wisely and profitably" intentionally and specifically. The patients were often benefited and in all instances received the best medical opinion without cost. The physicians had their diagnoses and treatment confirmed or modified by the best available experts. The students profited by the instruction received. As I have said, there was absolutely no hospital; for many years

University of Michigan Medical Building in the 'Seventies
The Medical Building in 1903
New University of Michigan Medical School, 1926

not even a receiving house. The doctors of the immediate vicinity did not bring their patients until the early morning of a clinic day. Those from greater distances lodged their patients in the hotel or in some boarding house. Invariably the physician accompanied his patient, or at least the exceptions to this rule were few. In some instances, probably in most, the professor had seen and examined the patient before he was brought before the class. Not infrequently the professor devoted his hour, sometimes more than one, to "some of the cases we are to see Wednesday or Saturday." As a student I saw more than one surgical operation performed on a cadaver, or illustrated on a manikin, or figured in detail on charts, the day before I saw the operation on the patient. More frequently I saw these demonstrations the day after the operation. These procedures were highly helpful to the student. As a laboratory assistant in charge of physiological chemistry I frequently examined the urine, the blood and later the stomach contents, both before and after the patient's presentation to the class. I remember with what pride I demonstrated leucemic blood and urine to the class; how I exhibited crystals of tyrosin and leucin in the urine in a case of cancer of the liver, a rare opportunity indeed; how I showed the presence of urea in the perspiration of a man dying of kidney disease.

When I went to Ann Arbor in the seventies one of the professors' houses on the north side of the campus was known as "University Hospital." It was, however, nothing more than a receiving home, in which patients brought in for the clinics could be kept before and after presentation to the class. There were no wards and no operating or dressing rooms, no place where students might receive bedside instruction. On Wednesday and Saturday mornings students carried patients on stretchers across the campus to the medical building, where the procedures I have already described were carried out.

It must not be inferred that during the twenty-five years (1850-1875) the School was without a hospital the clinical growth was exclusively along surgical lines. The year 1854 marked an epoch in the School's development, for in that year there came to it two great teachers. Of one and his work I have already written. This one was Corydon L. Ford, the great teacher of anatomy. The other was Alonzo B. Palmer, a great teacher of internal medicine. Palmer was a graduate in the class of 1839 of that large school known as the College of Physicians and Surgeons of Western New York, to which I have already referred. After some years as a village doctor, Palmer went to Chicago, became a partner of that Nestor of American medicine, N. S. Davis, and soon acquired a large, varied and remunerative practise. From Chicago he came to Ann Arbor in 1854 under the inclusive title of "professor of materia medica, therapeutics and diseases of women and children." How all-embracing and far-extending this title seems to-day, but if any man was in 1854 competent to give instruction in all these branches it was A. B. Palmer. His knowledge of medicine for that time was encyclopedic, as his diary, published by his wife after his death, will convince anyone who reads it. Nor was his learning confined to medicine. He knew English literature, was devoted to Shakespeare and graced the most intellectual society in both this country and in England. However, even surpassing his wisdom was his readiness to impart it. He delighted in talking to students, and no colleague had any difficulty in inducing him to fill an hour. I have known him to fill two consecutive hours, and still be ready for the third. He did no general practise, and would readily forego a consultation and the fee that might be attached to it if he could lecture. I must say that he continued to the end a diligent student, reading current literature and keeping posted, if not always fully appreciative of the latest advances in medicine. From the beginning of his work as a teacher he was as scientific as one could be at that time in methods of diagnosis. He drilled his students *ad nauseam* in the employment of instruments of precision; auscultation and percussion were not only his favorite hobbies, but in their use he showed great skill. I remember how proudly he exhibited to me the first laryngoscope I ever saw.

He spent the greater part of two years in Europe in the preparation of his *opus magnum,* a two volume work on the practise of medicine. I say "the greater part of two years" because he had to return occasionally to give a few lectures. He did not hesitate to make two extra trips across the Atlantic when he felt that he had some information which must be imparted to his students. His great work was published shortly before his death. Had it been presented fifteen years earlier it would have had a wide circulation, but it came just when the *new* medicine was supplanting the *old* and is now unknown and unused. He died in the harness in 1887 and now (1926) the ranks of his students are growing thin. Some have been strong enough to follow the new and keep pace with the present generation; some

are still following him. Only a few weeks ago I was
in the office of a village doctor while his patients came
and went and in the intervals between them he talked
of his great teacher, Alonzo B. Palmer, and showed me
the prescriptions he was then giving which he had taken
from his old teacher's lecture notes. I saw no evidence
that harm was being done his clientele and made no
unfavorable comment. The best that a teacher can do
is to impart to his students the latest and most authentic
knowledge of his time. He that is too far in advance is
stoned and he who is behind deserves no justification.
The most frequent complaint I had from my students
came in something like this form: "Why, doctor!
What you tell us to-day is not what you told us last
year." When this criticism ceases to bear the germ of
truth, the teacher should seek some other occupation.
The reader will see therein justification of my own
retirement.

After sixteen years of herculean endeavor to build
up a surgical clinic in Ann Arbor, Moses Gunn gave up
the effort in despair and became professor of surgery in
Rush Medical College in Chicago. The chair of surgery was immediately filled by that brilliant but erratic
man, William Warren Greene, who occupied it for only
one year. Greene was one of the first, if not the first,
in this country to operate successfully for goiter. This
operation was done as all operations were then done, in
the upper lecture room of the old medical building.
There is a story to the effect that when Greene reported
this case at some medical society, the elder Gross of
Philadelphia, then acknowledged as one of the greatest
surgeons in the world, arose and said: "You may call

that surgery; I call it butchery." Now even village doctors do this operation. That Greene did successfully perform this operation in the sixties is quite certain, but I will not vouch for the story, though I have no doubt that it expressed the attitude of the leading surgeons of the time.

Another man who contributed greatly to the building up of the surgical clinic was the first professor of ophthalmology, George E. Frothingham. He was a graduate of the School and worked his way up from demonstrator of anatomy. He was my preceptor and I can not speak of him without love and reverence. In my early days at Michigan he held out his helping hand and I took it and followed in a perfect confidence which I never found misplaced. It is true that later he and I differed radically about the removal of the Medical School to Detroit, but the relation of father and son between us was never broken. He began his lectures each year with a statement something like the following: "Gentlemen, I will be able to show you in the clinic throughout the year most of the diseases to which the eye is subject and many of the accidents and injuries to which it is exposed. Yes, I will show you many of these many times. I will operate before you twice a week, but you must know that you will profit none by my operations unless you know the anatomy and physiology of the organ thoroughly. I can demonstrate the fundamental principles. The world will be your clinic." He started many a great ophthalmologist on the right road. Among these I may mention such names as John E. Weeks of New York and Harold Gifford of Omaha. Frothingham's recorded contributions to his

specialty were not numerous, but all were sound. The
most effective argument I ever employed in asking the
legislature for hospital appropriations was the showing
of the number of cataracts successfully removed and the
number of partially or totally blind restored to sight.
These figures appealed to all, and besides I had the number of cases from each county.

In 1872 Donald Maclean, then teaching at a medical
school at Kingston, Ontario, a pupil of Syme, the great
surgeon of Edinburgh whom he revered, a Scotchman,
a graduate of Edinburgh, was called to the professorship of surgery in Michigan University. Like Gunn,
Maclean was a most fascinating man. I do not think
that any teacher in the University, within my time at
least, was so greatly admired by the students as he.
He captivated the hearts and won the admiration of all.
He was the beau ideal of the young men on the benches.
Handsome, bold and dexterous, he conducted his clinic
in a dramatic way. In speech he was somewhat hesi-
tating but this was not a defect. In him it was an
asset, emphasizing essentials and blocking superficialities.
He occupied the chair of surgery for eighteen years and
did much to build up the surgical clinic. Among the
profession in the state there were many who were devoted
to him, and would have the advice of no other when
they had difficult cases to deal with. He made many
great surgeons, some of whom have surpassed their
master. After all, is not this the highest criterion of a
great teacher? Like Gunn, Maclean left the University
on account of the paucity of clinical material. He urged
the removal of the Medical School to Detroit with such
earnestness that he was forced to resign.

In 1877 the wooden pavilion hospital, accommodating about 150 patients, with operating amphitheater, dressing rooms, and so forth, was opened. It may be of historic interest to state that this building was planned under the supervision of Edward S. Dunster, professor of obstetrics and gynecology. It was of the type employed in the latter part of the Civil War. Dunster had been an army surgeon and for a time after the war he was post surgeon at West Point; then he resigned, and taking up his specialty, became a pupil of Sims, Peaslee and Thomas. When built it was understood that this hospital would become so badly infected within ten years that it would be necessary to burn it. It served as a hospital until 1890 and for at least twenty years more as a class and laboratory room. It occupied the space now covered by the chemical laboratory.

James N. Martin, Dunster's assistant and successor (1885-1901), was a skilful operator and an excellent teacher, in both of which particulars he has been worthily followed by the present incumbent of the chair, Reuben Peterson.

The above are brief and inadequate sketches of the men and the work they did in the early development of the Medical School of the University of Michigan. They taught medicine, so far as it was possible in those days, in the scientific spirit and by exact methods. They were fully conscious of their weaknesses and these they remedied as far and as fast as was possible. Occasionally they called in temporary help and in doing this they showed wisdom. As a student I had my physiology from Burt G. Wilder of Cornell and my materia medica and therapeutics from Frederick Gerrish of Portland, Maine. It must be admitted that better helpers could not have been found.

Along with laboratory and clinical facilities the Medical School must have a good library and for the prosecution of scientific research the library must be selected along definite lines. I will admit that I am proud of what I did for the Medical School in this direction. While still only an assistant in the laboratory I found that the medical library was woefully deficient in both the number and character of its books. Each professor had about three hundred dollars a year for the purchase of books for his department, the total for the Medical School running from twenty-five hundred to three thousand dollars. I suggested to the medical Faculty that it would be wise to allow one person to select the books, having in mind the interests of all branches. I found that all the professors were glad to follow this suggestion and the task was turned over to me, although I was, as I have said, only an assistant and had no appropriation of my own. The shelves of the library were filled with textbooks which were out of date in a few years after publication. There were, it is true, a few sets, most of them incomplete, of American and English journals. The only French journal was the *Archives Générales de Médicine,* and the only German one was Schmidt's *Jahrbücher,* and neither of these was complete. Doctor Prescott and I talked over the matter and concluded that we would greatly limit the purchase of textbooks and devote the larger part of our money to the acquisition of complete sets of scientific journals in all languages. We also decided to interpret a medical journal in a broad way, including chemistry, physics and biology. Of course, cooperation between Doctor Prescott and myself meant a substantial increase in our common fund.

At this point I am going to confess to the only intentional and premeditative fraud I ever perpetrated on the University of Michigan. At that time the librarian was the Reverend Ten Brook—most college librarians at that time were Reverends. They seemed to have had a claim on the chair of mental and moral philosophy and the office of librarian, and most of them were suspicious of scientific books. This dear old man was grouchy, one of that class in whom I have been wont to say the milk of human kindness has undergone the lactic acid fermentation. To him I went with my carefully prepared list of journals. He received me with scant courtesy. I think that his mood was partly due to the fact that one below the rank of professor dared come to him. My list was for current subscriptions, as Doctor Prescott and I had decided to begin with these and fill up the back numbers later, since we knew that this would take a long time. The reverend librarian growled at the proposed purchase of so many journals in foreign languages and when he looked at the total cost he said with an air of finality and dismissal that it could not be done. I tried to argue and asked him to submit the list to the library committee. This he declined to do and turned me out of his room rudely. This rudeness probably saved my cause, because I am sure that the good old man thought it over and concluded that he had not treated me quite justly. The list which I had submitted carried the annual subscriptions, but many of the journals provided for semi-annual, and some for quarterly payments.

A few days later I faced the good old gentleman again with exactly the same list but with the prices cut down to the smallest time limit, most of the subscriptions being for only three months. The dear old man with no word of apology but with a face as full of kindness as he could mould it, signed his approval and before my eyes put the list in an envelope and addressed it to the European agency. Then he kindly dismissed me. I could have hugged him but I dared not. I left his room full of elation, tinged and softened with forebodings of what might happen when requests for renewals would come in. Nothing did happen, at least so far as I know, and the journals on that list, so far as war interruptions have permitted, are still coming to the library of the University of Michigan. Then Doctor Prescott and I set to work in procuring back numbers and in doing this I found one of the many joys of my life. Emboldened by success we appealed to the librarian, the Library Committee and the Board of Regents saying something like the following: "We have so many copies of *Annales d'Hygiene,* but we need the back numbers and therefore we are asking for a special appropriation for this purpose." In some instances we had to repeat this request more than once, but we never tired in doing so, and in the end it has invariably been granted.

This investment has proved as sound as one in real estate, situated most fortunately. Indeed, many of these old books could not now be secured at many times the prices we paid. When Doctor Sewall came to the faculty he became our coadjutor in this enterprise. When he left and Prescott was dead, this function developed upon Doctor Dock, and since he left it has been in the very

Doctor George Dock

Doctor Albert M. Barrett

Doctor Aldred S. Warthin

efficient hands of Doctor Warthin. Doctor Lewis
Pilcher and others have given the library priceless books
and now the medical library of the University of Michigan is one of the best for research students in the world.
If there be a great journal in medicine, including chemistry, physics and biology, in the world, a complete set
of which is not in the library I do not know of it. I
do not mean to say that this library has as many volumes
as that of the Surgeon General or some others. There
are many provincial journals, some of which contain
valuable contributions that are missing altogether or
in part. Many foreign government reports are lacking,
and the same is still true, I believe, of the transactions
of certain learned societies, but Doctor Warthin is
striving earnestly and intelligently to supply these de-
ficiences. The successive university librarians, Davis, Koch
and Bishop, have taken a pride in the medical library
and have rendered it every assistance possible. It is now
housed most commodiously under the direction of Miss
Bethen. If the present and future members of the
Faculty and students do not fully use it, it is their own
fault. A medical school without a good research
library is like an automobile without gasoline; it will
not go. The library is one of the strongest ties that
has held me to the University of Michigan when higher
financial rewards tempted me to go elsewhere. It is a
positive advantage to have it housed in the general
library since medical literature touches all other liter-
atures at so many points. This arrangement is good not
only for medical students and professors, but for all those
in other branches. In order to induce my students to
use the library I was in the habit of assigning to each

a subject and asking him to give an abstract of its literature as found in the library for a certain period. On the other hand, when I was preparing a paper, I would say to the librarian, "Next week I will begin writing on such a subject." When that time arrived I would find on my table every volume, bound or unbound, containing articles on that subject.

There are now certain organizations which for a definite price offer to supply an author with literature of reference. These organizations employ men and women to go through great libraries, such as those in Washington, Philadelphia, New York and Chicago, and make out the lists. I have never resorted to this short cut way of working up my literature. I prefer to make my own abstracts than to depend upon people who know nothing about the subject. Two persons may abstract the same article and reach radically different conclusions. Early in my career as a writer I had a valuable experience along this line. I was preparing a paper for a European journal and in it I had quoted an Italian authority through an English translation. I was reading over my paper preparing to mail it, when it struck me that the translation could not be correct. I laid my paper aside and sent to Italy for the original. I found that my suspicion was correct and in this way I was saved from a humiliation. A scientific man should make every endeavor to go to original sources. Abstracts are beneficial if they are checked up and verified.

I have stated that I greatly enjoyed the task of filling out sets of journals. Take the journal which I have mentioned. *Annales d'Hygiene,* the back numbers of which were secured by picking up one or more volumes here

and there. Of course I had the aid of a Paris bookman.
When the set was complete I was rejoiced to find that
certain volumes had come from the library of Trousseau
and others from that of Chevalier. I wonder if my
successors will prize these volumes as greatly as I did.
I should feel it a desecration if the control of these books
should ever fall into the hands of one who does not know
who Trousseau or Chevalier was. If every writer on
scientific subjects would consult the old literature there
would not be so many announcements of new discoveries.
Many would find that they had worthy even if unsus-
pected predecessors.

Greatly as I enjoyed filling out sets of journals,
I enjoyed even more the selecting of new professors.
There is no better index of the spirit of an educational
institution than the character of the men chosen to fill its
chairs. I had a long and interesting experience in this
direction. The first time I had anything to do with this
matter was when an independent chair in physiology was
established in 1881. The selection was largely left to me
because I was at that time teaching physiological chemistry, but it was necessary for me to convince my colleagues
and superiors of the wisdom of my choice. I had previously written a paper which had been accepted and published by Michael Foster, Editor of the *Journal of Physiology* and professor of physiology in the University of
Cambridge, England. Moreover I knew Professor H.
Newell Martin, who had been called to the newly established Johns Hopkins University at Baltimore. It will be
understood that this was twelve years before the Johns
Hopkins Medical School opened its doors.

Professor Martin took a deep personal interest in the

matter. He was intent not only on building up his own department in Baltimore, but in seeing the seeds of the new school of physiology then just coming into bloom in England through the efforts of George Harley, Michael Foster, J. Burdon Sanderson and Thomas H. Huxley, planted and nourished in the universities of America. I may add parenthetically that I then regarded that movement as the first real awakening of scientific medicine, and I have since had no occasion to reverse my opinion on this matter. I have placed Harley's name, the least known of the group, first on the list because I believe this position due him. In 1855 he became the first professor of practical physiology, which means laboratory instruction, in England by his appointment with this title in University Medical College, London. He held this chair for thirteen years, during which time he demonstrated the value of physiology to the scientific study of clinical medicine. On account of prolonged blindness he resigned this chair in 1869 and was followed in its occupation by Michael Foster. When Foster was called to Cambridge, Burdon Sanderson succeeded him in University Medical College and later went to Oxford.

On the recommendation of Foster and Martin I proposed to my Faculty the name of Henry Sewall for the new full chair of practical physiology at Michigan. I had the support of every member of my Faculty with the exception of one, but that one was no less a man than the dean, Doctor Palmer, who had another name. It is true that two other members of the Faculty were not deeply interested and did not greatly care which way the choice went. When Sewall came to Ann Arbor to inspect and more especially to be inspected, I was anxious that he should make a good impression upon our dean. Doctor Palmer's somewhat stately residence was located in a grove of giant *oaks,* greatly prized by their owner. Sewall and I were invited to a faculty reception given by the dean in the evening. We walked under the oaks and were ushered into the house. The first thing that Sewall said after his introduction was: "I have just been admiring your splendid *elms."* My heart sank; I could not hope for the dean's vote, and Sewall did not get it; but he got every other one and became our first full time professor of practical physiology.

Doctor Sewall had already done creditable laboratory work, but he had had little or no experience as a lecturer and I did not know how he would get along with two or three hundred medical students, sometimes inclined to be playful, to use a mild term, but after hearing him through a partially open door for a few hours I had no misgiving on this point. Doctor Sewall came early in the spring of 1881. The schedule was arranged for him to give a demonstration accompanied by a lecture three days each week to the freshmen, the higher classmen to be in attendance twice a week. When examination time approached in June, Sewall and I discussed the nature of the questions he should put to the students who had received such inadequate instruction. We could not hope that they had absorbed much of the knowledge which he had endeavored to impart to them. We decided that I should arrange an informal meeting between him and three of the best students in the sections to be examined. I sent to his room Frank Mall, afterwards professor of anatomy at Johns Hopkins; William J. Mayo, now the great surgeon; and Walter Courtney, afterwards in charge of the surgery of the Northern Pacific Railroad. Sewall soon ascertained that these men did not know much physiology, told them so, and predicted that no one of them would ever make a success in medicine. Several times in after years I had the pleasure of telling this story in the presence of Doctor Sewall and one or more of these students. Sewall admits that as a prophet he has not been a success. This confession, however, does not invalidate my statement that as a physiologist he has had but few equals. I am ready to defend this assertion before any scientific court by presenting the physiological literature produced since that time.

Twenty or more years after Sewall had been compelled by ill health to give up his work with us I received a call from a delegation of learned Frenchmen who introduced themselves by saying that they had journeyed to Ann Arbor to see the place where Henry Sewall had demonstrated that pigeons could be immunized to the venom of the rattlesnake, because they said that work had pointed out the way to the discovery of diphtheria antitoxin. Following Sewall's findings that animals can be immunized to snake venom Roux and Yersin showed that the poison generated in diphtheria is similar to snake venom. Then Von Behring and Roux independently immunized horses to the venom of diphtheria and produced diphtheria antitoxin, an agent which both prevents and cures the disease. If all my subsequent selections of new professors had been as fortunate as my first, and many of them were, I should now feel that I had not labored in behalf of the University of Michigan Medical School in vain.

Doctor Charles W. Edmunds   Doctor Arthur R. Cushny
Doctor Henry Sewall   Doctor James P. McMurrich

CHAPTER VII

MY SERVICES AS DEAN

WHEN Dean Palmer died in 1887, Doctor Ford nominally became dean but practically turned over that function to me. My relation to Doctor Ford and his family had been most intimate for many years. I was his family physician, the family consisting of himself, a very intelligent wife and two adopted daughters. I had all along urged advancement in the requirements for admission to the School and the lengthening of the course to four years. Good naturedly Doctor Ford had replied to my plan: "Have your way, but I will look forward to the time when I shall begin the opening lecture, which I will give as long as I live, with 'My dear *sir*,' since there will be only one student on the benches." But he saw the annual session extended from six to nine months in 1877, one year added in 1880 and a fourth year in 1890 with no prolonged decrease in the number of students. When the Medical School began operation in 1850, the requirements for admission included English grammar, rhetoric and literature, mental philosophy, mathematics through geometry and "enough Latin and Greek to enable the student to appreciate the technical language of medicine and to read and write prescriptions." In the earliest days each student had to write and defend before the Faculty a final thesis, which might be written in English, Ger-

213

man, French or Latin. A few, very few, were actually written in Latin. These specifications for admission to the Medical School were lowered during and after the Civil War, but began to grow stronger again about 1880, reaching that of matriculation in the collegiate department about ten years later and being carried onward to two years in collegiate work providing for certain specific subjects.

The work which I did in the Medical School, of which I am inclined to be most boastful, is the assembling of a great medical Faculty. At times there was not a weak thread in it. Of course this can not be true of any Faculty continuously, for at least differences in the strength of the threads will appear. In order that I might select professors wisely I made it a point to attend many medical societies, both in this country and abroad, with the purpose of estimating the value of young men. I read original contributions not only in my own specialty but in all branches of medicine for a like purpose. I decided upon the qualifications of a possible new professor along the following lines:

(1) The chosen man must be broadly educated and highly cultured, one whom I could introduce to my colleagues in other departments of learning in the University without shame. I sought men who would win the regard and respect of professors of Greek, Latin, law, and so forth. I knew that the appreciation of the Medical School held by the Regents, the President of the University and the professors in the various departments would be influenced by my selections. I saw about me the ill effects of unfortunate selections in other departments. Making a man a professor does not convert a bore into

an agreeable companion. It does not endow his brain with intelligence or clothe him in the garments of refinement. One of my University colleagues—not in the Medical School—told questionable stories, and capped these with a frequently repeated expression: "I done it." One morning I drove into the country and lanced "a bile" on the arm of a farmer. On returning to the village I saw a professor who had been vomiting "boil" all morning.

At one time in seeking a professor of anatomy I wrote Professor Waldeyer, who filled that chair at that time in the University of Berlin. He eulogized two of his countrymen greatly. I knew personally one of these men and was quite certain that he would not bear translation from Berlin to Ann Arbor but I came near yielding to the enticement of the other as pictured by the great Berlin authority on anatomy. I took Waldeyer's letter to the Regents; they too were pleased with the picture; authorized the appointment and urged me to complete the contract by cable, but I had already been bitten, and I wanted to go to Europe anyhow. I had not been in the company of the man recommended ten minutes before I was devoutly thanking heaven that I had not cabled. Possibly he knew anatomy, but he was not a gentleman. I may say that this time my search for an anatomist ended in inviting Doctor James P. McMurrich to accept the position. Anyone who has met the present professor of anatomy at Toronto will readily admit that in this case my choice was ideal in every particular.

(2) My chosen man must be a productive scholar. In this particular I admit that I made one or two mistakes. There are young men who start in this direction but soon

wither like a plucked flower. The causes of this catastrophe are many. Some marry a rich wife or otherwise unfortunately; some fall to the lure of a general practise; and some simply go to seed without obvious cause. When this happened there came the most unpleasant thing I ever had to do—get rid of an unfortunate selection. I would rather have the job of finding three professors than that of getting rid of one. In performing this function I have made a few bitter and lasting enemies, but in every case I have the consciousness of having best served the University.

When in 1890 we decided to have a real chair of pharmacology with laboratory instruction, I wrote to Professor Oscar Schmiedeberg, the dean of that science at that time at Strasbourg. He replied at length and advised me not to take a German, since he thought it a doubtful procedure to install a foreigner into a professorship. He said that he had in his laboratory two Americans but that one of them was more German than American and he recommended the other. Besides, he said that the man he was recommending was not only an American but a graduate of Michigan University. In this way John J. Abel became our first professor of pharmacology, as a real science. When the Johns Hopkins Medical School opened in 1893 Doctor Abel was called there and I had to find his successor. So I again wrote Schmiedeberg. He had in his laboratory no American whom he could endorse but he had a Scotchman. Thus through Schmiedeberg, Abel and Cushny, two of the great pharmacologists of the age, came to do their first teaching and to inaugurate their research work at Michigan University. Cushny remained with us long enough to train Doctor Edmunds, who is now his worthy successor. Cushny went from us to the University Medical School, London, and then became professor of materia medica at the University of Edinburgh. He died February 25, 1926.

Seeking a new professor I once wrote the distinguished head of a clinical department in Johns Hopkins Medical School. He recommended in high terms one of his assistants. I sent his letter to Professor Mall, a graduate of Michigan, and at that time professor of anatomy in the Johns Hopkins Medical School. Mall advised me not to take the man recommended. He said that Johns Hopkins professors are like fathers with marriageable daughters. They wish to get rid of the oldest and homeliest first. He added that the man to whom I had written had another assistant who would be worthy of the place. I have watched the development of these two men, though neither of them came to Michigan, during the intervening thirty years or more, and I am satisfied that Mall's estimate of the two assistants has been fully justified. This quest ended in the selection of Doctor Reuben Peterson whose students have testified by their works to his excellence as a teacher and an investigator.

About the time I was made dean (1891) there were seven chairs in our school to fill. This was in a way and in some particulars a most fortunate occurrence. It is seldom that a new dean has opportunity to select a Faculty to suit his own ideas, but it brought upon me my greatest strain as dean. I was determined to have men of general culture and of productive scholarship and none others. I knew full well that if I could fill all the chairs with men possessed of these qualifications the success of the School would be assured and the task of the dean would be easy. There was a strong appeal made for the selection of Michigan men. Ministers, lawyers, doctors and business men wrote to President Angell and to me asserting that the University is supported by the state and Michigan men should fill its chairs. Truth compels me to admit that this appeal met with some response on the part of the President. At least he used it in two cases, one successfully and one unsuccessfully. One Regent nominated his family physician while another Regent was urged to support a classmate. Fortunately my ideas had the support of the committee appointed by the Board of Regents to select the men. Without this important help I could not have succeeded as well as I did and I can not pass over this matter without personal mention of these men who, at a crisis in the history of the Medical School, rendered it signal service, and in my opinion saved it from utter wreck.

The chairman of the committee appointed to fill the vacancies was the late Doctor Herman Kiefer of Detroit, one of that large group, in which Carl Schurz and Doctor Abraham Jacobi (both of national reputation) were conspicuous, which the tyranny of Germany in 1848 drove to our country, much to our benefit. For years Doctor Kiefer had been not only the leading German physician in Detroit, but an outstanding man in his nationality in the Republican councils of the state and nation. Some time after the Civil War he had rendered important service to his adopted land in a mission to Germany. He was thoroughly acquainted with German medical education and fully conversant with the ideals of Billroth on this matter. He was a philosopher and a poet as well as a learned medical man. His collected prose and poetical works in German have been published in a large and impressive volume. He was the spokesman for the needs of the Medical School before the Board of Regents and he knew the matters in hand in every detail. He was convincing in speech and unyielding in his demands; consequently his pleadings carried great weight with his colleagues. One of his sons, a distinguished French artist, made the striking portrait of him which now hangs in the medical Faculty room and wins the admiration of every visitor. I wish to put on record the fact, now known only to his family and myself, that this portrait represents Regent Kiefer presenting the needs of the Medical School to his Board. During his regency he was a man of leisure and devoted his entire time to this office.

The other members of the committee were Stuart Draper of Saginaw, and Charles R. Whitman of Ypsilanti, later of Chicago. With this committee I visited Philadelphia, New York and Boston, and consulted leading medical and scientific men. It was Regent Draper who was urged to vote for one of his classmates, a highly honored practitioner, but without special qualifications for a chair in medicine. Draper declined to support this proposition and the name was withdrawn. On the recommendation of this committee, followed by exciting debates before the Board, the following appointments were made: Charles B. de Nancrede, surgery; George Dock, medicine; Paul C. Freer, general chemistry; William H. Howell, physiology; James P. McMurrich, anatomy; John J. Abel, followed after two years by Arthur R. Cushny, pharmacology; Fleming Carrow, ophthalmology. However, all these appointments were not made at one meeting of the Board and in some cases the contest continued for more than a year.

There was great objection to Doctor Freer. He had been a favorite pupil of Adolf Baeyer at Munich, had done some creditable research, but no teaching, or at least lecturing, to large classes. During his first year at Ann Arbor he failed utterly in the management of his lecture room. He was at first wholly devoid of tact and his attempts to secure discipline only made matters worse. His students were rude to him not only in the class room, but they smeared red paint on his residence. They brought their complaints to me as dean, but I extolled Freer's scientific qualifications, begged them to be patient and predicted that the time would come when they would point with pride to his name on their diplomas. In the meantime, I labored with Freer and tried to lead him into more conciliatory paths. Matters slowly improved with years. Freer put off the bearing of a Herr Professor. The students in his laboratory courses came to respect his knowledge and admire his skill, and when Doctor Freer left us to build up the greatest American institution in the Philippines, the Bureau of Science, he was not an unpopular teacher and the Medical School lost the services of a great scientist.

One Regent, no doubt prompted by an aspirant for the chair, organized and led an opposition to the appointment of Doctor McMurrich on the ground that he did not have a medical degree and consequently could not properly teach anatomy to medical students. I argued that we wanted the fundamental branches, anatomy, chemistry, physiology, and the like, taught as sciences and not exclusively in their applications to medicine and surgery. Doctor McMurrich had not been with us long before he won the approbation of every learned man on the campus. His encyclopedic knowledge, his modest manner, and his graceful courtesy toward all made him conspicuous even among peers. When his Alma Mater called him, we saw him leave with the full sense of our loss but with the consolation that our misfortune was Toronto's fortune. Doctor George L. Streeter, now of the Carnegie Institute, worthily followed Doctor McMurrich in the chair of anatomy.

When Doctor Howell left us, first to go to Harvard and then to Hopkins, we were inconsolable, but a break in the great faculty assembled by Stanley Hall at Clark University gave us Warren P. Lombard, whose researches on fatigue and tactile sensations have kept the school's reputation among scientific men, and whose general learning and genial bearing soon won the admiration of colleagues in all departments.

When Doctor Maclean resigned his position as professor of surgery in 1889, Doctor Charles B. de Nancrede was chosen to fill this chair and continued to render most devoted service to the University until his retirement in 1917, after which he was continued on the emeritus list until his death, April 12, 1921. I can not overestimate the service rendered to the University by this man. His presence was an inspiration; his diagnostic skill in both surgical and other conditions was unsurpassed; his devotion to his patients has been seldom equalled; many a midnight hour, without regard to weather, found him in the hospital, skilfully, unremittingly, without thought of self, devoting all his energy to the care of his patients. He and I were colleagues and co-workers in the Cuban campaign of 1898. Twenty-six years later, and after his death, his family received recognition from the War Department for his "gallantry on the field of battle." In the list of the names of those who have contributed to the honor and reputation of the Medical School of the University of Michigan, that of Charles B. de Nancrede has a most honorable place. In speaking of the great and devoted surgeons in this school I can not omit the name of Cyrenus G. Darling, who at first as Doctor de Nancrede's assistant and later as his immediate successor, honored his chief and himself in a splendid way. I am sure that I am not making an over-statement when I say that the love and admiration for him awakened by Doctor Darling in his students and professional colleagues throughout the state did much to cement and strengthen the bond of mutual helpfulness between the school and the profession of the state established by Moses Gunn in 1850.

From 1891 to 1908 George Dock served as professor of the theory and practise of medicine, and I am sure that in this capacity he had but few equals and no superiors. He lived in the laboratory and in the wards of the hospital. His original contributions to scientific medicine won recognition throughout the world. As a teacher he initiated his students in scientific investigations and demonstrated the value of research work in the treatment of disease. When Doctor Dock left us the late Doctor A. W. Hewlett came and filled the chair most acceptably for eight years.

When Doctor Carrow resigned in 1904, the chair of

Doctor Charles B. de Nancrede   Doctor Udo J. Wile
Doctor William H. Howell   Doctor Walter R. Parker

ophthalmology was divided into one of ophthalmology and one of otolaryngology, with Doctors Walter R. Parker and R. Bishop Canfield as their respective occupants. Both have demonstrated their fitness by their scientific contributions and their operative skill.

In 1890 Doctor William F. Breaky became lecturer and later professor of dermatology and syphilology and did excellent work with the limited material at his command. When he resigned in 1912, Doctor Udo Wile took up instruction in these branches and has built up a most satisfactory clinic besides making most valuable scientific contributions.

When Doctor William J. Herdman died (1906) his chair was split into psychiatry and neurology and these have since been occupied by Doctors Albert B. Barrett and Carl Camp, both of whom have fully justified their selection.

Doctor David M. Cowie has developed the department of pediatrics and has won recognition by his scientific contributions.

The medical Faculty of the nineties was in my opinion unsurpassed in any medical school in this country or abroad. When in 1893 the Johns Hopkins Medical School opened its doors and presented its Faculty par excellence of eight full professors, four of them, Hurd, Howell, Abel and Mall, held diplomas from the University of Michigan, and two of them, Abel and Howell, had been taken directly from the Michigan Faculty. In a recent Johns Hopkins publication, in which pretty nearly all advances in medicine during the past thirty years are attributed to its Faculty, I find no mention of the fact just stated. The Michigan Faculty of this time was what

might be called a full time Faculty on less than half time
pay.   No pecuniary inducement could tempt either the
professor of surgery or the professor of medicine to
neglect the instruction of his students or the care of his
patients.   In recent years much has been said about full
time professors in medical schools.   In fact the full
time professor is a myth, and it is fortunate that this is
true, because if he existed he would be worthless.   A professor in medicine or in any other branch of science must
have some diversity in his interests.   He must see his
subject from various angles, and especially is this true
of one whose students are being trained to live and work
under the diverse and complex conditions which attend
the practise of medicine.

I might, had I the knowledge, inclination or time to do
so, show quite convincingly, to myself at least, that many
of the great discoveries in science have come from men
who have had a wide range in intellectual activity.   I must
be permitted to cite a few examples taken from the history of medicine in our own country.   It was William
Beaumont, an army surgeon, stationed on the Island of
Mackinaw in the territory of Michigan, who by his patient
investigations on Alexis St. Martin, opened up the whole
field of gastric digestion.   It was Marion Sims, a practitioner in Montgomery, Alabama—then a village—who
discovered the means of relieving women of that hitherto
distressing and incurable condition, vesico-vaginal fistula.
Long of Georgia and Morton of Massachusetts gave to
suffering humanity the blessings of surgical anesthesia.
Up to our Civil War, American medical literature contained no references to cerebrospinal meningitis save those
that came from country doctors.   Lastly, but not least

of all, Banting of Ontario, hitherto unknown and unheard of, discovered insulin and made practical its application. Other illustrations might be drawn from the history of medicine in this country, and were I to go abroad I might fill pages with examples. It is desirable that those who teach in our medical schools should not neglect their duties as instructors, but even these functions can not best be performed by those whose range of activity and opportunity for observation are confined to the halls in which they live.

In three cases which I had to deal with in the early nineties there were assistants of varying terms of service and degrees of intelligence, left by the retirement of their chiefs. Naturally each of these had looked forward with more or less pleasing anticipation to the time which had now arrived when he could fill a coveted chair. Each had a just claim to consideration. Each had the personal friendship of the new dean. Should their claims, just as they were, outweigh the good of the school? This question had to be answered without equivocation. There could be no compromise. To retain these men and appoint strangers over them would be to them a greater humiliation than their retirement. My heart has always been larger than my brain, but in answering these questions I was compelled to neglect the promptings of the former and follow the dictates of the latter.

In another instance a most distressing condition arose. An applicant for the chair, a man of broad and deserved repute, was closely related by marriage to a member of the Board of Regents. For reasons which I will state later, I was compelled to contest this appointment before the Board. The matter became personal and to some extent vitriolic. Several times this man's name was presented to the Board for appointment to the chair. The vote had stood four to four and not having a majority, his election failed. On the eve of a Board meeting I learned that a member, who had hitherto opposed the appointment, had pledged his vote for the applicant, thus insuring his election. Before the rising hour the next morning I was in the bedroom of this Regent at his hotel. He admitted that he had pledged his vote and stated that he would deliver it. I then showed him letters from men whose standing and veracity he could not question stating that the applicant, though brilliant, was a drug habitué. The Regent was suddenly and seriously ill, too ill to attend the meeting that day and the applicant's name never again came before the Board.

During the years of my deanship there grew up within the school such men as Frederick G. Novy, G. Carl Huber, Aldred S. Warthin, Charles W. Edmunds and Carl Weller, all of whom were advanced to professorships. No one acquainted with American contributions to medical science can be ignorant of these names. Each has widened the boundaries of his own specialty by original research of the highest merit. Even to list their most important works would require more space than I have at my command. In their careers I have taken a paternal pride, since the highest honor that comes to a teacher lies in the productive scholarship of his former students. When I resigned from the University, a newspaper reporter came to me and asked for a list of my discoveries. I told him that I had made many important discoveries. He prepared to note them down. I mentioned the names listed above with many others. The

Doctor Moses Gomberg   Doctor Frederick G. Novy   Doctor John J. Abel

reporter was greatly disappointed and my great discoveries were left for me to chronicle. These men, with the new appointments already mentioned, made up the medical Faculty of the nineties and the years immediately following.

Having secured this excellent Faculty, my next endeavor was to see that each member had the best possible facilities demanded by his work and then to let him alone. I am sure that every one of these men now living will testify to the thoroughness with which I performed the last mentioned function. Each man arranged his own work, within the limitation that it must not interfere with that of others, named his own staff and gave instruction in his own way. The Regents ruled that if a dispute arose between two professors the dean should be the arbiter, with a possible appeal to the Board in case one felt himself aggrieved. If such an appeal was ever made I never knew of it. Of course, no man ever got all he wanted nor even all the dean asked for him. All worked in cramped spaces and with meager equipment. We had only a small acreage but it was cultivated intensively. Truth compels me to say that when the administrative forces of the University grew in numbers and in domination, the educational opportunities became more restricted, and the conditions under which professors labored sometimes became irksome. However at the time of which I am writing American university administrative policies were but slightly developed. This is a big subject and one upon which I would like to say much but will refrain so far as possible since I prefer to speak of more pleasing things. I must say, however, that it is now a question whether a university is a big business corporation or a seat of learning. It is galling to a research worker to have the conditions under which he labors dictated by an administrative officer who could not pass a matriculation examination.

Up to 1903, when we moved into the new medical building, Faculty meetings were generally held in my dining room. Here general policies were discussed in a spirit of perfect freedom, and I am sure that I never attempted to dominate. The majority decided and the dean was not always with the majority. After the reorganization and completion of the Faculty in the nineties I ceased to be responsible for appointments and for policies. These burdens were transferred from my shoulders to those of the Faculty as a whole. It is true that I remained the spokesman for the Faculty before the President, the Board of Regents and in some instances before the Governor and the Legislature, but I spoke as a representative and not as an individual.

There were two points about which I never agreed with the Faculty but as I did not have one supporter in that body, the Faculty had its way. In my old age, and looking backward rather than forward, I am not absolutely convinced which was right, the Faculty or I, on these points, but even an old man is slow to admit that he was ever in the wrong. The first of these concerned the utilization of the clinical facilities of Detroit. I never believed in the removal of the Medical School, or even its clinical teaching, to Detroit. It was on this rock that I broke with two of the best friends I ever had, Frothingham and Maclean. But I did believe that the Medical School could utilize the clinical facilities of the large city to the benefit of its students, and to that of the profession and the people. I can not enumerate all the propositions made on the part of Detroit physicians in this controversy which continued through two decades. For many years Detroit had no city hospital, but farmed out its sick poor to private and endowed institutions. The reason for this, as stated by the President of the Board of Aldermen, a graduate of the University, was that a city hospital was likely to become a bone of contention between the most corrupt politicians. This certainly has occurred in many city hospitals. The proposition was that the city build a hospital and absolutely and without reservation turn it over to the Board of Regents to be run for the city as the hospital at Ann Arbor was managed for the state. The Board should have the appointment of the staff, and the material was to be used for clinical instruction as a graduate school, or for sections of the senior class. This proposition had but one supporter on the Faculty and that was the dean. After Detroit had built and equipped one of the best infectious disease hospitals in the country—the Herman Kiefer Hospital—the city invited the Medical School to send sections of Seniors to it on Saturdays to avail themselves of the opportunity at least to see the infectious diseases in all their manifestations. This invitation was declined, but it led the University to build a small, model hospital for infectious diseases.

In the nineties Mr. Buhl, who lived in Pennsylvania, but who was born in Detroit and still had large interests in that city, sent his agent with the statement that he was ready to build and endow medical buildings in Detroit for such use as the Regents might choose. The only condition was that these buildings should be located in Detroit and accepted as a memorial to his father. This proposition was declined. Mr. Buhl, having his proposed donation rejected, put his money into irrigation projects on the Snake River in Idaho. Whether he made money in this venture or not I do not know, but recently as I motored through the abounding acres thus reclaimed from the desert and saw about me scores of smiling farms, and lunched in a clean prosperous village bearing his name, I concluded that Mr. Buhl's money was fortunately deflected from his proposed gift to the University.

The declination of this and many other proposals for the utilization of the clinical facilities of Detroit has led to the establishment of a small and inadequate medical school in that city, supported by the city, as a part of its public school system.

I have always insisted that the connection between a medical school and its university should be real and vital, and not simply a paper one. In this particular the school of which I was so long dean enjoyed an unique advantage. In addition to instructing its own students, to extending knowledge by research, to the preventing and curing of disease, it is a function of a university medical school to deserve and win the respect of learned men in other lines. Medicine is not a trade; it is one of the great factors in civilization, and should stand abreast of the foremost agencies in this great work. I am sure that the Medical School at Ann Arbor during my régime had the respect of the most learned professors in other departments. It had a good reputation among the more intellectual students in the college, and many a young man coming to Ann Arbor without definite decision as to his professional life has been turned to medicine in his college course. In some of the lecture courses medical students constituted a minority of those in attendance. The same was true in some of the laboratory courses. Then the medical student profited by his opportunities along other lines. The general library was for him as much as for any other students, while lectures, demonstrations, musical opportunities, and so forth, were within his reach.

I have received some credit, quite as much as I deserve, for building up a scientific medical school in a small city, but I have always regarded the location of the University of Michigan in Ann Arbor as a handicap not only to the Medical School but to other departments as well, but with that I had nothing to do. What an ideal campus Belle Island or Palmer Park would have made!

In making the above statements concerning the location of the University, I am fully convinced that my life could never have been so rich in intellectual associations and opportunities in a large city as it has been in the village of Ann Arbor. In a small community there is an intimacy of association between congenial people that is wanting in large aggregations of commercial enterprises, and all American villages are not Gopher Prairies.

The other point on which I had no support from the Faculty was the development of hospitals in all the larger cities of the state and their affiliation with the University Medical School. To claim that the profession of the state, many of whom are graduates of the University, is not competent to care for the sick is, in my opinion, to admit that the teaching at the University is not what it should be. However, this problem, like many others, will solve itself. Hospitals will be built in various sections of the state—indeed this is being done at the present time—and their affiliation with the Medical School is a matter in which I fortunately will have no responsibility. I am not inclined to waste my time or to trouble myself by vain regrets as to what might have been; nor do I claim to be a prophet as to what may be done in the future. I am an optimist, although I do growl, sometimes quite audibly, about existing conditions. The state of Michigan has done well in providing educational facilities through all grades, from the primary school to the University, for all its sons and daughters who have the energy and intellect to utilize it. It should go further and so provide that no citizen with a relievable infirmity need go without relief. I have faith enough in the intelligence of the people to believe that such provision will be made. I believe that every community should have a hospital and that every legally qualified physician should have at his command the facilities essential to the practise of both preventive and curative medicine. To do less is equivalent to sending an unarmed rabble to meet a thoroughly equipped army of invaders. However, many roads lead to Rome, and I do not claim to be wise enough to point out the one which the traveller should take. He should secure all possible information and then decide for himself.

One of my experiences while serving on the medical Faculty and on the State Board of Health was my biennal contact with the legislature. I look back upon this experience with great pleasure. I believe that there was not a legislature from 1883 to 1919 before some Committee of which I did not go, and I may say that in every case I met with sympathetic and intelligent response. During the period mentioned there may have been petty and even corrupt politicians among the legislators of Michigan,

but if so I never met them. As a whole the men who were
responsible for the affairs of State during the period
mentioned were of the highest integrity and devoted to
the welfare of the Commonwealth. It is true that some
of the men I had to deal with were denominated "politicians" as a term of reproach, especially by the opposing
party, but when a man awakens a somnolent community
and quickens it into doing something for its own good,
he deserves high credit, whatever appellation may be attached to his name. When the legislature of 1887
granted an appropriation of forty thousand dollars for the
hygienic laboratory, and that of 1889 one hundred thousand dollars for a new hospital, I regarded these sums
as colossal. In fact my conscience was somewhat troubled
because I had been a party to asking for so much, but
recent legislatures have appropriated for the University
in millions, and private endowments and gifts have come
in in like denominations. These are the fruits of the
trees of wisdom planted many years ago by President
Angell and nourished by President Hutchins. While the
present generation enjoys the harvest, it should not be
wholly unmindful of those to whose wisdom they owe
these blessings.

Although I had had previous experiences with the
legislature, especially as a representative of the Michigan
State Board of Health, my first appearance as chief
spokesman for the Medical School was in 1889, when the
medical Faculty asked for one hundred thousand dollars
for a new hospital. This was at a time when Doctors
Frothingham and Maclean were strongly urging the
removal of the Medical School to Detroit. With other
members of the Faculty I insisted that the school at Ann

Arbor should not be broken, although as I have already stated several times, I was in favor of graduate clinical teaching in Detroit. There were many warm discussions on this subject in the Faculty. At last there was an agreement that we should ask for an appropriation for a new hospital in Ann Arbor and I was authorized to present the matter to the Board of Regents for their sanction and then to go to the legislature for an appropriation. The first was easily secured, and Doctors Maclean, Herdman and I appeared before the Legislative Committee, the Chairman of which at that time was the Honorable Byron Waite, of Menominee, who was later a resident of New York City. Doctor Maclean violently attacked the Medical School, urged its removal to Detroit, and opposed the appropriation asked for by the Faculty of which he was a member, and sanctioned by the Regents. He was intemperate in his remarks which Herdman and I met with ridicule. Next morning the walls of Herdman's house and my own were covered with posters denouncing us as mountebanks, and one of these was found on the desk of each member of the legislature. Resort to this undignified and unwise procedure had just the opposite effect to that intended by those who resorted to it. The bill making the appropriation was immediately introduced, passed by a large majority and signed by the Governor.

Thus the first appropriation for the hospital on Catherine Street was secured by the unreasonable and undignified opposition to it. From time to time additional buildings were secured and the School which had started in 1850 without a hospital bed had accommodations some fifty years later for three to four hundred patients. From that time to the present no request for money for the

Doctor G. C. Huber   Doctor Moses Gunn
Doctor Donald Maclean   Doctor George E. Frothingham

University has been more popular than those asked for the hospital. The people of the state have come to regard the University hospital as their most profitable investment. There is scarcely a community in the state from which deserving poor have not gone to this institution and returned relieved in part or altogether of their infirmities. Indeed, I had occasion more than once to check the generosity of the state to the University hospital. A few years ago when the Regents asked for a large sum of money for a new library a proposition was made to me by influential members of the legislature to transfer that appropriation to the hospital. I admitted that the hospital was in sore need of better accommodations, but the University also needed a new library.

In the nineties one of my colleagues, the late Doctor William J. Herdman, began a movement to secure for the University a psychopathic hospital for the care and study of border-line mental cases. In 1901 the legislature made an appropriation for this purpose, but the building was not ready for occupancy until 1906, when Doctor Albert M. Barrett was made its director, and has amply demonstrated his fitness and ability. Unfortunately Doctor Herdman died in the same year and did not see the full fruitage of the tree he so wisely planted. The hospitals for the insane in the state are closely linked with this institution to their mutual benefit. This was pioneer work in this direction, which some other medical schools have followed. I think that I should add that this appropriation did not receive the warm support of all the individual members of the Board of Regents.

In 1903 rabies appeared in Michigan, and I was called in consultation to see the first case in man. This so deeply impressed me that I requested the Board of Regents to provide immediately a Pasteur Institute for the treatment of this disease, and this was promptly done. For many years this was the only institution of the kind west of New York, and those bitten by supposedly rabid dogs and other animals came to it in large numbers, and no one there treated succumbed to the disease. Now the material for treatment can be obtained and used by the family physician. It is with some pride that I record the fact that two of the improved methods in the Pasteur treatment have come from the researches of my former students, Doctor Downey Harris of St. Louis, Missouri, and Doctor James Cumming, now associated with the Health Department, Washington, D. C. I should add that my somewhat high-handed action in the prompt provision for this institute did not receive the approval of some of my own Faculty, but when I go over the list of more than two thousand patients treated in this institution without a death I am content.

President Hutchins and I appeared before a committee of the legislature of 1915 and asked for an appropriation of one million dollars for a new University hospital. In response to this request the legislature granted three annual appropriations of three hundred and fifty thousand dollars each, thus showing its liberality. However the War came on before this money was available and the erection of the building was delayed. As soon as I received my discharge from the army in 1919 I appeared before the Ways and Means Committee to discuss this matter. No discussion was necessary. Mr. Welch, the Chairman of the Committee, said, "We have given you one million dollars; the cost of building has doubled; we will make it two million." This was my last appearance before a legislative committee in behalf of the University. The new hospital has now been completed at a cost of about four millions of dollars, and although only a few weeks have elapsed since its opening, it now has a large waiting list. Those in charge claim that it is one of the largest and most complete teaching hospitals in the United States.

At the risk of repetition I must say that Michigan has not only been liberal in making appropriations for the University Hospital, but the state and the counties have made provision for sending the sick poor to this institution and providing for their maintenance while there. I do not think, therefore, that I am too optimistic when I believe that the people of Michigan will so provide that every remediable infirmity among its citizens will have the opportunity to find relief. Moreover the good examples set by Michigan in this direction have been followed by other states, like Iowa, Minnesota and Wisconsin, all of which have made similar provisions for the treatment of its poor in University hospitals. It can not be denied that sickness often pushes deserving people over the line from independence to dependency. It is therefore an act of wisdom on the part of the state to save its deserving poor from pauperism. When a family is placed under the necessity of receiving alms its members are likely to lose their self-respect and cease to be desirable citizens. The acquisition of property—food, clothing and shelter—is the first step in civilization.

I desire to say something about my experiences as a teacher. As I have stated elsewhere, I have documentary evidence that I declaimed before an audience in my eighth year. I was teaching Latin in Mount Pleasant College in my eighteenth year. I gave my first lecture as a member of the Faculty of the University of Michigan in January, 1876, and my last in June, 1921. I have indulged in many and varied avocations, but I have had only one vocation—that of teaching. I delight in unfolding a subject day by day to a bright, attentive and intelligent audience of young people. To watch their responsive faces as comprehension widens is to me a joy. I prefer giving many talks to one audience to repeating the same talk to many audiences. The task of a peripatetic lecturer has no fascination for me. I have tried it and find it irksome. My lecture soon becomes frayed out at the ends and threadbare in the middle. I lose interest in it myself and consequently fail to interest my hearers. It takes me hours to put myself in rapport with my audience, to establish an entente cordiale.

In lecturing to students I have developed my foibles, my likes and dislikes. I have never been satisfied with a one hour a week course. The breaks are too long for both teacher and student. The continuity in contact is interrupted. Other themes and interests intervene. I have never been satisfied with less than three hours a week and I prefer daily contact with my students. I do not like to stand on a rostrum and look down on the faces before me. I prefer to stand in the pit and look up. I want to be near those to whom I am talking. I look with suspicion on students who select the upper rows in the amphitheater when seats lower down are available. Although I am not a Baptist in creed, I believe in close communion in teaching. Indeed I enjoy walking up and down the aisles as I talk. It gives me opportunity to study faces from different directions and to estimate the interest and comprehension of each. When I am not satisfied on this point I like to stop and ask the one about whom I am doubtful some questions. I insist that each student occupy the same seat at each lecture. Then I have a mental picture of the class much as I hold my cards in a game of whist. Here is a club, there is a spade; here is a deuce, there an ace! I carry this mental picture not only when before the class but throughout the course and it occasionally happens when I meet a former student that I may not be able to call his name but can locate his face in my class picture, especially if he were a trump. I am always insistent that I can make my subject intelligible to students of average intellect giving average attention, but that I do not claim to supply brains or to instruct those who are not interested.

I never read a lecture and seldom used notes, because the employment of these procedures interfered with my study of the faces before me. Besides, my object was to make my instruction labile and not fixed; a living, breathing thing, and not a wax model. I counted a lecture hour wasted if I did not know more about the subject myself when I finished than when I began. As I proceeded in each lecture I saw my subject in a broader, or at least a modified form; or there flashed upon me some better way of presenting the facts and making them more comprehensible to my students. I have not been wholly averse to interjecting a joke or a bit of sarcasm, but this is a resort on the part of a teacher which may be easily overdone. I was never conscious of doing this to gain applause but I used it to illustrate, emphasize or clinch a point, or to give momentary respite from continuous cerebration on the part of my students.

I suppose that the time will come when lectures and lecture halls in our universities will be supplanted by the radio. Each student will sit in his room and when admonished to "stand by" will listen to a radio talk on "the functions of the pancreas," "encephalitis lethargica" or some other subject. I am glad that my teaching was done when teacher and student knew a closer and more direct contact.

I had opportunity to know and study Michigan students during the forty-seven years,—from 1874 to 1921—from the following points: (1) As a fellow student, (2) as an instructor, (3) as a practitioner of medicine among them, and (4) as an administrative officer. Moreover my viewpoint changed as I grew older. I knew them in my youth, during my mature life and as age grew upon me. I recognized the fact that my personal intimacies with students grew less with my advance in years. When I entered Michigan University the total number of students in all departments was less than twelve hundred; when I resigned in 1921 this number had increased to nearly as many thousand. In one of my early years as an instructor, on the occasion of the return of the dean of the Medical School from a prolonged stay in Europe, I introduced every individual student, calling each by name and giving his class. Although I have retained a fair memory of names and faces, when I resigned I would not have attempted to call by name those in my own classes. Quite naturally I am not inclined to account for this on the ground of advancing senility, but to attribute it to the large accumu-

Doctor Paul C. Freer   Doctor Reuben Peterson
Doctor Warren P. Lombard   Doctor George L. Streeter

lation of names and faces and to the multiplicity of my own duties and interests, some of which lay quite outside of the University. From the early years my wife and I kept open house for medical students. To these functions students from other departments frequently came. Besides we made it a point to attend student functions so far as possible. We frequently dined at fraternity and sorority houses and returned the courtesy, not neglecting the independents. This social intercourse led to some of the most cherished and lasting friendships it has been our privilege to enjoy. With advancing years this pleasure became less and less bounteous. Other duties interfered with "at homes." During the forty-five years I taught in the Medical School no graduate escaped an invitation to my home.

I must admit that these attempts to know the social side of student life were not altogether free from embarrassment. One of my own Faculty—only one so far as I know—said that I was seeking popularity with the students. This criticism did not worry me, but there was a more serious matter. Students who did not attend our "at homes" said that those who did were seeking to curry favor with the dean. This, I fear, had a tendency to cause me to be less lenient and possibly less just to my social friends. I can not regret, however, that I did cultivate the social side of my students. When some eminent scientist visited me it was a pleasure to have the students hear and meet him either at my own home or somewhere on the campus. The Michigan Union or club house now gives greater opportunities for functions of this kind. When Ehrlich, for instance, spent some days as my guest, every medical student had the privilege of at least seeing and hearing him. He evidently enjoyed it and I am sure that the more intelligent students profited by it.

To what extent my students profited by my attempts to cultivate their social life I can not say, but that I learned some things is certain. For instance one student whom I will designate as "Harry" occasionally "dropped in" on Sunday afternoons. His class record indicated that he stood near the head. When calling he seldom volunteered a statement and when questioned he answered in monosyllables. My wife and I came to refer to him as "silent Harry" and our prediction was that notwithstanding his superior class record, he would not be a success in practise; consequently we have followed him into his professional life with interest. After a short career as a village doctor he went to a large city, filled with eminent medical men. Within a few years he was leading all the rest in both the extent and excellence of his surgical work and was calling for young men to help him. This observation confirmed by similar ones demonstrates that the public, in some instances at least, recognizes a man's merit without waiting for him to announce it by word of mouth. Reticence in speech is not an insuperable bar to progress in practise.

On the other hand, I have had frequent proof that volubility in speech and being a "hail fellow well met" do not guarantee success. It is desirable that the medical man should listen sympathetically and be able to comment intelligently when conversation runs upon non-professional subjects. The educated layman can not highly regard the physician who is uncouth in dress and ungrammatical in speech. Human behavior should be a subject of the deepest interest to the physician and he should exemplify in his own conduct its best precepts. The dirty story is never more out of place than on the lips of the doctor. I must admit that I still have to blush with professional shame on this account when I attend social gatherings of Faculty and students. There is nothing more distasteful to me than to hear members of the Faculty vying with one another for students' applause in telling smutty stories. I have with difficulty been able to restrain myself from showing disapproval even at gatherings in which I have been the guest of honor.

The least of my worries has been the discipline of my students. I have never had much faith in the regulation of human conduct by rules and regulations. A wag once said that there were only two restrictions on the behavior of medical students at Ann Arbor: "One should not burn a college building nor shoot a professor." My Faculty and I encouraged a sentiment for gentlemanly conduct and I may say truly that this permeated the student body. I found that I could always trust my students to condemn any other behavior. It is true, of course, that occasionally a dissolute and wicked boy found his way into the school, but he met with such a prompt and unmistakable disapproval from his fellow students that he either improved in behavior or found his position so unpopular that he withdrew. A committee from one class came to me and stated that in the opinion of the class one of its members was morally unfit to continue as a student and become a member of the profession, and asked me if I wanted the details of the evidence on which the class based its opinion. I did not want the evidence. The finding of the class was sufficient and I assured the committee that the condemned student would withdraw from the School. I wrote the student's father, who proved to be a man of social and political importance in the state. The father came with fire in his eye and indignation in his heart. He threatened me in particular, and the University in general, with legal procedures. He would carry the matter first to the President, then to the Regents and if necessary, to the courts. He said that in condemning his son without a hearing I had violated all rules of equity. I let him relieve his anger, and when he had thoroughly exhausted his stored-up ferments of wrath I admitted that he had the right to appeal to any or all of the authorities which he mentioned. Furthermore, I admitted that any one or all of these authorities might disapprove of my action. But I pointed out that such procedures as he threatened would necessitate the making public of all the evidence which the students had collected, and if he succeeded in restoring his son, what would be the son's position in a class which had pronounced him morally unfit? The son was withdrawn from the School and this was the last of the controversy.

The most interesting function of my life as a teacher has been the study of my students. They have come and gone by the thousands and no two of them alike. Each has had his own individuality. In the first place, for many years I personally conducted all the correspondence with prospective students. This alone gave me a valuable insight as to fitness in an educational way, as to motives in choosing a profession, and as to character. Not the least valuable of my services to the Medical School lies in the fact that I kept hundreds of young men and not a few young women from coming to the University. I think that, in the majority of these instances, this was good for the applicant and I have no doubt that it was better for the School. When one wrote that he was wavering in his choice of a profession and asked me to advance reasons why he should prefer medicine, I invariably replied that in my opinion, he should not select medicine; certainly not until he came to the conclusion that it was the calling he preferred above all others. I wrote plainly that medicine demands of its devotees the hardest work in both preparation and practise, and its rewards in either wealth or fame are meager. No other profession demands more and returns so little. Most of my students came in the spirit I have indicated and those who, after coming, did not labor in this spirit, fell by the wayside.

In the second place, I always insisted on teaching the first or second year students, preferably those of the first. During my more than forty years as a teacher in the School, my full courses were limited to the first and second year students. My purpose in this was to distinguish early between the sheep and the goats, or the fit and the unfit. My colleagues, during these years, cooperated with me most heartily. The sheep we retained; the goats we eliminated. The usual mortality in the first and second years, mostly in the first, ran between thirty and forty per cent. The eugenicist dwells upon the desirability of an increase in the fit, in race betterment. I agree with him thus far, but insist that the more important factor in race betterment is the elimination of the unfit. Kill out the weeds and the corn will grow.

An incident connected with my teaching the freshmen may be of interest. Before the "germ theory" of disease had become so well established as it now is, Professor

Henneage Gibbes, a distinguished English pathologist, came to the school. He had not accepted the "germ theory" and his views were positively stated in his writings and lectures and were well-known to the Faculty. There was some joking among the Faculty members as to how Doctor Gibbes and I would get along together, inasmuch as I was a stanch germ protagonist. Doctor Gibbes had arrived and a Faculty meeting was called to arrange the schedule of lectures. The new man said he would teach only seniors, and I said that I would teach only freshmen. The other members were pleased to have matters so amicably settled and my new colleague thanked me for insisting that to him should be conceded the more honorable position on the lecture schedule. "Oh," said I, "I will teach the freshmen, and the seniors will not believe anything you say about the relation between bacteria and disease." The overwhelming confirmation of the work and theories of Pasteur soon left no ground for difference of opinion on this subject.

I freely admit that a satisfactory separation of the sheep from the goats in a class of one hundred or more is not an easy or a satisfactory task. The first few quizzes, especially when they have been both oral and written, enable the teacher to draw a general line of demarcation, but there are border-line individuals. This man is to-day plainly a goat and quite a scrubby one, but the teacher will give him another test to-morrow or next week. When the new test is applied, lo! your scrubby goat has become one of the most likely of your sheep. So the teacher applies test after test to this individual, until he recognizes the fact that he is devoting too much time to him. In these tests I hold that no individual student is entitled to more than his allotment of time. Having decided that certain members of the class are certainly goats, I have given them no more attention until the end of the semester when my colleagues and I compare our records. If a given individual is classified as a goat in the majority of the records, the only thing to do is to treat him as such and cast him out of the herd. I dare say that, at the time at least, some of my former students have felt that I did them an injustice. However I have always endeavored to have my students understand that being a goat in medicine does not mean that one is a goat in everything. Some of my goats have remained my good friends and have been highly successful in other lines. A few of them have had good cause to thank me for turning them from the medical profession. I have always strenuously objected to grading medical students as A, A+, A—, and so forth. This may do in high schools, and if the Faculties wish it in colleges, but it is wholly out of place in a medical school.

As I have indicated, I have been interested in the backward student only for the purpose of eliminating him. My continuing interest has been in the good student, and having found him, I have striven both as teacher and dean to give him every encouragement. After more than fifty years as a teacher it is my conviction that too little attention is given to the good student. Our schools, from the primary to the university grade, are dominated by the mediocre student, whose mere presence in the class holds all to a level far below that which would be set, were the needs of the more intelligent and more industrious consulted. The superior student does not need the incentive of grades. He studies because he enjoys it, and he needs greater opportunity; and above all, he needs to be relieved of the necessity of keeping step with the inferior men who now set the pace. As dean I was able to help the superior student, hungry for more than the routine course offered him. I saw that he had special privileges in the library and could linger among the book shelves at his own sweet will. If the books he wanted were not in our library (though it is one of the best in the country) they could be obtained from the Surgeon General's Library in a few days. If he wanted special experimental apparatus, he had it, were it possible. If he wanted to work over hours or during the holidays, he was entrusted with the keys. In all these helps I had the most hearty cooperation of the Faculty. I am fully convinced that the most potent factor in the development of young men while engaged in professional studies lies in the influence of one on the other. If a class is fortunate enough to have superior men, these set the pace and others are stimulated to follow.

If one should ask me if the Medical School of the University, during the time when I functioned in it as teacher or dean, was a success, I would paraphrase the motto of Michigan, and handing my interrogator a list of the students of those times, I would say: "If you seek the names of those who have honored the profession in various branches of science, you will find a goodly number on this list."

Far be it from me even to think that my connection with the school was the controlling factor in securing a high average of excellence among its students and graduates. With such a Faculty as I had, and with such students, being a dean was an easy job.

I had only rare occasions to complain of inattention, and then on the part of only a few. I am sure that my students bore my lectures with a forbearance worthy of sainthood. Inasmuch as it is never too late to ask forgiveness for sins in the past, I take this opportunity of offering an apology to my former students for the many hours during which they listened to my dull talks with a stoicism worthy of a better cause. Especially would I emphasize this apology to those students, who, in annual relays of from two to three hundred, for quite forty years listened to my talks on hygiene.

I had two definitions of hygiene. In the first I said that medicine consists of those facts gathered from the various sciences which may be utilized in the prevention or alleviation of disease. Hygiene is that bigger and more important part of medicine which concerns itself with the prevention of disease. My second definition was that hygiene includes anything and everything that I should choose to talk about.

The second of the above definitions was not altogether original with me. In the summer of 1888 I had the great honor and privilege of being frequently in the home of Mr. Jonathan Hutchinson (afterward Sir Jonathan) in London, thanks to the kindness of his gifted nephew, Doctor Woods Hutchinson, formerly one of my students. Mr. Hutchinson was one of the most learned and versatile men I ever knew. Indeed his learning was well-nigh universal, and, strange to say, at the same time accurate. At that time three of his sons were young practitioners. When we sat down to dinner Mr. Hutchinson invariably would ask: "What do you boys know about orchids?" or some fossil, or some extinct animal, or something equally remote from our intelligence. Perceiving our ignorance from our silence Mr. Hutchinson would occupy the dinner hour, much to our profit, in answering his own questions. However, the "boys" sought some way of getting ahead of the master, since rashness is a prerogative of youth. During his office hours Mr. Hutchinson's rooms were filled with a most diversified mixture of patients, especially were there all kinds of cutaneous disfigurements, and yet Mr. Hutchinson was a surgeon. It was arranged that I should be rude enough to attempt to forestall our senior by asking him a question. As we took our places at the table I asked: "Mr. Hutchinson, please define surgery for us." The reply came without hesitation: "Anything that comes to Jonathan Hutchinson, whether it be whooping cough, syphilis or broken bones." Then his question came and was followed by the usual lecture much to our edification, notwithstanding my chagrin.

Even more than the lectures I enjoyed the rapid fire quiz. With a class of not more than twenty before me this was the acme of pedagogical pleasure. I once asked first year students what is the normal temperature of the human body. Most of the class did not know. Finally one bright girl said that it is about 37 degrees C. I asked why she gave that answer. "Because that is the temperature at which we grow pathogenic bacteria."

In these quizzes, when wisdom ran low, wit sometimes came in most tellingly. I was once pushing a bright boy into an intellectual tangle, when he said that he had read so and so in a book. Then I dropped into the tangle myself. I told him that he must not take for truth everything he read, that his good sense should have shown him that what he had read not only could not be true, but on the face of it was arrant nonsense. In my mad haste I said that I would like to know in what book he had found such nonsense. Reluctantly he said that the name of the author was Vaughan. Needless to say, I subsequently handled this student more carefully. However, my experience did not save me from falling into other snares. Our admission requirement included courses in organic chemistry. Every freshman was supposed to know the chemistry of the amino acids, and in my lectures on physiological chemistry I began with the formation of these bodies in intestinal digestion. Realizing that some of my hearers were in deep water, I went cautiously and slowly. All through the hour I was annoyed by the fact that at least one man in the class was making no effort to follow me. A few minutes before the end of the hour I stopped and said: "The facts that I am giving to-day are the foundation stones of physiological chemistry. If you fail to comprehend them, it is useless to continue the course. One man in this class has not comprehended a word I have said. Throughout the hour I have watched his face and I have not seen a ray of intelligence in it. In order to convince you that I am right I will ask this man to arise and permit me to ask him a few questions." I pointed out the man. The poor fellow was so stricken with shame that for a while he could not move. Finally he managed to say: "Pardon me, Doctor Vaughan, I am not a member of the class. I am a clergyman with a letter of introduction to you. I am waiting to the end of the hour when I hope to present it." I asked the class to disappear, which it did with many a shout. As I read the letter it would have been difficult for an observer, had there been one, to determine which wore the darker garment of humiliation, the clergyman or I. However, we both had sense enough to see the joke, and became and long remained good friends.

Neither in lecture nor in quiz was I able to decide as to the fitness of the individual student so certainly as I could by going from table to table in the laboratory, stopping at each for a few minutes and talking with the student about the significance of the reactions he was studying and the interpretation he gave them. Many men are by nature wholly unfit for scientific study. They are wanting in the scientific attitude of mind. They start with certain premises which they believe to be absolutely, invariably and unalterably true, and from these they draw their conclusions. Some of these found their way into my classes, and my purpose, with their own interests at heart, was to turn them into some other channel. The most difficult and unpleasant task I had as a teacher and dean was to convince a student that he had mistaken his calling. Many took a suggestion to this effect as a disgrace, as a stamp of inferiority, and resented it with personal bitterness. However I am glad to say that some of these very men now thank me most heartily for the advice I gave them. One of my goats in medicine has proved to be a bull on the stock market and now cruises in the Mediterranean and voyages to the Orient in his own yacht. I may say that he is one of the most grateful students I ever had, and delights in entertaining his old teacher who turned him from the stony paths of science into the more pleasing and lucrative fields of finance.

I pride myself that I know the psychology of young men. I have certainly had opportunities to study in this field, since I have had five boys of my own and many thousands besides. I believe that much harm is done even in our universities by methods of discipline in use. To call a student before the Faculty and discuss his behavior is a procedure of barbarism scarcely excelled by the instruments of torture used in the Inquisition. During my years as dean I endeavored to prevent this practise and generally succeeded. There is no need trying to frighten a boy. He thinks that a special Providence waits upon him, and that he can sail safely among rocks where thousands of others have been wrecked. To call a student up before the Faculty and give him a bad name and to threaten him is, as a rule, an injustice and a punishment which does more harm than good. The rules of the Board of Regents, during my time at least, placed the discipline of students in the hands of the Faculty. Fortunately for me my Faculty was willing to entrust this duty to me. It is true that class room discipline was left to the professor in charge and I never interfered in this. I always upheld the professor, whatever he did, and acknowledged his authority as absolute and his decision as final. In matters of general morals the decision and the verdict was left to me. Sometimes I presented the matter to the Faculty after the verdict had been rendered, and invariably I was sustained. In the majority of the instances, however, my Faculty never heard of the matter. I could fill a small volume with incidents bearing on this point. I will content myself with giving a few.

I once had a letter from an uneducated German

farmer in Iowa. He asked how his son Fritz was doing
in school. I replied that there was no one of that name
in the School or in any department of the University and
that there never had been. Some days later there came
into my office an elderly man with a great, stalwart, fine
looking youth of about twenty years. The older man
introduced himself as Mr. Blank from Iowa, and then said
that this was the second year of supposed attendance in
the Medical School on the part of his son. On receipt
of my letter he came to Ann Arbor and he had found
that Fritz had never entered the School but was running
a gambling joint. He asked me what he should do. Of
course I flew into a passion and said that the young man
should be kicked into the street, that he deserved no consideration and that in deceiving his father he had committed a serious crime. In his great sorrow the father
fell into his native language and said: *"Aber, Herr
Doctor, er ist mein Sohn."* This went to my heart, and
after some conversation, Fritz, with nothing against him
on the books, entered the School on condition that he
was to come to my home every Friday evening at seven
o'clock, and that he should answer truthfully any question
that I asked him. We have had more brilliant students
but we never had one who worked harder. He
graduated in the late nineties, went to the Philippines as
an assistant surgeon, was honorably discharged some
eight years later with the rank of major, and is now a
prominent surgeon in a city of one hundred thousand
inhabitants.

This is not the only instance in which a father has
made inquiry about his son who has never entered the
University of Michigan. In a similar case I found that

the boy was living a riotous life in Detroit, coming to Ann Arbor twice a week, receiving and mailing his letters. I informed the father of these facts. I saw the boy and talked with him. The father disowned the son. Letters from him were burned unopened, and before the father died he did not know whether his son was dead or alive. Which was the better way of dealing with the boy?

At the 1915 meeting of the American Medical Association in San Francisco, I, as the retiring President, stood in the reception line. A handsome man, evidently a Spaniard, grasped my hand with fervor and said that I had greatly aided him in making a man of himself. I disclaimed any consciousness of having done so. He then told me that he entered our Medical School in the eighties, and that after a few weeks I figuratively had thrown him out, telling him that he was unfit to associate with decent men. After picking himself up he realized the truth of what I had said, went to the University of Pennsylvania, graduated and was now a representative from one of the Central American States to the meeting then in progress.

For some years, under a combination of circumstances, which I will not attempt to explain, I knew whenever a medical student came into contact with the police and also all the circumstances. I would drop Tom Jones a note asking him to call at the dean's office. When he came, I would say: "Tom, do you know you are going to the devil." The immediate reaction was one of indignation and denial; then I would tell him how many times he had been drunk, and where he had been drunk and who had taken him home, and all about his behavior for the past week or more. Then I would say: "Nobody but you and me know this. If you go straight, nobody but you and me will know it. If you go wrong, I will know it, and you will go home in disgrace." Some of these men, now grown gray, still drop me a note simply saying, "I am still straight."

I would not have it understood that I was always lenient in my consideration of the behavior of my students. When a man entered under forged credentials, as some did, when he stole or mutilated books, as some did, when he disgraced his School and the profession, as some did, the dean never waited for Faculty action but promptly told the boy to get out.

Most boys who are not morons—and morons seldom find their way into medical schools—are reached by appeals to their honor and chivalry. When I lectured to the students on venereal disease, I said: "Risk getting it if you want to. As an individual you are of no importance anyhow. You are only a grain of sand on the unlimited shore, but before you take the risk, you should know that if you acquire syphilis you can not sit at your father's table without danger of infecting your mother, your sister and other members of the family." Few boys are deaf to reasoning of this kind.

The greatest reward which comes to an old teacher lies in the love and respect shown him by his former students. Of these I am now receiving my full share, and my enjoyment of them surpasses all other pleasures. Some of my old students are now enjoying the highest rewards that come to scientific men; some have not reaped so bountifully, but the great majority are doing conscientiously and intelligently their daily duties as they lie before them. Wherever I go, in village or city, they

Doctor Charles W. Eliot

greet me. I have often attempted to classify the degrees
of success attained by my old students. It was long my
habit, at the end of each college year, to take the general
catalogue and go over the classes that graduated from
twenty to thirty years ago and try to group these men
according to their success in life. But the question arises,
what shall be the standard of this classification? This
question I can not answer, and I have given up attempts
to solve it.

The combined collegiate-professional courses naturally
evolved themselves in the University of Michigan; here
the conditions were most favorable. The collegiate and
the professional departments were on the same forty-acre
campus and students from one school or one department
frequently wandered into other lecture rooms. The
elective system, fathered by President Eliot of Harvard,
prepared the way for the combined courses, and in my
opinion, this is the greatest good that has come out of it.
Juniors and seniors in the college elected courses in
chemistry, anatomy, biology and physiology and after
taking their academic degrees entered the Medical School,
often with more credit in one or more of these subjects
than was required of freshmen medical students.
Naturally there was nothing to do but give them credit
in medicine for the work done in college. The medical
Faculty could not require them to repeat the courses,
which had been taken in the same laboratories and under
the same instructors who directed the work of medical
students. The combined collegiate-medical course was in
actual operation at Michigan University some years before it was recognized; then there were some warm
debates over it in the collegiate and medical Faculties, the

dean of the former, Professor Hudson, opposing, and I, as dean of the medical Faculty, favoring it. The vote authorizing it had to pass both Faculties. Dean Hudson argued that no study, which could be used in professional work, should be recognized for an academic degree, while I held that all real learning is useful; that I had found, *mirabile dictu,* that even old Virgil's teachings were useful in my professional life. Finally the combined collegiate-medical courses secured the approval of both Faculties and have been adopted in most universities in English speaking countries. The law Faculty followed and the six and seven year combined courses are generally recognized. President Eliot did not approve of the combined courses. At a session of the Association of American Universities at Ithaca, I was fortunate enough to engage in a discussion with him on this subject. I stated that through the elective system he was the founder of the combined courses. Good naturedly he denied "the bastard" but finally Harvard University recognized the combined course.

I served at Michigan under two presidents, Angell and Hutchins; quite unlike, but both worthy. Doctor Angell came frequently to the laboratory, and perched upon a stool he would say: "Go ahead with your work, tell me what you are doing and why you are doing it." He also asked me about other researches being conducted in the Medical School. I can say that for many years no research was carried on in our laboratories without Doctor Angell's knowing of it at the time. In his early life he prepared to teach chemistry and he never lost his interest in this and allied sciences. He was quick to comprehend and highly appreciative of productive scholarship. His questions and comments were to the point. He was also interested in the scientific books which I kept in my laboratory for ready reference, and he read French so much more readily than I that he quite embarrassed me. One day I was telling him about my work then in hand and added that I found myself anticipated many years ago by a Russian who had published a short paper in a French journal. I showed him the article; he glanced through it and said: "Yes, the story you have told is all here." I never knew a man who cerebrated so quickly and at the same time so accurately. His mental grasp was broad and firm. His keen intellect fastened instantaneously on essentials and brushed away non-essentials. Quite naturally his interest in research lessened with advancing years and his visits to my laboratory became less frequent. On administrative matters he and I often differed widely. He did not believe in forcing reforms. He was an evolutionist, while I, at times at least, was willing to resort to revolution. In most instances time demonstrated that he was right. He was a great college president, but during his administration much intellectually dead timber was permitted to stand in his Faculty. I believed in using the ax; he preferred to await the hand of time.

President Hutchins, handsome and dignified, with a strictly legal mind, was also appreciative of scientific work but with less ready comprehension of its scope and importance. He attended all medical Faculty meetings but declined to preside. He was ready to give advice as to methods and forms of requests to the Regents and to the legislature. He had an intimate knowledge of the ideals of the Medical School and was ever ready to champion its claims. He rendered invaluable service in urging better facilities and in the retention of good men on the Faculty. As dean of the Medical School and as an earnest advocate of research work in all departments of the University, I was fortunate in having the approval and cooperation of these men.

If I am leaving any memorial of my life's work, it lies in the Medical School, and my interest and pride in it have not been abated by my detachment from active duty. I served it faithfully if not always intelligently, and I left it without regret, being fully conscious of a desire to wander in other fields before reaching the shore of that river where old Charon awaits me in his boat. I may add that I am in no hurry to reach the trysting place, knowing full well that the faithful old boatman will be there on my arrival. However, I would not be human were I not solicitous for the welfare of what I am leaving behind. Every man who adds a worthy stone to the old structure will, so long as I am conscious, receive my blessing. If anyone should weaken its walls he will have my curses.

I owe much to the University of Michigan—more than I can repay. When I had exhausted the best educational resources my native state then afforded, Michigan held out a helping hand. I profited by its facilities and learned wisdom so far as I was capable from its great men of the seventies. When it took me into its service I was advanced in authority and emoluments quite as rapidly as my merit deserved. The University has conferred upon me all the honors it can bestow; in 1900 it gave me the LL. D. degree; in 1903 my colleagues, students and friends presented me with a memorial volume,

President Harry H. Hutchins

filled with their own researches and commemorating my twenty-fifth anniversary in medicine; in 1915 my colleagues, students and friends presented the University with my portrait, painted by that skilful artist and prince of good fellows, Garry Melchers.   When I was retired in 1921 the members of the Research Club, consisting of the scientific workers of all departments of the Universities, gave me a testimonial which I prize more highly than any diploma.   Not being a prophet, I have not been without honor in my own country.

CHAPTER VIII

THE PRACTISE OF MEDICINE

I ENGAGED actively in the practise of medicine for twenty years (1878-1898). After the Spanish-American war I occasionally saw an old friend in consultation, but gave my time to research in my laboratory and to teaching, with an occasional diversion as an expert. On my graduation in medicine it was my intention to devote myself exclusively to scientific work, but this seemed impossible. Dean Palmer was at that time doing some consultation work and he frequently called me in to make analyses and treated me as a consultant. Dr. Frothingham, my beloved preceptor, had a general practise besides his specialty as an ophthalmologist, and he desired to make me his successor in the former. Through these men I found myself shortly after graduation doing a large local practise in the families of my university colleagues. Quite naturally I took care of sick medical students, and this function quickly extended to students in other departments. I soon found that I loved the calling. I do not believe that many young doctors have had a more intelligent clientele than I did during these twenty years. The general practitioner, of that time at least, got near the hearts of his patients. I formed intimate friendships among the professors and their families and among the students which have lasted through the intervening years, and which I number among my richest possessions. I will not deny that the financial reward was pleasing. My charges were less than moderate, but supplemented by my small salary and expert fees, they were sufficient to enable me to provide a comfortable home, educate my boys and entertain my friends in a modest but respectable way. In no one of the forty-five years that I served the University did my salary balance one-half of my family expenses, and still we always lived plainly. I might have been courageous enough to live in poverty in order to devote my energies exclusively to science, but I was never willing to subject my family to want.

In my busiest years of practise I kept some research going, and by adding to the small salaries paid by the University to my assistants from my own pocket I secured competent help. In this way I could direct the work and leave the details to my assistants, while I was out earning the "damned guinea," after the manner of the famous John Hunter. Besides I was benefiting my helpers by increasing their incomes up to the cost of living. In this way Doctor Mary Leach, now professor in Western College, Oxford, Ohio, and Doctor Sybil Wheeler, now Mrs. Charles E. Keeler, rendered invaluable aid in my work on the "protein poison," while they won their Ph. D.'s. Both of these women were more skilful in chemical manipulation than I. In earlier years Doctor Charles T. McClintock, now dead, and Doctor Julian McClymonds, now of Lexington, Kentucky, were my efficient helpers. To all of these I gave credit in my current publications.

I first hung out my professional shingle on the house at the corner of North State and Lawrence Streets, near the Catholic Church. My nearest neighbor was Father

Van Erp, a charming Belgian priest. He looked after the spiritual health of his flock, and I after the bodily health of such as chose to come to me. In the exercise of my function I had his support while I kept him informed about more material things. Father Van Erp and I spent many hours in his study or on my porch in discussing all things within the range of human knowledge except religion; this was never mentioned between us, but whenever I heard the step of approaching death in a Catholic family I resigned my function in favor of the consolations offered by the Reverend Father. Instinctively we respected each other, and I am sure that if my spirit is denied admission to Heaven's gate, Father Van Erp will be there to intercede for me. The good Father, returning from an early mass at the alms house, was thrown from his buggy in front of my house and killed. *Requiescat in pace.*

Then came a German priest, and between him and myself there was a mutual repulsion. We started out badly. A good Catholic lady, under my care, laboring under the delusion that she was about to die, insisted on having the last rites of the church. Knowing that the death rate from hysteria is not high, I postponed from day to day calling the priest. The nurse, a Catholic, told the priest of the condition of affairs and he came to me with unchristian words. The lady did not receive the rites and lived some thirty years longer and died under the care of some other doctor, but not from hysteria. Then there were words between this priest and myself concerning the hygienic or unhygienic conditions of the sisters' home and school. This controversy brought to me a splendid testimonial worked by the hands of the sisters which I greatly prize. The German priest was replaced by that prince of gentlemen whom I am proud to number among my best friends, Reverend Father Kelley, later Bishop of Grand Rapids; also now dead.

I must say something about the nurse mentioned above and how she cured the patient with hysteria. I honored this nurse by giving her the name of "Sarah Gamp." She asked why I so named her. I told her that Sarah Gamp was a distinguished personage in the history of nursing, and after that she adopted the appellation with pride. The hysterical patient was given to retching and vomiting. One day as I entered the room, the patient called for the wash bowl. The nurse presented the bowl half full of dirty water. The patient in great anger called out: "How dare you bring me a dirty bowl? I will not vomit in a dirty bowl." And after that she was well. I want to bear testimony to the efficiency of Sarah Gamp's treatment of hysteria. It cured when some of the most lauded drugs in the pharmacopeia had failed.

Sarah was rich in devices of her own. I once found her giving a patient an alcohol rub. Her procedure consisted in filling her mouth with Bourbon whiskey, retaining it for an appreciable time, and then ejecting it into her palms. She explained that it was desirable to bring the lotion to the temperature of the human body before applying it.

It must not be inferred that all my nurses, even in the earliest days of my practise, were Sarah Gamps. I had two, a German woman, Mrs. Durheim, and an Irish one, Miss McCarty, who were most conscientious and skilful. Then I had as a male attendant that English gentleman, Doctor Brewer, to whom I have referred elsewhere. In the early nineties came my first trained nurses, Miss Clark and Miss Bowen, quite equal to the best products of the schools of today. I have watched the evolution of the modern nurse, the worthy handmaiden of progressive medicine, have seen her function in civil and military hospitals and in private homes and I revere the memory of Elizabeth Fry, Florence Nightingale and other founders of this most worthy profession.

I had one serious disqualification in the practise of medicine—a lack of self-confidence. I have had the misfortune to go through life in a critical attitude of mind. I never hear a lecture or read a book without a sharp outlook for weak points in argument, partial truths and biased statements. This has detracted greatly from my intellectual enjoyment. I have a strong desire to contest the statements of author or speaker, and the suppression of this has caused me much effort at self control. Openly I have been able to do this for the most part, but inwardly I have often strained at the leash. Fortunately a fairly well developed sense of humor has allayed my disquietude. I have never been a hero worshipper. Indeed I have never been able to make of myself a hero. I have been my own unrelenting critic. I never give a talk before an assembly without spending an hour or more in inwardly reviewing its many imperfections. It has seemed to me that I have simply spluttered without saying anything, or spoken badly what might have been said much better. I do not know to what extent this sense of self-criticism affects others, but now that my participation in public affairs is near its end, I am admitting that with me it has amounted to almost a mania, and it was one of the factors that led me to relinquish practise without regret.

Once in a group of fellow practitioners the question arose as to the fitness of Doctor Blank to practise. I said that it was not the fitness of Doctor Blank to practise but my own fitness that I questioned. I had an abnormal fear of making a mistake in diagnosis or treatment, and I have no doubt that this fear was often well grounded. I suppose that modern, more precise and more scientific procedures release the physician of much of this anxiety. I carried but few drugs and generally wrote prescriptions; then I would have horrible dreams in which a certain prescription stood out before me undeniably showing that I had ordered a dangerous dose. I was one of the first to use a duplicating prescription book. This I placed on a table by my bed every night and when a dream testified to a mistake I would turn on the light and read it. The dream was never confirmed, and Freudism has never found a disciple in me.

I know of no better field for the study of human psychology than the practise of medicine. One sees ignorance and credulity in their most diverse forms. At one time a fakir went through the villages and rural districts of Michigan claiming to diagnose tuberculosis in children for from twenty-five cents to one dollar per head. His equipment consisted of bottles of limewater and glass tubes. The child blew through the tube into the limewater. If the water became cloudy the child had the disease. This fakir added many small fees to my bank account. In Ann Arbor I saw the entrails of a black cat, killed in the dark of the moon, bound on the head as a sure cure for epilepsy.

A man came to my office with an inoperable cancer. He told me that he had sold his small farm in Indiana for two thousand dollars, and that the doctor who would cure him would get this money. I said, "No, not the man who will cure you because he does not exist, but the doctor who will promise to cure you." As I have stated, the bulk of my local practise was in the families of the Faculty and among the students. From my patients I learned much, and, best of all, I came to a fairer and higher appreciation of the intellectual life. I saw men and women of the best type, not in a conventional, drawing-room way but in their anxieties and troubles. I knew them in health and in sickness, and I drew from this knowledge an inspiration and reverence which did much to mold my own being. My patients gladly paid the small fees for my services, each according to his ability, but my greatest rewards did not come in the currency of the realm but in their friendship and confidence. I once heard a great man pronounce an eloquent and sympathetic eulogy on a greater man whose home I had visited daily for months and less frequently for years. When the speaker referred to the dead wife of the subject of his eulogy, as one Mary Blank, I came near shrieking with horror. I could have told of a wifely devotion and heroism which would have done honor to a Spartan mother. However, wise old Hippocrates sealed by oath professional lips.

Soon after I began practise in Ann Arbor old students and other medical friends located in Michigan and adjacent states, began to call me in consultation. In a few instances I was able to render valuable service, but in most I could only help the doctor and console the relatives. During the twenty years mentioned I visited most cities and villages in Michigan and many in northern Ohio and Indiana. When I hear business men tell of their troubles in 1893, I recall that from January first to August first of that year I traveled ten thousand miles on the Michigan Central Railroad, and unknown miles on other roads and did not take in enough cash to pay my railroad and hotel bills. I must add without delay that it was all paid in 1894 and this was just as well. During a long distance call in the first half of 1893, the patient was sure to ask two questions: (1) Will I get well? and (2) Am I going to get well soon enough to go to the Exposition? If I could answer both these questions favorably the patient was willing to have me charge on the books any fee, but he reserved the cash for the Exposition.

My friend Muir Snow was superintendent of motive power on the Michigan Central and he would stop any train at any point to let me off or pick me up in case I was on a medical mission. I had much fun out of this incidentally. In fact I could fill a leaflet with testimonials as to the kindnesses shown the wandering doctor by the railroads in the old days when they were not shackled by the government.

Some of these trips necessitated long drives over corduroy roads and through pine forests. One dark night I was driven over the ice the length of Baraga Bay on Lake Superior. The man who had called me stationed men with torches every few miles to show the way. There were ropes about the horses' necks so that they might be choked and thus kept from sinking if the ice should break. But now doctors are making consultation trips in aeroplanes and my stories are out of date.

In my class (1878) there was a handsome, elderly Englishman, Robert Henderson, who located at Buchanan, Michigan, a small village, the next station on the Michigan Central Railroad west of Niles. Henderson always wore a high hat, a Prince Albert coat and striped trousers, and would have been wholly in place on Piccadilly. His face had the ruddy glow so characteristic of the English gentleman, and was adorned with gray burnsides while his head was covered with white hair. He was much older than his classmates and reserved in manner, respected by all but intimate with none. From his village home he would occasionally drop me a note of the following purport: "Come over Friday night; see patients with me Saturday; give me the latest medical information and return Saturday night or Sunday." I would take the half-past ten Chicago train, reach Buchanan about five A. M., walk to the doctor's residence and enter the kitchen, where I was sure to find him cooking breakfast for us. The aroma of his coffee, bacon, or ham and eggs, have refreshed me many a time when my meal has been too long delayed. After breaking our fast we would attach Galen, a beautiful, smooth-limbed horse, to the gig and make our round among the doctor's patients, most of whom were farmers.

One fair October day we had driven many a mile among the highly cultivated farms of the valley of the St. Joseph River, had tarried for short periods at the homes of the sick, when we turned aside into a short lane leading to a dilapidated house. The contrast between the farm we were entering and those we were leaving was striking, although all were in the same rich alluvial soil. The fences along the short lane were rapidly crumbling into Mother Earth. The gate at the end lay on its side; its rusty hinges parted from the rotting posts. In the yard which we had now entered, rank weeds, proclaiming the fertility of the soil from which they sprang, partly hid rusting plows, harrows, hoes and other agricultural implements. About the falling barn stood two lean kine and a crippled horse, all exhibiting the sad visage of pauperism. The house had never known a coating of paint, and half-naked children standing on the uncertain stoop stared at the approaching visitors through cadaverous eyes. The doctor had told me that I would be greatly interested in the case we were to see. The master of the eighty acres of untilled soil was a bleeder and had been bleeding at the nose for twenty-four hours or more. We alighted and threw the rein around a limb of a barren fruit tree, thus hoodwinking Galen into the belief that he was securely tied.

In a bare room in the house, the interior of which proclaimed the destitution of the family more loudly than the exterior, the master sat over a broken bowl into which every few seconds a drop of blood fell. I made a saturated solution of alum, soaked cotton in it and plugged the nose first posteriorly and then anteriorly. The operation was simple, but Doctor Henderson had never seen it, and was greatly pleased. Leaving the doctor in the house I returned to Galen, relieved him of his phantom tethering, got into the buggy and turned toward the broken gate. After some time the doctor came at a swinging gait through the weeds; his long coat tails and flowing burnsides moving in the breeze, his silk hat sitting back on his head and his right hand grasping some greenbacks. When he reached the buggy he extended his right hand saying: "I have a small fee for you—enough to pay your railroad fare, at any rate." I gave Galen a flick with the whip on the back, causing him to start suddenly. The doctor fairly fell by my side. As soon as he could get his breath he said: "That was a nice trick you did in stopping the hemorrhage." "Not half so nice as the trick you are attempting to play on me. You are trying to make me believe that that man paid you twenty-five dollars. If you had shown the man that money it would not have been necessary to plug his nose. Every drop of blood in his body would have stood still in astonishment. You are a damned old fraud. You are not only attending this family without compensation but you are feeding them. What did those packages contain which I saw you put into the back of the buggy this morning and carry into the poor man's house? Do you think that you are the only man who can help the poor? Do you deny me a privilege which you grant yourself? Return the bills to your pocket from whence they came." Thus I lectured my dear old classmate as I drove Galen down the short lane and turned to more pleasing scenes. The old village doctor and Galen are dead, but I am sure that if there are errands of mercy in Elysium they are on their rounds. I know not what heroes of war it has supplied; what eminent men it has sent to legislative halls, but I do know that the village of Buchanan would honor itself should it erect a testimonial to the doctor who once served as a ministering angel to his neighbors. I suggest a Henderson Memorial Hospital.

One night as I sat in my office, the following long distance telephone message was received: "This is Mr. X, of Peru, Indiana. It is now ten minutes of eleven; at ten minutes past eleven a train leaves Ann Arbor for Detroit; take that train; at Detroit take a sleeper on the Wabash; arrive at Peru at seven a. m.; most urgent."

At seven A. M. I found Mr. X. on the platform at Peru. As we took our seats in his car I asked, "Who is sick?" "A poor Irishman, a section worker on the railroad. I told him that he should have a good doctor. I am paying all bills." I found the patient receiving the last rites of the church, and, within ten minutes after my entry to his room, he was dead.

At dinner in Mr. X's comfortable home, he asked me if I did not want to go to Europe. I replied that that condition was chronic with me. He then stated that he was having the last thing in the way of a touring car built at Kokomo and that he and I, with our wives, would "do" France, adding, "I am paying all bills." I must have been unusually stupid that day, for even after this speech I did not realize that Mr. X, and not the poor Irishman, was my patient. A few days later Mrs. X called me up from Chicago saying that Mr. X was going through Marshall Field's great emporium, buying every-thing, and ordering them sent to Peru, while she was following him, countermanding his orders and that they would arrive in Ann Arbor that night. The next day she and I took Mr. X to a retreat for the mentally disturbed. On the train we had lunch in the dining car. As Mr. X was slow in paying the bill, I drew my pocketbook. Pushing me back into my chair, Mr. X, with a handful of bills, arose and announced to the astonished diners that he was a millionaire traveling with his private physician and paying all bills. Since this experience I have carried a ready made diagnosis for anyone who offers to take me to Europe or around the world. For-tunately I have had only rare opportunity to use it.

One summer day I was in consultation at Rensselaer,

Indiana. When through with my professional call, a son of the patient drove me to the station. A train from the East was approaching. The boy told me that was my train and as his horse was frightened he turned for home. I walked down the platform meeting the slowly approaching train. I put a foot on the step; then to my horror the train moved faster. It did not stop and soon was going at the rate of sixty miles or more per hour with me standing on the only accessible step of a vestibule car. I clung to the vestibule door, shouting for help, while the telegraph poles barely missed my back as they rushed by. Finally I was rescued by a porter who was passing from one car to another. I blessed that negro and he seemed satisfied with the more material reward I transferred to his possession. When the train finally rested at the Chicago station both my pulse and respiration rates were above normal.

A preacher whom I had once heard and who had been a guest in my home confided to me his trouble. While a student in college some one recommended a proprietary medicine known as savapnia for a catarrh. He tried it and finding its effects agreeable, continued its use. In crossing to Europe he found that he had not laid in a sufficient supply and asked the ship's doctor for some. The doctor told him that he had no savapnia but had a plentiful supply of opium and that the two were identical. Thus the preacher found that he was an opium addict. As a rule the stories of opium addicts are not to be credited. Most of them prefer falsehood to truth even when the latter would serve them better, but I never found cause to doubt this story. My patient had tried various advertised opium cures and found satisfaction in

all so long as he continued their use, but on discontinu-
ance he was as miserable as ever. One of these poison
vendors had recently threatened to expose him and the
poor preacher was in great distress. After talking the
matter over, we made a contract that he was to place
himself absolutely under my control. I rented an
isolated farmhouse about two miles from Ann Arbor and
installed in it the patient, his wife and two reliable attendants. I visited the house daily. On going into his
room I would find him with a colored bath robe over his
shoulders, his long hair hanging down, pacing to and fro
in the greatest disquietude. He would fall on his knees
and say: "Just one more dose! I would sell my soul
for one night with morphin."

On this patient I perpetrated the only intentional and
gross fraud I ever practised on a patient. In providing
for his comfort I made one serious mistake. I permitted
a telephone in the house. This discovery of modern
science was then new, and but few of those who used it
knew anything about its mechanism and operation. One
cold, rainy night, I had just returned from the house
when my telephone called me most peremptorily. My
patient told me that his heart was going all to pieces. I
asked him to put the receiver over his heart and hold it
there for one minute when he could return it to his ear.
I assured him that the heart beats were perfectly normal
and hung up my receiver. The patient, after some months
of confinement, was really well again after years of
physical and mental torture. He passed out of my orbit,
became the efficient and inspiring president of a denominational college and passed some twenty or more years
in this position. One day I received a telegram asking

me to come to him immediately. I found him dying of cancer of the stomach. His physicians wished to give him morphin, but he would not take it until I came and relieved him from his oath.

During my patient's imprisonment I obtained and analyzed every advertised opium cure in the United States and published the results. There were then about twenty, and I found that all except one contained opium in some form. The exception was advertised under the taking designation of the "double chlorid of sodium and gold." Analysis showed that it was the simple chlorid of sodium. The gold part of it passed from the gullible victim to the vendor. If I remember correctly, the price was ten dollars for an eight ounce solution—quite dear for table salt. This led me to devote much time for some years to the exposure of patent and proprietary medicines. This crusade was later greatly aided by the facile and biting pen of Samuel Hopkins Adams in *Collier's Weekly* and by the propaganda department of the American Medical Association. I am, however, to-day (July 25, 1926) informed by my local druggist that he still has frequent calls for these panaceas. No respectable newspaper now admits their advertisements to its columns. This is another feather indicating the current of civilization is moving in the right direction.

In both my local and long distance practise I saw many Jews, and I wish to say that I found them most desirable patients. Were I compelled to resume the practise of medicine, I should select a Jewish community. They want the best service; they follow the physician's directions most implicitly; they are never given to quackery; and as a rule, they pay their bills without a murmur. For years the largest clothing store in Ann Arbor was Jewish. I was almost daily at the home of the proprietors in a professional capacity. In January I received the yearly bill. I took mine to settle accounts. The proprietor compared the two bills, his and mine, and said: "Doctor, what is the use of keeping details. You doctor my family and I will clothe yours." As I had five growing boys this proposition was quite acceptable. Recently, my wife and I have been most hospitably entertained by the children of these families in two of the larger cities of the Pacific coast.

I had despaired of meeting the so-called typical Jew until I had the following experience: The doctor who had called me met me at the station, and as we drove down the street, he told me that the patient was a young lady, a Jewess; that her father was a dealer in second-hand furniture, but that her uncle was the richest man in the county; that the young lady had been infected with a pin in a bolt of cotton which she as a clerk was handling in her uncle's store, and that as soon as she recovered she was to be married to a Jewish millionaire from Chicago. The doctor concluded by saying: "Make your usual charge and it will be paid." When my return train time was near I went from the sick room into the parlor. There I found the father and the rich uncle. The father asked my charge and on my reply he fell on the sofa calling, "Rachael, Rachael." The wife, Rachael, came. "Say it again, doctor, I just want Rachael to hear it. I never saw so much money in my life. I go on to the street and see if I can borrow it." Then Rachael took up her lamentation which ran something as follows: "*Ach! Lieber Gott, Herr Doctor, wir haben so viele*

Kinder. Sie kosten so viel! Sie mussen die Piano immer spielen!—but I put my trust in you and God." When she had exhausted herself the father renewed his psalm of lamentation. I felt like a thief, and said that I would make no charge. Then the father began with offering me fifty per cent. and slowly going up. I shook my head, and the doctor and I were leaving the room when the father opened a drawer, pulled out a roll containing more than twice my fee, and paid me in full. Evidently the uncle had brought in about what he thought I would charge and told the father to beat me down. As among other people, there are all kinds. I was once traveling with a well-to-do man, not a Jew, who annoyed me by petty and persistent objections to every charge. I remonstrated. Then he put it to me in a new light. He said: "Your business is science and you delight in making discoveries and you welcome even little ones. My business is to accumulate money, and I live to save it, even a little at a time."

There is a common prediction that the family physician, especially the village variety, is doomed to speedy and certain extinction. I do not believe this, and I certainly hope that it is not true, though I admit that his present position is precarious. He has been a most potent factor in civilization. Take from scientific medicine the contributions made to it by the country doctor and you rob it of half its glory. I stand ready to support this affirmation, though I have not the space here to do it. Through the centuries the country doctor has been the most learned man in his community, often the only one. The old Latin proverb, "Where there are three doctors, there are two atheists," taken literally may be regarded as a term of opprobrium, but it means that among every three doctors there are two who contend with superstition. The promising medical graduate of the present will not locate in a village because he does not have the facilities to practise his profession as he has been trained in it. Give him these, and many of his kind will prefer the country to the city. Some years ago a wealthy man, who practically owned a Michigan village in which his manufacturing interests lay, came to me and insisted that I prevail upon some bright man in the senior class to locate in that village. He admitted that he did not live there because it was not a fit place in which to rear his children. Indeed he shamed himself by his own admissions. I told him to make the village a fit place for a man of education and refinement to live in and rear his children in, and promised him that when he had done this I would find a suitable physician. This has been done, and a good doctor now has charge of the small but well equipped hospital, and as his children grow up they will attend a model and a modern school. I hope that wealthy men of this class will multiply, and if they do, the village doctor will continue.

CHAPTER IX

EXPERIENCES AS A MEDICAL EXPERT

THE study of poisons, their chemistry and their effects upon animals have always had a fascination for me. As I have stated, my first published papers were on arsenic and antimony and much of my research has been devoted to poisons, mineral, vegetable, bacterial and animal. My experience as a medical expert has been confined almost exclusively to cases in which poison is supposed to have played a part. I know nothing about other branches of legal medicine or expert testimony. I admit, now that I am through with all this, that but few experiences ever gave me greater thrills than come from cross-examination by a bright lawyer. In such instances I only hoped that my antagonist would fight fair, but if he should strike below the belt I generally managed to direct my thrust at a like part of his anatomy. I do not claim that victory has always been with me or the laugh on my side, but I have escaped grievous wounds. I have faced many eminent criminal lawyers, most of whom have remained my good friends. In a few cases the contest has ended in mutual aversion. There is no other state in which my brain remains so clear and acts so promptly as when I am in the witness chair.

My varied experience as an expert has caused me to formulate certain rules for my own conduct when serving in this capacity. These may be of service to younger men:

(1) Never accept service in a case unless you are convinced that the claims on your side of the case have scientific justification. It is often said that the expert swears for the side which offers him the biggest fee, and that the larger his fee the harder will he swear. In my experience the usual procedure has been as follows: The lawyer comes, lays before the expert the facts that he intends to establish and asks what would be the expert's testimony provided he did establish these facts. In my own experience quite as frequently as not this consultation has ended in the lawyer not wanting me as an expert. In such an instance the lawyer provides for the payment of my charge for the consultation, and I am free to accept service for the other side if offered.

In the drainage canal suit between the State of Missouri and the Sanitary District of Illinois I declined employment by the latter. The State of Missouri never asked my help, but I am sure that I should have declined had it been asked. At that time I was quite sure that the sewage of Chicago could be poured into the Mississippi River without endangering the health of the citizens of St. Louis, but I did not believe that the plan then proposed and since practised, was the proper method of disposing of the sewage of Chicago. In the final days of the hearing I did testify as to the interpretation of the vital statistics presented by St. Louis. This helped the Chicago side and I am told that it had some weight in the decision rendered by the court of last resort. Now (1926) I am even more certain than I was twenty years ago that the drainage canal was not then, and is not now, the wise and scientific method of disposing of the immense waste of Chicago.

A prosecuting attorney in Ohio was trying an old man for the murder of his wife. Someone in Toledo had reported strychnia in the remains. The symptoms were those of gastro-intestinal irritation and showed not the slightest evidence of strychnia poisoning. The prosecutor came to me twice and urged me to serve as an expert for him. On his second visit I told him that if he did not discontinue the case or modify the charge I would appear as a voluntary witness for the defendant at the trial. This I did, and the accused was acquitted.

An aged couple lived in a Michigan village. Early one morning the husband found the wife dead in bed. About 10 A. M. a large amount of embalming fluid was injected into the abdomen. A few hours later an autopsy was held and various organs in separate receptacles were sent to a competent chemist who reported sixty-eight grains of arsenic in the liver and only a fraction of a grain in the stomach. A sample of the embalming fluid was also sent to the chemist and in this he found no arsenic. Both the prosecutor and the lawyer for the defense consulted me. I advised them that the husband did not administer the poison, that the poison had not reached the liver through the stomach and that the embalming fluid used was arsenical and not that sent to the chemist. Neither would believe me and the prosecution was proceeding when the conscientious embalmer found that he had "mixed" his bottles and had injected an arsenical fluid into the abdomen.

(2) Sentiment should not concern the medical expert. He should confine himself to scientific facts. Sentiment has no place in a trial for murder and certainly the doctor should not resort to it.

(3) The expert should be modest in giving his qualifications. He should ask his lawyers not to magnify his greatness on direct examination; it may cause much embarrassment on cross examination.

In a famous trial in New York City a justly eminent man qualified as an all-round, unlimited medical expert. The next day he was compelled to admit that he knew but little physics, chemistry, physiology, anatomy, and so forth. I have learned by both personal experience and observation to bring to the smallest possible limit my expert qualification.

In a Federal Court in Chicago many years ago when I was young and inexperienced, I qualified as a chemist. I spent the whole of the first day on cross examination in answering questions about the chemistry of the alcohols, though no one of this chemical group had anything to do with the case in hand.

That evening, as my cross-examiner and I sipped our beer, I asked why he had consumed so much time in his irrelevant examination. He replied that he had recently tried a whiskey case and felt posted on the alcohols, adding, "I am working by the day and I hope you are."

(4)' Answer questions on cross-examinations as readily and as good-naturedly as on direct. I have noticed frequently that when the medical expert is turned over for cross-examination he is likely to assume a hostile attitude. He does not sit at his former ease. His face speaks defiance and his tone becomes antagonistic. The medical expert should not try to be facetious or smart but should leave the opening of this dangerous procedure to his interrogator. The man who begins this play is likely to awaken dislike in judge and jury. If the lawyer begins it, the sense of fair play, both on the bench and in the box, will justify the witness in replying in kind; then the deadly duel is on and the first to lose his temper is lost. In the heat of battle the expert should pray that he may not swear too strongly. I admit that in my own experience this prayer has not always been fully granted.

(5) The expert should know that he has the right to qualify his answer, a right which I have never known a judge to deny. If his own lawyer neglects to secure this right for the witness he should himself appeal to the judge. The interrogator often demands that his question be answered by an unqualified "yes" or "no." There are many questions that can not be so answered. Of this every judge and juryman is fully aware.

(6) The expert should express no opinion of the guilt or innocence of the accused. In one's social relations with those connected with the case in and outside of the courtroom the expert should make no distinction between those on one side and those on the other.

I will now give brief synopses of a few of the more interesting cases in which I have served. Before doing this, however, I must say something about my qualifications; in other words, I must qualify. When I began giving instruction in physiological chemistry in the University laboratory, work in toxicology was included in that subject and was required of students in pharmacy and optional with medical students. At that time the senior pharmacy class averaged about thirty; each of these was required to supply ten animals; to each of these animals, with only an assistant present, I administered some poison. Then the student in charge was admitted to the room and began his protocol which contained a full record of time of administration, appearance and progress of symptoms, time of death, observations at autopsy, processes of chemical investigation and the exhibition of findings. The poison administered might be of mineral, vegetable or synthetic origin. With some three hundred cases a year quite a wide range was possible.

THE HALL CASE

In September, 1880, I read a paper or gave a talk to a local medical society at Holly, Michigan. There I met a Doctor Hall, who had graduated at the University some years before and had since practised at a village near Holly. He told me that his wife had died the preceding spring after a somewhat prolonged illness, during which he had frequent counsel; that now his neighbors were insisting that he had poisoned her; that he proposed, with the approval of the prosecuting attorney, to resurrect her body, have a toxicological examination made, and with the evidence stop the talk. Within a week he, accompanied by an under sheriff, brought me the stomach, telling me not to proceed with the analysis but to hold the organ until further word from him. He said that he was undecided about further procedure. A few days later the same under sheriff came with a letter from Doctor Hall instructing me to turn over the stomach to the bearer. This I did. That day Doctor Hall and the officer met in Detroit and the former went to the city physician, Doctor H. O. Walker, told him that he wished to procure a human stomach in order that he might make some diffusion experiments with it. The city physician, making many autopsies, complied with this request. The same day Hall took a stomach to Doctor Lyons of Detroit, a perfectly competent chemist, and instructed him to test it for poison and make a report. Doctor Lyons could find no poison; but the exhibition of this evidence of innocence to his neighbors did not stop their talk. Gossip grew louder, and the prosecuting attorney, S. W. Smith, for many years since a most worthy and valuable member of Congress, felt compelled to move in the case. He provided for the exhumation of the body of Mrs. Hall, but the grave was found empty and the remains could be discovered nowhere.

At this stage Doctor Hall was brought to trial, in which I was a witness as to fact. I had no expert testimony to give. The jury disagreed. The next year children playing in a straw stack near the cemetery discovered a flour barrel in which was the body of Mrs. Hall. Doctor Prescott found weighable quantities of arsenic in the liver and other organs and a trace of the same poison in the brain. At the second trial the undertaker testified that he had bathed Mrs. Hall's body with an arsenical fluid, and the question of the diffusion of arsenic through the dead body came up. Doctor Prescott and I answered this question, he in the negative and I in the affirmative. Doctor Hall was convicted and sent to the penitentiary. In this trial the judge admitted some most incredible testimony. For instance, a man, who had been in jail with Hall, was permitted to testify that he had heard Hall tell in sleep how he had poisoned his wife. On account of the admission of testimony of this kind the Supreme Court ordered a third trial. In this the question of the possible diffusion of arsenic through the dead body, or post mortem imbibition, grew more important. Doctor Prescott, aided by others and supported by Taylor's great book, the authoritative text in a toxicological case at that time, said that arsenic would not diffuse through dead tissue. I now had the cooperation of another colleague, Professor John W. Langley.

Several humorous incidents occurred at this trial, one of which I must relate. The chief counsel for the prosecution, Judge Baldwin, and I were warm friends and our contest in this case did not lessen our friendship. One day while we were lunching he remarked: "I understand that you are to come on the witness stand this afternoon and I tell you now that I have a question that will leave you without a foot to stand on. I will tell you now what it is, since I know that there is but one answer to it. The body of this woman was found in a sitting posture in the barrel where it had been during the greater part of the time since her death. Admitting that the undertaker did wipe the chest, abdomen and limbs with a towel soaked in an arsenic fluid, how could traces of the poison get to the brain? How could arsenic violate the law of gravity and go up instead of down? I am going to ask you if you can mention a substance which thus violates the law of gravity?" I replied: "Langley is to precede me on the stand; knock him down with that question first and then I will take my turn."

I did not tell Langley of the misfortune which was to come upon him. The kerosene lamps lighting the courtroom were burning and Langley was on the stand. I could see Judge Baldwin preparing to deal the blow. It came; Langley's quiet features were not perturbed as he promptly answered: "Yes; the kerosene goes up in the wick." I did not have to answer the question, and Doctor Hall was acquitted. I entirely lost sight of Hall's guilt or innocence in the bigger question of the post mortem imbibition of arsenic. If not guilty, Hall was certainly insane; he may have been both. It was known that he was a morphin addict and he died a few years after his acquittal in an insane asylum. However, the Hall case did not finally and fully settle the question of the post mortem imbibition of arsenic.

THE MILLARD CASE

Scarcely had the Hall case reached its final disposition when the Millard affair came in evidence. In the early eighties Matthew Millard was the leading citizen of the village of Paoli, Ionia County, Michigan. He owned a small bank, manufactured agricultural implements in a small way and had a general furniture store in which he sold cradles for the babies and coffins for those of all ages. Millard's wife died after an illness of about three weeks, during which time the village doctor saw her as frequently as he deemed desirable, and twice he called in an older physician from a nearby locality. After her death Millard, explaining to his friends that he did not have in his establishment a coffin good enough for his wife, determined to embalm her body while he sent to Detroit for a more costly casket. With this explanation he went to the druggist and asked for some embalming substance. Millard testified that he asked the druggist for arsenic and that he received this substance. The druggist testified that

Millard asked for strychnia. Unfortunately the druggist made no record of the sale of the poison as the state law even then demanded. There appears to have been no doubt in the minds of the judge or the jury that Millard secured white arsenic from the druggist. Millard and his brother testified that they took a teaspoonful of the powder obtained from the druggist, suspended it in a teacupful of water and injected one Davidson's syringe full into the mouth and the remainder into the rectum of the dead woman. No one else was present when this was done. Millard did not send to Detroit for a coffin but finally used one taken from his own stock. The body lay in the grave one hundred and five days before it was exhumed by order of the prosecutor. The post mortem examination was made under a shed with many citizens, some enemies and some friends of Millard standing about. The various organs were placed in a common receptacle and this was taken to Doctor Prescott at the University for chemical examination. Doctor Prescott found large quantities of arsenic in the lower bowel and liver and appreciable quantities in the other tissues sent him. At this time the brain was not removed and consequently was not examined. The question put to the experts was as follows: "Grant that a teaspoonful of white arsenic was suspended in water and injected into the mouth and rectum of a corpse, might arsenic be found widely distributed and in large quantities after the body had rested in the grave one hundred and five days?" Doctor Prescott, supported by Doctor Samuel Duffield, a recent pupil of the great German chemist, Fresenius, answered this question in the negative; Professor Robert Kedzie of the

Michigan Agricultural College and I answered it in the affirmative. Doctor Kedzie and I made in the courtroom demonstrations of the diffusion of arsenic which we thought convincing. Two of these I will briefly indicate: We prepared two batches of gelatine, one containing arsenic and the other containing hydrogen sulphid. We poured an inch or more of one of these in a test tube and after complete consolidation of this portion, poured on top of it the other preparation. Then day by day in the courtroom we called attention to the extension both downward and upward of the yellow coloration which first appeared at the line of contact of the two layers of gelatine. It made no difference whether the arsenic was originally in the lower or upper layer.

In a second demonstration we suspended a loop of human intestine containing an arsenical suspension in a saturated solution of hydrogen sulphid in a glass beaker and daily called attention to the formation of a yellow precipitate in the outer fluid. At that time Taylor's book on toxicology was supposed to be the latest and most authoritative work dealing with poisons, and Taylor said that the finding of arsenic in the liver is unquestionable proof of its administration before death and that arsenic could reach that organ only through the circulation. As a result of this trial Millard was convicted and sentenced.

The review of this case by Justice Campbell of the Michigan Supreme Court, ending in an order for a new trial, materially modified procedures in cases of suspected poisoning in several particulars. I will mention briefly some of these. During the many days of this trial all experts were required to sit in the courtroom and listen

Doctor Vaughan in His Laboratory

to all witnesses as to fact. After an attendant on the woman in her last illness had testified as to the symptoms as she observed them, each expert was asked something like the following question: "Having heard the testimony of Mrs. W., do you believe that deceased came to her death by poisoning by arsenic?" Justice Campbell ruled that this was clearly error.

In the trial, sentences and paragraphs from Taylor's book were admitted as evidence. Justice Campbell ruled that this was error; Taylor was not there and could not be cross-examined: he might have been wrong in his statements; knowledge might have advanced since Taylor wrote; and books could be introduced only to contradict a witness. If a witness testified that an author said so and so, his book or other writing might be introduced to contradict this testimony; under no other circumstances could a book be introduced in evidence. This ruling has been generally accepted. At least it has been supported in every murder case in which I have subsequently served. This ruling has relieved the expert from a most distressing condition. In the first Millard trial the witnesses were compelled to answer such questions as these:

You recognize Taylor's book as the most authorita tive work on posioning there is, do you not? I do.

Taylor was a great toxicologist, was he not? Yes.

Quite as great as you, was he not? Yes, much greater.

Then do you dare dispute him? Yes, on this point.

Thus the tangle went on, becoming more and more complicated.

The local physician who attended Mrs. Millard testified that her symptoms were such that he suspected arsenical poisoning some days before she died; still he made no attempt to justify or correct this suspicion by examining the vomited matter or by having it examined; nor did he administer any antidote. Justice Campbell ruled that if this testimony was true the physician became *particeps criminis* and should stand in the dock with the accused husband.

Of course the druggist was scored in Justice Campbell's decision for not keeping a record of the sale of the poison as the law required.

At the trial an undertaker qualified as an expert, and testified that a suspension of arsenic injected into the rectum of a corpse would be immediately and completely returned without retention of any portion. Justice Campbell ruled that this man could not be qualified as an expert, since an expert should have scientific knowledge as well as practical experience.

During the months that elapsed before the second trial Doctor Kedzie and I were busy in both the laboratory and the library. We wished to make a demonstration of the post mortem imbibition of arsenic that would convince all. Doctor Kedzie tested the matter out on animals. I took a human body, dead only a few hours, and on this I carried out exactly the procedure claimed to have been practised by Millard and his brother. Having first demonstrated that the body did not contain any arsenic, I suspended a teaspoonful of white arsenic in a teacupful of water and made the injections into the mouth and rectum and buried the body and finally tested every organ in it. Arsenic was found in every tissue. These results were published and later were confirmed by Witthaus of New York, Rees of Philadelphia, the American editor of the latest edition of Taylor, and others in this country and abroad.

Doctor Prescott watched the progress of my investigations and was as glad as I when the question, which we had interpreted differently through so many months, had been answered by scientific demonstration. During this prolonged controversy Doctor Prescott remained my respected master and I his beloved student. Our personal relations were never in the slightest degree disturbed. I have often wondered if I should have been as honest about it as he was had the final verdict been different. The second Millard trial was short. There was no difference among the experts and it ended in acquittal. I am told that Millard still lives as a humble but law-abiding citizen. Whether he, aided by his brother, made an injection as they testified, I do not know. The question asked me on the witness-stand assumed that they did. My search through the old tomes in the library resulted in a real surprise—indeed quite a shock. I found that the post mortem imbibition of arsenic had been recognized and taught by the great French toxicologist, Orfila, many years ago, and that it had been practically demonstrated by an Irishman, Kidd by name, some years later.

This is not the only one of my scientific discoveries whose halo has been dissipated in a similar way, as I shall have occasion to relate elsewhere. How many recent discoveries in science have a like ancient prototype I will not attempt to estimate. That there is in the realm of knowledge "nothing new under the sun" may be too broad a generalization, but that many facts have been discovered, lost and afterwards found, is certain, while the number of those lost and not yet found is uncertain. Seneca, who lived in the first century of our era, says that he had seen a model of a house heated from a central plant by means of flues, led under the floors and through the walls. More remarkable yet, he had seen a device which recorded in legible characters words as fast as they were spoken. That St. Augustine, when Bishop of Hippo, in northern Africa in the fourth century, utilized the services of stenographers, there seems to be no doubt. Examples along this line might fill a volume. How much of our present science may be lost and when it will be found I can not say.

I wish to hint at another line of thought awakened by these experiences and leave it for those who care to do so to develop. A great authority, like Taylor, may teach error as well as truth, and the greater the weight given to his teachings the greater harm will his error do. Grains of error in mountains of truth are errors still. In science at least, there must be no Pope, no *Ipse dixits*. I must not forget that Pliny, nineteen centuries ago, called attention to the harm that might come from a great author's acceptance of a false statement.

The Hall and Millard cases did much of good, besides that which I have already mentioned. They led to the legal interdiction of arsenical embalming fluids, to more care on the part of druggists in dispensing poisons, and to the better protection of patients by their physicians.

THE CARVETH CASE

A man in Hastings, Michigan, in attempting to poison his wife by administering strychnia, insisted on calling in a notorious quack from a city near by. The husband asserted that none of the Hastings doctors were competent to treat his wife. He employed an ignorant woman to take care of the sick wife. Indeed this was before a trained nurse had invaded that community. After a severe spasm, his wife, without her husband's consent, sent for the old doctor who had administered to her ills since early girlhood. The wise old doctor immediately recognized the symptoms of poisoning with strychnia and reported to the prosecutor. Then the two set a trap for the suspected husband. The doctor prepared a glass of medicine, perfectly harmless, emphasized its potency and gave strict orders that no dose of it should be administered until the clock struck a certain hour. A few minutes before this time the doctor dropped in, but found that he had forgotten his thermometer, stethoscope or something else. He sent the husband to his office to bring the article. During his absence the doctor emptied the contents of the prepared glass into a bottle and put another glass of water by the bedside. He took the bottle to the prosecuting attorney, who sent it immediately to me. The husband, growing more impatient because the symptoms did not develop faster, put more and more strychnia into the glass. Indeed the contents of the last glass which the doctor emptied into his bottle contained undissolved crystals of the alkaloid. I reported my findings to the prosecutor over the telephone as fast as the tests were made, and it will be understood by any chemist that no great time was required. The husband was arrested, tried and sentenced while his intended victim recovered.

Years afterward, during an outbreak of typhoid

fever in the state penitentiary, I was examining one of the patients, when looking into my face, he said: "You are the man who sent me here." "No," I said, "it was not I, but wise Doctor Woodmansee."

.   THE HUGHES CASE   .

The scene of this trial was also in Hastings, Michigan. In the country near that village, in a house quite away from a frequently traveled road, there lived an old man, who was reputed to be a miser, but if he ever had any money to hoard no one ever found it. There was in the same neighborhood a ne'er-do-well by the name of Hughes, who was a jack of all trades and a master of none. One morning, according to Hughes' story, he went to the home of the recluse. Finding the door slightly ajar he pushed against it and in this way entered. He saw the old man stretched on the floor with his skull crushed and a bloody ax lying by his side. The body was quite rigid and one foot against the door accounted for the resistance Hughes had met with in trying to open it. The marks showed that in the opening of the door the whole body had been moved along the floor. It developed that Hughes had spent the day before in painting the window blinds of a farmer's house in the vicinity. The paint was green. There was a smear of green paint near the end of the ax helve where the left hand would come in contact with it in wielding the weapon. The ax and a piece of the blind were brought me and I was asked to compare the paints on the two. This I did by microchemical methods.

On the stand I testified that the paints had the same composition, the same adulteration, and that the granules were of the same size, showing the probability that they were ground in the same mill. I had informed the prosecutor that I had studied thirty other samples of green paint found in neighboring places and that all agreed in the particulars mentioned above. I had not regarded my testimony as of importance. It was a plain statement of fact, but when taken with the finding in the thirty other samples, this fact would be insignificant. I sat in the witness chair and heard the prosecutor beating into the heads of the jury, into the consciousness of the court and into the hearts of the crowded room: "These two paints, one from the blind Hughes had painted and one from the ax helve he had held when he committed the murderous deed, were one and the same in composition, in adulteration and in size of granule." I watched the faces about me and I began to realize that my testimony which I had not considered of importance was deciding the fate of the accused. At this stage I allayed my fear and consoled myself by the thought that the cross-examination would relieve my direct testimony of the exaggerated significance being attached to it. The chief attorney for the defense had more than a local reputation as a criminal lawyer and to him I confidently looked for relief. It was with pleasure that I heard the prosecutor say: "Take the witness." To my horror I was asked a few irrelevant questions; then, "That's all." I sat rooted in the chair. The defense repeated, "That's all." The prosecutor said, "That's all, Doctor." Still I sat benumbed. The judge leaned forward and gently said: "Doctor, do you understand that they are through with you?" Then my tongue was loosened and turning to the judge I said: "Your Honor, may I make a statement before I leave the stand?" Then I told of the examination of thirty other samples of paints sold in that county. However, even this did not apparently interest the defense. The prosecutor was, I suppose, justly furious but had no more questions. Hughes was convicted but served only a short time when he was pardoned. I do not know how much weight was given to my testimony by either judge or jury. Possibly it was not a determining factor in the verdict and that I magnified its effect. Had it been a civil case involving only property loss, I would have kept silent, leaving the lawyer to protect his client as is his duty, but in a murder case I could not do so. Whether my action lay within the legal limit allowed an expert witness I do not know. What the judge, a most esteemed personal friend, thought of it, I never learned. It certainly did not help Hughes in the verdict, though it may have done so in the pardon. This is not the only time when, as a witness, I have thrown a helping line to the other side, generally more adroitly; sometimes it has been eagerly seized, while in other instances it has been wholly disregarded or thrown back with a snarl.

A BROKEN SKULL OR MORPHIN?

In a flourishing city beyond the Missouri River there lived, some thirty years or more ago, in a cottage set back from the street and partly hidden by cedars, a man and his wife. Fortunately there were no children. This pair did not live in harmony. Frequent altercations, at times limited to epithets, at others emphasized by blows, reached the ever open ears of the neighborhood. All sympathy was with the meek and somewhat subservient husband. The wife excelled in the violence of her epithets and the husband could not conceal all evidence of her physical dexterity and superiority. In short he was so plainly the under dog in the fight that he won the individual and collective pity of all who knew the pair. The neighbors believed that there was nothing too mean for the wife to do. In this state of affairs a justly prominent physician in the city was called to the cottage in the dawn of an early morning. He found the husband in bed in a state of coma with pupils contracted to pin points and attended only by his sorrowing spouse. Soon after the physician's coming the man died. The stertorous breathing and the contracted pupils quite naturally suggested morphin poisoning. In communities like this death throws open the doors to both enemies and friends, and the house and small front yard were soon filled with the former, for of friends the wife had none. After listening to the stories whispered in his ear by the visitors, the suggestion of morphin poisoning was accepted by the doctor as a certainty, and he so reported to the prosecutor. The wife was put under arrest and the stomach of the dead man removed and sent to me. I was instructed to test for morphin and informed that further toxicological search would be superfluous. This seemed reasonable. The man had been seen in apparent health on his way home the evening before. There were no symptoms of gastro-intestinal irritation or strychnia poisoning, and there was the doctor's report of coma and contracted pupils. I went to work in my search for morphin thinking that I had an easy task before me. There was no question of the interference of putrefactive bodies because there had been no putrefaction. I expected to see the color tests develop one by one in all perfection, but they did not come. I was compelled to send in a negative report. A few days later the prosecutor himself found me in my laboratory; he said that I was incompetent; I admitted that I had doubts about my own competency and that he might be right. He went away bearing the organ, but slightly reduced by my investigation, and saying that he would take it to a *real* toxicologist. This he did. For some days, Professor Haines of Chicago searched for morphin; then he made a negative report and like myself he was denominated an incompetent. At last the prosecutor did find a chemist who was competent and who did report the presence of morphin in the now much curtailed organ.

The case came to trial and the prosecution rested without Dr. Haines or me appearing. The leading counsel for the defense concluded that he would like to ascertain what we knew about the case; therefore he came to Ann Arbor by the fastest train. I declined to give him any information, invited him to dinner and informed him that the next train for the West was due at 10:40. Did I do right? I have often asked myself this question, and not being able to obtain a satisfactory answer from this source I carried it to a learned legal friend. He said that the defense should have put the prosecutor on the stand and found out from him what part Haines and I had in the matter. Be this as it may, it does not interrupt my story.

The wife was convicted and sentenced; some years elapsed. A negro arrested for some other crime confessed that he, in the pay of the wife, had killed the man. Hidden in the cedars in the front yard, he had struck the man across the head with an iron crowbar, and he said that he had assisted the wife in carrying the body into the house and placing it in the bed. The man's body was resurrected and a fractured skull was found to corroborate the negro's confession. I might draw two morals from this story. First, stertorous breathing and contracted pupils do not always justify a diagnosis of morphin poisoning; second, in a medico-legal post-mortem examination every part of the body should be thoroughly inspected.

A NAMELESS CASE

In a western state some years ago an irregular practitioner of medicine was accused of killing his wife after obtaining a heavy insurance on her life. In order to save the state the cost of investigation the prosecutor turned over the body of the woman to the insurance company for autopsy and chemical examination. An unknown chemist reported morphin, and the man was tried for killing his wife by the administration of this poison. After a somewhat prolonged investigation of the case I was thoroughly convinced that the man had not killed his wife by giving her morphin, but I was not sure that he had not killed her by other means. I consented to go on the stand on behalf of the defense, provided questions on direct examination should be limited to the validity of the tests for morphin, submitted by the prosecution. The defendant was acquitted.

A CONNECTICUT CASE

A few years ago Mr. Alcorn, state attorney, and Doctor Wolff, a toxicologist and chemist, both of Hartford, Connecticut, consulted with me concerning a prospective murder case likely to come within the jurisdiction of the former. A Mrs. Andrews had managed an old folk's home at Windsor, Connecticut, for many years. She had borne a good reputation in the community; had met her financial obligations promptly and had never been accused of cruelty to her wards. She accepted people by the month, by the year, or after a certain age for life. In the last mentioned instances she demanded a fixed price to be paid on entering the institution. Finally, someone called attention to the fact that while those inmates who paid by installments showed no remarkable mortality, those who paid up for life on entering did not live long. This talk spread and the state attorney felt that he must move in the matter. He had known Mrs. Andrews for many years and had no personal prejudice against her; on the other hand, he was disinclined to believe the insinuations as to her character. We decided to proceed in an ideal way, preserving her honor so far as possible, and at the same time securing justice for all. The prosecutor arrested the woman, gave ample time for her to secure legal advice, and announced that on a certain day five of the bodies would be resurrected. The autopsies would be conducted legally and each organ would be divided into three parts, one to be turned over to the state chemist, Doctor Wolff, one to a chemist selected by the defendant, and the third to me. The defendant secured able attorneys and her experts were Professor Underhill of Yale, Professor Benedict of Cornell, and Doctor Schultze, expert for the prosecuting attorney of New York City.   There was no dispute between the chemists about the presence of poison in the bodies.   The chief contest centered on one of the bodies in which large quantities of arsenic were found.   The embalming fluid contained no arsenic. The experts for the defense were inclined to hold that there had been a mistake, as in a case I have already reported and referred to on page 282 and that an arsenical embalming fluid had actually been employed. They claimed that the large quantities found in the liver and other organs could not have reached these tissues through the stomach during life.   In this they were undoubtedly right, but they could not deny that diffusion after death had gone on.   Moreover, in this case it was only necessary to examine a drop of the almost clear contents of the stomach under the microscope in order to see the most perfect crystals of arsenic trioxid.   The experts for the defense admitted that these could not come from a solution of arsenite of sodium or potassium injected as an embalming fluid.   In short, the evidence was plain that the poison had gone into the stomach as white arsenic.   The defendant was found guilty and sentenced to death.   The Supreme Court found some error and ordered a new trial.   The second trial had not proceeded far before the woman changed her plea to guilty and threw herself on the mercy of the court.   She was then sentenced for life.

An amusing incident connected with the first trial of this case may be related.   I never felt altogether comfortable in uniform.   The high tight collar and the heavy shoes irritated me, and I cast them off at every opportunity, sometimes in violation of the rules and regulations. At Siboney, in the Cuban campaign, with other medical officers I stood almost continuously at the operating table from Friday evening until the following Wednesday morning, but during most of this time I wore only my pajamas. A wicked correspondent snapped me in this apparel and sent the photograph to his paper.

When the telegraphic call came to me in Washington to come to Hartford, I exchanged my khaki for a Palm Beach suit and the next morning I was in the witness chair. On cross-examination the lawyer tried to embarrass me by inquiring why I was not in uniform. This did not worry me but he was not content and finally drew from me the admission that I was absent from my post in Washington without leave. Of course he threatened to report both of my violations of the rules and regulations. Even this failed to embarrass me. I was excused from the witness chair about noon. I hastened to New York and secured a lower berth on the midnight train for Washington. About ten P. M. I was in my berth. I found that I could not lower the shade over the rear window, but as the night was hot I pronounced this a happy incident. I hung my trousers by the rear window. When the train pulled through the tunnel there was a rush of air through my berth. This awakened me sufficiently to thank heaven for the breeze and to pull the sheet up over me. The next thing I knew the train was standing in the Washington station and the porter was vigorously trying to bring me to consciousness. When I opened my eyes I saw the open rear window without screen and I realized that the breeze, for which I had been thankful, had carried away my trousers. I tried to be severe with the porter for neglecting the screen. The poor negro disappeared but was soon back with a pair of his trousers but I could not get in them. I gave him a ten dollar bill, told him to take a taxi, go down town and bring me a pair forty-two inches about the waist, and without regard to length, texture or color. In an unbelievably short time he was back with a nondescript pair in which I encased my nether extremities. I did not lose my equanimity until I stood on the platform and found many inquiring eyes turned upon me. I made a rush through the gate and there it seemed every officer in the United States Army stood singly and in groups. With downcast eyes I fled through them. I was near the last door on my way to the taxi stand when I faced the Chief of Staff, in whose presence I had breakfasted, lunched and dined daily for three months. Again, thank heaven! While his eyes were on me his mind was on bigger things as was proper. Hidden in a taxi I drove to the ladies' entrance at the Army and Navy Club, which I knew would be untenanted at that early hour. Soon I was in my room on the second floor and donning with joy my regimentals. A few minutes later I was breakfasting with my comrades. The story of my early morning escapade was too good to keep. No one enjoyed it more than General Gorgas, who in speech made all kinds of threats of dire punishments, but whose eyes belied his tongue. Our British liaison officer, Colonel Goodwin, skilled in pen and ink drawing, made a recognizable sketch which he labeled: "A Highland

Officer Reaches Washington." This hung on the wall of the club for some days and is now in our possession. After this experience I took more kindly to khaki.

THE BUCHANAN CASE

I served as an expert in three important murder trials in New York City, in the first for the defense and in the others for the prosecution.

Buchanan was charged with poisoning his wife by the administration of capsules containing morphin and atropin. The body had been in the grave many months before the tests were made. The chemical experts for the prosecution were Doctors Witthaus and Doremus, Jr., while those for the defense were Doctor Wolff of Hartford, Connecticut, and I. Besides the chemist nearly every medical specialty played a part in the prolonged procedure. The prosecution was conducted by De Lancy Nicoll and the defense by Charles Brooke. These were among the great criminal lawyers of New York City of that time. The judge was Recorder Smyth and I wish to say that he was a terror to evil-doers. He was always alert, not only listening to what was said, but seeing how it was said. Frequently he would interrupt an examination and take a hand in it himself. His questions admitted no equivocation. Nothwithstanding the uprightness and strength of the bench and the excellence of the bar the trial became a most sensational affair. The experts became absorbed in the accuracy of the color tests for morphin in amylic alcohol extracts from putrefying organs. Shortly before there had been a very sensational trial involving the same questions in

Portugal. In the Portugal case nearly every recognized toxicologist in Europe had become involved, and the weight of expert evidence was that these tests under these conditions were uncertain and non-dependable. In the New York case the experts for the prosecution had relied wholly upon these tests, the accuracy of which was questioned by the defense.

Some one—I do not remember who—suggested that a demonstration be made before the jury. The judge and I retired to his room. I had two porcelain dishes containing putrefactive substances. To one of these a small amount of morphin was added. The judge marked the one to which the morphin had been added and gave the dishes to the experts for the prosecution. The tests were applied and resulted in their locating the morphin in the wrong dish. Besides this, atropin had been reported because a drop of a solution of the extract of the putrefying tissues dilated the pupil of a cat's eye, but the one who made this test gave the wrong direction to the long axis of the cat's pupil. There were other breaks, some on one side, some on the other.

To me, and I have no doubt to the other experts, the trial became a most regrettable affair. It made a break in the friendship between Professor Witthaus and myself, which lasted for some years, but which, I am glad to say, was at least partially repaired before his death. Buchanan was convicted and finally executed. I declined to sign a petition for clemency in his case because I was not convinced about his guilt or innocence.

Only older toxicologists can appreciate the trouble we had in distinguishing between the color reactions of certain alkaloids and those induced by unknown putrefactive bodies. For a short time the work of Selmi and others made us quite doubtful about the validity of some of our alkaloidal tests. The amylic alcohol of that time was notoriously impure. There is no longer trouble in this particular. Fortunately science clears away the fogs which it raises. They are only temporary mists which for a time obscure our vision. Sooner or later the rising sun enables us to see clearly. The scientist is sometimes bewildered by his own observations, but ultimately he or some successor lifts the veil.

In the first century Seneca wrote: "Nature does not disclose her mysteries in a moment. We think ourselves initiated; we stand but at her portals. These secrets open not promiscuously nor to every comer; they are remote of access; enshrined in the inner sanctuary."

THE FLEMING CASE

A Mrs. Fleming could come into the possession of a large fortune only after the death of her mother; neither could the mother enjoy it, since she had already dissipated her part, while the residue was to go to her children only after her death. Under this state of affairs both mother and daughter lived in comparative poverty. The mother persisted in living, showing no inclination to suicide. One day the daughter, it was claimed by the prosecution, prepared a clam broth for her mother. The mother ate and after a few hours died. The daughter was charged with murder.

The case was tried before Judge Goff. John McIntyre, most capable, conducted the prosecution and Charles Brooke, the defense. The chief experts for the state were Valentine Mott, Jr., a young German by the name of Scheele, and I. I do not remember the names of the experts for the defense. At any rate they were not required to play an important part in the trial. In this case I saw one of the most dramatic exhibits I ever witnessed in a courtroom. It was so thrilling that it practically determined the fate of the defendant and gave her an acquittal. My version of this story is in some respects so different from that told by my old friend, Doctor Allen McLane Hamilton, in his admirable volume entitled *Recollections of an Alienist,* that I must go into some detail. Hamilton says: "A German expert, of apparent slight experience and reputation, testified that he had found a certain poison in the body of the deceased, and was then pinned down to admit that his operations consumed an impossibly short time. The defense knew that this was doubtful, so they made him enumerate all his reactions and the way they were obtained; and without suspecting the drift of the questions he proceeded to entangle and contradict the testimony he had given when he first went on the stand. It really ought to have taken many days to perform all these investigations, instead of the few hours he claimed. Contradictions of this kind are dangerous in poisoning cases. The jury acquitted the prisoner."

In a general way Doctor Hamilton's statements are in harmony with my memory, but he does not touch upon the critical and dramatic point.

Walter Scheele, a handsome young German, a recent pupil of some of the most renowned German specialists in toxicology, had recently come to New York, armed with letters of introduction from his masters. He was prepossessing in manner, and soon after his arrival presented his letters to Doctor Mott, who at the time was examining the remains of the defendant's mother. Impressed by his bearing and by the letters he bore, Doctor Mott asked the prosecutor to employ Scheele as an assistant in the case. This was done and Scheele checked up on Mott's findings. How honestly or dishonestly he did this service I do not know. I never saw Scheele until the trial had begun. Doctor Mott had given his testimony in a masterly and scientific way. Then Scheele was put on the stand to confirm Mott. Scheele went through his direct examination with credit. Brooke, one of the shrewdest cross-examiners I ever knew, took the witness in hand, asked him if he had not recently joined a certain Turnverein and was answered in the affirmative. Then he was asked if, at a recent meeting of that society, he had not openly boasted of his employment as an expert in the coming trial and had stated that he held the key to the prisoner's fate. This Scheele vehemently denied.

Then came the climax. Member after member of the society took the witness chair, and when the procession ceased Scheele stood before the court a discredited man, guilty of perjury. If any eyes of either pity or hatred had rested on the accused they were now turned upon the handsome young German. My turn for the witness chair followed this most surprising and astounding dénouement. I never functioned as an expert under such depressing circumstances and it took all the nerve I could command to answer the questions. I dimly heard the prosecutor as he turned to Brooke and said: "Take the witness." Then, I saw Brooke stand up and turn to me a most kindly face as he said: "The defense does not desire to cross-examine this witness; it admits the truth of all his answers and regards him as a true scientist," or words to this effect. This was of course most gratifying to me, but it carried venom for the poor broken German by implication.

Of course all this was in the newspapers and it meant worse than death to Scheele. He could never hope to go on the witness stand again as an expert. He sought work even in menial fields. He left New York and found a precarious living in a Baltimore drug store. For years I lost all sight of him. During the World War his name again appeared in the newspapers as one of the German conspirators engaged in the attempt to dynamite the Welland Canal; but I have no personal knowledge of this.

THE WAITE CASE

A young man, whom, so far as I know, I never saw until we faced each other in the criminal court of New York, he in the prisoner's box, and I in the witness box, graduated in the Dental School of the University of Michigan, married a daughter of a wealthy citizen of Grand Rapids and took an expensive apartment on Riverside Drive, New York City. On the death of her parents the wife would inherit a large fortune, but the husband was impatient and apparently decided not to await the slow moving steps of nature. He opened an office in one of the palatial buildings downtown and posted his professional shingle on the door of his attractive waiting room. Everything except the doctor's practise moved along rapidly and smoothly. The father and mother of the wife were insistently invited to make a visit to the New York home of their children, to see how happily they were living and how prosperously the new son-in-law was winning practise. The simple old people went, saw and were pleased with the demonstration. They opened wide their purse in the purchase of costly furniture and adornments. They were rejoiced that their daughter had selected a husband so wisely. After a short illness the mother died but she was advanced in years and no suspicion was aroused. The father was persuaded to prolong his visit, and where could he expect to find more consolation in his bereavement than in the home of his daughter? Soon he followed his wife. Still there seems to have been no suspicion awakened by the physician in attendance or by the undertaker. Both bodies had been embalmed and sent to Grand Rapids for burial. The old friends in the smaller city began to ask questions. The family pastor, Reverend Wishart, and the family physician, Doctor Schurz, became detectives and spent some time in this capacity in the metropolis. I was called upon to make an examination of the remains of the father. I found arsenic in more than fatal quantities. The district attorney of New York, Mr. Swann, took charge. Professor Benedict of Cornell, and Doctor Schultze, city pathologist and toxicologist, confirmed my findings. The proceedings moved with almost English smoothness and swiftness, and Doctor Waite went to the death chair.

CIVIL LITIGATION

Happily my services as a medical expert have not been confined to criminal cases but have extended into the more pleasing fields of civil litigation. Some twenty or more years ago there was a great discussion, and honest difference of opinion, concerning the poisonous or otherwise harmful action of certain preservatives used in foods and beverages. There were many royal battles along this line before certain states first, and Congress later, enacted the pure food law. In some of these contests I had the pleasure of participating, sometimes being victorious and at others meeting with defeat.

I was employed by the food and dairy commissioner of Pennsylvania in his endeavor to check the use of sulphites in improving the appearance of stale and decomposed meats. The meat men of Philadelphia brought over from Berlin Professor Liebreich to assist in their defense. The hearings were in Philadelphia and Reading, though the chief contest was in the former city. Liebreich had to admit that his own country, Germany, forbade the employment of these chemicals, but he said that the prohibition in that country was for political reasons and was not justified on sanitary grounds. Furthermore, he granted that he would not have meat thus sophisticated on his own table, but he held that the use of this preservative permitted the sale of cheap meat and thus benefited the poor since the sulphite was in no way detrimental to health. We, for the prosecution, held that sulphites should not be added to meats for two reasons: (1) Such addition enables the butcher to sell as good meat that which should have gone into the waste can; (2) the sulphites are in and of themselves harmful.

As it turned out, the testimony of the distinguished German scientist did not help his clients. Indeed, it made the jury think quite properly that the poor man should not eat that which the rich discarded.

Probably the biggest and most interesting contest was concerning the use of a limited amount of benzoate of soda in catsup and fruit syrups. The State Druggist Association of Pennsylvania had a law framed which permitted the employment of one-tenth of one per cent. of this substance, and pronounced any addition of more than this, or the addition of any other substances, illegal. This bill was passed by the legislature, but the Governor threatened a veto. I had a long argument with him. He was immovable and said that if the bill was brought to him for his signature, as it must be before it could become a law, he would certainly veto it. He then recommended that the bill be withdrawn and suggested that another be prepared, forbidding the use of as many substances and whatever substances we might desire to prohibit but omitting any reference to benzoate of soda. I tried to show him that such a bill would permit the use of any substance not specified in it and would place no limit on the amount of benzoate of soda added. The Governor was firm and asserted that while he was Governor no bill permitting the use of any food preservative should become a law in his state.

There was a big contest on this subject in Indiana and minor ones in other states. Those who opposed the admission of this limited amount of benzoate of soda had to admit that in every dish of cranberries one eats he gets a larger amount than we proposed, but one of these insisted that God made a mistake when he put benzoate of soda in cranberries. This fight finally went to Congress and wisely the matter was referred to a referee board of distinguished chemists and we may still find on a bottle of catsup that it contains one-tenth of one per cent. of benzoate of soda. So far as I know there is no evidence that either the morbidity or mortality rate has been increased by the use of this preservative.

There is an impression that the pure food law was conceived, developed and first brought into existence by Congress. This is a mistake; these laws were in force in several states before they were enacted into a national law by Congress in 1906. One of the early states to move in this matter was North Dakota under the leadership of the late Professor Ladd who subsequently became a United States senator.

The contest concerning the addition of saccharine to foods continues in a desultory way. While I am sure that saccharine in the quantities used in foods is not poisonous, I do not believe that it should supplant sugar in the sweetening of commercial foods. When a man eats a sweet food he assumes that he is getting sugar, which has a high food value, and not saccharine, which has none.

In a spirited contest in Ohio the offending substance was a roasted coffee bean which was coated with white of egg. This fact was plainly stated on the label, and the claim was made that this manipulation tended to retain the flavor of the bean. Professor Harvey W. Wiley, at that time the head of the Bureau of Chemistry of the United States Department of Agriculture, and I contended that this was not an adulteration. I testified that in my old Missouri home this trick of coating the roasting coffee bean with the white of egg and for the same alleged reason was practised. This brought a laugh from my opponents who suggested that I belonged to a prehistoric age.

There was a great array of experts in the coca-cola

case tried in Chattanooga, Tennessee, under Judge Sanford, now of the United States Supreme Court. The question was the supposed poisonous action of caffein, the active principle of coffee. One dropping into the courtroom would suppose that a course of lectures in physiological chemistry was being given. A chart showing the chemical constitution of caffein and the xanthin bases formed in the human body, taken largely from one of my books, hung near the witness box, and the jury, consisting in part at least of mountaineers, must have been amused, if not instructed. Each expert brought his qualifications down to the smallest limit, and having so qualified he was not permitted to stray beyond bounds. All lived in the excellent hotel near by. Court hours were short and there are many beautiful rides about the city. I renewed my acquaintance with Chickamauga Park under aspects wholly different from those of 1898. Little did I suspect that in 1917-18 I would again visit this spot as a soldier; again see it as a tented field and again seek relief for the sick and dying soldiers.

Our wives were with us, and we spent a month under these pleasant surroundings. I had a chance for a friendly wrestle with Doctor Wiley who led the government champions. I crossed swords with some of my old students and admired the skill with which they handled their blades. I fought side by side with others and had equal pride in their dexterity. There was a glorious breaking of skulls, and I am sure that we all left this goodly company hoping that a coca-cola trial would be established as an annual event. The assault against the use of coffee has not yet found its Volstead and opportunity awaits our successors.

In the early nineties an English syndicate operated a silver mine somewhere in the Rocky Mountians. The ore was crushed and deposited in a large reservoir. The heavier and valuable parts subsided. The supernatant fluid was passed into a second reservoir where further subsidence occurred and from this the lighter part emptied into a mountain stream, honored by being designated as a river and finding a place on the map of the region. The water from the reservoirs, which had been deflected from the river higher up, was returned to that channel when it had served its purpose. It made up one-tenth or more of the volume of the river as it continued its descent. In the valley below, the waters of the river were spread out over the surface of the pastures on which thousands of cattle fed. For a year or two there had been a high death rate among these animals, which the owners could not account for. Suspecting that the water bore a poison, the cattle men began suit against the owners of the mine. Evidently the former were not themselves wholly convinced that the epidemic among the cattle was due to the water and they were slow in pressing their suit. The owners of the mine consulted me. I laughed at the idea that the water used for irrigating the valley could be implicated. I talked widely if not wisely about anthrax, black-leg and other diseases that afflict horned quadrupeds, but I undertook to make an analysis of the water as it returned from the second reservoir to its normal channel. To my surprise I found in each gallon of this water half a grain of arsenic and a slightly larger quantity of antimony. The owners of the mine were greatly agitated, and I greatly humiliated. Fortunately these poisons were not in solution; they were in suspension. A cheap filter was constructed. The water passed rapidly through but the poisons were held. A few months later chemists for the cattle owners analyzed the water and found it free from poison. The epidemic among the cattle did not reappear the next summer and the suit was dropped.

For many years I was almost continuously employed as scientific adviser in some enterprise. In the early eighties I assisted the owner of several paper mills in the construction of a lead-lined tower for the manufacture of sulphurous acid used in the preparation of wood pulp. The result was not artistic but it served the purpose. One manufacturer wished to raise his dam. This necessitated the overflow of a considerable area which he owned. The neighbors objected on the claim that increasing the depth of the water and keeping the ground constantly covered would favor the spread of malaria. I held that these changes would tend to lessen malaria. It must be remembered that at that time (1883) we knew nothing about the plasmodium, and the demonstration that the mosquito is the vector in this disease was a long way in the future. The best-supported belief was that malaria is due to emanations or miasms arising from stagnant water. My contention was that deepening the water and keeping the marshy area covered would lessen the malaria. In this opinion I had the support of Colonel Charles Smart, U. S. A., and Doctor Irving Watson of New Hampshire who testified in the case. The dam was raised, and there is no evidence that there was any increase in malaria.

One of my earliest papers on a sanitary subject was on the purification of water by filtration through the soil. I showed experimentally, using urine for pollution and estimation of urea as the measure, that purification by this process had been over-estimated. This awakened wide discussion. Nearly every home in rural Michigan at that time relied upon a small charcoal filter for its drinking water. It was believed that the filthiest waters poured into these receptacles were satisfactorily purified in passing through the small layer of sand and charcoal. Doctor Prescott and I took up this matter and showed that this faith was not justified. We were assailed by the manufacturers of the filters and, what was more difficult, had to face the prejudice of those who had long used them. However, charcoal household filters were slowly replaced by porcelain and stone ones, and for a time by the practise of drinking only boiled water. At that time the drinking water throughout the smaller cities, villages and rural districts was obtained mostly from shallow wells or cisterns in close proximity to privy vaults, all in the same gravel bed. Many contentions and some lawsuits grew out of these questions. Someone found "in a book" a statement that all the water that reaches a well is that which falls as rain within a circle the radius of which is the depth of the well and the center of which is the mouth of the well. On this foolish dictum we lost our first case involving this question, notwithstanding the fact that my colleague, Professor John Langley, had demonstrated its fallacy by mathematical computation and by practical tests showing the diffusion of lithium salts through the soil. The well water, having been shown by spectroscopic examination to be free from lithium, soluble salts of this metal were deposited in the soil many rods distant from the well and were found to appear in the well water subsequently.

In one instance involving the water supply of a place

of some five thousand inhabitants, the question was whether the water in the city wells came from a polluted lake or from the adjacent hills. The amount of sodium chlorid in the water of the wells and in that of the lake was determined by chemists employed by the contestants. As a neutral I made the same determinations. The three findings agreed to a decimal point; then fifty barrels of salt were dumped into the lake. A repetition of the analyses showed conclusively the source of the water in the city wells. Demonstrations of this kind generally satisfied both parties. At least they gave the court definite and unbiased information. I participated in many of these contentions as a member of the State Board of Health and without remuneration. I was glad to have this relief from the suspicion of personal interest in the questions involved.

Later, along with these chemical studies and finally overwhelming them, came the more difficult and complicated questions of bacterial contamination of foods and drinks, and thus I was drawn from the exclusive field of sanitary chemistry to the much broader one of bacteriology. I had no choice in this matter. I wish to testify that in my own experience in public health matters, experimental work began in chemistry. For years my studies on milk supplies were confined to determinations of solids, fats, proteins and carbohydrates. We, or at least I, knew nothing about the bacterial contents of these important foods. I went to the dairies and took samples; I followed the milk man as he distributed the lacteal fluid and took samples from his wagon; then I induced students to purloin glasses of milk from the boarding house tables. Eagerly my students determined the solid contents of the successive samples under my directions. It is needless to say that these analyses showed quite constantly a decrease in total solids. As early as 1877, G. G. Groff and I made similar but more superficial studies of the milk supply of Philadelphia, depending largely upon observations, questions and the occasional use of a lactometer. The good old Quaker dairyman in Chester County honestly believed that the milk as it came from his Holsteins was too rich for city people to drink. He added water and shipped to the wholesale dealer; having the same belief, even if of different faith, he added water and sold it to the retailer. Of course, it could not be expected that the last mentioned would break the rule. We concluded that an average sample of milk increased in volume about thirty per cent. from the time it left the udder of the cow until it reached the lips of the baby.

Then there came a short time when adulterants and preservatives in milk were burning questions and the basis of some lawsuits. It was said that the milkman added bicarbonate of soda to raise the specific gravity which he had lowered by the addition of water. I was never able to confirm this report. In one sample I did find powdered carbonate of lime, but this quickly subsided and could not have been widely employed. This recalls an amusing incident: A woman brought me a sample of well water, stating that after being boiled for a while it deposited a chalky substance which she believed to be arsenic dumped into her new well by a vicious neighbor. I had difficulty in convincing her that the deposit was carbonate of lime which became insoluble when the carbonic acid gas was driven off by the heat.

Salicylate of soda is said to have been used as a milk

preservative; I never found it. The same is true of borax and boric acid. I did at one time favor permission to use borax in exported butter, and I believe that the English laws still permit it. Formaldehyde was for a short time widely used as a milk preservative, and I participated in some of the cases which came before the courts. In this connection I have a good joke upon myself. Having decided to determine definitely the question of the poisonous action of formaldehyde in the quantities employed as a preservative in milk, I arranged my guinea pigs in batches: number one had nothing but milk, with no preservative; number two had only milk to which one part of formaldehyde in ten thousand had been added; number three had one part in twenty-five thousand; number four had one part in fifty thousand. To my bewilderment all died mostly between twenty and thirty days after beginning the experiment. The controls died quite as promptly as those receiving formaldehyde. Had I been a scientist like Pasteur, I would have seen that I had a problem before me and would have proceeded to interrogate, but I did not. Then, I missed the opportunity of discovering experimental scurvy. I had opened the door and a voice had kindly bidden me enter, but I did not hear it, or at least did not heed it.

This is not the only time I have been deaf to the bidding of science. We bought from a firm manufacturing diphtheria antitoxin five hundred guinea pigs for a small price because the firm had found that animals that had received one injection of horse serum died with promptness on a second injection of the same substance, after manifesting most striking symptoms. Since then I have taken off my hat with great respect to Theobald Smith who first described this phenomenon and to Richet, who gave it the euphonious but inappropriate name of anaphylaxis. Nature hangs out many signals, which mean "come and learn of me," but man is slow to see. For untold centuries clouds flashed such signals, but it remained, according to accepted belief at least, for Benjamin Franklin to respond with his kite. Many are called; but few respond. Time has kept a diary of her own acts and has deposited her records in the solid rocks, in fossils, in buried forests and elsewhere, and still there are those in this, the twentieth century, who assert that it is wicked to read and interpret these records.

During the first years of my medical practise in Ann Arbor my best paymaster was typhoid fever. Each home in the village had a cistern or a shallow well located in a gravel bed with a privy vault nearby. The contents of the vault leached into the water supply and the people drank an extract of their own alvine discharges. One well was the source of considerable revenue to the doctors. It was used not only by the family of its owner, but he generously invited his neighbors and friends to share his blessing. The health officer condemned the well, but this did not diminish the use of its water. He removed the pump for which kindly office he received only curses and experienced a loss in his clientele. Finally he and I became politicians. I was elected to the Board of Aldermen and Ann Arbor introduced a public water supply and slowly the morbidity and mortality from typhoid fever fell. This experience in Ann Arbor was only one of many similar ones in small cities and villages, and only a miniature of what took place in our larger cities. In this country the term "politician" has become one of reproach and there are many good reasons which I will not attempt to enumerate why this is justified. But in my opinion the genus politician can be divided into two classes—the good and the bad. The man who induces the masses, even against their inclination, to do that which results in their own betterment belongs to the good class and performs one of the highest functions of citizenship. How far he may employ political methods in the accomplishment of his purpose depends upon the circumstances under which he works, his own conscience and judgment. The bad politician is one who is not working for the betterment of the people, but for party or personal aggrandizement. Among the good politicians in sanitary betterment I have known I give the names among the dead of Henry B. Baker of Michigan, Herman Biggs of New York and Jerome Cochrane of Alabama. This list might be greatly lengthened, and I may state that they had many peers in their time and have left many worthy followers.

My work as a public health expert extended rapidly. During the twenty years between 1880 and 1900, epidemics large and small, of typhoid fever, diphtheria and scarlet fever in the Northwest were frequent, while the occasional appearance of cerebrospinal meningitis and poliomyelitis caused even more alarm. Not a city taking its water supply from the Great Lakes from Duluth to Buffalo, on the American side at least, escaped typhoid fever. A like fate disturbed many communities on small lakes and on the rivers. I served as expert adviser in the great outbreaks of this disease in the nineties at Grand Forks, North Dakota, at the Sault, at Saint Clair, and in lesser epidemics. I made frequent examinations of the water supplies at Chicago, Omaha and elsewhere. My contest with this disease culminated in the work of the Typhoid Commission in 1898 which I discuss in another chapter. If there is anything in the epidemiology of this disease which I have failed to see, and I am sure that there is much, it has been because I have been too blind to see.

These experiences in the field should have made me a better teacher of the branch then scheduled under the all inclusive designation of "hygiene." Whether they did so or not I can not say. I only know that the lecture hours were too short for me, however tiresome they may have been to my students. My lectures probably took on too much the nature of the "relation of personal experiences." In fact one of my colleagues thus designated them, not inaptly.

CHAPTER X

AFTER the sinking of the *Maine* in the harbor at Havana, the proclamation of war against Spain, and the call for volunteers, I was anxious to enlist; but having a wife and five children dependent upon me, I could not conscientiously do so. There was quite an outbreak of enthusiasm for enlistment among the students of the University of Michigan. President Angell was then in Constantinople as United States Ambassador to Turkey, and President Hutchins, who later became permanent President, was acting in that capacity. One day he came to me and said that the students were all astir about the war, wanted to hold a mass meeting with speeches, and might be stampeded into enlistment. He advised that the mass meeting be permitted, that representatives of the students be invited to talk, and that the older and wiser members of the Faculty pour the oil of caution upon the troubled waters of youth. As dean of the Medical School I was asked to attend the meeting and to do my part in allaying and cooling the enthusiasm and patriotism of the students. Reluctantly I consented to do my small share in this work.

University Hall was crowded. Even the students who made speeches, for the most part at least, evidently had been selected from among those most likely to be moderate in speech. I sat on the platform and listened to talk after talk by my older and wiser colleagues. One admonished the students that their first duty was to their parents, that they should not enlist without consulting them, and that they had parents distributed from the Atlantic to the Pacific. Another said that the student's first duty was to the University, that if he enlisted he interrupted his course of study, would probably not be able to regain his place in his class, and would suffer delay in graduation. A third told the students that there were enough unemployed in this country to fill the quota called for by the President, advised waiting until the unemployed had enlisted, and if it appeared that the ranks were not filled by these, enlistment by the students might be considered. I had promised President Hutchins that I would be at least moderate in my speech and I went to the meeting fully determined that I would comply with my promise. I have long known that in speaking I labor under a serious defect, but I had no realization until that night of the extent to which this defect dominates and determines my actions. Whatever I may intend to say, when I am to make a speech, when I actually begin to talk, I always give expression to my convictions. Many a time I have gone before an audience intending by my words to palliate and to compromise, but after I begin to talk I have always been led by my convictions rather than by my intentions. At the mass meeting I was called upon to follow the colleague who had spoken of filling the ranks with the unemployed. This drove me into a mental frenzy, and standing before the audience, I said: "God pity the country whose tramps must fight its battles;

it is true that you are here to acquire an education with the purpose of fitting yourself for the work of life; but I would rather see these walls crumble into dust than to see you hesitate to go when your country calls. You have duties towards your parents, but your first duty is to serve your country." Along this line I rushed on in a verbal flood until my time limit was reached.

The next afternoon Governor Pingree, in his office at Lansing, called me by telephone, informed me that he had read my speech, had signed my commission, and that I would report for duty at Camp Alger, Virginia, without delay. Some enlist because they like the soldier's life, some for patriotic reasons, but I received my commission at the outbreak of the Spanish-American War because I talked too much.

On the third or fourth evening after my arrival at Camp Alger we had had our mess, and were sitting in front of Colonel Boynton's tent and listening to an Irish officer from a nearby Massachusetts regiment read Mr. Dooley on the war, when an orderly from brigade headquarters rode up and handed the Colonel a piece of paper. Finishing the reading Colonel Boynton arose and said: "We strike tents to-morrow morning at seven o'clock, entrain at Dun Loring, go to Alexandria and there take boat for Old Point Comfort. To-morrow we will be on our way to Cuba." This order applied to the brigade consisting of the 33rd and 34th Michigan and the 7th Massachusetts under command of General Duffield.

At this point I perpetrated my first blunder in military affairs. I sent my orderly to the office of the division surgeon, Colonel A. C. Girard, with a note saying that up to that time my brigade had received no medical supplies and that I *protested* against going to Cuba without full medical equipment. I was subsequently told by one who was with the colonel that he was indignant when he read my note and as I appreciated later, he had a right to be angry. In an incredibly short time the colonel's orderly rode up to my tent and handed me the piece of paper I had sent and on the back was written: "First endorsement, sir: To protest to a superior officer is unmilitary; you should have requested. However, five ambulances are now on their way to your regiment with more supplies than you can possibly need in Cuba." I may say that the excess disappeared long before those wounded at the Battle of Santiago had been dressed. I am criticising no one when I say that the hospital tents at Siboney were the property of the State of Michigan and not of the Federal Government.

At Alexandria, before embarking, we were addressed by the Secretary of War, General Alger, who spoke to us not only as our commander, but as our neighbor and friend. He told us that every possible provision had been made for our comfort and that we should be permitted to carry with us not only our regulation equipment, but whatever additional luxury we might within reason demand.

After a pleasant night's ride down the Potomac we reached Old Point Comfort in the early morning. The officers breakfasted and lunched at the Hotel Chamberlain, wrote parting letters and sent telegrams to their families and friends. In the afternoon two regiments, the 33rd Michigan and the 7th Massachusetts, went aboard the auxiliary cruiser, the *Yale*, and before nightfall we stood out at sea. The voyage was accompanied by enough excitement to make the time pass interestingly. It may be of historic importance to say that, although this was long before the time of the wireless, all kinds of information and misinformation, especially the latter, reached our ship. One hour we were hearing that Santiago had capitulated; the next the news spread over the decks that the Spanish fleet had emerged from the harbor and destroyed all the American men of war there assembled. Later in the day we learned that both of the above rumors were false but that Cervera's fleet had reached the scene of action and had sunk our flagship, the *New York*. Of course these rumors had their origin in the fancies of some active brain and were without any basis. Off San Salvador an unknown vessel came within the range of our vision. This gave rise to the wildest surmises which were intensified when the unknown vessel neglected to respond to our interrogation as to her name, her nationality, and her destination. The decks of the *Yale* were cleared for action and I was ordered to prepare the sick bay for the reception of the wounded. I might say that I had selected for hospital space and operating room what had been the second class dining room when the *Yale,* under the name of the *Paris,* was a transatlantic liner.

The *Yale,* failing still to get an answer to her interrogatories, sent a shell over the bows of the unknown ship, which being thus awakened into politeness, informed us that she was English and bound for British Honduras. After this little flurry the sailors and soldiers of the *Yale* enjoyed a siesta which continued until the eastern end of the island of Cuba showed itself above a placid sea. We passed around Cape Maysi at night with all lights out and under considerable excitement, sufficient to breed wild rumors again. I was up late and was awakened in the morning by the sun, now quite above the horizon, throwing its full glare into my face. Excitedly and hurriedly I dressed and rushed to the upper deck which I found to be deserted, but on looking landward I saw, apparently at no great distance, the flag of Spain proudly floating over Morro Castle. As I looked a peculiar sensation permeated my being. I could not analyze or define it, nor have I been able to do so subsequently. I am inclined to the opinion that it contained elements of both pleasure and pain. The flag was convincing evidence that the crisis had not arrived and that we were in time to witness and possibly participate in the struggle. This constituted the pleasurable or satisfying element in the sensation, but it was accompanied by an unpleasant apprehension. If a battle or battles were to be fought on land or sea men must suffer and die. As my years of practise had multiplied, I had become more and more sensitive to human suffering and to death. There may have been in my mixed sensations something of personal fear.

As I have said, the side of the upper deck on which I stood as I looked up at the Spanish flag was wholly deserted. I ran quickly to the other side and found that the *Yale* was lying alongside the flagship, the *New York*, and its officers were receiving orders. As I looked up and down the long line of our warships lying off the mouth of the harbor of Santiago, I thrilled with national pride. After a few minutes the *Yale* turned its prow to the east and soon we had dropped anchor off the tiny village of Siboney. There is really no harbor at this place. The shore presents sharp, jagged coral rocks.

Immediately along the sea there is a mesa or table land
varying in width from a few to some hundreds of yards.
This is backed by an almost perpendicular hill of two or
three hundred feet with but few points of easy ascent.
On this mesa and only a short distance from the sea lies
Siboney, which had become the depot of our supplies,
including food, equipment, and ammunition.

Disembarkation began in lifeboats and this slow process was not completed until late in the afternoon. The
soldiers, with their arms and blankets, were first transferred. There were on board a few horses and mules.
These were suspended by cranes and lowered to the sea
when they were set free. Most of them struck for the
shore, but some turned and passed seaward where they
were lost. Late afternoon had arrived when a naval
officer rather rudely ordered me to assemble the hospital
corps, consisting of about thirty men, and go ashore with
them. I politely said that I would not go until all my
medical supplies had preceded me. By this time the medicine and instrument chests had been assembled on the
deck, and I insisted that I would not leave the ship until
these had been carried to the shore. The naval officer
repeated his command and this time accompanied it by an
oath. I looked at his shoulder straps and then at mine
and again refused to go, accompanying my statement by
a more violent swear word. This ended the colloquy, and,
after I had seen that all my supplies and men had reached
the shore, Major de Nancrede, my colleague, professor of
surgery in the University of Michigan, now division surgeon and my superior officer, and I took our places in a
lifeboat. This was steered by a little cockswain from
an undergraduate class at Annapolis. The boat had

reached about one hundred yards from the shore when the helmsman was suddenly seized with *mal de mer* and lost control of the rudder.   The next instant our boat was swamped and we were in the sea, but being fair swimmers and the distance short, we easily reached shore. Following the advice of the Secretary of War I had gone to Cuba fairly well equipped with changes of underclothing.   My good wife had packed these in a trunk which carried her name and address plainly marked on one end. Among other things she had provided me with a soiled clothes bag of ample proportions closed with a draw string.   My trunk was on the *Yale* and before leaving the boat I had transferred all my soiled clothing to the trunk and had filled the bag with clean underwear.   I had taken the bag in the lifeboat with me.   When I swam ashore I saw my bag dancing on the waves a short distance out.   Acting on impulse I returned to the water and soon captured my bag, the contents of which, as it turned out, were to be of more service to others than to me.

For a few days our regiments were encamped on a lowland along a little stream which flows into the sea just east of Siboney.   Here we were in close proximity to a part of what was known as the Army of Insurrection commanded by Garcia.   So far as I could see, these troops, if they could be called troops, consisted of a rabble of half-clothed, half-starved men, women, and children. It was the first time I had seen a starving people, and I could hardly believe what I saw.   My mental picture of starving people had consisted of individuals uniformly emaciated from head to foot, but the first impression made upon me by these people was that they had eaten too heavily.   The limbs and the chest were greatly emaciated, while the abdomen was markedly protruding. The only food which they had in great abundance was the mango and this was consumed in unbelievable quantities. The bulk of this food accounted for the abnormal protuberance of the abdomen, while its deficiency in food principles accounted for the waste of the other parts of the body.

Our first camp was by no means a pleasant one. There was an abundant growth of palmettos, the blades of which were cut and used for bedding, but they were neither smooth nor springy. Our ponchos, which were spread over the boughs, were constantly slipping in one or another direction. It rained heavily every day and nearly every night. With the regularity of the clock there was sure to be a heavy shower at two P. M. After a few days in this camp we were permitted to go to a location about a mile west of Siboney where the mesa was narrow and where we had on one side the sea and on the other the mountains, which rose almost perpendicularly to a height of several hundred feet. This location was much dryer than the other, but its special advantage was in the fact that it took us from the immediate vicinity of the Cuban troops. This relief was made more secure by forbidding the natives to enter our camp. If I remember correctly this was suggested by the medical officers on the ground that it might afford our soldiers protection against possible infection. A critic might have pointed to the fact that our soldiers were not prohibited from mingling with the Cubans and that infection might be acquired quite as readily in their camp as in ours. However, the arrangement did add somewhat to our comfort and at the same time to the protection of our personal property.

Nearly every American soldier carried a toothbrush and when not in use it was stuck in his hatband. The natives were very curious about this article which they believed to be a new weapon of warfare.

We had not been in this camp a week before the Battle of Santiago was fought. The part played in this battle by Duffield's brigade was small, but inasmuch as it is the only time I have ever been under fire, I must be permitted to gratify my inclination to tell something about it. The plan of attack was explained to the brigade officers, both of the line and of the staff. I shall not speak of the main Battle of Santiago, but of Duffield's attack on Aquadores which was a small part of the large battle. Running along the mesa between the sea and the perpendicular hills there is a railroad which, coming from the east of Siboney, passes through that village, continues along the mesa, crosses a high bridge at Aquadores and continues into Santiago. Along this road there are laid on top of the ground pipes which carry the drinking water from the mountains east of Siboney into the city of Santiago. I may say here, parenthetically, that five minutes of destructive work on our part might have completely cut the water supply to the besieged city, but to the credit of our nation, this was never discussed or thought of as even a possibility. It is true that along the pipe line, where the American soldiers were encamped in part, we did not hesitate to drive a hole with a pick in order to get an abundance of water not only for drinking but for bathing. The water was known to be absolutely free from any dangerous contamination. It came through the pipes where we were encamped under great pressure and when a hole was driven into a pipe the water was discharged with sufficient force and abundance to give a shower bath to whole companies at a time. I believe that the frequent employment of the baths saved my life and I am sure that it added greatly to my comfort, but our soldiers had strict orders to plug these pick-driven holes when not in immediate service.

I wish to speak a little more fully concerning the manner in which we passed our time during the few days before the battle and while we were encamped on the mesa a short distance to the west of Siboney. The mesa consists of a barren, rocky soil supporting but little plant life, and that of sparse and scanty growth. At that time, at least, it was traversed especially at night by thousands of crabs as large as a man's fist. Their physiognomy was both attractive and repulsive. They looked half human and half devil. I do not believe that they were capable of inflicting any injury upon man by either bite or claw, but their presence awakened great animosity and the human tendency was to fall upon and destroy them. They crawled at night over the soldiers sleeping on the ground, in or outside of their dog tents, and their presence did not favor unbroken rest. Personally, I slept in a hammock and was not disturbed by this unwelcome visitor. There were stories told that the crabs would crawl up the scrubby trees from which hammocks were suspended and drop upon the occupants, but this did not happen to me. When I repaired to my hammock for a night's rest I hung my blankets on a bush within easy reach. I slept soundly until about two A. M. when I awoke frozen through and through. The temperature at two P. M. averaged one hundred and twenty degrees in the shade; that of two A. M. stood about sixty-four degrees. It seemed to me that the whole island suffered a malarial paroxysm once a day. Awakened, I would reach for my blankets which were wringing wet with dew or with rain, wrap them about me, and possibly secure an hour or two of broken sleep. The early morning was announced by swarms of mosquitoes and by a deadly stillness of the atmosphere. I may say that from five or six A. M. to about nine A. M. were the hardest hours I had to bear. Covered with mosquitoes, stifled with the absence of any breeze, I would free myself violently from wet blankets, leave my hammock, strip myself of every article of clothing, go to the pipe line, pull out a plug and enjoy a shower. We had only an army ration consisting of hard tack, bacon and coffee. The coffee was parched but unground. The cook pounded the grains with the blunt end of his bayonet in a tin pan, added water, boiled it, and we had a most delicious coffee.

The railroad from Siboney to Santiago had been torn up in places, the bridge had been destroyed, and the rolling stock put out of commission, but our engineers had repaired some of the engines sufficiently for limited service and had put the track in shape as far west as within rifle fire of Aquadores. At three A. M. the morning of the Battle of Santiago, General Duffield, with several hundred men, boarded coal cars and started west with the intention of making a feint attack on the small garrison at Aquadores. It has been said that General Duffield's mission was to capture Aquadores but I know this is not true. There is a deep ravine just east of Aquadores and the railroad bridge across this had been destroyed. There was no other bridge which led over this ravine and the possibility of attacking the fort at this place with the idea of capturing it would have been absurd.

By early dawn our train had gone as far west as it was safe to go on account of the Spanish guns which we knew were located at Aquadores. We detrained and the soldiers proceeded westward through the dense chaparral which lined the seaward side of the railroad. Through this we went within rifle fire of the ravine and its broken bridge. I was lying in the chaparral with one of the companies of the 33rd Michigan. The gun boats, lying off the shore and easily within our vision, were sending shells over our heads, supposedly into Santiago. I have no reason to believe that in my physical, mental or moral makeup I differ from the average man. The company with which I was lying in the chaparral on the seaward side of the railroad kept this position for an hour or more, during which time the shells from our gunboats were screaming through the air over our heads. Lying there I thrilled in every fiber of my being with sensations which I never felt before and which I have never experienced since. These sensations were of the most pleasant kind. I believed that our shells were destroying the enemy. It proved afterwards that they had no effect. Why the belief that our enemies were being destroyed should have given me pleasure I cannot understand. I said to myself, "If I am killed the next moment the pleasurable sensations which I am now having would be worth all they might cost." I believe that in the presence of war man returns to the savage state. He becomes a beast of prey, ready to seize and devour, full of fierce hate, and he loses all the finer sensibilities which he has inherited through generations and which he may have acquired in his own short life.

The company with which I was lying was ordered to

form in columns of four and cross the railroad. About half the men had crossed when a Spanish shell came down the road, struck down and horribly mangled eight men. Six were killed instantly. Across the road from me a boy was lying on his back holding up his right arm, from which the hand had been amputated at the wrist. The blood was spurting from the severed vessels as water flows from a hose under pressure. I rushed across the road and the boy cried: "Take care of me first, Doctor Vaughan; I am an Ann Arbor boy." I stopped the hemorrhage by the application of an Esmarch bandage and had the boy carried under a railroad water tower which stood nearby. The dead and the other wounded men were brought to the same location. Soon bullets were piercing the posts which supported the tower, and General Duffield coming along, advised me to change my dressing station and go behind some large rocks which were nearby. The Spaniards were shooting at the water tower, not because we were using it as a dressing station (they did not know this), but an American boy of the Signal Corps was on top of the tower directing the fire from the ships. Into our improvised dressing station wounded men were brought. Every few minutes a Spanish shell came down the railroad track, while on each side their Mauser bullets peppered the rocks. I may say that the Spaniards proved themselves good marksmen. Our men had only black powder and with each discharge the location of the soldier was indicated, and but few of those who exposed their position in this way escaped without a wound and several were killed. Duffield's brigade succeeded in preventing the Spaniards located at Aquadores from going to reinforce those engaged in the greater battle.

The day wore on slowly; we were exposed to the full rays of the tropical sun; before the battle I had urged the soldiers that on going into action each man should carry a canteen filled with boiled water and that he should drink from no other source. Before noon I had emptied my canteen by drinking from it myself and by refreshing the wounded. Later I found myself kneeling and drinking from a puddle which I had every reason to suppose might bear infection. I believe that I would have drunk this water if I had known it to be a culture of typhoid germs or of the Asiatic cholera bacillus. There comes a period in thirst, especially when exposed to the direct action of the sun, when one will drink if opportunity affords, whatever the supply may be. Behind the big rocks my hospital corps men and I were safe from both shell and rifle fire.

As evening approached I was filled with horror at the idea that some wounded man might be lying in the chaparral uncared for. I determined, therefore, to search through the rocks and bushes. I scattered my men in this search. I found a man shot in the foot. He could not walk; I alone could not carry him. I saw two of my hospital men on the other side of the railroad. I called to them to come and help me with the wounded man. At this time, as all through the day, a Spanish shell was coming down the railroad track at irregular but frequent intervals. Although I was within easy hearing of my hospital corps men neither of them heeded my call. They continued their search and did not look in the direction from which I hailed them. I begged, I implored, that they cross the railroad and assist me in carrying the wounded man to shelter. They gave no heed; they failed

Major Vaughan in Spanish-American War

to hear. Then I sent in their direction a call accompanied by violent oaths. This brought them to attention. Both quickly sprang across the road and soon we had the wounded man under shelter. I am convinced that under certain circumstances even a command by an officer is not sufficient unless accompanied by an oath to bring men to obedience. That evening we returned on the train to Siboney bearing our dead and wounded. With us the day had not been a glorious one, but I had acquired an experience which was new and of value to me.

I may add that in 1924—twenty-six years after the Battle of Santiago—I received a citation for "gallantry on the field of battle." Uncle Sam may be slow in conferring honors but he seldom wholly forgets.

That night the wounded from the greater battle began to pour into the base hospital at Siboney. In the next few days some twelve surgeons took care of about sixteen hundred wounded men. Practically all the missiles passed through the body. I saw but one lodged bullet. For the most part the surgery was easy and could be done by one without experience in this line of work. I selected as my assistant a barber. I had him lather about the wound with a lysol soap and shave the area. This being done in front, the patient was turned over and the wound of exit treated in the same way. My surgical work consisted in applying to the wounds of entrance and exit dressings of iodoform gauze and strapping them in place. In this way my colleagues and I treated many cases in which the chest had been pierced and the fatality from these wounds was small. When the bullet passed through the abdomen the patient was turned over to more skilled surgeons than I. From Friday night until the following Wednesday morning we stood almost continuously at the tables dressing wounds.

The land battle was fought on Friday. On the following Sunday morning as we were still dressing the wounded someone said to me: "There is Admiral Sampson." I looked up and saw the flagship, the *New York*, just dropping anchor in front of our tents. Admiral Sampson was starting down the ladder in order to reach a life boat which was lying below ready to bring him ashore. As I looked I heard the boom of great guns and turning to the westward I plainly saw the Spanish fleet coming out of the mouth of the harbor at Santiago, while our warships were enveloping them with a tremendous fire. As each Spanish ship emerged it turned to the westward and the naval battle soon passed beyond our vision. In the meanwhile the *New York* lifted anchor and was proceeding under full steam to join in the battle. At this moment a warship from the east was apparently coming towards shore. Wise men, through their glasses, pronounced it a Spanish vessel and we believed that Cervera's fleet was just in time to participate in the battle and might possibly determine the result. Evidently some of those engaged with the Spanish at the mouth of the harbor also mistook the approaching vessel for a Spanish man-of-war. At least we soon saw the *Iowa* detach itself from the fighting line and proceed eastward to meet the incoming stranger. Admiral Evans, in command of the *Iowa*, subsequently told that he suspected the vessel to be Spanish and how he came out to meet it. The new warship proved to be Austrian and was of course neutral, and had no participation in the conflict. It was on the approach of this vessel that my hospital corps men cut my red blanket (see page twenty-two) and with a sheet for background made a large Red Cross flag.

The long afternoon passed away. The battle had gone westward and was beyond both sight and hearing. We did not know what had happened. Night had fallen and we were operating by the light of lanterns hung from the ridge poles of the tents when a bugle call for doctors came from the sea. With others I rushed to the small improvised dock. The *Harvard* had dropped anchor a short distance out and a lifeboat was approaching us. Its occupant proved to be the English attaché and when within hailing distance he shouted, "You should have been with us; we gave them hell. There is not a splinter left." The *Harvard* carried about eight hundred wounded Spanish sailors. For a while we delayed the dressing of our own wounded in order that we might attend to the most seriously injured of our enemy.

While we were disembarking from the *Yale* on our arrival at Siboney the German attaché came on board and I was detailed by General Duffield to take him over the ship and show him what disposition we had made of the soldiers during the voyage. In words he made no criticism, but with the characteristic movement of the shoulders, in practise by his countrymen, he expressed not only disapproval but contempt for what he saw. I do not blame him for this. Our provisions for carrying soldiers were by no means commendable. A day or two after the battle, while I was standing at the operating table, the Swedish and German attachés came and stood by me. I felt called upon to say something complimentary, or at least pleasing, to my visitors. In lieu of anything else I ventured to say that the American army was less well disciplined than European armies. The German said nothing, but the Swede said something for which I inwardly thanked him at the time and which I have subsequently greatly treasured. He said: "I do not know about discipline. There are different kinds of discipline. From a safe place I watched your men go into battle last Friday. A division was ordered across the little river. It proceeded up the hill towards the Spanish lines. It did not do this in good military form. I thought how differently a German division would have moved, but after it had crossed the river and the Spaniards began firing, each American corporal took command of his squad and went up the hill. Until that time I had believed the German army to be the best disciplined in the world, but I now recognize that there are different kinds of discipline. You have captains that might lead brigades and corporals that might lead companies. I believe the American army to have the most intelligent discipline I have ever seen."

On Wednesday morning following the battle the stress of caring for the wounded had been relieved. Every wound had been dressed once and some of the most serious had been looked after a second or even a third time. I had just reached my hammock, feeling that I could sleep almost anywhere and under any conditions, when men bearing another on a stretcher came along. They told me that they had brought the man some miles from up near Aquadores, that he seemed very ill, but that just now he was asleep. Satisfying myself that at least the last part of their statement was true I advised that the stretcher be placed beneath my hammock, utilizing in this way the only shade available. The man on the stretcher and I in the hammock slept I know not how long, but at least an hour, possibly two. I was awakened by the vomiting of the man. I sprang from the hammock and although I had never seen a case of yellow fever, an incorrect diagnosis was impossible. *El vomito negro* was plainly in evidence on the face and over the clothing and blankets of the man left in my care. Immediately, giving the patient but scant attention, I ran to the camp calling for Doctor Guiteras, the yellow fever expert, a native of Cuba, a distinguished professor in the Medical School of the University of Pennsylvania, and, I may add, a man of not only big intelligence but of great heart. As soon as I saw him I shouted: "Come, doctor, we have a case of yellow fever."

So far as I know, this was the first case of yellow fever seen among our troops. After providing for the comfort of the patient and placing him in competent hands Doctor Guiteras and I on a handcar started up the mountain railroad to the east of Siboney with the intention of selecting a site for a yellow fever hospital. This we soon agreed upon on the mountain side some hundreds of feet above the sea level. The site selected was on the northern slope of the coast range looking out upon a valley filled with magnificent royal palms with the highest peaks of the Sierras opposite. To this location we carried a few tents, medical supplies and cooking utensils, and made ready for a yellow fever hospital. Before the close of the first day we had three cases. During the second day thirty or more were brought in. Before the end of the week our hospital had grown so as to house several hundred patients. I believe that altogether there were among our troops in and about Siboney at that time some thirteen or fourteen hundred cases of this disease. Fortunately, the death rate was not so high as it often is, running, I believe, about fifteen per cent.

We had now to consider two important problems. One was whether or not we should burn the village of Siboney in our efforts to stamp out yellow fever. Among the members of the board asked to make recommendation on this subject were Major Gorgas (who, with the rank of colonel, stamped out yellow fever in Havana and later in the Canal Zone, and became Major-General Gorgas, Surgeon General of the United States Army) ; Major La-Garde, commander of the surgical hospital at Siboney; Captain Ireland, (now Surgeon General Ireland) ; my colleague, Major de Nancrede; Captain Fauntleroy, myself and possibly others. We recommended that the village should be burned. The inhabitants and their belongings were accommodated in tents and the houses reduced to ashes. The only ones to profit by this procedure were the owners of the houses, inasmuch as the United States Government for the time being, provided them with shelter and food, and subsequently rebuilt the village. Among those who participated in giving this recommendation to burn Siboney in order to suppress yellow fever the matter has been in late years a joke, which we have tossed one to the other from time to time. "So you call yourself an epidemiologist? Did not you recommend that Siboney should be burned in order to eradicate yellow fever? How many infected mosquitoes were destroyed in that conflagration?"

The other problem was much more serious and for-

tunately we answered it more wisely. What should be
done with the more than sixteen hundred wounded men
in the tent hospital? It was decided that they should, to
a man so far as possible, be immediately sent to the
United States. There were enough transports idly lying
off the shore to carry these men. Their embarkation
began immediately and if my memory serves me right,
by the end of the second day after the recognition of the
first case of yellow fever every wounded man was safely
and comfortably, so far as comfort could be secured for
every wounded man, on board a transport and on way
to the United States. So far as the records give us information, no one of these wounded men developed
yellow fever, or if such was the case the disease was
not recognized.

Our surgical hospital at Siboney was now cleared out.
We had a hospital for malaria, one for typhoid fever,
and a third located, as I have stated, up on the mountain
side and quite a distance from the others, for yellow
fever. Doctor Guiteras and others showed great skill
in the differential diagnosis of these diseases. As a rule
the history of the case gave sufficient distinction between
malaria and typhoid fever. We had no microscope for
the detection of the plasmodium. We had no facilities
for making the Widal test for typhoid fever. The distinction between typhoid fever and yellow fever was
largely determined by the test for albumin in the urine.
We did have some test tubes and a bottle of nitric acid.
Besides these we had alcohol lamps. So far as the
records show, patients with these three diseases were
classified as definitely as would have been likely to
happen if we had known more about specific tests or

had had abundant laboratory facilities. This success in differentiating between the diseases was due to the long clinical experience which such men as Guiteras, Gorgas and La Garde had had.

One week from the day on which I saw the first case of yellow fever I had charge of policing the grounds at and about Siboney where our large tent hospital, now empty, still stood. I had been moving about rather briskly in the sun with the temperature as usual during the afternoon somewhere about one hundred twenty degrees in the shade. About four P. M. I began to feel a pain in the small of my back which rapidly grew more severe; in fact, I could hardly stand or walk, or at least in either of these positions I suffered rather severely. It required no diagnostic skill on my part to tell what was happening within my anatomy. I went to my tent, or at least to my field desk and wrote to my wife telling her, I believe, the biggest falsehood I ever perpetrated upon her. I told her that I had been ordered into the interior of Cuba, that as near as I could calculate I would be gone two weeks, and that during that time she must not be anxious if she had no letter from me. I then went to the chief correspondent of the Associated Press, telling him that I was coming down with yellow fever, and asking that he say nothing about it in dispatches home. This he promised, and he kept his promise. Then I went into one of the long hospital tents in which there were standing in two rows somewhere between fifty and seventy cots, all of which had been vacated by the surgical patients sent home. I had an orderly change the sheets on one of these cots into which I dropped as soon as it was ready.

After nightfall I sent for Doctor Guiteras. He came, examined me most carefully, and said: "Only a little malaria. You will be all right in a few days. To-morrow I shall give you quinine." Having directed the hospital corps man to provide for my immediate wants he left. I soon dismissed the attendant. I am quite sure that Doctor Guiteras came to the side of my cot during that night a half dozen or more times. Each time I pretended to be asleep. Actually I did not sleep a wink during the whole night. He would come up so gently, put his finger on my pulse so lightly and so cautiously, scan my face, with marked anxiety in his own, as I could see through my partially closed eyelids by the flashes of lightning that came every few minutes that long night. With the first dawn Doctor Guiteras came, swinging his arms, making an effort to whistle a tune, and trying to make me believe that he had had a night of unbroken rest. Later in the morning he came, went over me again, and repeated, "Only a little malaria. Don't you think that the air up at the yellow fever hospital on the mountain side is much better than it is down here on this low wet ground?" I expressed my agreement with him and my readiness to proceed to the yellow fever hospital and I made a movement to sit up in the cot. Gently but firmly, he held me down and then he explained. "Your temperature is above one hundred five degrees; your pulse is below forty; a change in position, even the sudden lifting of an arm, might stop your heart. You will not move on any account. Men will come, lift your cot, place it on a flat car, and you will be carried to the yellow fever hospital. I shall go with you."

Soon I was at the yellow fever hospital on the mountain side in a tent with eight or ten others. Inasmuch as Doctor Guiteras had other duties in the yellow fever hospital, I was placed so far as treatment was concerned at first in the hands of a very able Cuban physician, Eccheverria. Pretty soon I was vomiting the characteristic black, almost tarry stuff, which gives to this disease its Spanish name of *el vomito negro*. My stomach would begin to contract its walls slowly, but most painfully. I could feel it constantly growing smaller and harder until it had apparently proximated the density and size of an ivory billiard ball, and then with a spring the walls would dilate, accompanied by a gush of black vomit. It seemed as though the blood in the capillaries of the stomach walls was being forced out under such pressure that even the red blood corpuscles were broken into the finest particles. Doctor Eccheverria's treatment, for which he had at that time a great reputation in Cuba, consisted essentially in the administration of a large dose of calomel, twenty or more grains, to be followed by the frequent drinking of a half pint or more of a saturated solution of Epsom salt, flavored with sliced limes or pressed lime juice. In an interval between the contractions of my stomach walls I managed to get down about twenty-five grains of calomel, but I am sure that no trace of it remained in my stomach longer than half an hour. The solution of Epsom salt, known among patients as Doctor Eccheverria's lemonade, served to wash out the stomach frequently. In addition to the large dose of calomel and the continuous administration of the lemonade, Doctor Eccheverria starved his patients. Nothing but the calomel and the lemonade was to pass down one's gullet. My vomitings grew less and less frequent, and so far as I can remember, my stomach became tranquil and free from pain in the early afternoon of that first day in the hospital.

On the second or third day Major Gorgas took charge of my treatment and his nephew, Theodore Lyster, (General Lyster in the World War) then a student of mine in the University of Michigan but with us in Cuba, assisted in caring for me. To their devotion and tenderness I owe, in all human probability, my recovery. Some eighteen years after this General Gorgas, as we were enjoying our postprandial cigars, confided to me that at Siboney he had given an unfavorable prognosis in my case and had told Lyster that in his opinion I would live but a few hours. For the first few days I was too sick to be hungry. The pain in my back continued, although it gradually grew less. My temperature hovered around one hundred five. My pulse was constantly below forty.

Just across from me in the little tent was a large man, the postmaster to the corps. One day he called to me, saying that he had a bottle of ginger ale, the contents of which he kindly offered to divide with me. Ginger ale! How joyously the words struck upon my ear drums. The only thing that had passed my lips for days had been Doctor Eccheverria's lemonade, the water component of which was taken from the iron pipes on top of the ground, with the air temperature at one hundred twenty degrees in the shade. This water in and of itself, just warm enough to be nauseating, was not made more appetizing by its saturation with Epsom salt or the addition of lime juice. I knew that the ginger ale could not be very cold, but I remembered the pleasant tingling sensation induced in one's gustatory organs, even by carbonated water, and then I felt that the flavor of the ginger ale would go to the right place. However, being a physician, I could not do otherwise than caution my comrade. I told him he had better put the ginger ale bottle aside, that in a few days we would enjoy it all the better, but he insisted. He sent the orderly out of the tent and told me he would open the bottle himself. Along with the bottle he had a corkscrew and he began to get up out of his cot. Then I pleaded with him earnestly. I said, "Do not move. If you must drink the ginger ale, call the orderly and have him pull the stopper. Your heart is crippled and a change in position may kill you." He laughed at my excessive caution, but had just reached the erect posture when he fell dead across my cot, breaking it down and lying on top of me, stone dead. I tinkled the little bell at my side, the orderly came, and the dead man was removed. This was not the only instance in that hospital when death was caused by change in posture. I fear that even physicians do not always appreciate the danger incurred by change in posture when the heart is so disturbed.

For several days I was in a peculiar mental condition. I had a double consciousness. I was not ill, but I had a friend who was dangerously ill and in some way, which I could not explain to myself, I was responsible for his illness. If he should die I would be morally guilty. I think the mental suffering which I experienced was largely due to this condition. I had frequent short naps and after each I would be in a cheerful frame of mind. I was sure my friend was going to get well. Then I would feel less and less certain about it, and finally I would be equally sure he was going to die. Fortunately when

I had reached the point of deepest despair on account of
my friend, I would fall asleep, and after a few minutes
awake again in the cheerful frame of mind. Being sick
myself I did not have opportunity to observe others to
any great extent. However, I am sure that the state of
double consciousness was not peculiar to me. I know
that one man in our tent, after displacing the mosquito
netting by his own movements, would lie looking at his
own leg covered with flies and ask why the damned fool
did not cover himself. From the testimony of others I
am sure that in that epidemic at least, a state of double
consciousness was frequent.

About the sixth day my fever having greatly declined
so that at no time of the day did it go above one hundred
two, I began to grow hungry, and as the fever went down
my hunger grew more and more intense. I spent the
seventh day without food, but with constant visions of
the dining room table at home with the full complement
of good things to eat which my wife was wont to prepare. I saw the table loaded with stewed, boiled, fried,
and baked articles of diet, each one for the moment appearing in its most attractive and alluring form, but
whether the dinner seen in my vision was boiled, baked
or otherwise prepared, the most prominent position was
occupied by the great silver pitcher filled with ice water
and covered with beads of perspiration. Oh, how I did
long to eat! I felt as though I would sell my soul for a
mess of pottage. In at least one case a patient at this
stage, an occupant of the same tent with myself, by brib-
ing an orderly secured a can of beans and ate the entire
contents. Within a few hours he was dead.

On the morning of the ninth day of my fast Major

Gorgas told me that I could eat. I asked what I might have. He told me that for the first day it would be wise to confine myself to meat extracts and asked how much I wanted. I told him to roll in a hogshead. With his greater wisdom, he sent me a small medicine cup of this beverage. I found that one or two swallows sufficed; more nauseated me. I took the small quantities two or three times during the day and found that my stomach gradually resumed its natural functions. By the next morning my hunger had greatly increased and about this time two Cubans came to the tent with two wild guinea hens which they had shot and which they offered to exchange for hard tack and bacon. We filled their bags with government rations and for an hour or more sat around with hungry eyes waiting for our cook to prepare the guinea hens. A most delicious stew was finally offered us, and I am sure that the eight or ten who partook could not have been more pleased had we feasted at the table of a king. Appetite grew most amazingly and every hour or two during the day we passed up our tin cups to be refilled with the delicious broth.

I wish I could satisfactorily describe the pictures I saw as I lay in the tent with a temperature at times going as high as one hundred six degrees. From my cot I looked out to the north over the valley of royal palms into the crags of the highest peaks of the Sierras. About these, each day at two P. M. with the regularity of the clock, short, broken lines of lightning would begin to play. These quickly grew longer, more frequent, and more brilliant. At the same time clouds, some small, some large, from apparently every point of the compass began to gather about the peaks, shutting off their features until I saw nothing but an intense blackness, the depths of which were constantly being pierced by most vivid lines of lightning. These formed figures, some grotesque, some heroic, all intensely fascinating. I was entranced, enraptured, held by a spell of enchantment, such as a normal brain has never known. I fancied some god or demon residing in the peaks sending out through the limitless air summons after summons for the assembly of his cohorts which, obeying the call, rode in as invisible spirits on the clouds coming from the furthermost parts of the earth. The clouded area with its center about the peaks grew wider and darker until it cut out the light of the sun and enveloped the whole earth. Then the thunders shook the mountains, the earth trembled, the rain fell in torrents, the sheets of water descending the mountain side swept my tent clean. The storm disappeared more quickly than it came, the clouds having spent themselves passed into nothingness. I was now conscious of my immediate surroundings. The next day as the hour approached I watched with eager anticipation, and so long as my fever continued I was not disappointed. Of such are the visions of a diseased brain.

On the tenth day after I had come down with yellow fever Captain Ireland came to my assistance, placed me in a little dummy train, and took me down to the base hospital at Siboney. When I left the United States to go to Cuba I weighed two hundred and ten pounds; when I returned to the United States I weighed one hundred and fifty. On the morning when, assisted by Captain Ireland, I reached Major La Garde's tent, he said: "You will go home on the first transport." I assured him that I had no such intention, that I was now an immune, and that my usefulness in the camp was thereby increased. I expressed my desire to rest for a few hours and then be permitted to go back to the yellow fever camp and assist Major Gorgas in taking care of the patients. The skill with which Major La Garde handled me was not then fully appreciated, but has since stood out in my memory as one of the greatest favors ever done me. He was my superior officer, and he would have been perfectly within his right had he ordered me home, but this was not his way of doing things. He employed more pleasing and more effective measures. He had a cot prepared for me in a small tent and he told me that I should rest for a few days and if I then found myself able my request to return to the yellow fever camp would be granted. A few feet from the small tent in which I rested there was a mess tent, on the table of which there stood constantly articles of diet, the aroma of which floated out to me with an enticement I could not resist. Several times during the day I got out of my cot and attempted to walk to the mess table, but invariably I found my legs so weak I could traverse the short distance only by getting down on my hands and knees and crawling. After one or two attempts of this kind Major La Garde had an orderly bring to my cot frequently various tempting dishes. Every now and then he would come in, sit down and say: "To-morrow morning a transport leaves for the United States with convalescent soldiers and I haven't a doctor to send with them. I do not know what to do." He made no further reference to my going, but continued hour by hour to bemoan the fact that he had no medical officer to place on the transport. The day was a long and wearisome one. At last the sun was rapidly sinking and as it went down my confidence in my physical strength waned. I began to doubt the wisdom of my staying on the island.

Again Major La Garde confided to me his trouble about securing a medical officer for the transport. The *City of Santiago,* the transport in question, was lying just off the shore and was receiving sick soldiers, carried out in life boats. At last I said: "Major, do you want me to go on that transport?" He made no reply to my interrogation, but called to Captain Ireland saying, "Bring a stretcher with bearers and put Vaughan on the transport." I raised no objection; in fact, by this time I was perfectly willing to go. Captain Ireland accompanied me to the transport and secured for me the most comfortable stateroom on the vessel. This room was to serve not only as my living and sleeping room, but also as the office of the doctor in charge. I was placed on board the *City of Santiago* about sundown on Sunday. At that time, unaided, I could not walk from one side of the deck to the other, but from the moment of going on board I began to recover my strength with almost miraculous rapidity. The *City of Santiago* did not leave Siboney until Monday afternoon. We passed around the eastern end of Cuba and paralleled its northern coast for many miles, when we struck out for Tampa.

For a day and more a great shark followed closely in our wake. There was a crate of live chickens on the rear deck and a wicked boy let some of these escape. I witnessed the incident and was sure that it was done with a deliberate intention of feeding the shark. Within two days after going to sea I was able to visit any and every part of the ship. I went down to the galleys and saw that food was prepared for the sick. I had a list of the sick made, saw each one several times a day and kept a case record which proved of value when I was asked to make out papers for pension claimants. We carried about three hundred convalescents from yellow fever. When we reached Tampa Bay the state health officer of Florida came aboard and asked me whether we carried yellow fever or other infection. I showed him a clean bill of health from the Spanish health officer of the port of Santiago. I may say here that for some time after the capitulation of that city Spanish civil officers were continued on duty. The clean bill of health, however, did not satisfy the observant health officer. He forbade our landing, telling us that the Marine Hospital Service had made preparation for us on Egmont Key, that the ship would lie at anchor and its passengers would be carried in life boats to this destination.

The transfer from Siboney to Egmont Key was in no way an improvement. In our new location we found the mosquitoes more numerous, larger, and more vicious than their Cuban relatives. However, my old friend, Surgeon Giddings, of the Marine Hospital Service, was in command of the camp and had done everything within his power to provide for our comfort. He told me, with some pride, that he had secured a large mosquito-proof tent especially for General Duffield and myself. A Cuban general, whose name I forget, had accompanied us on the *Santiago* and had informed us that he was on his way to Washington as the political representative of the new government which was to be established in Cuba, but at that time did not exist, except in the brain of the wily diplomat. When Surgeon Giddings brought General Duffield and me to the big mosquito-proof tent we found it already in the possession of the Cuban hero. With characteristic modesty, General Duffield made no claim on account of rank, but he and I took possession of a nearby tent of ordinary size and construction. We slept as best we could while fighting mosquitoes, but in the middle of the night there came a West Indian hurricane. We were thankful for the storm, because the wind scattered our uninvited visitors. When the storm became wilder and the rain was pouring in torrents we heard cries of distress. On going out we found that the storm had overturned the great mosquito-proof tent and that the Cuban hero, entangled in its meshes, bound hand and foot, was lying in the open field fully exposed to the downpour and loudly crying for aid. While others extricated the helpless man we returned to our simple cots and again wooed Morpheus.

We had two or three days on Egmont Key and I hope never to see it again. By this time four or five transports, all bearing convalescent yellow fever soldiers, had accumulated in Tampa Bay. I received a telegraphic order from the Secretary of War to select one of the transports, put all the sick soldiers on board, and proceed to New York. Furthermore, the order authorized me to purchase everything that in my opinion might add to the comfort of the soldier so far as I could find such material in Tampa. One afternoon, seated in a life boat, I started out to inspect the transports lying in the Bay. I had been received courteously by the captain of every ship which I had visited until I was approaching the *Segurança*. As I came near this vessel the captain, a

Scandinavian, ordered the ladder raised and refused to permit me to come aboard. I rowed up under the boat and pulling out my order from the Secretary of War, I said: "I thank you, Captain, for your courtesy. I have an order from the Secretary of War to inspect your ship. I shall immediately telegraph the Secretary that you refuse to permit me to come aboard. I bid you good day." The ladder dropped instantaneously, the red-headed captain quickly descended and with great formality and courtesy assisted me in reaching the deck. This was by far the best ship in the Bay and I selected it for the voyage to New York. By the time the captain and I had visited every part of the *Segurança* and I had finished my inspection the Bay was swept by a moderate hurricane. I could reach my life boat only by going down a rope ladder and I was instructed that when commanded to do so I should let loose and drop into the boat. When I did let loose of that rope I had no idea that I would stop before I reached the bottom of the Bay, but the men in the life boat caught me as deftly and as easily as if I had been a bag of feathers and stretching me in the boat they were quite on their way to another ship before I fully realized what had happened.

On one ship there were a few negro soldiers and forty negro stevedores. With two other officers and the captain of the ship I was in the captain's room making out an order to be sent to Tampa for food. We four were the only white men on board the ship. The day was warm and we had laid aside our blouses carrying insignia of office. From the deck there came an agonizing cry of *"Help! help! murder!"* Fortunately, one of the officers, a regular army man and far wiser than I, fairly forced my blouse on me and saying that I was the ranking officer, pushed me out of the door. As he did so a negro soldier running for his life dashed into the room and I faced a mob of twenty or more negro stevedores each with a razor and one with a pistol. These villains had robbed the negro soldiers, one of whom had run to us for protection. The stevedores at once recognized the authority of Uncle Sam in my shoulder straps and cap. I held up my hand and ordered them to stop. Every negro stopped immediately and then I told the one with the pistol to advance and give me his gun. This he did. Then we ordered all of them down into the hold and I did not breathe a peaceful breath until the last woolly head had disappeared and the manhole cover had been lowered and double locked. We soon transferred the negro soldiers to the *Segurança* and two or three days later as this ship was lifting anchor to proceed on its voyage to New York, the captain of the ship carrying the stevedores came over in a life boat to ask what he was to do with his prisoners. I told him that their sentence was indefinite and so far as I was concerned they could remain in the hold until some one else ruled upon the period of their captivity.

The *Segurança* needed coal and water and we needed food for the voyage. It always happens that an individual or a corporation is able to secure whatever it desires and is found in the market quicker than the government can act. A certain amount of red tape retarded my attempts to secure provisions from Tampa. Long before I had finished this job the steward of the *Segurança* had filled his storeroom with food and drink, which he was to sell to the officers at extravagant prices on the way to New York. There was always some excuse ready on the tongue of the man who ran the little tug boat between Tampa and the *Segurança* as to why my orders were delayed while those given by the steward were promptly delivered. It was during this state of affairs, the steward's storehouse filled with provisions and my orders yet unfilled, that I took from a recently arrived transport some twenty-five men who had been on inadequate ration since leaving Cuba and had had no food for twenty-four hours or longer. I went to the steward of the *Segurança* and proposed that he either sell me some of the provisions which he had on hand or that he permit me to use some of them with the promise that as soon as the government supplies were received his loan would be fully returned. He told me plainly that no enlisted man should have a bite of food or drink from his supplies; that they had been furnished by the ship's agents in Tampa, and that they were to be sold to the officers on the way to New York. Fortunately, there were on board this ship some five or six able-bodied, armed soldiers, subject to orders and ready to obey. When the steward of the *Segurança* was given his choice of opening his storehouse or being placed in irons and thrown into the hold of his own ship, he unhesitatingly chose the former, and our hungry soldiers were fed.

It is laughable now to look back at the precautions taken by the health officer of Florida to prevent the introduction of yellow fever from the transports into Tampa. A tug from the city brought to the ship with frequent visits a few tons of coal at a time. In discharging the fuel the tug lay along side the ship and the

men from the tug went on to, and some of them, through
the ship. When a telegram was brought out on a tug it
stood at some distance from the ship and through a
megaphone the contents were transmitted, or in case of
official dispatches, they were placed in a box or roll,
attached to a string and tossed aboard. When food was
brought down, men on the tug passed freely and un-
interruptedly through the ship and men belonging to the
ship visited the tug.

After some days of delay the *Segurança* lifted anchor
from Tampa Bay and proceeded on its four-day voyage
to New York. This trip was not without its tragedy and
its comedy. We had gone to Cuba without ever dreaming that we might need such a thing as diphtheria antitoxin. From the time of leaving Old Point Comfort on
the outward voyage to reaching New York harbor on
the home coming there were cases of malignant diphtheria among the Michigan regiments, with an occasional
death. One of these occurred off Cape Hatteras and at
the request and advice of General O. O. Howard, who
had been to Cuba as a spectator and was now our honored
guest, the ship was stopped and a burial at sea with all
its attendant ceremonies took place. I may say here
that when the *Segurança* reached New York harbor,
there were some fourteen cases of malignant diphtheria
on board. This was the tragedy of the trip.

Among those quite recovered from yellow fever was
a colonel of regulars, a man who had led his regiment
heroically in the Battle of Santiago. He was, unfortunately, a dipsomaniac and in some way while we were
detained in Tampa Bay he obtained an abundant supply
of whiskey and before we were fairly out to sea he was

drunk. His intoxication in no way hampered his organs of locomotion. Stripped of every thread of clothing he boldly walked the decks indulging in obscene and profane salutations. I tried confining him to his room and detailed a signal corps man to guard him. Soon both were drunk and parading the deck in nature's clothing. I sought the advice of General Howard, who told me to put the colonel in irons. This I did not have the courage to do, but I did, after removing all drinks from his room, succeed in locking him in and in finding a reliable guard. I am glad to say that when we reached the battery in New York the colonel, sober and clothed in his uniform, without having attached to him any suspicion of wrong doing, was met by his charming wife and two daughters who greeted him as a hero deserves.

Judging from this experience, which may not be a wise thing to do, I believe that a northward sea voyage is highly beneficial to those convalescing from yellow fever and tropical malaria. The *Segurança* left Tampa Bay with at least thirty soldiers apparently *in extremis*. They were not only physically exhausted, but were so mentally clouded that they were not inclined even to accept help. I was also greatly impressed with the value of hypodermic injections of strychnia in these cases. This, I believe, was the only drug we used on the trip. The more seriously ill were placed on cots or lay on blankets on the upper deck. I visited them nearly every hour during the daytime and less frequently at night. I would walk among them asking who wanted milk or broth. Most of them were wholly indifferent and did not signify by word, movement or look that they desired anything. An attendant would kneel by the side of one

General O. O. Howard

and, raising his head, place at his lips and pour down his throat a portion of some well-prepared nourishing food. Within a few days most of these men were leaning over the rail or sauntering up and down the deck, and it was a great pleasure to watch their rapidly increasing strength and mental vigor. I believe that when we reached New York, with the exception of the cases of diphtheria, every man was on his feet and able to take care of himself. In all my experience as a practitioner of medicine I was never more pleased with results secured; this gave me a firm faith in the efficacy of proper medication and wise feeding.

As ranking officer on the ship I wore my blue blouse tightly buttoned. One hot afternoon on deck General Howard put his hand on my shoulder and said: "Relax, unbutton and take off your blouse. There is no need of strict adherence to military form." I unbuttoned my blouse, showing that there was nothing between it and my naked body. The good old general asked whether I had no shirt. My bag filled with underclothing, rescued from the sea at Siboney, had served others in greater need of clothing than myself. I was invited to the general's room and on the remainder of the voyage I had the honor of wearing one of his shirts. After this I walked the deck with my blouse unbuttoned and often without it.

Another experience with the big-hearted old general may be worthy of note. He was deeply religious and I fear that he had heard me on certain occasions use expletives which did not fall kindly on his ear; at least, one day he took me aside and gave me quite a lecture on the iniquity of swearing. I told him that I agreed with everything that he said, and that indulging in oaths was not a fixed habit with me. Then I related to him my experience in calling my hospital corps men across the road to assist me in carrying a wounded man on the battle field. He put his hand on my shoulder, looked steadily into my face, and with twinkling eyes, he said: "I admit that at times swearing seems to be absolutely necessary. I confess to you that on rare occasions I have been compelled to clothe my command in strong words."

In the last hour of the fourteenth of August, 1898, the day the armistice was signed, the *Seguança* dropped anchor at the quarantine station in New York harbor. I had been warned by the Secretary of War while in Tampa Bay to bring the ship into New York with the soldiers in such a condition that even the yellowest of journals could make no complaint. After the ship had come to rest I ordered every one off the deck, pulled a chair to the rail, lit a cigar and waited. It was not long before it happened. A tug came along side filled with newspaper reporters. In reply to their interrogatories I gave the name of the ship, the ports from which it had sailed, and a satisfactory account of those on board. I was asked whether there had been any deaths on the voyage, and I replied that one soldier had died and the cause of death was paralysis.

The next morning my good friend Doctor Doty, health officer of the port, came aboard with a newspaper in his hand, saying, "I see that you had a death from paralysis on the way." I answered in the affirmative and taking him by the arm, I said, "First of all, I will show you thirty other cases of the disease from which the man with paralysis died." I took him to the forecastle where

I had quarantined as best I could cases of diphtheria. Doctor Doty promised to care for these and he did it so skilfully that now for the first time, so far as I know, it appears in print that the *Segurança* brought into New York harbor cases of diphtheria. At Governor's Island each soldier laid off his clothing, passed through a bath and disinfecting room, and donned a new suit. The *Segurança* then proceeded to the wharf at the Battery where the officers disembarked.

On the voyage to Cuba I often sat on deck admiring our young officers as they passed. I thought that I had never seen finer looking, more intelligent, cleaner young men, and I was filled with pride of my country and of those who were ready to defend it. A few weeks later one of these young men whom I had so greatly admired would present himself or be brought to the hospital. His cheeks were sunken, his eyes glazed, his skin wrinkled, the fine glow of youth and health replaced by a cadaverous coppery hue. On being asked his name and the military organization to which he was attached, he would often answer slowly and stupidly. Some times he was unable to give the answer. His brain was benumbed and paralyzed by the plasmodia of tropical malaria. On the return voyage I had under my observation some of these same young men. Some left Tampa as I have said, almost moribund. One of these, the son of an ex-governor of Michigan, then a major, a general in the World War, was my special care. I took him to the Murray Hill Hotel in New York and left him under the care of a skilled confrère. His recovery was speedy and complete.

My summer vacation in Cuba was ended. I had had

an experience which I would not have missed and from which I learned much. I can not refrain from saying that when it was known among my colleagues in the University of Michigan that I was going to Camp Alger one of my dearest friends came to me and made an earnest plea that I had no right to risk my life by going to the war. About the time I left for Camp Alger he left for a summer vacation in France and went to his death on the ill-fated *Burgoyne*. Man proposes; God disposes.

CHAPTER XI

THE TYPHOID COMMISSION

ON REACHING New York on my return from
Cuba in August, 1898, I found an order to report
to the Surgeon General in Washington. Within a few
days the Typhoid Commission had been appointed, instructed and set to work. This Commission consisted of
Major Walter Reed of the regular army, chairman,
Major Edward O. Shakespeare, brigade surgeon, and
myself as division surgeon.

For some days we went every morning to Camp Alger
in Virginia nearby Washington, spent some hours in camp
and hospital and our evenings in discussing the work
assigned to us. It may be well to state the views we then
held concerning the epidemiology of typhoid fever.
Briefly, they were as follows: (1) Typhoid fever is a
specific disease due to infection with the Eberth bacillus;
(2) it is disseminated by the contamination of drinking
water, or, as we said, it is a water-borne disease. Naturally, milk or other foods or beverages might be vehicles
for its transmission; (3) it is not known to be transmitted
through other agencies, though flies have been suspected;
(4) it can be scientifically diagnosed by the agglutination
test during life and by the pathological findings after
death; (5) malaria, with which it is most likely to be
confounded, can be diagnosed by the finding of the plas-

modium in the blood; (6) typhoid fever will be found to
be most prevalent among those who are under par in
health, especially among those who suffer from gastro-
intestinal disturbances; (7) the mortality from this disease will be found to be greatest among those manifesting
these disorders. These were the views held by the most
competent medical men at that time.

Our visits to Camp Alger gave us much concern.
There we saw hundreds of cases which we believed, from
the clinical symptoms, to be typhoid fever, but which were
pronounced malaria by the majority of the physicians in
attendance. Autopsies were not in favor at that time.
Therefore we could not expect to get information from
the dead. To order autopsies would increase the public
furore which at that time was running high among the
people. Besides, it would be best, since it could be done,
to make the correct diagnosis during life. There was not
a microscope in any camp. Indeed, there were but few
medical men in this country in 1898 who could make the
agglutination test for typhoid fever or recognize the plasmodium of malaria and there were still fewer of these in
the army. An army diagnostic laboratory had never been
thought of. Plainly the first thing to do was to determine
the nature of the disease we had to deal with. We went
to Surgeon General Sternberg and asked authority to establish a diagnostic laboratory in each camp. No man
could have been more appreciative of this suggestion than
the pioneer bacteriologist of this country, and we were
given the authority asked. We were told to select the men
to operate these laboratories and to spare no cost in
equipment.

Doctors Gray and Carroll of the Army Medical

Museum soon began diagnostic work at Camp Alger, transferring their equipment to Fort Myer when the troops left Alger. Later, Carroll was established at Jacksonville, Florida, and Assistant Surgeon Curry took charge at Fort Myer. Doctor George Dock of the University of Michigan made investigations at Chickamauga, Knoxville and Meade. Assistant Surgeon Craig took charge of the diagnostic laboratory at Sternberg Hospital, Chickamauga Park, when Doctor Dock left. Naturally it took some days to get these laboratories into operation and in the meantime the Commission must move on. We left Washington feeling that we were proceeding properly in our attempts to secure a correct, scientific and unassailable diagnosis of the disease. We recognized that our evidence when presented must be overwhelming. At Camp Alger some of the medical officers agreed with us that the dominant disease in their hospitals was typhoid fever, but these men were in the minority. The majority held to malaria and there was the bogie of typhomalaria which had come into existence in the Civil War and during the more than thirty years which had elapsed since that conflict had been accepted as a reality by many of the best in the profession. It is needless to say that we read and re-read and discussed time and again the history of the fevers in our armies in the sixties. I have condensed this information in my work on epidemiology.

The seventh army corps under the command of General Fitzhugh Lee was in camp near Jacksonville, Florida. The water supply for the troops and that for the city came from four artesian wells varying in depth from six hundred and thirty to one thousand and twenty feet. These wells were located between the city and the camps. Pipes carried the same supply in one direction to the city and in the other to the camps. The population of the camps and that of the city were each in round numbers thirty thousand. Civilians and soldiers drank water from the same source. We could find only seven cases of typhoid fever in the civil population at a time when each of the three division hospitals was receiving a score or more patients with this disease each day; it was evident that typhoid fever in the seventh army corps could not be water-borne unless the water became infected after leaving the city pumps.

By this time we were informed that our diagnosticians at Fort Myer and at Chickamauga were at work. The medical officers at Jacksonville, like those at Camp Alger, were at variance about the diagnosis of the disease; but the dominant designations were typhomalaria and malaria, the latter for the milder and the former for the graver cases. We explained the matter to General Lee and asked him to provide a commission of three or more from the medical officers of the camp, to instruct this commission to select fifty cases that they believed to be malaria or typhomalaria and to turn them over to us. This caused considerable grumbling which reached the line officers. I heard a division commander protesting against the order to General Lee. He said that three men had come from Washington, and full of conceit had questioned the diagnosis of the prevailing disease as made by the medical officers in charge. These Washington men had been on the ground only a few days and had studied the cases only superficially while the medical men of the corps had watched the development of the epidemic from the beginning and had observed every phase of the disease. His discourse ran along this tenor for some time and as I stood near and heard it I had to admit to myself the truth of much that he said. General Lee heard him with good humor on his face, but ended the monologue by saying that the order would stand.

We put the fifty men, thus selected, on a hospital train and sent them to Fort Myer. Carroll reported every case typhoid; no malaria; then the grumbling became louder. It was hinted that the laboratory men at Fort Myer were our creatures and made a report to suit our views. The first part of this insinuation was true, but the second was not. However, we determined to make the demonstration so strong that no one could question it. Therefore, we asked General Lee to instruct the board of medical officers to select one hundred and fifty more cases. This was done and we distributed them among all the best hospitals in Baltimore, Philadelphia, New York, Boston and Cleveland. From each and all of these came confirmation of Carroll's report from Fort Myer. By this time Dock and Craig were sending in their findings from Chickamauga and from that time no one questioned the diagnosis of typhoid fever. Typhomalaria disappeared from the morbidity lists, not only in army sick reports but shortly in civilian records.

Another favorable condition for the study of the epidemiology of typhoid fever was evident in the camp near Jacksonville. The first division disposed of its fecal matter by water carriage. The installment for this purpose was crude in construction and faulty in operation, but the number of cases developed in the six regiments of this division was one thousand and thirty. In the second division the tub system of disposing of fecal matter was employed. By this method infected fecal matter was scattered all along the company streets and the roads. The number of cases of typhoid fever in the nine regiments of this division was two thousand six hundred and ninety-eight. In the third division regulation pits served as receptacles for fecal matter. In the seven regiments of this division there were one thousand two hundred and ninety-two cases. The tub system was immediately condemned. Water carriage was recommended. When the latter was not practicable it was urged that all fecal matter should be disinfected with freshly slacked lime, removed in odorless excavators and buried. For some years after the Spanish-American War this was done at many army posts.

It was at Jacksonville, if I remember correctly, that the idea of contact or, as we then called it, comrade infection began to obtrude itself upon us. There were certain companies and even certain tents that supplied more than their proportionate number of cases. Then we began a most laborious research which we did not complete until many months after our return to Washington. I shall go into some detail about this later. About this time also we began to be convinced that flies had some part in the dissemination of typhoid fever.

Our stay at Jacksonville was pleasant apart from our special duties. We were members of General Lee's staff and enjoyed his mess and his stories, one of which I shall repeat since I have never seen it in print. After the surrender at Appomattox, Fitzhugh Lee on his way home was riding along a dusty lane. Seeing a farmer sitting on the rail fence he stopped and began conversation. General Lee: "The war is over." Farmer: "I heard that but I

General Fitzhugh Lee

don't believe it." General Lee: "Yes, it is over; Lee has surrendered." Farmer: "I heard that too; maybe that little runt, Fitzhugh Lee, has surrendered, but Robert E. Lee, never."

Among the regiments inspected at Jacksonville was the 3rd Nebraska whose colonel was the late Honorable William J. Bryan. As we were instructed to do, we found our way to the colonel's tent, presented our credentials and asked him to join us in the inspection of his regiment. I shall only say that we found the sanitary condition no better than in other regiments. When we were through with the inspection Major Reed said to the colonel: "Shakespeare and Vaughan are on this commission because they know something of camp sanitation. I am here because I can damn a colonel," and he proceeded in plain terms to speak of the responsibility of a commanding officer in looking after the health of his troops, and so forth.

A few days later General Lee reviewed the troops from a platform near the Windsor Hotel. He insisted on our standing on the platform with him. We stood back until a certain moment when Lee signified his wish for us to come forward, saying: "Here comes the 3rd Nebraska; salute the colonel as he passes." This was the only hint we had that General Lee may have heard of the incident in the camp.

We went from Jacksonville to Chickamauga Park. This had been the largest camp in the country. During June and July, 1898, it had been occupied by two corps, sixty thousand troops, but before our arrival many regiments had been sent away. Some had gone to Porto Rico, some were sent to Newport News, and more recently large detachments had been transferred to Anniston, Alabama, to Lexington, Kentucky, and to Knoxville, Tennessee.

Nature has made Chickamauga Park an attractive place. That it is the stage on which one of the great battles of the Civil War was fought lends it a historic interest. In 1898 there was only one objection to it as the site of a great camp. The rocky surface made the digging of latrines difficult and the scanty soil, when thrown out in making the excavations, soon became hard clods with no absorptive property. There are within and about the park large springs and in 1898 the government might, at less cost than was actually expended, have carried an unlimited supply of pure water to every soldier and washed all his excrement beyond the bounds of the camp. I can not but feel that the engineer corps was largely responsible for the 1898 tragedy at Chickamauga, but the ignorance of camp sanitation at that time displayed by the army engineer was surpassed only by that of the line officer. It is true that the medical officer was not up to the times on this subject, but his recommendations were often regarded as unwarranted suggestions from an inferior and treated with contempt. A corps commander went ostentatiously daily to a well condemned by the medical officers and drank of its water. Fortunately for him he had doubtlessly drunk so much polluted water in his life that he had secured a high degree of immunity.

The frail rip-rap dam which was built to deflect the water of Cave Spring Branch, the open sewer of the camp, as it flowed into Chickamauga River was a travesty on sanitary and engineering skill. Besides, the pure waters of the springs were dipped by hands, often bearing infection, into headless barrels not free from the possibility

of infection and hauled in wagons to the troops. Here
the barrels were emptied by a repetition of the dipping
process. There was testimony that men seeking absence
without leave often rode in the empty barrels on their
return to the springs. The result was that water supplies
for regiments thus provided were always short and frequently exposed to specific infection. Some organizations were supplied with piped water which came from
Chickamauga River but the intake was protected from
the sewer only by the flimsy rip-rap dam already referred
to and this was broken by the first heavy rain. In and
near the park are a few shallow wells in a soil traversed
by fissures in the rock and subject to pollution from
latrines. Such in brief was the water supply of the camp
at Chickamauga Park in 1898. It was fortunate for us
that we had studied the camps at Alger and Jacksonville
before we came to Chickamauga; we never could estimate
the extent to which typhoid was water-borne at this camp.

I have never seen so large an area of fecal-stained
soil as that which we looked upon and walked over in
Chickamauga Park in 1898. This area was a checker
board, marked with woody spots of irregular contour and
open spaces, some of which had known cultivation. The
woody lands were smeared with alvine discharges. As I
have said, most of the soldiers had been removed before
our arrival, but even then one could not walk under the
trees without soiling one's shoes with human excrement.
Behind every considerable tree it lay in heaped-up cones.
The falling leaves and twigs did not suffice to hide it.
The gentle winds had not wholly dispersed it; a hot September sun was drying it out. An occasional rain was
sinking the pollution below the surface and down into the

soil where the typhoid bacilli may retain their vitality and virulence for a long time.

At Chickamauga regiments came and went; many brought the infection; none left without it; no organization lingered within its precincts without contributing to the morbidity and mortality lists. With every considerable accession of new troops the flames of the epidemic flared up, consuming not only the newly added fuel but burning deeper into the charred logs. This phenomenon was noticed especially in certain Pennsylvania regiments, which originally consisted of only eight companies. Those in the park early had experienced their first epidemic, when the additional four companies arrived. Soon the sick curve began to rise and both the new and the seasoned soldier contributed. This seems to be a frequent occurrence in military organizations. The recruiting of veteran organizations may be accompanied by greater loss than battles, and is always fraught with danger.

Regiments moved out of the park, leaving their grounds not only untidy but highly and dangerously infected. New regiments came in and occupied the vacated areas without attempt to clean up. Tents were in some instances pitched over scantily covered latrines. The rains washed the excreta of certain organizations into the company streets and even into the tents of lower lying ones. Nothing is more conducive to sanitary neglect than the expectation of "moving on" in a few days. What does it matter? We are going to vacate these grounds to-morrow or next week. There were organizations at Chickamauga Park when we visited it in September that had been on waiting orders since May or June. "We are going to-morrow or at farthest next week to Newport News and embark for Cuba or Porto Rico or possibly for Spain." It is deadening in every particular for an army to be on "waiting orders," which never come. It breeds a psychological state of mind which begins in elation and soon settles down into an apathy which is destructive in its effect upon every man from the commander-in-chief to the lowest private in the ranks. The Treaty of Peace had been signed in Paris, August 14, and when our inspection was made, military pride had disappeared and every soldier was brooding over personal grievances. Add to this, the physical and mental effects of the deadly epidemic, prevalent in every camp, and it is not surprising that we found in every military organization a spiritless, despondent gloom covering the whole. There had been no peace treaty with disease and death.

The night after our arrival the commander-in-chief took me into a grove of trees and in a whisper asked if I knew the meaning of the Indian word Chickamauga. I did not. Then he said, "it means the river of death and this disease is not typhoid fever nor malaria. It is Chickamauga fever and is due to a miasma that arises nightly from the river and permeates the camp."

I can not speak for the other members of my board but I admit, now after twenty-eight years, that I became in a way morbid. I have said something of the morbid fancies that invaded my brain cells in my struggle with yellow fever in Cuba in July. I had lost sixty pounds in this contest. I had been entrusted with the command of a hospital ship when I was too weak to go from one side of the deck to the other, save by crawling on my hands and knees. My experiences in Tampa Bay had not acted as a sedative on my over tense nerves. On the inspection tour I had managed to behave quite normally. At least I am sure that my comrades would not have testified to my insanity. I relished my food as I had never done before—although I have had only rare occasion to complain of the efficiency of my gustatory nerves or my digestive organs. An imperative diarrhea annoyed me and persisted in doing so.

When we were preparing to leave Washington the manager of the Southern Railroad kindly placed at our disposal a private car. It had a kitchen presided over by a most competent cook. His viands were well selected and tastily prepared. There was an obliging porter and we had separate bedrooms. The front end of the car served as our office and reception room and in it sat our competent stenographer. In short, we had every modern comfort in our journey. To me there was but one discomfort. That car had to stand at night at our stopping places in the switch yard with trains passing, bells ringing and whistles screaming throughout the long hours. At Jacksonville General Lee had been kind enough to permit our car to be brought to the vicinity of his headquarters. This gave relief for the time. But never since that time have I ridden on a train through the switch yards at Jacksonville or Chattanooga without a painful shudder.

At Chattanooga our car stood at the switch yard. We left it in the morning after a delightful breakfast and returned in the evening to a more abundant dinner. The first Sunday morning of our stay at Chattanooga I asked permission to rest for the day. I went to the Reed House, secured a room and went to bed swearing by all the gods that I would respond to no call until I had a good sleep. I had but a few minutes in bed before there was a loud knocking at the door. I tried to ignore it but it became louder and more peremptory. With an unspoken oath on my lip I opened the door. In walked William Lasley, who, while a student at Michigan, had gone through a long siege of typhoid fever during which I had served as his physician. I had forgotten that his home was in Chattanooga. He told me that his father's carriage was waiting and that I was to go to his home. I went to the commodious house on the bank of the river, where my time until morning was divided between chats accompanied by smokes, sleeping and eating. I went back to my work greatly refreshed Monday morning.

But during the following days of our stay at Chickamauga I suffered much in both body and mind. As we rode in an ambulance through the camp, tramped the long corridors of the Sternberg and Leiter Hospitals with the crowded cots on each side, consulted with the officers, both medical and of the line, visited with and received the reports of my good colleague, Doctor Dock, in charge of the diagnostic laboratory, and planned our work, I really envied some of the more comfortable looking patients. Once in passing an empty cot I was sorely tempted to throw off my blouse and drop on it. But I was restrained by seeing the mental picture of my wife in the "cottage in the woods" at Old Mission holding before her the Detroit *Free Press* bearing on its front page the head line, "Major Vaughan of the Typhoid Board becomes a victim of the disease." This braced me up and I went on with my comrades. When we had finished with Chickamauga and had spent a few days in getting statistics at the camp at Knoxville, I incidentally suggested to my comrades that we go to Asheville, North Carolina, and spend a few days in getting our papers in shape. They readily assented. By some means we succeeded in having our car parked at or near the Biltmore station. We employed an old, garrulous negro driver with an ancient carryall, and riding over this beautiful region we spent some days before returning to Washington.

In the memory chambers of my brain there hang many pictures. Some are the joy of my life, too sacred and too personal to describe to any save my most intimate friends. But there are also ghastly ones which I would tear down and destroy were I able to do so, but this is beyond my power. They are a part of my being and will perish only when I die or lose my memory. Some of these are hospital scenes. Two were painted on my memory walls during the inspection tour of which I am now writing. By some inscrutable device these pictures, although painted on the microscopic cells of my brain, are full life-size and each shows hundreds of human figures. They are not pictures of still life, for I see every movement of each figure. Sometimes their eyes turn toward me or toward a comrade. In some, the eyes are full of meaning, bespeaking a brain in action; in others they are dull and staring, indicating benumbed or comatose intellectuality. Some faces show the hectic flush of high fever; some the pallor of approaching death; some of the figures are full and rounded, showing but slight departure from health; others are wasted and skeleton like; some are motionless; others are picking at the bedding or plucking imaginary objects from the air. All are prostrate on cots but some are attempting to rise and unreasonably impatient of restraint. These pictures are not all silent ones; some are gentle in their speech; others are violent and denunciatory; some are muttering in low delirium; others are shouting in wild mania. The pictures of which I am speaking just now are of the Second Division hospital at Jacksonville and the Sternberg Hospital at Chickamauga. The colors in which they are painted are indelible, strong in contrast, without harmony; but always painful in their effects upon their possessor. The artist who painted these pictures is typhoid fever.

While I am engaged in describing the horrors of my memory picture gallery I might as well say something of the others, and then I will promise never to touch this grewsome subject again. A third picture is in some respects the most horrible of all. The figures are as numerous as those in numbers one and two, but all are children, mostly from five to ten years of age. Most are paralytic in one or more limbs, but this is not the most distressing feature. The paralysis is gradually extending to the muscles of respiration. Suffocation is advancing slowly but painfully and fatally. The little ones, as they pant for breath, turn their beseeching eyes to the doctor. They utter no word of complaint; but with their eyes they beg for help. The pump that brings the air into the lungs grows less and less efficient and finally stops; the lamp of life flickers, fades and goes out. This picture was painted on my memory walls as I stood in a ward of the Willard Parker Hospital in New York City during the great epidemic of infantile paralysis in 1916.

The fourth canvas is quite as large as the others. I see hundreds of young, stalwart men in the uniform of their country coming into the wards of the hospital in groups of ten or more. They are placed on the cots until every bed is full and yet others crowd in. The faces soon wear a bluish cast; a distressing cough brings up the blood stained sputum. In the morning the dead bodies are stacked about the morgue like cord wood. This picture was painted on my memory cells at the division hospital, Camp Devens, in 1918, when the deadly influenza demonstrated the inferiority of human inventions in the destruction of human life.

Such are the grewsome pictures exhibited by the revolving memory cylinders in the brain of an old epidemiologist as he sits in front of the burning logs on the hearth of his "cottage in the woods." As he looks, he prays that his successors may be spared this infliction. I am growing sentimental and I have condemned this tendency. When I am detected I am ready to plead *peccavi,* but confession is not atonement.

At Chickamauga the agencies concerned in the transmission and spread of typhoid fever fairly obtruded themselves on our vision. I will briefly discuss them. It had been suggested that the house fly might be a vector in this disease. I do not know who first suggested this. In Circular Number One, issued by Surgeon General Sternberg under date of April 25, 1898, there occurs the following: "No doubt typhoid fever, camp diarrhea, and probably yellow fever are frequently communicated to soldiers in camp through the agency of flies, which swarm about fecal matter and filth of all kinds deposited upon the ground or in shallow pits and directly convey infectious material, attached to their feet or contained in their excreta to the food which is exposed while being prepared at the company kitchens or while being served in the mess tents."

Our statistics show that the percentage of typhoid was

much less among those who ate in screened tents. We sprinkled lime over the contents of the latrines and soon saw flies with feet whitened by the lime walking over the food on the mess tables. Later Doctor Alice Hamilton demonstrated by cultural methods the presence of typhoid bacilli in flies which had fed upon typhoid dejecta. This has been abundantly confirmed and *Musca domestica* has been pronounced guilty and is now figuratively dubbed "the typhoid fly."

Our board estimated that the fly was responsible for about fifteen per cent. of the cases of typhoid fever in our camps in 1898. This was taken up by civilian health authorities, exploited in the press and has done much to reduce the number of these pestiferous insects and to render life more comfortable as well as safer from infection, not only with typhoid fever, but tuberculosis, diarrhea, dysentery, and so forth.

Had a conscious effort been made to demonstrate the epidemiology of typhoid fever it could hardly have been better staged than it was in Chickamauga Park. At first there were practically no trained nurses or hospital orderlies, either males or females. Before us every morning regiments were drawn up and so many men detailed from the ranks to serve in the hospitals as orderlies for the day. We followed these men to the hospitals and saw them handling bed pans in their awkward, ignorant way, often soiling their hands as well as the bedding, floors and the ground. At noon they went to lunch mostly without washing their hands, to say nothing of disinfecting them, handling their food and passing it to their comrades. A like demonstration was repeated at supper. The next day a repetition of this cycle was reenacted. Of course, the Board interdicted this show which had already been running for some weeks.

The men, both when off and on duty, soiled their feet in going through the wooded spaces and tracked the infection into their tents. In this way, the person, the food, the clothing, the bedding, and the tentage became the source of this specific infection. The members of the Board saw plainly that contact or comrade infection was the chief agency in the spread of typhoid fever in our camps in 1898 but they realized that their conviction would need to be verified by voluminous and reliable statistics before they could ask the scientific world to accept it. This meant a sentence for them to hard labor for an indefinite period. I shall return to this.

Before beginning our statistical studies it was desirable that we have some idea of the minimum period of incubation in typhoid fever. We might be able to figure this out from the sick reports of the Pennsylvania regiments that had come to Chickamauga Park short and had received their additional companies on certain recorded dates, but it might be possible to get the desired information elsewhere. About this time fifty trained female nurses from Chicago arrived at Leiter Hospital. We were compelled to assume that all were free from typhoid infection when they arrived and began their hospital work. Each of these was carefully watched and the first came down with typhoid fever ten days after her arrival. Our conclusion was that the minimum period of incubation in typhoid fever is something less than ten days. This has been repeatedly confirmed. Many accidental infections with pure cultures have been recorded and in one instance, at least, a culture was swallowed with suicidal intent. It is true that the period of incubation in typhoid fever is not so constant as in measles, but the knowledge that it may be shorter than ten days has been of great service in the study of its epidemiology. Of course, with our present knowledge we would have vaccinated these girls and the probabilities are that all would have escaped the disease.

After a few days in Washington our Board went to Camp Meade near Harrisburg, Pennsylvania. Here the medical men, notified of our studies, had begun handling typhoid fever as a contagious as well as an infectious disease. Tents, bedding and clothing were disinfected and under these procedures typhoid fever rapidly decreased in the camps, some of which were continued for months. A short visit to Montauk Point, New York, preceded our inspection of Camp Meade. In the former we studied the diseases prevalent among the soldiers returned from Santiago, Cuba. Here we found not only typhoid fever but tropical malaria and convalescents from yellow fever. Later we studied the sick reports of the Fifth Army Corps, the army of invasion, but we did not include these findings in our final report, since our orders were interpreted as confining our work to diseases acquired in the United States. I admit that I was somewhat irritated by a statement coming from the Surgeon General's office about the close of the World War saying that we had no medical report on the Spanish-American War and not mentioning the work of the Typhoid Commission. I have regarded our report as the medical history of the Spanish-American War with the exception of those diseases acquired in Cuba, Porto Rico, the Philippines, those in our navies and the battle casualties. It is true that these are important omissions, but an official report of our medical histories that makes no mention of the work of the Typhoid Commission is certainly defective, and in memory of Majors Reed and Shakespeare I entered a protest.

Our term of sentence to hard labor began in October, 1898, and continued without intermission until the last of June, 1899. The place of our detention was the Army Medical School at Washington. We had before us the monthly sick reports of one hundred and eighteen regiments. From these, every name with rank and company was copied and arranged alphabetically. Each man was traced to a hospital and to final disposition. The records of twenty regiments were so defective that they were discarded. Of the remaining ninety-eight regiments we charted all of the sick in eighty-four, but some of these had been furloughed and it was impossible to follow the individuals. We appealed to the superintendents of civilian hospitals to which sick soldiers had been sent as shown by our records. Only one large hospital, Cook County, Chicago, declined to give us the information asked. However, we did get the data we wanted from this institution. When the superintendent declined to aid, we appealed to the members of the medical staff, prominent Chicago physicians, and they, at their own expense in both time and money, supplied us with the data. In sixty regiments all cases of typhoid, all short and long so-called malarias, and all diarrheas were charted according to the date of their occurrence. In the remaining twenty-four regiments only cases of typhoid fever were charted. In forty-eight regiments we traced the subsequent history of every man with a short diarrhea or supposed mild malarial attack in order to see whether these individuals afterwards showed an immunity to typhoid fever. Bearing on the theory of contact or comrade infection we located by tents and in the order of their occurrence every case of typhoid fever in a number of regiments, both in isolated, small camps and in the larger camps, both north and south of the Mason-Dixon line. These data were furnished by medical officers and by company commanders.

Having found the first case of typhoid fever we endeavored to ascertain where he acquired the disease and how he transmitted it to others. This necessitated our going back to his enlistment and making inquiries concerning the existence of the disease in the community from which he came. Local health officers and physicians, for the most part, came promptly to our aid. We were able to show that in 1898 typhoid fever was so widely distributed in this country that in the assembling of a volunteer regiment, about one thousand three hundred men, there would be from one to four men already bearing the infection. These brought the infection into the camp. In no case did typhoid fever originate *de novo*. This effectively killed the theory first formulated by Murchison, defended and strengthened by the teachings of Pettenkofer and accepted and elaborated by Davies and other medical officers in the British army, that typhoid fever originates in a ripening process in normal excreta deposited in the soil. It re-established the theory of Budd that there is no typhoid fever without a preceding infection and that typhoid fever is spread only by introducing the alvine discharges of an infected man into the alimentary canal of another man. Thus, apparently well but infected men brought the seeds of the disease into the camps, deposited these in the latrines or elsewhere in their discharges, soiled their own persons and clothing and thus communicated the disease to others.

War with Spain was declared April 21, 1898, when Minister Woodford was handed his passport at Madrid. At that time our regular army numbered 28,183 officers and men widely distributed in small posts throughout the country. This number was augmented to approximately 275,000, thus making about one regular to ten volunteers. The regulars with but little aid, probably with more detriment, fought the land battle at Santiago, the only big land battle of the war. After Dewey's victory in Manila Bay there was but little for the army to do but to go in and occupy the country. The greatest contest was with disease. Why was this? The greatest bacteriologist in the country was the Surgeon General. Why then were our camps without any scientific equipment? On March 9, 1898, when war was inevitable, Congress appropriated fifty millions of dollars for "national defense." This sum was placed at the disposal of President McKinley, but he could use it only for defense. It was spent liberally in coast defense, when any fool might have known that a Spanish soldier would never step on our shore save as a prisoner. Not only the medical department but the quartermaster and the commissary did not get a cent of the fifty millions of dollars. We have always boasted that we would fight only a defensive war. We still hear this foolish and hypocritical cry. The nation that prepares only for defense, prepares to lose. The exceptions to this rule are indeed rare. In our War for Independence, John Paul Jones and his comrades did not confine their operations to our own coast. In the war of 1812 we invaded Canada. The Mexican War was wholly aggressive. If the southern troops had followed up the rout at Bull Run, the fate of the Civil War might have been quite different. The Spanish-American War was offensive from start to finish and the nation paid dearly for the foolish congressional procedure. I think that no man saw more of the American soldiery in rank and file than I did, and, in my opinion, it consisted of the flower of the nation. How many potentially great men sleep in the graves of that war no one can estimate. Many of those who survived have demonstrated both in civil and military life their worth to their country.

During our inspections and the continuance of our work there was no lack of wise men who were willing to tell us the cause of the epidemics in the camps. Many said that it was due to the transfer of northern men to the south. To this we had only to point to the high prevalence of typhoid fever in certain regiments that never crossed the Mason-Dixon line.

Some said that it was due to the unwise selection of camp sites. There is no spot on earth so salubrious that man may not convert it into a hotbed for the breeding of disease.

Since Major Reed had many other duties, Shakespeare and I had to do most of the clerical and tabulation work. We spent the working hours of the day in the Army Medical Museum and the evenings in our rooms on K Street. Here we had a commodious workroom with a great table in the center. We spread out our sick reports and continued the work. I am a fair worker when I have a task, but at midnight I want to go to bed and I did so, invariably leaving my comrade at the table. I have never known a more persistent worker than Major Shakespeare.

In June, 1899, Shakespeare and I were informed that the finances of Uncle Sam were so reduced that he could no longer keep us on his pay-roll and we were discharged; I should say honorably. But this did not stop our work; we divided the remaining sick reports and went to our respective homes. We planned a temporary resurrection of the defunct Board at Atlantic City, June 2, 1900. I was on my way when I had a telegram announcing the sudden death of Major Shakespeare. I attended his funeral and returned home. In preparation for this meeting I had prepared an abstract of our report. This was published by the government, but I knew that a bare statement of our conclusions without supporting evidence would not be convincing. In the meantime, Major Reed was carrying out his brilliant and successful researches on the transmission of yellow fever. Thank God! he lived long enough to see this work accepted and his name written among the great benefactors of his race.

Foreign governments began to ask that the report be published in full. Doctor Christopher Childs of the London Epidemiological Society came over and studied the manuscript with me. I owe much to his suggestions and generous help. In 1903 Congress, largely through the influence of Mr. Root, then Secretary of War, made an appropriation for the publication of the full report which appeared in two volumes, one of text and one of charts, late in 1904. These volumes were sent to the war departments of all nations. Some years later it was announced from Germany that Professor Robert Koch had discovered that typhoid fever is largely distributed by contact, giving the percentage of cases due to this cause at practically the same figures given by us. It is needless to say that this announcement did not mention our work begun ten years, and published four years previously. Since this is my autobiography it is my duty to disclose some of my vices as well as magnify all my virtues; therefore I will admit that I was not greatly depressed when I learned that in the invasion of Belgium in 1914 the German army suffered from typhoid fever more seriously than did the English or French.

In my official report I summarized our findings and conclusions in non-technical language to the lay reader. In the chapter on typhoid fever in volume two of my work on epidemiology I have reproduced the summary in more abbreviated form. It may be of interest, however, to mention some of these briefly and to inquire how far the original views of the Board were modified by its own work. These views I have already formulated on page 369. Our work demonstrated beyond peradventure that typhoid fever is a specific disease. It converted a theory into a demonstrated fact. We greatly modified numbers two and three of our previous beliefs. Before beginning our inspection we believed that typhoid fever was exclusively a water-borne disease. Our investigations showed that water-borne infection played a relatively small part in the spread of this disease; that contact or comrade infection was responsible for sixty-two and eighty-hundredths per cent. of cases; that flies caused fifteen per cent.; that the remaining twenty-two and two-

tenths per cent. was due to water or air-borne infection
and possibly undetermined agencies. Of course, a given
local epidemic may be disseminated exclusively by any one
of these agencies. Water-borne epidemics, as in the case of
polluted water supplies, are usually characterized by ex-
plosive outbreaks, while those due to other agencies are
more insidious and gradual in their spread.

Our original views numbers four and five were confirmed; numbers six and seven were found to be quite
wrong. In the beginning we had not the slightest doubt
that we would find typhoid fever more prevalent among
those who were frequently on the sick report than among
those in more robust health, but thinking that it would
be well to substantiate this, we collected much statistical data. The evidence against our assumption was
overwhelming. More than ninety per cent. of those who
developed typhoid fever had no preceding intestinal dis-
order. In other words, the disease was almost wholly
confined to the robust and vigorous. Those frequently
on sick report for the most part did not develop this
disease. The reasons for this are multiple. It had long
been known that typhoid fever is more prevalent among
men than women, and more prevalent among young
adults than in childhood or in advanced age. This fact,
well founded, was believed to be due to some inexplain-
able influence of sex and age. The true explanation is
more simple. The husband has a much wider range of
activity than the wife and his exposures to infection are
much more frequent. The same is true of the young
adult compared with the child and the aged. There are
other more technical reasons for the greater prevalence
of this disease among young adult males. Many men

Doctor Robert Koch

in more advanced years have had slight unrecognized attacks and have thus secured some immunity.

But the results that came from our study of the proportion of deaths among the frail and the robust shocked us. The figures showed that the more robust the patient the more likely was he to die. We went over these figures time and time again. We discussed them from every angle. We did not want to believe them; but there they stood. We could find no error; we were compelled to accept them. Then, we thought that we had made a discovery. I began to delve into the old literature; to my surprise this same thing had been observed in the typhus epidemics in Ireland. Among the half-starved Irish cotters one out of twenty-three of those attacked died; among the doctors, priests and nurses who became infected one out of every three died. Poor, lousy, infested men were haled from the prisons into court and tried for some misdemeanor. The jailer, the barristers, the jury and complainants would sicken and die while the prisoners would recover. This it was that gave the name "Black Assizes" to these trials. This it was that led the English to establish the first fever hospital and to improve the conditions of their jails. It is frequently said that these reforms were due to the pictures drawn by Charles Dickens; they were wrought by a more potent force, the high death rate among the upper classes when brought into contact with the disease.

One old writer in describing the epidemics of typhus in Ireland and England wrote that the disease went through a community, much as you or I would go through a flock of sheep, picking out the "handsomest, healthiest and lustiest." So our discovery turned out to be nothing more then the picking up of lost facts. This tendency of certain infections to kill off the most robust was confirmed in the pneumonia and influenza epidemics of the World War. These diseases do not improve the race by killing off the unfit as Herbert Spencer believed, but like war, they destroy the best in the nation. Occasionally we still hear the assertion that the doctors are injuring the race by preserving the lives of the unfit, who were formerly killed off by disease especially in childhood. I believe in weeding out the unfit but disease is not the agent through which this desirable result may be secured.

I ventured to offer a simple explanation of the fact that certain infections are more deadly among the robust than among the weak. When one becomes infected with the bacteria of these diseases the body cells begin to destroy the invading germ cells. The strong man kills his invaders rapidly, at the same time liberating their poisons, and in this conflict the patient either recovers promptly or dies quickly. I have said that nothing more surely fatal to the typhoid patient can occur than the sudden destruction of all the bacilli in his body. Nature often overdoes its work; it is a brave but reckless leader in battle. At first I advanced this theory tentatively and without absolute conviction as to its truth, but I have heard it from so many men and have read it in so many books without reference to its author that now I am fully convinced of its truth. It is said that one may repeat an imaginary incident so often that he finally believes it actually occurred. From observation among my friends and my own personal experience I believe that this old saying has much truth in it. But nothing can be more convincing of the truth of one's own story than to hear it repeated by those whose judgment and wisdom one respects as coming within their own experience, or as deduced from their own intellectual processes. It is all the more a compliment to the author because it is not intended as such.

As disgraceful in some respects as they were to our country and to England the Spanish-American and the Boer Wars were necessary preparations for the World War. I am sure that this is true in a medical and sanitary way and I believe that it is true from every military standpoint. I lived through the years between the Spanish-American and the World Wars, grumbling more or less audibly, swearing inwardly, sometimes vociferously, and asserting that our government had learned nothing from the Spanish-American War and that we would enter the next as unprepared as we were in 1898. However, I was not altogether inactive during this interval. I never lost my interest in the medical corps and I kept as closely attached to it as the law permitted a civilian to be. During the Spanish-American War I had come to admire many men in the regular army, especially in the medical corps. I knew something of the handicaps under which they worked, sympathized with their attempts to improve matters and continued to enjoy their personal friendship. In 1908 the medical reserve corps, the first of the army, was authorized and I became a lieutenant subject to orders. The Surgeon General on one or two occasions called men of this corps to Washington in consultation.

The organization of the reserve corps was a wise step which was soon adopted by other chiefs of the

army. In the medical corps it was done by Surgeon
General O'Reilly with the aid of Majors Kean and Ireland.
Every progressive physician in the country wanted a commission. The sanitation of all posts was greatly improved.
In 1898 the death rate in the army from typhoid fever
per hundred thousand was eight hundred and seventy-
nine; in 1899 it was one hundred and seven and continued with some fluctuations to fall, reaching nineteen
in 1907, the lowest point before the introduction of typhoid vaccination. With compulsory vaccination there
were no cases in 1913; three per hundred thousand in
1914; none in 1915; three in each 1916 and 1917. In
France in 1918 and 1919 it was five and three-tenths and
seven and one-tenth respectively. In 1898 a civilian enlist-
ing in the army was quite sure to have typhoid fever; one
in every five did. In 1917 the civilian who wished to
escape typhoid fever could find no safer place than the
army.

In 1910, twenty per cent. of our troops were vaccinated against typhoid fever. In 1911, thirty per cent.; in
1912, this procedure was made compulsory. This method
of increasing resistance to this infection was first practised by Sir Almroth Wright, of the Army Medical
School at Netley, but England ignored the discovery
of its wise son and went through the Boer War without
this protection. The losses from this disease in South
Africa were even greater than ours in the Spanish-
American War. Ours was the first army in the world
in which vaccination against typhoid fever was made
compulsory and therefore universal. This was largely
due to Colonel F. F. Russell, who recommended it after
a thorough study of the optimal procedures in Euro-

pean armies. Of course all nations engaged in the World War made it compulsory. Had typhoid fever been permitted to run riot in the World War, as it did in the Spanish-American and Boer Wars, the loss of life, great as it was, would probably have been doubled.

Our troops went to Cuba in 1898 without hospital equipment. The tents used as hospitals at Siboney belonged to the State of Michigan and not to the Federal Government. In the World War our first assignment to France consisted of hospitals and the first of our soldiers killed in France was a medical man, Doctor Fitzgerald, of Kansas City. Before the World War the Red Cross hospitals in this country, under the direction of Colonel Kean, were made ready for an emergency and were transported to France well-equipped and well-manned.

Before the Spanish-American War medical officers detailed to West Point, Annapolis, Leavenworth and other points of instruction took care of the sick, but gave no instruction to the cadets. This was changed and the graduates from these institutions had opportunity to learn about sanitation, preventive medicine, and their duties concerning the health of the troops who should come under their command. Our nation did profit by the lessons of the Spanish-American War and my grumbling, swearing and forebodings were happily without justification as such things often are.

CHAPTER XII

DURING our Civil War the authorities became aware of the fact that science could be of service in war as well as in peace, and the National Academy of Sciences was chartered by Congress in 1863. This is a self-perpetuating body, selecting its own membership, receiving no financial aid from the government, but ready at all times to put itself at the command of Congress or the President. Immediately on its organization, the Academy was entrusted with the solution of problems, ranging from "the preservation of paint on army knapsacks" to "the protection of bottoms of iron vessels from corrosion." In peace, committees from the Academy have, on request, given advice on an equally wide range of subjects. At its annual meeting in April, 1916, the Academy, by unanimous vote, tendered its service to President Wilson and this was immediately accepted. A committee of members of the Academy with authority to enlarge its membership from the scientists of the country was appointed and christened "The National Research Council."

The first meeting of this body was held September 20, 1916, in the Engineering Foundation Building in New York. About forty of the most eminent scientists, including every department from astronomy to bacteriology, were present. An organization was effected and an executive committee, which should meet at short intervals, was appointed. We had no money, but to its great credit the Engineering Foundation gave us office space in its building, furnished a secretary, and granted five thousand dollars from its treasury for immediate expenses. It is not my purpose to give in any detail the work done by the National Research Council. This has been done by its prime mover and leading spirit, George E. Hale, of the Mount Wilson Observatory, Pasadena, California, and by others in a volume entitled *The New World of Science* by Robert M. Yerkes. Doctor Hale was the dynamo that generated and supplied the motive power, reinforced by such men as Michael Pupin, Gano Dunn, Robert Millikan, A. Michelson, William H. Welch, Edward Conklin, J. J. Carty, A. A. Noyes, and many others. The scientific men from every department of government were brought in in cooperation with this organization. In other words, the scientific forces of the nation were mobilized and began to work without a creak or jar, as a perfect machine should. Indeed, the mobilization of science extended beyond our country and soon we were in close cooperation with the scientific men of all the allied nations. Immediately after the appointment of the committee known as the National Research Council, Doctors Hale and Welch went to Europe and established a liaison with our friends. It was found that the scientists of our allies were ready to supply us with all the knowledge they had gained, and our work was largely directed by their experience and advice.

My part in the National Research Council before we entered the war was to look after medical affairs. As a member of the executive committe during the fall and winter of 1916-17, I made frequent visits from Ann Arbor to New York and Washington. I would make a night journey to one of these places, spend a day in consultation with my fellows and return that night and continue my University duties. Quite naturally we could not talk about these matters with those outside of our organization. Our country was still endeavoring to practise neutrality in deed, word and thought. During this period President Wilson was re-elected largely on the slogan that he had kept us out of the war. Even among ourselves we did not speak of our work as a preparation for war, but as preparation for an "emergency."

Our organization had no official standing, no government support. The National Academy of Sciences had volunteered its services to the President and he had accepted, but we were not under his direction nor that of Congress. It is true that the President, with the authority of Congress, appointed in the spring of 1916 a Council of National Defense but with this we had at the time no official connection. To me, and I dare say to all the members of the National Research Council, this was a period of work under high tension. During this time I passed through phases of great elation and distressing hours of mental depression. I felt a moral and intellectual enthusiasm when I saw, as sometimes I did, the approach of the day when our disgraceful procrastination, so it seemed to me then, could be broken; then I felt like shouting from the house top. In this condition of mind I did at times speak out more plainly than I intended. At a Faculty meeting one day when I had returned that morning from New York I said something—I do not remember what—but it must have been spoken with fervor because it led dignified President Hutchins to remark: "Doctor Vaughan, we are not all so enthusiastic about entering the war as you are." I admit that I became somewhat morbid. I did not see how my University colleagues could go on engrossed in their daily routine while the nation faced a catastrophe. Indeed, the only regrettable words I uttered to a colleague were spoken when in this state of mind. I immediately saw the injustice of my remarks and apologized. But unjust accusations are never forgotten. I had my hours of depression when I reviewed the number of German insults heaped upon us answered only by polite notes from our President and I wondered whether he could ever be prodded into action.

Of course, during this period I kept in close touch with General Gorgas and his staff and was largely advised by these men. However, there were certain things which an outsider could do better than one in the service. The following are some of the many subjects which were discussed: (1) The sterilization of drinking water for troops in cantonments, on the march, and on the firing line; (2) the ventilation of barracks; (3) soldiers' clothing; (4) rations; (5) the best methods of vaccination against both smallpox and typhoid fever; (6) the treatment of wounds; (7) the treatment of poisoning with deadly gases; (8) the provision of supply of medicines; (9) the protection of the ear against high explosives; (10) the detection of disease carriers and their treatment; (11) provision of diagnostic laboratories in both equipment and personnel; (12) the bacteriology of wounds. On all these points my confrères in the regular medical corps were better posted than I.

Digitalis was considered an essential agent in the treatment of pneumonia. The "emergency," if it came, would be accompanied by a high morbidity from this disease. All the digitalis used medicinally in this country had come from Germany. There was not enough in stock here to serve a small hospital six months. A species of the plant from which medicinal preparations are made grows wild in this country, especially in the states of Oregon and Washington, but this is not the species from which the preparation had been made. Would this species serve our purpose? Boy scouts in Oregon and Washington gathered the wild leaves; these were assayed at the University of Minnesota and when the "emergency" did come we had enough of this drug to supply the world.

Surgical needles were not made in this country. A firm was induced to build a plant for this industry. This it did at its own expense and our surgeons in France were able to stitch wounds with American made needles. We would need the most efficient disinfectants in large numbers; what are they? And how should they be used? Professor Zinsser of Columbia University and Professor Richards of the University of Pennsylvania put their services and their laboratories at our disposal in answering these questions and continued this work for some months after we entered the war.

We knew that body lice infested the soldiers of our allies, as well as those of our enemies, and the natural history of these parasites and the most successful method of destroying them became matters of concern. We secured recipes for insecticides from our allies and did our best to improve them.

On February 28, 1917, the Council of National Defense invited the National Research Council to cooperate with it in scientific matters.

On the day preceding the entrance of the United States into the war, the following cablegram was sent by the National Academy of Sciences to the Royal Society of London, the Paris Academy of Sciences, the Accademia dei Lincei of Rome, and the Petrograd Academy of Sciences—leading scientific bodies, then engaged in the study of war problems, with which the National Academy had cooperated for many years in scientific research:

"The entrance of the United States into the war unites our men of science with yours in a common cause. The National Academy of Sciences, acting through the National Research Council, which has been designated by President Wilson and the Council of National Defense to mobilize the research facilities of the country, would gladly cooperate in any scientific researches still underlying the solution of military or industrial problems."

As I have already indicated, during the war the National Research Council acted as the scientific component of the Council of National Defense. Since the war the National Research Council has received five millions of dollars from the Carnegie Foundation, large grants from the Rockefeller Foundation, and the General Education Board and smaller grants from other sources. Its function is to encourage research in all branches of science and to foster cooperation in this work.

CHAPTER XIII

THE WORLD WAR

A S I have already said, more than once, I was
impatient for our nation to get into the war. I
felt that our tardiness was a national disgrace. Reared
in the midst of the Civil War, war has always been to
me abhorrent. The trappings of war and its displays
never had for me any fascination. The nearest I ever
was a convert to Freudism was when a medical colleague
put me through its catechism. After he had asked me
many questions and had me fill out partial sentences, he
inquired if in childhood I had ever been frightened by
a soldier. I had to admit my experience with the pistol
in my face. He said that I had hesitated whenever I
came upon the word "soldier" in his inquisition. With
the other members of my family feeling as I did, it is
not surprising that my five sons and I had our commissions in 1917 as soon as they could be obtained. I
was promoted from a lieutenant in the reserve corps to
the rank of major and assigned to duty with the medical
division of the Council of National Defense in Washington.

During my first weeks in khaki my duties were many
and diversified. Questions pertaining to every phase of
the preservation of the health of our soldiers were

referred to me. Some of these had already been determined in the National Research Council and only awaited official sanction. Daily, men and women with suggestions, some wise and many otherwise, filed through my office; some were prompted by patriotic motives and sought no personal gain; others were seeking a financial return; some protested vigorously against vaccination; some wanted the soldiers prohibited from smoking, with special emphasis against cigarettes. All kinds of curealls and preventives were offered the government; some free, but most of them on the payment of a substantial reward. The number of nostrum manufacturers and vendors was large, heavily fortified by testimonials. It was a great opportunity to study psychology. I listened to all courteously and decided nothing, but said to each that his proposition would be referred to a board. In all instances in which there was doubt in my own mind this was done. My wide acquaintance among physicians and other scientists enabled me to refer most things to one or more experts and of these all were willing to serve. There were more methods of purifying drinking water than I had ever heard of and I thought myself fairly well posted on this line. Frauds and exaggerations were easily detected. For instance, one man had a new and wonderful method of purifying drinking water. He mentioned a dozen places in the United States and Canada where his method was in successful operation. He had hardly got out of the building before telegrams were on their way to the health officers of these places and on his return a few days later, all I had to do was to show him the answers. The baseless lies told me must have kept the recording angel busy.

Within a few days such men as Colonels Lyster and Darnall of the regular medical corps, with such experts as Whipple and Sedgwick of the Massachusetts Institute of Technology, and Phelps of the Hygienic Laboratory, had formulated every detail for the purification of drinking water in cantonments, small and large, on the march and in the field, and these were officially sanctioned. After this if a man came with a new method I told him that his process might be the best in the world but that the matter had already been settled and was in operation and no change would be made. One poor fool came with a horrible story of the injuries being done the British soldier by wearing brass buttons. According to him brass buttons on the blouse were killing more British soldiers than German shells. I asked him to disclose this important and dreadful fact to Colonel Goodwin of the British Army who was in the next room. According to another, certain insects were feeding upon French soldiers and he had a wonderful insecticide. He described bugs unknown to the most learned entomologist. Colonel Dercle and Major Rist were informed of the great injury and the immediate danger to their soldiers. I may say here that our liaison officers were of untold value to us; they brought to us the experiences and observations which they had accumulated during more than two years of the war. The stream of would-be benefactors through my office ceased as abruptly as it had begun and my occupation in this line terminated.

Simultaneously with the above and continuing longer, applications for commissions from physicians in civil life were coming in by the hundreds and the thousands. Each of these had to be scrutinized, accepted or rejected, and suitable rank and special duty suggested. A committee consisting of Colonels Noble, Miller and Caldwell of the regular corps with Doctors Welch, Mayo, Simmons, Martin and myself had this task. The only ranks then open to such applicants were lieutenant, captain and major. I never knew of but one man who thought that the rank assigned him was too high, but I may say, in honor of my profession, that audible dissatisfaction was rare. Moreover, I record with most satisfaction that political influence was seldom brought to bear. There were a few shameful exceptions, but these were rare. In the Spanish-American War I served with Major Reed and Shakespeare on a similar committee, and nearly every man whom we rejected was soon back with a letter from my friend, then Secretary of War, saying that Senator so and so or Congressman so and so asked that the applicant have another examination; then the examination was written and such that no man in this group passed. If this occurred in the World War, I do not know it. When I am asked if politics in Washington is improving I cite this example and give an emphatic affirmative answer.

In the World War a physician from Ohio wanted a commission and would not be satisfied with anything but the highest rank. I had my suspicions as to his personal character and professional standing and put him off from time to time while I was endeavoring to get more exact information. One day he came to me with a look of triumph on his face, saying, "I have a letter from my Congressman." For a moment I wondered if we were dropping back into the customs of 1898. He handed me a sealed envelope which I opened, and read the following: "Dear Colonel: This man is from my district. He claims that he voted for me and probably he did. He thinks that he should have a commission and he wants to be a major. Do not let him bulldoze you but do as you think wise in the matter." I informed the applicant that the letter was eminently satisfactory and with this information he took his departure. I never saw him again.

No age limit for medical officers was fixed, though sixty-four was supposed to be the limit, but the honored dean of American surgery, Doctor W. W. Keen, in his eightieth year, looked like a boy in khaki and at my solicitation wrote a valuable handbook on *War Surgery,* up to date in every particular.

When in 1916 President Wilson, by congressional authority, appointed a Council of National Defense, as a member of this important organization he named a medical man, Doctor Franklin Martin of Chicago. This selection proved to be a wise one. Soon after his appointment Doctor Martin, aided by Doctor Frank Simpson of Pittsburgh, began organizing the medical profession of the country. At that time there were in the United States about one hundred and forty thousand legally qualified physicians of both sexes and of all ages. About half of these were believed to be fit personally and professionally for military service of some kind. State committees classified and graded all of these, giving the special fitness of each. These lists were in the possession of the Surgeon General by December, 1916. In this work Doctor Martin had the hearty cooperation of the American Medical Association, the College of Surgeons and all their component organizations. In short, the medical profession of the United States was mobilized for war, so far as the law permitted, by the close of the

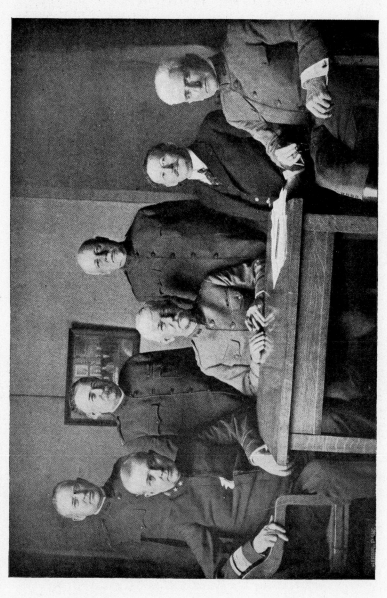

EXECUTIVE COMMITTEE OF THE GENERAL MEDICAL BOARD

Standing, left to right—Doctor Frank Simpson, Professor Vaughan, Professor Welch

Seated, left to right—Surgeon-General Braisted, Surgeon-General Gorgas, Surgeon-General Blue, Doctor Franklin Martin

year 1916. I may add, since I will not return to this subject, that nearly forty thousand physicians enlisted in the army and navy and quite as many more served on draft boards or were engaged in other government services. The medical profession was not altogether unprepared for war when it was proclaimed, and if any other profession enlisted or served in proportionate numbers I do not know it.

After war was proclaimed the Medical Division of the Council of National Defense, under the direction of Doctor Martin, continued and amplified its work. The executive committee, of which I was fortunate enough to be a member, had frequent meetings in which propositions were presented and discussed with the greatest freedom. This committee consisted of the three Surgeons General, Gorgas, Braisted and Blue, and Doctors Martin, Welch, Simpson, Grayson, Mayo and Vaughan. General Gorgas presided at the executive meetings with the same gentleness with which he had ministered to me when I had yellow fever in 1898. I never knew another man who could receive the highest honor without any facial evidence of emotion or face criticism without the slightest sign of embarrassment. I knew him as Captain Gorgas in Cuba; worked with him as Major General Gorgas, and can testify that the acquisition of stars made not the slightest difference in him. I stood by his side when at Atlantic City the American Medical Association decorated him with a medal, the gift being accompanied by a most laudatory speech by Doctor Reed of Cincinnati. As we left the platform I said: "I do not see how you could go through this ordeal without emotion." He replied, with a twinkling in his eyes: "You do not see what is going on within." I was with him when a United States Senator asked why he did not commission osteopaths. He replied: "Because the laws which you make do not permit; will you change the law?" On an inspection tour he decided to stop and visit a camp unannounced. We alighted from the train, he with two grips, I with one. I picked up one of his. "No," he said, "you forget that I am younger than you." On reaching the street, he said, "You watch the grips and Willie will find a cab." One day we were walking along Pennsylvania Avenue when we met Senator McKellar of Tennessee. The Senator put his finger on the "R" on my collar and said, "We are going to take that off." I replied: "Pray, do not; it confers many privileges on me; I can be saucy to a superior officer, who seeing the 'R,' says to himself, 'Oh, well, he is only a reserve man and does not know better.' Here I am walking on the right side of General Gorgas when I should be on his left. We have met several line officers and I have noticed disapprobation on their faces until their eyes fell on the 'R.' "

When we entered the World War the highest rank that a reserve officer could have was that of major. This was true in all corps. General Gorgas determined to remove this restriction in the medical corps. With this purpose he appeared before congressional committees. This awakened resentment not only among his own regular officers but in the whole army. General Gorgas was summoned before the Secretary of War and accused of violating a regulation which forbade all army officers lobbying before Congress. He pleaded guilty, but in perfect candor said that the heads of other departments could do as they saw fit, but that the good of the medical

corps justified his action, pointing out that in the hospitals
and on the battlefields of France our medical majors would
have to consult with brigadier and major generals in the
European armies, and although their professional equals,
could not be treated as such by their European confrères.
His candor and the justice of his claim won over his
accusers, and the restriction in regard to promotion was
removed in all corps. Mrs. Gorgas and Mr. Hendrick
have told of this episode in their most admirable biography of General Gorgas. I should add that in this contest
General Gorgas had no difficulty in winning the approval
of congressional committees. He plainly stated that most
of his regular officers would, during the war, be needed
in administrative work while reserve officers would be
in the hospitals and on the firing line.

Before the War College his reception was not so
pleasant, but Congress makes the laws, and even the
War College has to obey them. Thus the "R's" were
removed and volunteers and regular officers stood on equal
ground. Truth, however, demands that I record the fact
that in the medical corps at least this benefited the regular
officer more than it did the volunteer. This new law
provided that in the newly constituted corps there could
be a certain per cent. of colonels, we will say three. In
1918 there were less than one thousand regular medical
officers and quite thirty thousand volunteers; now three
per cent. of thirty-one thousand is more than three per
cent. of one thousand and it can not be denied that promotions were not proportionately distributed. However, this
is a small matter. To the regular officer, rank is of great
importance; to the volunteer, it is of only temporary value
in so far as it enables him to do better work.

I have only one grievance concerning the rewards conferred on medical men during the war. When we entered the conflict and Mr. Balfour and General Joffre came over, their first request was that we send them medical men. It was decided to call for one thousand picked doctors under thirty-five years of age and send them to the British army as a training school with the promise that as soon as our soldiers reached France they would be transferred. With others I was sent out to drum up these, and I am not unduly boasting when I say that no one could have been better acquainted with the life conditions of the recent medical graduate than one who had been dean of a large medical school for twenty-six years and still occupied that position. All these young men had recently finished years of costly college and professional training; were just establishing themselves in practise; those who were not married intended to be; many had one or more children and were anticipating more; many had purchased homes on credit, had established hospital connections which must be broken, and so forth. It has always been a consolation to me that I presented no false hopes. I said to these young men: "You can not afford to refuse this invitation. Some time in the future your son will ask if you were in the World War and if not, why. However, you should not accept without full knowledge of the price you will pay. You will leave your practise and it will take you a long time to recover it. When the war is over the man who goes must be content to live on a side street, while the man who stays at home lives on the avenue. The former will be fortunate if he can make small deposits in a bank in which the latter is a director. Those of your colleagues

who stay at home will pass a resolution pledging the
members of the local medical society to send fees collected
from your former patients to your wife, but if she is
dependent on this income she and her children will live
in poverty." These things and many others along the
same line I said to them.

Many of these young men called at my Washington
office on their way to the port of embarkation. They were
handsome in khaki. It was only by direct questioning
that I was permitted to see the mental burdens some of
them were carrying. A few were ordered back home;
more were temporarily assigned to camps in this country;
but they went more than nine hundred strong to the
British Army and were forgotten. The British could
not promote them; they did confer decorations on some.
Most of them were a credit to our country, but when the
Armistice was signed, all were lieutenants still. After the
war was over an attempt to right this grievous wrong
was made, but promotion in rank is of but little service
to a volunteer when the war is over. No one paid more
dearly for his patriotism than the young medical man
and I dare say that if a like emergency arises in the
next generation his sons will follow his example. I must
admit that the young men among my former students who
shirked the call to war and stayed at home for profit lost
my esteem. I am glad to add that they were but few.

General Gorgas was fond of driving a car, and in our
official journeyings in and about Washington he frequently
performed this function. We dubbed him our chauffeur,
criticized his driving and had much merriment about it.
He detested war but would have led a corps in battle with
the same calm with which he managed the largest medical

corps ever created, providing as it did for the lives, health and comfort of more than five million men. He was anxious to have the war done with, when he could take up his life work, the eradication of yellow fever from the world. The day after the Armistice was signed his term as Surgeon General expired and soon thereafter he was on his way to West Africa to continue his yellow fever studies. He died in London after having been knighted by the king in person.

In the early spring of 1917, before a barrack had been erected, General Gorgas, Doctors Martin, Welch and I were granted an audience with Secretary Baker. Our purpose was to offer suggestions concerning the ventilation, floor space, cubic capacity, and so forth, of the barracks in the cantonments. The other gentlemen had spoken, basing their arguments on what we know of the epidemiology of cerebrospinal meningitis. Lighting his pipe, the Secretary turned to me and said: "Doctor Vaughan, what have you to say about this matter? All I know about hygiene I learned from you. When I was a boy, my father was a health officer in West Virginia. When he found something you had written he brought it home and asked me to read it aloud to him. Now, as I understand it, the disease these gentlemen have been talking about is one of infancy. What has it to do with soldiers?" The opportunity for a little humor was irresistible, so I said: "Mr. Secretary, permit me to take up my rôle as your instructor. It has been thirty years or more since it was interrupted." Good naturedly he said, "Go ahead; you will find me a willing pupil." I told him that he was thinking of infantile paralysis while my

Secretary of War Newton D. Baker

colleagues had been talking about cerebrospinal meningitis, a disease most prevalent among young adults and
especially among recently recruited soldiers in crowded
barracks.

The Secretary, after hearing us, called for the chief of
staff and gave orders that all barrack plans should have
our approval; of course this was not done. I did not
come in contact with Secretary Baker frequently or intimately, but when I did he listened attentively and answered
sympathetically. I once suggested that the cantonment
hospitals should be built more permanently and preserved
after the war as sanatoria for different diseases. The
Secretary seemed quite pleased with the idea and promised
it serious attention; more pressing demands doubtlessly
drove it from his mind. I never drive through a wrecked
cantonment without recalling this conversation and wishing that the suggestion had been given more consideration.
tion. We wrecked our cantonment hospitals and then
proceeded to build hospitals for veterans, but at the cost
of millions, to say nothing of national scandals. In my
opinion, Secretary Baker has had to bear much undeserved
criticism. We have had great Secretaries of War in times
of peace but none in war, if the critics of the times be
right. In the Civil War the first Secretary, Cameron,
held his position but one year. His successor, Stanton,
was criticised by the people and had other troubles. In
the Spanish-American War Secretary Alger bore the
brunt of criticism and Mr. Baker has met with a like
fate.

One afternoon I was called to the office of the Secretary of War and on arriving I was directed to a certain
room. On entering I found Assistant Secretary Keppel

in the chair. In front of him were several men in long-tailed coats and one man wearing the uniform of a major in the quartermaster's department. This man greeted me and said that he was glad to see another uniform. Mr. Keppel asked one of the long tails to explain the purpose of the meeting to me. He said that he and his colleagues represented the "Purple Cross," that this organization supplemented the Red Cross, and that the latter looks after the soldiers during life, while the former looks after them when dead. He and his friends were asking for an order turning over all soldiers that should be killed or die from any cause in France to the "Purple Cross" to be embalmed and returned to their homes. He went on to say that the "Purple Cross" had a board of supreme directors, made up of the most eminent scientific and medical men in the country. This board supplied the directions for preserving the dead. He held a paper in his hand and said: "Here is a list of our directors." I asked to see the list and near the head was my own name. I said, I fear with some warmth, that since entering the room I had learned much. I had never before heard of the "Purple Cross." Now I find that I have the honor of being one of its directors. I ended with pronouncing it a fraud. Failing to get the desired order from the Secretary of War these men had a bill introduced into Congress with a like result. I have been told that the official organ of the "Purple Cross" roasted me brown, but I was never conscious of going through the process.

During the early summer of 1917, Doctor Martin very wisely called the most prominent men in the medical profession for consultation in Washington. Topics for consideration at these gatherings were carefully considered

THE WORLD WAR 419

and were presented for general discussion. Every visitor was encouraged to speak plainly and without restraint. The topics brought before these assemblies were of varying importance. I will mention here only one. The conservation of food was then a most important matter. The United States had been for two years feeding Belgium, England and France, the first-mentioned gratis and the others to the profit of the American producer. It was universally believed that starvation was proving to be a most important factor in determining the result of the war. The price of wheat was fixed by the Federal Government as a war measure. First helpings at table were scant and a second discouraged. It was urged that the daily consumption of sugar should be brought down to the lowest limit compatible with health and the rapidly advancing price of this article contributed to compliance with this suggestion. The American people were complying with these requests with wonderful unanimity. Elaborate dinners were discountenanced. Simple two or three course dinners were, even among the wealthy, the rule. Our soldiers must be fed without stint because we must rely upon their strength in the great struggle. But civilians must be moderate in eating.

To-day those of us who lived through that period can but feebly recall the intense interest taken in food conservation, especially by the better-to-do and more intelligent classes. We look back upon it as a kind of hysterical display of patriotism; but *then* it was a question of paramount importance. We must feed our soldiers and those of our allies even if we must deprive ourselves of a certain amount of gustatory pleasure. At that time we were not demanding that France back our loans by a mortgage on its shell-torn acres or wantonly ruined cities and cathedrals. Thousands of moderately well-to-do women among us were each feeding and clothing at least one French orphan. Then we recognized that France, England and Italy had been fighting our battles as well as their own. We read with horror, backed by hatred, how French mines were being dynamited after the machinery had been shipped to his own country by the barbarous Hun. We cried to our allies: "You can have all our surplus food, all our wealth, yea more, even the blood of our sons; persevere in your courageous contest; we are coming to your aid with our great resources." Men are brothers when they face a common danger; alas, this statement is true only under the condition therein given!

The above is a feeble and inadequate statement of the psychology of our nation when on a Sunday morning in June, 1917, the wisest men in the medical profession assembled in one of the large rooms of the Willard Hotel. The subject was food conservation; the discussion was strictly scientific; nothing was said about the degrading effects of alcoholic drinks. The chief speaker was Doctor Alonzo Taylor, now of Stanford University, California. He had recently been in Germany as a food expert. His audience was to have first-hand and exact information. Indeed, there was then and there is now, no one more competent to speak on the subject of foods. His words came clothed in the unsurpassed virility characteristic of the man. He showed that in the conversion of carbohydrates, starches and sugars, into alcohol there is a marked loss in food value. He calculated this loss mathematically. The figures stood before his auditors and convinced them. I can not speak for others but in my mind his speech was much as follows: "We need to conserve our foods; an efficient way in which this may be done lies in the prohibition of the conversion of carbohydrates into alcohol." Probably many in the room were fully aware beforehand of the truth of Doctor Taylor's statement but it had, as presented by him, a telling effect. Add to this the following facts which must have been in the mind of everyone in the audience: alcoholic drinks must not be permitted our soldiers; civilians must be equally patriotic; therefore the latter must willingly deny themselves what they forbid the former. I, at least, and I believe all others in the room, was convinced that a national prohibition law was not only justified but, for the time at least, necessary.

At the close of the meeting Doctor Martin appointed a committee to draw up resolutions expressive of the sentiment of those present. These resolutions were formulated and presented to the Council of National Defense the next day. We never thought of what effect a prohibition act might have on the nation after the war. When one is held up by a highwayman in a dark alley or on a lonely road and is fighting for his life or his pocketbook or for both, his mind is not likely to be occupied in planning what he will have for breakfast the next morning. About the same time the American Medical Association, at an annual meeting in New York, passed a resolution favoring prohibition. How much these movements, inaugurated in medical organizations, had to do with the enactment of the eighteenth amendment I can not say. I have heard the profession accused; I have never heard it praised in this connection. I have given the details as they came under my observation and in which I participated. It is not within my province to approve or disapprove of the eighteenth amendment as it has operated or failed to operate since the World War.

In my opinion, another hysterical move inaugurated during the war was the undue and unjustified importance attached to the so-called "Intelligence Test" as used in the promotion of officers. I had a small part in the introduction of this procedure, but in my opinion it ran beyond bounds and secured unwarranted commendation. I thought that it might be an aid in the selection of those who might be entrusted with rank and increased responsibilities, but I never dreamed that it would become a dominant factor in these matters. The test, as applied in our army, was a rude measure of mental alertness, but this is only one factor in intelligence. It was not used in any other army and of those in our army to whom it was applied, but few if any ever participated in battle. It is one thing to be a model officer in a cantonment and another thing to perform the same function on the firing line. The so-called "Intelligence Test" as employed in our mobilization camps in the World War will need to be subjected to more crucial trials before it can justly deserve the high encomiums then and later bestowed upon it.

In the extension of his office force General Gorgas was kind enough to put me in charge of the division of communicable diseases. This post was the one for which I thought myself best fitted. General Gorgas must have had the same idea, since no word passed between us concerning it either before or after the assignment. On going to my desk one morning I found a sign bearing the words "Communicable Diseases" hanging over it. The tables of all my assistants had been moved to that part of the room and on my desk were the reports from all the camps on the prevalence of communicable diseases. I made no remark but went to work.

Writing as I am of the experiences of an epidemiologist of the World War it would be criminal in me not to mention the mistakes which, in my opinion, were made in my own department. I leave it to the heads of the other sections and divisions to do as they please. I will trespass on their fields only so far as it is necessary for me to do in discussing my own problems. When this is necessary I will go as far into other fields as I deem necessary, "with charity for all and malice towards none." It is now generally admitted that the conservation of the health of troops is a matter of prime importance. I had nothing to do with battle casualties, the care of the wounded nor even with diseases which are noncommunicable. When can one consider the health of a military organization, so far as communicable diseases are concerned, satisfactory? The answer to this question, which my helpers and I formulated, was: When the morbidity and mortality rates from these diseases are no higher among the soldiers than they are in the same age group at home. This is a high standard, one seldom reached, and one less frequently maintained for a long period. We did reach it in some camps, but in most we fell below it; in a few, far below. The more densely people are packed together the more difficult is it to control the spread of infection. There are no other conditions under which men are so closely and so continuously in contact as in an army camp. In the field men are not so crowded and consequently infection is less prevalent. From September

29, 1917, to March 29, 1918 (six months), five out of twenty-nine great camps complied with the standard named in both the morbidity and the mortality rates. Three others were satisfactory in mortality but with an excessive morbidity. Taking the twenty-nine great camps together the death rate from pneumonia during the six months mentioned above was twelve times as great as in the same age group of the civilian population of this country. Only one other disease, cerebrospinal meningitis, showed a higher case mortality than pneumonia, but the cases of pneumonia far outnumbered those of meningitis. So far did pneumonia overshadow all other diseases that the history of this disease is the medical history of our cantonments. The typhoid fever of the Spanish-American War was practically negligible.

The procedures followed in the mobilization of our soldiers in the World War brought into every cantonment every infection then existent in the areas from which the men came. Drafted men were assembled at some point in each state. They came from every community; they came in their ordinary clothing; some clean, some filthy. Each one brought many samples of the bacteria then abounding in his own neighborhood. They brought these organisms on and in their bodies and on and in their clothing. They were crowded together at the state rendezvous and held here for varying periods of time, long enough to pass through the stages of enlistment. Then they filled troop trains and were transferred to their respective cantonments. On the trains the men from the first to the last car mingled freely. Not a troop train came into Camp Wheeler (near Macon, Georgia) in the fall of 1917 without bringing from one to six cases of measles already in the eruptive stage. These men had brought the infection from their homes and had distributed its seeds at the state encampment and on the train. No power on earth could stop the spread of measles through a camp under these conditions. Cases developed, from one hundred to five hundred a day, and the infection continued as long as there was susceptible material in the camp. It is true that measles is not in and of itself a deadly disease, but it predisposes to pneumonia and increases the death rate from pneumonia. These facts are stated in my work on epidemiology as follows: (1) Of every one thousand men with measles, forty-four had peneumonia and fourteen died; (2) of every thousand men without measles, seventeen had pneumonia and two died; (3) a person who has recently had measles is ten times more likely to die from pneumonia than is the person who has not recently had measles.

In armies, measles is a disastrous and dreaded disease for two reasons. In the first place, the number attacked by it simultaneously is overwhelming. For instance, all susceptible individuals, on the troop trains mentioned, came down practically on the same day or within two days. The period of incubation in this disease is more definite and fixed than that of any other. This has been demonstrated in more than one instance in which measles has been introduced into communities from which it has long been absent or has never been known. The following are illustrations from my work on epidemiology:

In 1781 measles disappeared from the Faroe Islands and did not reappear until 1846. During this period of sixty-five years there was not a case of this disease anywhere on any of the seventeen islands constituting the inhabited parts of this group. On the reappearance of measles the total population of the seventeen islands was 7,782. These were gathered for the most part in small villages of from twenty to two hundred persons. Thorshavn, the administrative capital, was the only village with a population of more than two hundred, and it numbered only eight hundred. Measles was brought into the islands by a cabinet maker who left Copenhagen March 20 and reached Thorshavn on the 28th in perfect health. From this case it was easy to trace all subsequent cases. It was found that every individual who had not had the disease sixty-five years or longer before acquired it. When a man visited a village in which the disease prevailed and returned to his home everybody with whom he came in contact developed the eruption fourteen days later. Age and sex had no influence upon susceptibility. The man of sixty succumbed quite as promptly and as certainly as the boy of six.

So far as is known measles never touched the inhabitants of the Fiji Islands until 1875. At that time the king of these islands visited Sydney in New South Wales preparatory to turning over the government of his islands to the British. During this visit the king's son and one of his servants developed measles. When they landed on the island the king called a conference of prominent men from all parts of his country. It is estimated that the population of the Fiji Islands at that time numbered about one hundred and fifty thousand. Practically all acquired the disease and forty thousand died. This instance is frequently quoted by authors who hold that it is evidence of the deadliness of this disease when introduced among a people who have hitherto not known it. It is more likely that the high death rate was due to the fact that all the people came down simultaneously, or nearly so, and consequently the sick were left without care. There was a small detachment of natives, one hundred and forty-seven strong, under English military discipline. Every one of these developed the disease but were well cared for and the death rate was only six per cent. while among those uncared for it was about twenty-six per cent.

Study epidemics of measles wherever they appear and you will find that the mortality rate is influenced by the care and attention given to the sick more than to any other agency. Measles when the sick are ideally cared for is a disease of low mortality; when the sick are inadequately taken care of, this disease may rank in its fatality among the great plagues of the world. When introduced into a population with a susceptibility of one hundred per cent. it strikes down so many at practically the same time that adequate care for the sick is impossible. The resistance of the body already reduced to a minimum by the virus of the disease is easily overcome by secondary infections (especially pneumonia), by exposure to cold, by thirst and by hunger. This is true of measles, whether it appears for the first time in a virgin population as it did in the Fiji Islands in 1875 or whether it appears as it did in the camps in the United States in the winter of 1917-18.

In the second place, the large number attacked by measles simultaneously overwhelms hospital facilities, breaks down the most ample provision for the care of the sick and renders successful isolation impossible. What is true of measles is largely true of mumps. In civil life mumps is negligible because only a few are attacked simultaneously; among soldiers it may temporarily render an efficient army helpless.

In Missouri and Kansas and in South Carolina, cerebrospinal meningitis had been known to be endemic for some years before we entered the World War. This disease is spread by carriers, who personally remain well, but transmit the infection to more susceptible individuals. It required no prophetic gift to predict outbreaks of this disease in the cantonments to which the quota from these states were sent. The records from Camp Funston, Kansas, and Camp Jackson, South Carolina, show just what did happen.

The dangers in the mobilization procedures followed by us in the World War were pointed out to the proper authorities before there was any assembly, but the answer was: "The purpose of mobilization is to convert civilians into trained soldiers as quickly as possible and not to make a demonstration in preventive medicine."

No time is gained by hurrying sick men or the bearers of infection into camp. They simply fill the hospitals and lower the effective strength. The line officer has advanced greatly in his appreciation of preventive medicine since the Spanish-American War but I hope that his education in this direction may be greatly extended before the next mobilization of troops will be necessary.

We recommended that the drafted men should be assembled in groups of not more than thirty in places near their homes. There they should be cleaned, bathed, barbered, clothed in clean garments, subjected to their vaccinations, held in isolation for from ten to fourteen days, examined for carriers, tagged with the infectious diseases they have had, sent to the cantonment in locked cars and there restricted to barracks holding not more than thirty men for some days. During all this time they should be exercised or drilled by officers. That thousands of young men may be assembled without suffering from infectious diseases is demonstrated annually on the campus of each of our great universities. The most insane procedure carried out in 1918, from the viewpoint of an epidemiologist, was the sudden and complete mobilization of the students in our universities in the Students Training Corps. How many lives this procedure sacrificed I can not estimate.

In some of the cantonments the last building completed was the hospital. This, with its diagnostic laboratory, should be the first. The epidemiologist with his assistants should be the first officers on the ground in the preparation of a training camp. They should have medical supervision of the workmen engaged in the construction. There were cases of cerebrospinal meningitis in Camps Funston and Jackson before a soldier arrived. The mobilization of an army is a medical as well as a military problem.

It can not be denied that there was a deficiency in heavy clothing and bedding at some of the camps in December, 1917. I never came so near freezing as I did at Funston at that time. I shivered at Doniphan (Oklahoma) and I felt a norther at Bowie (Texas). In each of these camps I saw shivering guards. The winter of 1917-18 proved to be the coldest on record east of the Rocky Mountains.

During the World War pneumonia from the beginning to the end continued the most potent cause of death. Taking the calendar year of 1917 there were in our army 8,479 cases, with 952 deaths, a fatality of eleven and two-tenths per cent. It will be understood that mobilization of the new army did not begin until October, 1917. During the winter months of 1917-18 (September 29, 1917, to March 29, 1918) the cases numbered 13,393 with 3,110 deaths, a fatality of twenty-three and one-tenth per cent. During the summer months of 1918 (April 5 to August 30) the cases were 8,912 with 1679 deaths, a fatality of eighteen and eight-tenths per cent. During the autumn months of 1918 (the influenza period) the number of cases was 61,198 with 21,053 deaths, a fatality of thirty-four and four-tenths per cent.

When we had charted the pneumonia morbidity and mortality in each of the large camps, one thing stared us in the face most strikingly. This was the astonishing difference in the number of cases in the several camps. Camp Hancock, located near Augusta, Georgia, showed a morbidity of six and seven-tenths and a mortality of one and one-tenth; while Camp Wheeler, near Macon, Georgia, showed a morbidity of ninety-five and a mortality of twenty-three and six-tenths per thousand. Good and bad camps were mixed in nearby locations. Then we made other charts, placing the camps not where they were, but in the states from which their soldiers came. Then all the good camps, with the exception of Lewis near Tacoma, Washington, were in that portion of the United States east of the Mississippi River and north of the Ohio and Potomac Rivers. Next we determined the incidence of pneumonia among urban and rural men. It was found invariably low among the former and high among the latter. Now we had the key to the situation. The area from which the men of the good camps came is the most urban, or densely populated, part of the country. City dwellers acquire some degree of immunity to respiratory diseases because they live in an atmosphere frequently or constantly bearing these infections. Country boys are more highly susceptible to the respiratory diseases. This suggested that we increase the resistance of the rural soldiers by vaccinating them with dead cultures of the bacteria of the respiratory diseases. This was attempted during the summer months of 1918, notably by Major Cecil and Captain Vaughan at Camp Upton on Long Island and at Camp Wheeler in Georgia, but this work was overwhelmed by the great and deadly epidemic of influenza. I am glad to say that in all this study of the distribution of pneumonia throughout the camps I had the valuable assistance of Captain George T. Palmer.

Attempts to secure artificial immunity to the pneumonias have been continued by many of the best men in the profession. The problem is a difficult and complicated one because so many bacteria may cause pneumonia, but I have no doubt that it will be solved in time.

In August, 1918, Colonels F. F. Russell, William H. Welch, Rufus Cole and I made an inspection trip through the camps in the Southern States. With the memory of the visit to Asheville, North Carolina, in 1898, in mind, I proposed that we stop in that region for a few days, which we did. But there I contracted a most severe coryza. We reached Washington one Sunday morning and I went directly to the Surgeon General's office, where General Richard was officiating, as General Gorgas was in Europe. Scarcely looking up from his papers the general said, as I entered the door: "You will proceed immediately to Devens. The Spanish influenza has struck that camp." Then, laying aside his papers and looking into my suffused eyes, he said: "No, you will go home and go to bed." I took the next train for Camp Devens and arrived early the next morning. I am not going into the history of the influenza epidemic. It encircled the world, visited the remotest corners, taking toll of the most robust, sparing neither soldier nor civilian, and flaunting its red flag in the face of science.

Soon the Huns were slowly but stubbornly retreating and in November the Armistice was signed, but there can be no armistice between medicine and disease. The conflict will continue as long as man walks the earth and the victory will ultimately be won by death. But as I see it, man's mission on earth is not to seek immortality either for himself as an individual, or for his race, but to strive for wisdom. To what heights he may lift himself in this effort I can not say. I do know that if he ceases to strive for wisdom he will sink into ignorance to which there is no bottom. Man has by long effort acquired a degree of intellectuality which enables him to serve as a co-worker with his creator. The wheels of evolution are never standing still; they are constantly moving; they may go forward or backward. We are concerned with the things of this life, not with the possible or probable hereafter.

The war brought to my wife and myself the greatest sorrow of our lives. As I have said all of our five sons enlisted. Our eldest (Victor C. Vaughan, Jr.), with his brother Walter, went to France in June, 1917, where he served in the hospital at Chaumont until the Armistice. After this, General Ireland assigned to him the duty of working up the typhoid statistics in our expeditionary

THE FAMILY IN THE WORLD WAR

Colonel Victor C. Vaughan

Lt. Colonel Warren T. Vaughan   Lt. Colonel J. Walter Vaughan

The Late Major Victor C. Vaughan, Jr.

Captain Henry F. Vaughan   Lieutenant Herbert H. Vaughan

forces. He did this work at Dijon and then went to St. Aignan preparatory to starting for home. He was to leave the next morning when he and a comrade, late in the evening, went bathing in the Cher River and he was drowned. He began practise in Detroit in 1905 and, instead of waiting for patients, he, with the permission and assistance of Doctor Guy L. Kiefer, health officer, opened the first tuberculosis clinic in that city. He continued this work and in 1923 the Detroit Board of Health dedicated the infirmary of the new municipal hospital at Northville to his memory. He served the poor so efficiently that the well-to-do began to seek his advice, and when he went to France, he had a well-established reputation as an expert in tuberculosis. He married the splendid woman who had been his assistant in his early work. He was an ideal practitioner, devoted to and beloved by his patients, always bringing to them the best skill acquired by experience and study. He made several contributions of scientific and practical value. There was apparently before him a bright and useful career. I shall not discuss the sad emotions awakened in his parents by their great and irreparable loss. These are too sacred to trust to words.

CHAPTER XIV

MEDICAL AND SCIENTIFIC SOCIETIES

I AM an ardent believer in cooperative efforts in professional and scientific work. The man of genius may make his most valuable contribution to human knowledge in isolation, detached from his fellows, but recognizing that I have no claim to this distinction, I have been a zealous, if not always an intelligent, worker in medical and scientific societies. This has been prompted by mixed motives, some selfish and some more or less altruistic. With the purpose of extending my own knowledge, I have sought association with men whose intellectual superiority I have recognized. In this particular I have been most fortunate in receiving instruction and continuing my pupilage. However, I have found it well to preserve a critical attitude under these conditions for I have heard much misinformation from the lips of reputedly great men. Error is not converted into truth by the stamp of authority. The processes of evolution are not arrested by the dictum of the late Mr. Bryan.

A simple organization from which I have drawn much pleasure, enthusiasm and information is the "Scientific Club" of the University of Michigan, formed in the early eighties and still functioning. It consists of twenty research workers, meets at the homes of members, devotes one hour to listening to and discussing the problems of the host, one hour to a lunch and two hours to smokes and good fellowship. It is not considered good form to leave without satisfactory explanation before the clock strikes twelve. The only official is the chief servant who is selected by lot and whose functions consist in notifying the members of meetings, keeping tally on attendance, and serving as custodian of the club property, limited to a jack knife and a corkscrew, which he must produce on demand. Alas! The corkscrew is now limited to the plebeian function of opening ginger ale bottles.

I can not say how much other members have profited by this simple organization but it has done much to broaden my intellectual horizon and make me appreciative of the research problems my colleagues had in hand. To hear Calvin Thomas talk on German literature; Edward Walter discuss the great treasures housed in the Bibliothéque Nationale; Henry Adams explain Chinese finance and transportation; Dean Worcester or J. B. Steere tell of explorations in the Philippines under Spanish rule; Albert Prescott unfold the fascinating story of the benzene ring; Moses Gomberg dwell upon the chemistry of carbon compounds; Edward Campbell speak of solutions of carbon in steel; William Hussey describe double stars; Charles Greene exhibit and explain the details of the structure of the first cantilever bridge; these and many more of like interest and value were treats to one whose chief occupation was the study of the effect of bacteria on guinea pigs, rabbits, monkeys, and the like.

No other agency has done more to stimulate productive scholarship in the University of Michigan than the Research Club which was organized in 1900. I will permit the historian of this club, Doctor Lombard, to tell the story:

"Up to the time of the founding of the Club, Michigan had been an excellent teaching College, a glorified High School, and a University only in name. Graduate work was too often only a prolongation of undergraduate studies. There was nothing to stimulate student, instructor, or professor to original investigation. Any research work that was done was the result of the initiative of the rare individual who found pleasure in such work, but who received little external encouragement. It is not strange that the men most interested in research felt the need of mutual support and that they must get together and help one another through their sympathy and interest in each other's problems. Moreover, there were many problems involving the University as a whole, which they felt could only be solved through the coordinated action of the men who were interested in research work. Perhaps the most pressing of these was the way that the work of the graduate students was conducted, and the fact that a large proportion of the Faculty was doing no research work. Many of the older members of the Faculty were of course hopeless cases, but there was great concern lest the younger men, having nothing to stimulate them to original investigations, would slide into the teaching rut and stay there, as so many of their chiefs had done.

"The club was formed with the object of uniting, as set forth in the Constitution, 'those members of the academic staff of the University who were actively engaged in research and to originate and support such measures as are calculated to foster and advance research.'

"From the first it was recognized that the hope for the future depended on arousing the interest of the younger men. There were a number who had already shown promise through their work, and these were gradually taken into the club, but as Associate members (a class which was abolished in 1904)'. Why was a class of Associate members instituted? Because the founders of the Club felt that if it was to accomplish anything, a lot of delicate questions would have to be handled without gloves, and that discussion would be more free if confined to the older men, whose sympathies were well known. Those of us who were present at the early conferences will recall that they were very interesting and enlightening.

"Certainly the Club was never at the beck and call of any coterie, but has sought to serve all who had like interests at heart. That it was not a close corporation, ruled by a few, and that all interests of the University devoted to research could have fair play is evidenced by the fact that twenty-two different men have served as President during the first twenty-five years (only Vaughan was President more than once, all feeling the need of his leadership during the first four years, after which he declined to serve). Moreover, forty-eight men have served on the Council, ten of these having been elected twice, and one three times. About thirty-five different departments of the University have been represented on the Council at different times."

Up to the organization of this Club, the Medical School was the only department of the University in which productive scholarship was officially recognized and encouraged and in this it was demanded; it was made an important factor in the selection of Faculty members and in promotions. The bulwark of conservatism was in the literary Faculty whose dean, John O. Reed, although a teacher of physics, was opposed to reform and in this was supported by many venerable and lovable professors who believed that their highest function was to teach the elements to the masses of students. But the Research Club has made progress and now (1926) even the President of the University is a man distinguished for his contributions to biological sciences. In 1900 the membership of the club numbered twenty-four; in 1925, one hundred and twenty, with a showing of three hundred and sixteen original contributions during the twenty-five years.

I took an early and continuing interest in the local and state medical societies. In the eighties a meeting of the state medical society bore a close resemblance to a political convention; it was a contest for offices; there were contesting delegations; one year the Michigan Central Railroad carried free those named by its chief surgeon; sectional strife was in evidence; personal animosities were aired. I will have to admit that under these conditions I was one year elected president. However, the sting of this admission is somewhat relieved by the fact that I was opposed by the railroad surgeon. Now, the medical profession of the state, at least the intelligent part of it, is directing its energies to scientific work; its annual meetings are harmonious and enlightening and its journal is a credit to it.

The annual meetings of the American Medical Association in the eighties were of the same character as those of the state society, but on a larger scale. In my opinion, Doctor John H. Rauch, Secretary of the Illinois State Board of Health (1877-1891), was the John the Baptist of reform in medical education in this country. He exposed many diploma mills, causing a score or more of them to close temporarily, and urged the extension in time and improvement in the curricula of medical schools. But the low-grade medical schools had too much political influence at that time and Doctor Rauch was forced out of office. His elimination was followed by the rapid multiplication of low-grade schools and a decline in the intellectuality and morale of the profession. I know about the work of Doctor Rauch because some of his papers were written in my home in Ann Arbor and I assisted him in the collection of data. I may say that medical education in this country reached its lowest ebb in the ten years following the elimination of Doctor Rauch.

In 1901 the *Journal of the American Medical Association* published statistics obtained from the schools themselves and although the data were presented in the best possible coloring, the revelations were most deplorable. In 1904 the American Medical Association appointed a Council on Medical Education. I had the honor of membership in this Council for many years, but I wish to say that the excellent work it did was principally due to Doctor Arthur D. Bevan, long its president, and Doctor N. P. Colwell, continuously its secretary. The Council had not the slightest legal authority, but it determined to ascertain the facts and to give them to the public, relying on their belief that inefficiency and fraud are best suppressed by exposure. The only legal support the Council had lay in the state boards of medical registration and licensure and these could not with good grace give the right to practise medicine to graduates of inferior schools.

During the school year of 1906-07 everyone of the one hundred and sixty medical schools in the United States was inspected and the results published. "At the lowest extreme were a few institutions which were actually selling diplomas; in a large number only didactic, lecture or recitation courses were given, sometimes by the one teacher who constituted the entire Faculty. Most of the schools had no laboratories save an old time dissecting room and occasionally an excuse for a chemical laboratory. One institution was found which turned out one hundred and five graduates in 1905, without having completed any laboratory work, not even dissecting, nor had they had the opportunity to see a single patient in either a dispensary or a hospital. Less than half the colleges had affiliations with either dispensaries or hospitals in which patients could be utilized for clinical instruction, and the schools were few, indeed, in which students had the opportunity to study patients in small clinics at the bedside or as clinical clerks."

On the publication of the first report of the Council on Education, there was great furore among those interested in low-grade schools. Most violent denunciations were hurled at the Council and its members. Then the Council asked the Carnegie Foundation to make an inspection of the medical schools, using an eminent educator who was not a medical man. Mr. Abraham Flexner did this so thoroughly and impartially that all opposition was silenced; the poorest schools went out of existence; weak ones combined their resources; and now (1926) there are eighty medical schools, where there

were one hundred and sixty (1904), sixty-four of which
are departments of universities and among these some
are unsurpassed in equipment and teachers. There has
been in the history of education no parallel to this advance
in professional training.

However, I must not paint this picture in too brilliant
colors; nor must I give the Council unlimited credit for
its accomplishments. The world had moved between
1877, when Doctor Rauch made his attempt to improve
medical education, and 1904, when the Council was organized. In 1883 Doctor Rauch attempted to close a
diploma mill known as the Boston Bellevue Medical College. This institution was charged with selling diplomas
and degrees "to individuals grossly ignorant of any
medical knowledge, and either with or without attendance
upon its alleged courses of instruction." The officers
under this charge admitted everything of which they were
accused, but claimed that they were not violating the
postal laws by sending their literature through the mail.
This matter was referred to a United States commissioner
who rendered the following decision: "The state has authorized this college to issue degrees, and it has been done
according to legal right. . . . The law makes the Faculty of the college the sole judges of eligibility of applicants for diplomas. There is no legal restriction, no legal
requirement. *If the Faculty chooses to issue degrees to
incompetent persons the laws of Massachusetts authorize
it.* This is, therefore, not a scheme to defraud under the
statute. The defendants are dismissed." I think that
this decision should be preserved as evidence of how our
Federal Government protected its citizens from fraud in
1883!

There is a more serious side to this matter; in 1925 medical diploma mills were exposed in Missouri and Connecticut, owing to corruption of state boards of licensure, and in other states cult schools, osteopath, chiropractic, and the like, are pouring out annually numbers of men and women, who are feeding on the credulity of the people. There are ebbs and flows in the general intelligence of successive generations and so long as there is abundant pabulum charlatanism will continue. Jenner demonstrated the protective value of vaccination against smallpox by repeated demonstrations in the years from 1796 to 1800, but there were thousands of cases of smallpox among us in 1925. However I, at least, am not going to worry about this. Morbidity and mortality rates depend upon the intelligence of the people and each generation gets about what it deserves. It is the problem of pure science to interrogate nature and to discover truth; it is the function of medicine, engineering, law and other professions to demonstrate the useful application of these discoveries; and finally the acceptance of these discoveries and their applications depend upon the intelligence of the people. I know of no scientific discovery which has not ultimately benefited the masses, but through ignorance or for other reasons, too numerous and complicated to be discussed here, scientific advances may be ignored, misinterpreted and even converted into agencies of human destruction. The advantages that have come to the profession from the labors of the Council can not be blotted out whether the benefits to the people are lasting or temporary.

At the close of the last century most newspapers in this country carried advertisements of patent and proprietary so-called medicines and some of the manufacturers of these worthless and often harmful nostrums accumulated great wealth and influence. The American Medical Association began a crusade against these frauds. Their contents were determined and their worthlessness exposed. This good work soon received the support of the best publications, some of them at great financial loss, and this iniquity has been markedly curtailed, though not completely exterminated. Under the able management of Doctor George H. Simmons, supported by excellent men on the Board of Trustees, the *Journal of the American Medical Association* has become the most authoritative medical publication in the world. In my opinion, the best work done by the medical profession in the past twenty-five or thirty years is to be found in the moral and intellectual cleansing it has done in its own house; of course continued scrubbing will be necessary. The medical profession has on its own initiative closed its inferior schools, has raised the requirements for admission, has lengthened and strengthened the courses of instruction, has stimulated the betterment of hospitals, has endeavored to educate the laity in the prevention of disease and has encouraged more exact observation and research among its members. All of these advances have brought benefits to the people in lower morbidity and mortality rates, in an improved standard of health, and in the keener enjoyment and appreciation of life and in greater efficiency. That the intelligent laity appreciates these services is shown by the fact that medical education and research are now receiving both private and public support with a liberality unequalled in history. The names Pasteur, Lister and Gorgas are as familiar in educated society as are those of kings, mighty warriors and divines.

In 1913 the American Medical Association conferred upon me its highest honor—the presidency. This token of appreciation of my work by my professional colleagues is highly prized.

In the eighties the sections of the American Medical Association were so barren in scientific interests that many special societies came into existence. In some of these I found most nourishing intellectual food. Of one of these, the American Association of Physicians, at first limited to one hundred members in the United States and Canada, I became a member in 1889, president in 1909 and honorary member in 1915. The annual meetings of this society were rich treats, affording abundant opportunity for the extension of my intellectual horizon; for having my own ideas confirmed or confuted; for crossing swords with the ablest men in my profession; for receiving and inflicting wounds; and for social intercourse of the highest character. Of the original members of this society only four (William T. Councilman and Frederick C. Shattuck of Boston, James C. Wilson of Philadelphia and William H. Welch of Baltimore) are now (1926) living. To these I extend my greetings; to the shades of the dead I bring votive offerings; to all I acknowledge my indebtedness.

A short time before the death of Doctor Oliver Wendell Holmes the Physiological Society, numbering then not more than ten or twelve, met in Boston. Through the kindness of the late Doctor Henry P. Bowditch, then professor of physiology in Harvard University, Doctor Holmes received the members of this society. We entered his home, two by two. Doctors Holmes and Bowditch stood in the library, and to the surprise of all, when each man was presented, Doctor Holmes knew something of his work. We marveled at the extent of his reading and at the tenacity of his memory. I went with Doctor Abraham Jacobi of New York. When he was presented Doctor Holmes spoke of Doctor Jacobi's recent book on *Diseases of Infancy*. The next day Doctor Jacobi and I entered a street car, where we found Doctor Holmes immediately in front of us. The following conversation occurred between Doctors Jacobi and Holmes:

"Good morning, Doctor Holmes."

"Pardon me, I do not know you."

"I am Doctor Jacobi."

"Do you reside in Boston?"

"No, I live in New York."

"Are you a practitioner of medicine?"

I shall leave the reader to explain how Doctor Holmes knew so much about Doctor Jacobi in the evening and how he managed to forget it all the next morning. Doctor Jacobi and I suspected that Doctor Bowditch had something to do with the wonderful knowledge temporarily possessed by the Autocrat of the Breakfast-table at his reception. I admit that my chief use of *Who's Who* and *Men of Science* is to inform myself of the achievements of an expected visitor, and the occasion having passed, my memory soon fades.

I was elected a member of the American Public Health Association in 1883 and then became acquainted with the great men who laid the foundations of preventive medicine in this country. The fruit of the work they did we are now enjoying. I occasionally hear a young sanitarian speak with some contempt of the qualifications of his predecessors; then I delight in telling him that if he and his generation do as well as those of whom he is speaking, the world will have cause to bless and honor his name. In the forty-five years that have passed since 1880, the annual death rate in this country has been reduced from above twenty to about twelve per thousand; that from tuberculosis has been halved; yellow fever has been swept from the Western Hemisphere; typhoid fever has been reduced to almost negligible figures; diphtheria has been largely robbed of its terrors; and the average of human life has been increased by about sixteen years. If the same pace in betterment in life conditions is maintained for the coming period of like duration, the death rate in 1970 will be between six and eight and the average man will live out the biblical allotment. It is dangerous to prophesy and the wise man avoids it; but I venture to predict that this achievement will not be reached.

For the American Public Health Association, I wrote in the early eighties the Lomb prize essay on "Healthy homes and healthy foods for the working classes." This was an early attempt to popularize the recent improvements in house construction, ventilation, heating, and the caloric values of foods, their economic selection and their scientific preparation. The essay contained daily menus of balanced rations costing from twelve to fifty cents. It was printed in several languages, was sold at cost, and to those who would not buy, it was given. Mr. Lomb endeavored to ascertain how widely it was read and what influence it had on those for whom it was intended. A copy was placed in the home of every working man in Paterson, New Jersey, and some weeks later a visitor called to find out how many had read it. The number of these was small. Those who bought it, read it; those to whom it was given, did not. The moderately well-to-do read it and often followed its advice. Doctor Irving Watson, of Concord, New Hampshire, reported that the essay was widely read by thrifty New Englanders and that there was only one objection to its teachings. "Those who lived on the fifty cent ration developed gout." I think I can say without undue self laudation that this essay was a contribution to the popularization of the needs for a balanced dietary.

About the same time, the American Public Health Association appointed a committee on the practical investigation of disinfectants with Doctor Sternberg (later Surgeon General), as Chairman. The final report of this committee, constituting an octavo volume of one hundred and thirty-seven pages did much to establish differences between deodorants, preservatives and disinfectants and the findings therein given have not been materially modified by subsequent investigations. My part in this work was largely confined to the study of the germicidal action of mineral acids and mercuric chlorid.

When the United States Public Health Service was reorganized about 1903 and its splendid hygienic laboratory was opened, an advisory board of civilians was appointed and on this board I have continued from the time mentioned. The United States Public Health Service renders the people of this country a service which but few appreciate and about which most people know nothing. Its functions are devoted largely to the prevention of infections

entering this country and their extension from one state
to another. This service has charge of all national
quarantine stations and in more than one instance has
kept Asiastic cholera, bubonic plague and other infectious
diseases from landing on our shores. It has charge of
interstate quarantine and its machinery is at the service
of the state and local authorities when requested. The
service is charged with the protection of the people in
the manufacture and sale of all vaccines and serums
while from its hygienic laboratory researches of the
highest character and of the greatest value to the people
are constantly coming.

To be a member of the International Health Board
is in and of itself equivalent to receiving a graduate
course in public health. This organization, supported by
the Rockefeller Foundation, began operation about fifteen
years ago in showing the people of the Southern States
how they might eradicate hook-worm disease. This
function was soon enlarged so as to include malaria. At
first the Board paid for all this work, but now the people
in the Southern States, having been convinced of the
benefits thus secured for themselves, are bearing the
costs. Then the Board extended its demonstrations to
nearly every part of the globe. It has made a special
effort to eradicate yellow fever totally from the world
and at this writing (February, 1926), it can be said that
there has been no case of yellow fever in the Western
Hemisphere since May, 1925. Recently (July, 1925)
the Board has sent an expedition to West Africa to
ascertain whether or not yellow fever exists on that con-
tinent, and if it does, to proceed with its extinction.

In the American Philosophical Society and the National Academy of Sciences I find it difficult to comprehend some of the papers presented by those whose researches lie quite beyond my own limited field of endeavor, but the effort is stimulating and beneficial. It gives me some comprehension, inadequate as it is, of the wide range of human knowledge and awakens dreams of the possibilities of human achievement. As I see it, one of the highest functions of man is to study the operations of nature in the construction, maintenance, and development of the universe, and to adjust the race to its environment. Man is a part, probably a small part, of creation, but even the smallest cog in a complicated mechanism has a function, the proper performance of which is essential to the harmonious working of the whole. Man, as a part of the great machinery of the universe, unlike the components of man-made machinery, is capable of self improvement and better adjustment. How far this capability is possessed by other components, I do not know, but there are reasons for believing that growth, or the spirit of the creator, pervades, animates and directs all things, whether they be material, intellectual or spiritual. Even the chemical elements are not inert, but are labile, are born and are modified by environment. Nothing in the universe remains indefinitely in a fixed state; growth characterizes all; even the stars are born, flash into activity, fade and die, their substance supplying material for other growths; some of these changes are recorded in astronomical time, some are measured in solar terms while others are counted in geological ages. Law governs the universe; it is inexorable; and the unfit is eliminated. Suns and planets and all things pertaining thereto, when they fail to keep progress with the great mechanism, are cast out as waste and their substances and energies are converted into agencies which no longer interrupt the harmonious evolution of the universe.

Mrs. Vaughan

CHAPTER XV

OLD AGE

OLD AGE! The greatest paradox in the life of man! All wish to reach it; every one dreads it; few acknowledge it when it comes; it is always a liability, never an asset; some may respect it, none love it; many would give all they possess to acquire or retain it; many who possess it die in poverty; as it hangs on the tree it is an alluring fruit; many of those who pluck it find it filled with gall and bitterness. Philosophers, pagan and Christian, have discussed it, some with wisdom and sympathy; others in contempt and bitterness; painters have portrayed it, some in truthful fidelity; others in idealistic colors; artists have chiseled it in marble and cast it in bronze, some showing it in strength, others in weakness; men in every calling of life have honored it by worthy achievement; others have disgraced it. It has been held out as a reward for virtue; to many virtuous men who have acquired it, it has proven to be an apple of Sodom; it is not wholly withheld from the vicious.

Old age is frequently denominated "second childhood." In one particular—that of dependence and guidance by others—there is reason in this comparison, but fundamentally there are great differences. The normal child is growing in strength; the old man is losing. In the child

451

constructive biological processes are dominant; in the aged destructive processes prevail. Childhood is arrival; age is departure. On the threshold of the House of Life those who have preceded welcome and guide us; on leaving, each goes out into the unknown with no word of cheer or guidance from those who have gone before. Curiosity and adventure are the dominant motives in childhood; in the aged these are waning. Investigation and the acquisition of knowledge are basic in the mentality of the child; indifference and forgetfulness mark the declining years of life. Great expectations stimulate the child; frequent disappointments have made the old man wary of promises. To the child the future beckons; to the old man the past calls. All the cells in the body of the normal child are gaining in momentum, in multiplication and in function; in the old they are losing in all these activities. Youth moves lightly, free from care; multiplying burdens bend the shoulders and retard the steps of age. The child is a top, just released from the string, abounding in energy, moving with speed and grace; the old man is the same toy, with energy spent, beginning to totter and soon to fall.

Individual characteristics inherited or acquired in early life are likely to become intensified with age. The egotist is prone to boast more loudly of his achievements while the modest man becomes more retiring and reticent. The former embarrasses his family and friends while the latter becomes less social. To some, old age, or the consciousness of it, comes suddenly. Such a one realizes that his strength, either physical or mental, is seriously impaired. The recognition of this is a crisis in life and may terminate in serious tragedy. It is a severe blow to a strong man to realize abruptly that he must fall out of the race, that his work is done, that his ambitions are never to be realized. Fortunately, to most this realization comes slowly, and fortunate is he who is the first to recognize his own weakness and doubly fortunate is he who still has a strong enough grip upon himself calmly and wisely to set his house in order and yield gracefully to the inevitable. This is a crucial test of a man's sanity and too often it breaks his reason. In the face of such disaster some find consolation in religion, which offers them hope in a future and unending life, with freedom from the cruel limitations placed on man here below. Man's mind has been fertile in the invention of schemes of personal immortality and these have done much to smooth the pathway of advancing years. Pagan Seneca declares: "Old age is the fruit of sobriety and supplies opportunity to go on to happiness unhindered by passion. Life's duration should be measured by deeds done and not by years lived. He who has lived without good deeds has been long dead. Man does not come upon death abruptly; he approaches it day by day; we reach the end, but we have been long on the way; everything comes to an end; nothing perishes; this death, which we regard with terror, does not take away life; it only suspends it; seeming destruction is only change in form."

Every one who has reached seventy should read and reread that unsurpassed essay on old age written by Cicero. For wise counsel it has no equal within the whole range of literature. Age curtails one's participation in current events. The old man must lay aside many duties, and sadder still, must forego honors to which he has been accustomed. As a leader he is supplanted by a younger man. For a while he may struggle along in the front rank, but soon he finds that his own progressive enfeeblement and the more insistent strength of the new generation force him to retire to the rear, and if he is wise he finally realizes that his proper place is that of a spectator, and not of a participant in the combat. Under these circumstances he must choose between becoming a fool or a philosopher. In the rôle of the former he shows himself as a harping critic, embitters his own life, makes himself obnoxious to his friends and the quicker he goes to his grave the better for all. If he chooses to become a philosopher he may enter upon enjoyments unknown at any earlier period of his life. As a spectator he may find amusement and even bits of instruction in the passing show with the full recognition of the fact that he is no longer responsible for results. It has been said, quite truthfully, that the old man is denied the sensual pleasures of youth and early manhood. Fortunately desire grows feeble with advancing years and when it is no longer felt the sense of deprivation ceases. Doubly cursed is he in whom desire outlives capability of enjoyment. There is nothing in human form more disgusting or more pitiable than the aged roué who seeks rejuvenescence in the filthy pools of sensuality.

While old age unfits man for certain activities, it does not necessarily assign him to a life of idleness. There are still light physical exercises in which he can employ his days with profit and pleasure. Agriculture, in its multitudinous phases, holds out alluring charms for the aged. No branch of science has been exhausted. No species of animal or plant has revealed all its life secrets to man. Neither the flora nor the fauna of any locality, however limited, has been completely catalogued. Fortunate is the old man who has a scientific hobby which he may ride, with joy to himself and without disturbance to his neighbor. Greatly blessed is the old man who has learned to commune with the dead through their writings. The richest treasures of earth are his to enjoy. Gorgias, the tutor of Isocrates, lived one hundred and seven years and continued to devote himself to study. When asked about his comfort, he replied: "I have no reason to complain of old age." Fontenelle (1657-1757) said that the happiest part of his life was between sixty and eighty. Chevreul (1786-1889) is reported to have said as he was dying: "I only find a little difficulty in living."

Moderation in eating and drinking should grow more strict with advancing years in recognition of the fact that the processes of digestion, absorption, assimilation and elimination decline. Between the sexes the serene love of Philemon and Baucis is more suitable to old age than the stormy passions of Romeo and Juliet. An Arab proverb says the two worst things for an old man are a good cook and a young wife.

In normal senescence every organ and every function is involved and harmony is maintained as the machine slows down and finally comes to rest. However, in many instances decline in function is more marked in one organ than in others. Montaigne observed: "It is the body which sometimes yieldeth first to age; and other times the mind; and I have seen many that have had their brains weakened before their stomachs and legs."

Not infrequently disease precedes or accompanies senescence and has an intensifying effect. Among those who consume carbohydrates in excess, diabetes, either mild or grave, is a frequent precursor to senescence. In other instances disease of the circulatory system involving the coats of the arteries or the valves of the heart may supervene. Indeed, there has been a tendency to measure the progress of senescence by the state of the arteries as ascertained by the blood pressure. "A man is as old as his arteries" has become an aphorism first employed by physicians and now repeated by the laity. Like other proverbs it contains both truth and error. The walls of the arteries do tend to harden with advancing years, but normal blood pressure does not insure great longevity nor does it license its possessor to continue the heavier tasks of his earlier manhood. Paton says: "The somatic changes beginning after the prime of life has been reached are demonstrable in practically all the organs of the body and include a variety of different forms depending upon the character of the tissues in which they occur. No categorical definition of these alterations is possible, since it is necessary to distinguish carefully between the signs of normal aging and the changes precipitated by the action of disease. Besides these two distinct sets of conditions, definite pathologic processes may arise as secondary complications of physiologic old age. Moreover, it is sometimes not possible to state when the normal or average physiologic rate of progressive changes going on in the body has been accentuated by disease; nor can we, as a matter of fact, say why it is that we grow old."

Goethe, both scientist and poet, puts it as follows: "By appointed hours we enter into life; the days are numbered which make us ripe to see the light; but for the duration of our life there is no law. The weakest thread will spin itself to unexpected length; and the strongest is cut suddenly asunder by the scissors of the fates."

In my work on epidemiology I have written: "Among the aged and those suffering from chronic diseases, pneumonia is the kindly friend who, having prepared the bed for the body worn out with the work and worry of life's short day, administers the soporific which induces the sleep of the eternal night. On the whole, the old man who is rowed across the Styx by pneumonia is not compelled to pay a heavy toll in pain."

Thoughtless youth, unmindful of the fact that it hopes to reach his status, is prone to throw jibes at the old man. When he enters into the conversation with enthusiasm he is said to be garrulous. When he is silent, he is said to be morose. When he dresses neatly he is denominated a Beau Brummel. When his coat is of last year's variety he is a slouch. When he entertains liberally he is called an old spendthrift. In his thrift he is a miser. When the wise old man finds himself in such company he turns to his books.

I suppose that when one has passed his seventieth birthday he may justly claim to be old. During my younger days, while I was professor of hygiene, I thought that it would be a reflection on my teaching to die young. Having escaped that disgrace I find myself quite as willing as ever to postpone my departure from earth.

> "Unmeaning is the old man's wish to die,
> Or age complaining of life's lengthened course.
> For at th' advance of death, none has the will
> To die; old age is no more grievous to them."

In my seventieth year (1921) I resigned from all duties and functions at the University of Michigan. In September we rented a pleasant home in Chevy Chase and

I took up the duties of the chairmanship of the Medical Division of the National Research Council, then housed in the old Charles Francis Adams home, 1701 Massachusetts Avenue. We are not strangers in Washington, having resided here in 1898-99 following the Spanish-American War and in 1917-19 during the World War, besides making frequent visits to the capital in intervening years. We have always enjoyed Washington; here we have many of our most highly prized friends. My wife, in the Washington Club, and I, in the Cosmos and Army and Navy, find those, association with whom satisfies our highest ideals of social and intellectual companionship. When I wish authoritative information I have only to engage one of my acquaintances in conversation. The libraries are unsurpassed and no one needs to suffer from intellectual hunger in Washington.

The position of the chairmanship of the Medical Division of the National Research Council being for only one year, in October, 1922, we took temporary residence in Chicago where I assisted in launching *Hygeia,* a journal devoted to individual and community health, and published by the American Medical Association. Both at work and at play in Chicago we passed the time most pleasantly. My associations in the office were ideal in every respect and we did enjoy the opera which, in our limited experience, we believed to be unsurpassed anywhere in the world. We spent the winter of 1923-24 in Washington giving our time to reading and writing. In October, 1924, with a skilful and trustworthy chauffeur, we journeyed to Florida, went by boat from Tampa to New Orleans, and from thence to California, passing up the Pacific Coast to Portland and back to "the cottage in the woods" which we reached the last of May, 1925. This trip, the most delightful we have ever taken, was marked by no unpleasant incident. We found friends and made pleasant acquaintances at every stop. We left no place without regret or without the desire to return. In September, 1925, I again assumed the duties of the chairmanship of the Medical Division of the National Research Council, now located in the splendid building near the Lincoln Memorial, and am engaged in this most pleasant occupation as I write these lines.

In the eighties we became aware of the fact that we should seek summer pasturage for our rapidly growing and multiplying boys. We gave a few weeks of two vacations to the search. At first we secured a location at the "Snows" (les Cheneaux), but later, straying into the Grand Traverse Region, we changed our plan. Some twenty congenial families combined, bought a woodland tract on Old Mission Bay, divided the shore line into locations and drew lots for choice. In 1890 we built a modest cottage in "the woods beyond the world." The lover of William Morris will know from this quotation what books we were reading at the time. Here our five boys grew up, reading Fenimore Cooper and playing at Indians in the woods, swimming in the bay and sailing both near and afar. Here each of the four married ones brought his bride, and here they assemble each summer with their wives and children, not neglectful of the widowed wife of their eldest brother. To the stranger Old Mission has but little attraction; to us it is hallowed ground. Grandmother and grandfather, surrounded by happy, romping, laughing children, often see in their features and hear in their voices reminiscences of their lost son. Then the old pair grow sad, but tears must be brushed away and sad memories hushed, for we live for the living and can only mourn in silence for the dead.

A condition made by my wife on going to Old Mission was that the boys should not sail. I kept mute, and she, interpreting silence as consent, seemed satisfied. The first summer the older boys with their fellows were crossing the bay with their canoes moved by sails improvised out of torn pillow cases and bed sheets. Then wise woman as she is, she said that if sail they would, they must have instruction in the art; under the skilful direction of Mr. Aiken Montague and in the company of his sons, our boys were soon sailing in the *Onawa* to Mackinaw, Detour, up the Saint Mary's River, through the locks, and along the Canadian shores of Lake Superior. On many of these trips I was the only passenger, my function being that of a self-adjusting ballast, while the others constituted the officers and crew, taking turns as cook and dish washer. The *Onawa* was a sloop, about forty feet over all, drawing less than two feet, but supplied with a heavy iron center board. As a harbor and picnic boat she was ideal, providing for as many as twenty or twenty-five in the cockpit. In heavy seas in the open waters of the Great Lakes she was trustworthy in skilful hands as was demonstrated in more than one gale. My wife became an ardent sailor and frequently the whole family, including the babies, went for a sail of from forty to sixty miles, to Charlevoix and Petoskey. On one of these trips we were caught in a heavy gale which wrecked at least one steamer. Our dingey filled with water and had to be cut loose. The main sail was torn into shreds but enough of the jib was

The Cottage in the Woods
The *Red Arrow* on the shore of Lake Superior

left to keep her head on. We managed to creep into Charlevoix some time in the night. In the storm no one lost his head, bells announced the hours at proper intervals and no one told the captain what he should do. In the storm a large watermelon rolled from one side of the cockpit to the other. When opened on our return voyage under restricted sails and with fair winds the boys asserted that the gale had blown the seeds out of the melon. The log of the *Onawa* was recorded in doggerel lines without meter and with many questionable rhymes, the main thing being an attempt at humor. She was a gallant little craft and sailed the lakes before auxiliary motors were known.

In larger boats, the *Kayoshk* and the *Gem,* built and owned by Mr. Montague, we have had many delightful cruises. Our son Walter's more pretentious *Red Arrow* now serves all of us.

Our time at Old Mission is not given wholly to the water. I step from the back door of the cottage into a bit of the primeval forest of Michigan, the Leffingwell Forest Reserve, donated to the people by the Reverend Charles W. Leffingwell, now of Pasadena, and a true lover of nature. In this forest one walks beneath towering pines, white and Norway, giant hemlocks and spreading beeches, interspersed with clumps of birch bark, and may look out into the open expanse of Grand Traverse Bay and beyond into Lake Michigan. The dear old doctor left evidences of his love of the beautiful in the names he gave to points of interest. Now we are climbing "Prospects Heights"; now standing on "Inspiration Point"; now walking through "Wintergreen Hollow." His markers are growing illegible and soon will be blotted out. His children and mine in loving fun added such appellations as "The Milky Way" to designate the path they took to bring the daily supply of lacteal fluid to our homes. Our table never groans from the weight of imported viands, but carries a sufficiency of native food, prepared by Mary Gruner who has been in charge of our culinary department for thirty-five years.

The Peninsula is devoted to fruit growing, especially cherries and apples with an abundance of berries in season. As one drives along the Ridge Road in late May or early June the blossom display, while not so extensive as that seen on descending from the mountains into the Santa Clara Valley, is pleasing, and when one eats the fruit there is no comparison between the California and the Michigan products, the preference being universally conceded to the latter. The thick, yellow cream which we have from well-fed Guernseys is unknown on even the most expensive hotel tables. Of other food products of both the vegetable and animal kingdom there is no dearth. Of cold storage eggs there is not one, and when Joe Mulujek lifts his nets filled with white fish we have the most delicious food produced in the waters of the earth, fresh from its native element.

Nor are we in danger of social and intellectual starvation here in "the woods beyond the world," for Mr. Bishop, the kindly University librarian, keeps us supplied with the best literature, both old and recent. Many others, with inclinations like our own, find pleasant places in the Grand Traverse Region and every cottage door is open to all visitors.

To my elderly brothers I would say: When your friends will not listen to your oft told tales; when you tire of standing on the side lines and seeing the procession go by; when the young turn to you a cold shoulder and a deaf ear; don't worry, but thank God and take to the woods. When you think that the new generation is going to the devil, do not preach to it, do not trouble about it; let it go, and come to the woods. Come and saunter in the forest by day and learn contentment from Mother Earth; sit on the shore or lie for an hour at night in your boat; look into the starry heavens and realize how small and insignificant is man and how glorious are the works of God.

I can truly say that with old age, so far as I have experienced it, I am content. The pleasure in living has grown, and indeed the fast revolving years have only increased my interest in my environment. It is true that I am apprehensive—not of what may happen to me after death, but of what may happen before that event or may happen to my loved ones before or after my departure. In other words, only the things of this life concern me greatly. To paraphrase a saying of George Sand, I may say that my anxiety is not with death but with life. No one grows so old that he fails to realize that some misfortune may come upon him before he dies; therefore Sophocles, twenty-three centuries ago, wrote: "O citizen of Thebes, my country, behold this Œdipus, who solved the famous enigma and was the most exalted of mankind, who, looking with no envious eyes upon the fortunes of others, into how vast and stormy a sea of tremendous misery he hath come! Then, mortal as thou art, looking out for a sight of that day, thy last, call no man happy ere he shall have crossed the boundary of life, the sufferer of naught painful."

I have had the pleasure and the honor of traveling with many of the best men and women of my generation and have profited by their advice and example. My ancestors did not transmit to me any gross defect. My parents nurtured me in wisdom and love. I have not been pinched by poverty, nor exalted by riches. Above all I have been blessed in my wife whose unfailing love has cheered me in both fair and foul weather and whose wise counsel has been my staff and support along the way. She has borne to me and reared to maturity five sons no one of whom has ever caused our cheeks to blush with shame. In the death of our eldest the heaviest sorrow known to parents has been imposed upon us, one which time can not relieve, but we know that his fate awaits all and that ultimately we shall join him either in the eternal sleep or in whatever form of conscious existence the wise creator of the universe has provided for mortals when their earthly duties are ended.

The End

INDEX

INDEX

INDEX